D1615037

LECHER'S LEXICON

LECHER'S LEXICON

An A-Z Encyclopedia of Erotic Expressions and Naughty Bits

By
J. E. SCHMIDT, M.D.

Bell Publishing Company
New York

To

Oliver

This 1984 edition is published by Bell Publishing Company,
by arrangement with Brussel & Brussel, Inc.

Originally published under the title *Cyclopedic Lexicon of Sex.*

Manufactured in the United States of America

Library of Congress Cataloging in Publication Data

Schmidt, J. E. (Jacob Edward), 1903–
Lecher's lexicon.

Reprint. Originally published: Cyclopedic lexicon of sex. 2nd ed.
New York : Brussel & Brussel, 1967.
1. Sex—Dictionaries. 2. English language—Slang—Dictionaries.
I. Title.
HQ9.S28 1984 306.7'03'21 84-18399
ISBN: 0-517-455463
h g f e d c b a

RAISON D'ÊTRE — A PRELUDE

This book brings together, for the first time, the substance of the scientific or learned terminology and the bulk of the esoteric slang which constitute the vocabulary of sex and the libido. The material is presented in the new combined format of the *Reversicon* and the conventional dictionary. In a conventional dictionary, the progress is from a word to its meaning; in the *Reversicon* presentation, the direction is from *meaning* toward *word*. In this work, therefore, it is possible not only to find the meanings of words, but also the words themselves, on the basis of the idea or concept the particular word represents.

The new approach to lexicography is of special interest to writers and speakers, who are more likely than others to be searching for words and expressions. In this book, too, the reader will find hundreds of hitherto unrecorded words and phrases which, until now, formed the so-called oral lore of the sexual lingua.

The demand for a dictionary devoted to the vocabulary of sex-love has been appreciated for a long time, but the fulfillment was delayed chiefly because of the general timidity inspired in lexicographers by the unblushing tongue of Eros. But lexicography should be immune to timidity when transfusion of sense into words is the issue. It is because of such pusillanimity in this area that so much semantic precision and philologic beauty has already been lost, irrevocably.

In the matter of definition, it is a lexical sin to be pauciloquent because of modesty, especially in the field of slang where there are so many recondite overtones, so much fervor and *haut goût*.

I have, in my files, some 990 words and phrases designating in very special ways the sex organs of a woman. Should these be dismissed with such obtunded generics as *vulva* or *pudendum muliebre*? Can semantic justice be done to the 876 terms referring with various ingenious allusions to sexual intercourse by translating them into the classic but jejune *coitus*? There are also 714 words referring in one way or another to the female breasts, and 837 words and phrases symbolizing the monolithic phallus. Almost every one of these numerous synonyms has its own *raison d'être,* its own inalienable intimacy, which should not be sterilized by diffidence.

Here, in the dictionary, I am divesting myself of this human frailty, for smothering modesty has no more justification in the art of defining words than a timid and inadequate vaginal examination has in the practice of gynecology. Thus, to cite a mild example, the slang phrase *sweater dandies* is defined as *the prize pectoral bunnies of a young female,* because it means that—not the effete *mammae.* Words are here regarded as so many patients up for a thorough physical examination.

I have certainly made no attempt to offend anyone; on the other hand, I have not sidestepped from my aim to endow each word ensconced in these pages with its justly ordained mantle of semantic flesh, regardless of the alleged or presumed indelicacy of this flesh. For example, in rendering the slang term *nun* as *a female who limits her pudendal activities to urinating,* I have not meant to be vulgar or disrespectful to the classic term of the same structure. In this particular compass of slang, a *nun* means just that—not one scintilla of nuance less.

All definitions and interpretations are mine. So are the auras and the semantic décor. And it follows, therefore, that the onus is also mine. But I hope that, under the circumstances, I have succeeded in handling this teeming horde of acrid vocables with the least amount of acerbity, even for the more sensitive reader.

In this book, **boldface lower case** type indicates slang terms. Standard words are set in SMALL CAPITALS, while foreign words, standard in meaning but not fully naturalized, are printed in **BOLDFACE CAPITALS.** Derivational forms, references, etc., are expressed in *italics.*

PREFACE TO THE SECOND EDITION

The enthusiastic acceptance of the first edition of this book by the public, the critics, and the medical profession made the publication of the present Second Edition almost mandatory. During the several years that passed since the original publication, the author has produced as well as collected a substantial number of new and additional terms which appear in this new edition under the title Addenda.

The caldron of human expression is forever boiling and bubbling with new ideas and with new words for old and new concepts, especially in the field of mankind's second strongest urge – the libido. New trends in thought and in fashion add to the need for new words and expressions with which to describe them.

Thus, the advent of the miniskirt, microskirt, and other adjuncts of feminine allure, resulted in the creation of corresponding terms (e.g., *brachycraspedonia*) with which to express the innovations as well as their libidinal reverberations. The tendency of older men to marry young girls, which reached new heights in 1966, also called for a new terminology (e.g., *alphamegamia*).

The bare feminine leg and the scintillating knee of the *haute couture* logically begot *gymnoscelia*, *knemelatry*, etc. Other proclivities of man and maid – normal, abnormal, and questionable – are termed and expounded in the Second Edition. There are a total of more than 1,300 additional medical, scientific, lay, and slang entries in the new book, replete with comprehensive definitions and etymologic derivations. It is hoped that the reader of the Second Edition will find the material even more educational and entertaining than he found it before.

LEXICON OF SEX

Exotic Practices, Expressions, Variations of the Libido

A

A cappella . . . Engaged in, or performed, without the benefit of a phallic condom or a vaginal diaphragm; used, obviously, with reference to sexual concourse, in allusion to choral singing without instrumental accompaniment.

A little conversation . . . An off-the-record or an extracurricular, as it were, engagement in phallo-vaginal needle-threading.

A . . . For other entries beginning with **A**, see under more significant part of the expression.

Abdomen, distended, as seen in anticipating women . . . **Bean belly.**

Abdomen, female, sexual interest centered on the . . . ALVINOLAGNIA.

Abdominal plaster . . . A patrician metonymy for a desirable female pudendum, regarded as a salubrious application to the male counterpart.

Ability of phallus to attain and sustain a functional erection . . . POTENCY.

Ability of phallus to impregnate . . . **Knock-upability.**

Ability of phallus to penetrate introitus vaginae . . . INGRESSABILITY.

Ability of phallus . . . See also under *Phallus, Penis,* etc.

Ability to have an orgasm in quick time . . . TACHORGASMIA.

Ability to have an orgasm only after prolonged effort at phallation and with the aid of mental stimulants, by the male . . . DYSORGASMIA.

Ability to have an orgasm only when thinking of a more desirable female than the one being phallated . . . ALLORGASMIA.

Ability to have an orgasm . . . See also under *Sexual intercourse, Phallation,* etc.

Ability to satisfy sexually; applied to the female . . . GYNOPHELIMITY.

Ability to satisfy sexually; applied to the male . . . OPHELIMITY.

Abnormal sexual craving or instinct . . . EROTICISM; PARAPHILIA.

Abstain from beans . . . To be a sexual teetotaler. Also, of the female, to refuse the seminal injection.

Abstain from phallation until one is married; said of the male . . . **Save one's fat.**

ACANTHOPHALLIC . . . Having a rough or spiny penis. From *akantha* (thorn).

Accept the male ardently . . . **Roast brown.**

Accept the male in coitus . . . **Play the bitch to; Play the ace against the jack; Stand bitch to.**

Accept the male in coitus, by spreading that which needs spreading . . . **Do a bedspread; Do a spread.**

Accept the male pudendal emissary in a reclining position . . . **Lie down and take nourishment.**

Accept the phallus into a warm home . . . **Roast the meat.**

Accept the phallus orally . . . **Blow; Take a drink;** FELLATIZE.

Accept the phallus pudendally . . . **Take beef.**

Accessory penis . . . PARAPHALLUS.

Accost a whore . . . **Flag down.**

Ace poker . . . A phallus of the size and consistency that desirous females like.

Ace poker . . . A male who phallates with admirable virtuosity.

ACEPTIATRIST . . . A physician expert in the field of contraception. From *a* (not), *capere* (take), & *iatros* (physician).

ACEPTIATRY . . . The branch of medical science dealing with the prevention of conception. Ex *a* (not), *capere* (take), & *iatreia* (medical treatment).

ACMEGENESIS . . . The induction of the sexual orgasm.

Act involved in sexual intercourse . . . PHALLATION.

Act of acts . . . The introduction of the membrum virile jejunum into the pudendum muliebre jucundum.

Action of male in sexual intercourse . . . PHALLATION.

Action of male in sexual intercourse, verb designating . . . PHALLATE.

Actor's mistress or harlot . . . **Lakerlady.**

Actors' pads used to camouflage the contour of the genital apparatus . . . **Decencies.**

ACUCULLOPHALLIA . . . The condition of having a circumcised phallus. From *a* (without), *cucullus* (a hood), & *phallos* (penis).

ACUCULLOPHALLIC . . . Having or pert. to a circumcised phallus.

ACUCULLOPHILIA . . . A woman's fondness for a circumcised phallus. Ex *a* (without), *cucullus* (a hood), & *philein* (to love).

ACUCULLUS . . . A circumcised phallus. Ex *a* (without) & *cucullus* (a hood).

ACULEOPHALLIC . . . Having a pointed or conical penis. Ex *aculeus* (a prickle).

ADECTIA . . . The unwillingness or inability of the female to accept the male in coitus. From *a* (not) & *dektos* (acceptable).

Adult female who accepts the phallus by mouth . . . FELLATRICE; **Sword swallower; Beef eater; Jaw artist; Mouther.**

Adult female who accepts the phallus by rectum . . . SODOMANTE; SODOMEE.

Adult female . . . See also under *Female, Woman,* etc.

Adult male who accepts the phallus of another by mouth . . . FELLATOR; **Beef eater; Jaw artist; Mouther.**

Adult male who accepts the phallus of another by rectum . . . SODOMANT.

Adult male who continues the role of a catamite . . . **Auntie.**

Adult male . . . See also under *Male, Man, Person,* etc.

Afternoon lustfulness, esp. in men . . . DELINOLAGNIA.

Afternoon sexual indulgence . . . **Blanket drill.**

Agate . . . A diminutive phallus, in allusion to a small size of type.

AGENOBIOSIS . . . The living together of husband and wife without sexual relations, by mutual consent. From *a* (not), *genos* (sex), & *bios* (life).

Agfay . . . A male homosexual.

Aggressive sexual elements of a romantic male . . . **Animal spirits.**

AGYNOPHELIMITY . . . The inability to give sexual satisfaction by the female.

AIDOION . . . The Greek form for the vulva, in allusion to something deserving of respect.

Air one's pores . . . To be, or go about, naked.

ALGOLAGNIA . . . The derivation of sexual pleasure from the infliction or suffering of pain.

ALGOLAGNIST . . . A person who derives sexual pleasure from inflicting and/or suffering pain. Ex *algos* (pain) & *lagneia* (lust).

ALGORGASMIA . . . Painful sexual orgasm in the male.

ALGORGYNIA . . . Sexual frigidity in the female. Ex *algor* (coldness) & *gyne* (woman).

ALGORSENIA . . . Lack of sexual desire in the male. From *algor* (coldness) & *arsen* (male).

All-night man . . . A recently married man, to a provocatively compiled female.

ALLINSEMINATION . . . Artificial insemination with semen taken from a male other than the husband.

ALLOANDRISM . . . A trick of the imagination of a woman in coitus whereby she pretends that her phallator is another, more desirable, male. Ex *allos* (another) & *aner* (male).

ALLOGYNIA . . . The pretending by a man in coitus that his sexual partner is another woman, whom he would like to phallate. From *allos* (another) & *gyne* (woman).

ALLORGASMIA . . . In sexual intercourse, the ability to have the orgasm only when thinking of a female more desirable than the one subjacent, or of a situation particularly erotic to the phallator.

ALLOVALENT . . . Of a male impotent with his wife, potent with other women. (Ex *allos,* other, & *valere,* to be strong.)

Alluring display of cleavage . . . **Wappenschawing.**

Alluring display of female breasts . . . **Bubby circus.**

Alluring display of female legs . . . **Leg bait.**

Almanac . . . The pudendum muliebre, conceived as a repository of a thousand and one little and big surprises, for the amative male with a capable plunger.

Alphonse . . . A pimp or go-between of a harlot.

ALVINOLAGNIA . . . Sexual interest of the male centered on the female abdomen. Ex *alvus* (abdomen) & *lagneia* (lust).

Amateur prostitute, i.e., one who gives, but not to earn a living by it . . . **Dolly-mop.**

Amorous contribution to the enjoyment of the sexual act volunteered by a harlot . . . **Blessing.**

Amorous escapades indulged in by young males to relieve the first twinges of seminal pressure . . . **Wild oats.**

.Amorous favors granted by a girl to her escort on their parting at her door, as after a dance, to entice him to return . . . **Boodle.**

Amorous favors, niggardly with, when parting with the escort at her door, as after a dance . . . **Boodle-pinching.**

Amorous shenanigans between man and maid, upon the blanket-covered bed, usually restricted to digital exploration of her fleshy charms . . . **Blanket ruffling.**

Amorous . . . See also under **Erotic.**

AMPHIMIXIS . . . The direction of one's early interests and energies toward the sexual organs.

AMPHISEXUAL . . . Both homosexual and heterosexual. From *amphis* (both).

Amputation of the female breast by a fiend, either as an expression of sadism or as an act of vengeance . . . MAZOPEROSIS.

Amputation of the male sex organs as an act of jealous retaliation . . . COLOBOSIS.

AMULIEROSIS . . . Mental disorder resulting from lack of association and/or intercourse with women. Ex *a* (without) & *mulier* (woman).

ANACLISIS . . . Sexual gratification conditioned by a basic instinct, as hunger.

ANAL EROTICISM . . . 1. Erotic sensitivity of the anus. 2. Sexual satisfaction derived from stimulation of the anus. 3. Sexual gratification derived from defecation.

Anal eroticism combined with urethral eroticism . . . AMPHIMIXIS.

Anal eroticism, person with persistent . . . ANOCRAT; ANAL CHARACTER.

Anal eroticism, strong and persistent . . . ANOCRATISM.

Anal phallation with a child, usually a boy . . . PEDERASTY.

Anal phallation with an adult male or female . . . SODOMY.

Anal region, conceived as an occasional trumpeter; also, such trumpeting . . . **Ars musica.**

Anal region of buttocks . . . **Back yard.**

ANAPHRODISIAC . . . A substance, usually a medicine, which calms sexual desire.

ANAPOCRISIS . . . Lack of response from the female coital partner. Ex *apokrisis* (response).

Anatomical . . . Erotic, provocative, etc., as parts, but also wit, stories, and the like.

Androgen . . . Hormone which stimulates development of secondary sex characteristics in the male.

Androgyne . . . Female hermaphrodite.

Androgynia . . . Hermaphroditism in the female.

Androgynism . . . Pseudohermaphroditism in the female.

Androgynus . . . Female pseudohermaphrodite.

Andromania . . . Excessive sexual desire in the female. Ex *aner* (man).

Androphilist . . . A female especially fond of men.

Androphobia . . . Strong dislike of men by a woman.

Androsodomy . . . Rectal sodomy practiced upon a male. Ex *aner* (male) & *sodomy*.

Androzoon . . . A male animal trained to perform the sexual act with a woman. Ex *aner* (male) & *zoon* (animal).

Anesodia . . . The inability of a female to have sexual intercourse because of partial occlusion of the vaginal introitus by hymeneal tissue. Ex *an* (not) & *eisodos* (a coming in).

Angel . . . A male homosexual.

Angel . . . A girl as the alleviator of the membrum virile erectum.

Angelina . . . A child, usually a boy, in whose anus and rectum a pederast insinuates his phallus.

Angelina sorority . . . Catamites collectively; the world of catamites.

Angel's gear . . . Girls' or women's clothes, esp. the garments covering the unmentionables.

Angel's suit . . . No suit at all, i.e., nakedness.

Anglican length . . . 1. Of the phallus, a satisfying length. 2. A length of phallus administered in the conventional manner.

Angular party . . . A male escort with a persistent angular protrusion on either side of the fly, resulting from an unsatisfied mind.

Anililagnia . . . Sexual desire for old females. Ex *anus* (old woman) & *lagneia* (lust).

Animal, licking of vulva by a trained . . . Zoolinction.

Animal, male, trained to perform the sexual act with a woman . . . Androzoon.

Animal, sexual intercourse of a human being with an . . . Zooerastia.

Animal spirits . . . The aggressive sexual overtures of an amorous male.

Animal used by a man in the practice of zooerastia . . . Gynezoon.

Animals, sexual desire directed toward . . . Zoolagnia.

Anisomastia . . . Inequality in size of the two breasts. From *anisos* (unequal) & *mastos* (breast).

Anisonogamia . . . A marriage or mating involving spouses of markedly disparate ages, esp. one in which the female is much younger. From *anisos* (unequal), *aion* (age), & *gamos* (marriage).

Ankle . . . A girl, in allusion to one of the lower attractions.

Ankle, female, especially erotic about the . . . TALOPHILOUS.

Ankles, having beautiful . . . CALLISPHYROUS.

ANOCRAT . . . A person dominated by anal eroticism.

ANOCRATISM . . . Strong and persistent anal eroticism. (From *anus* and *kratein,* to rule.)

Anoint . . . To honor with the seminal spurt.

Anolinguist; female who licks a man's anus . . . **Buttock and tongue.**

Anolinguist; male who licks the anus of a female . . . **Bum sucker; Fart sucker.**

ANOMEATIA . . . Phallation by rectum with a female. From *anus* & *meare* (to go).

Anonyma . . . A female professional thigh spreader, in allusion to the practice of operating under an assumed name.

ANOPHELIMITY . . . Inability to satisfy sexually; said of the male. Ex *an* (not) & *ophelos* (help).

ANOPHILE . . . A male sexually attracted to elderly women. Ex *anus* (old woman) & *philein* (to love).

ANOPHILEMIA . . . Sexual perversion in which the male derives pleasure from kissing the anus of a female. Ex *anus* & *philema* (kiss).

ANOPHILOUS . . . Of the male, especially erotic about the anus of the female. Ex *anus* & *philein* (to love).

ANORAPT . . . Rapist of old women.

ANORAPTUS . . . Rape by force involving an elderly woman. Ex *anus* (old woman) & *raptus* (a violent attack).

ANORAST . . . A male who phallates a female per rectum. From *anus* & *erastes* (lover).

Another man's woman, pay pudendal homage to . . . **Cop a phinney; Beat one's time.**

ANTHOLAGNIA . . . Sexual lust aroused by the aroma and/or sight of flowers. From *anthos* (flower) & *lagneia* (lust).

ANTHROPOPHAGY . . . A form of cannibalism in which sexual pleasure is derived from the practice, often expressed in the eating of genital parts from a person of the opposite sex. Ex *anthropos* (man) & *phagein* (eat).

Anti . . . A condom as an anti-infection and anti-impregnation device.

Antipodes . . . The amatory underside of the female, in allusion to its comparative inaccessibility, as New Zealand and Australia, and its position on the other side or end of the trunk.

Antiquated rogue . . . A retired, because of impotence, but formerly dashing, phallus.

Antony pig . . . A smallish phallus; in allusion to the smallest pig in a litter known as St. Anthony's pig.

Anus as pederast's or sodomite's heaven . . . **Hinder entrance.**

Anus as substitute vagina . . . **Wrong font.**

Anus; conceived as an occasional trumpeter . . . **Ars musica.**

Anus, erotic licking of . . . HEDRALINGUS.

Anus, erotic sensitivity of the . . . ANAL EROTICISM.

Anus, esp. as a sodomite's target . . . **Hole.**

Anus, esp. as vaginal substitute . . . **Roby Douglas.**

Anus, female, male who licks . . . **Bum sucker.**

Anus; in allusion to its occasional cacophony . . . **Bum-fiddle; Ars musica.**

Anus of the female, especially erotic about the . . . ANOPHILOUS.

Anus, person who licks, for his own or the other's pleasure . . . **Fart sucker.**

Anus, sexual gratification derived from stimulation of . . . ANAL EROTICISM.

Anus, suckle or lick the, of the female . . . **Bite the brown.**

Apartments to let . . . Females with rentable pudenda.

Ape leader . . . A maid no longer young having a chaste pudendum.

APHALLATA . . . A female still a virgin. Ex *a* (without) & *phallos* (penis).

APHALLATIA . . . The condition marked by lack of outlet for the sexual urge.

APHALLATIC . . . Designating virgin females.

APHALLATOSIS . . . Mental disorder resulting from lack of satisfaction in one's sex life.

APHRODISIA . . . Sexual excitement, esp. when urgent. Also, not often, sexual concourse. Ex *Aphrodite,* the goddess of love.

APHRODISIAC . . . A substance which stimulates the sexual appetite.

APISTIA . . . Unfaithfulness in marriage.

Apostle's grove . . . The female pubic turf and the environs.

Apparatus . . . The male external genitalia.

Apples . . . A girl's breasts, junior size.

Ardent and dedicated phallator . . . **Road hog.**

Areolated retrobrassiereans . . . The fleshy perquisites of the female chest, in allusion, obviously, to the, in the young, attractive circumnipplear coloration and the normal habitat, behind the brassierean cups.

Aristocratic vein . . . The vulva of an aristocratic female.

Armored division . . . A parting of the female nether labia by a condomed phallus.

Armpits, female, especially erotic about the . . . MASCHALOPHILOUS.

Armpits, female . . . See also under *Axilla.*

Arms, female, especially erotic about the . . . BRACHIOPHILOUS.

Arousing of a male by exposure and denial of female desirables . . . TANTALIZATION.

ARRHENIDIA . . . The external and internal sex organs of the male. From *arrhen* (man) & *aidoia* (genitals).

Ars musica . . . The anal region, in

allusion to the occasional anal trumpeting.

Arse . . . 1. The buttocks; the rump. 2. The anus or rectum. 3. The female lipped underbelly.

Arse . . . To phallate per rectum, in sodomy or pederasty.

Arse cooler . . . A short skirt.

Arse crawler . . . A submissive husband.

Arse crawler . . . A sodomite; a pederast.

Arse, drop anchor in one's . . . To intromit the phallus in the rectum of a catamite or a sodomant.

Arse from elbow down . . . Of a female, having very provocative hips and rump.

Arse from elbow down . . . Of a female, attractive from the waist down, but not pretty of face or bosom.

Arse grease . . . A sodomite's or pederast's phallic ejaculant.

Arse up . . . Of the female, to present the back in pudendal denial.

Arse worm . . . A contemptible phallus good only for the anal introit.

Arseduke . . . A boy whose anus and rectum serve as vagina to a pederast.

ARSENOSADISM . . . The derivation of sexual pleasure from the infliction of cruelty upon males. From *arsen* (male) and *sadism*.

Arser . . . 1. The phallus of a sodomite. 2. The bearer of the phallus of a sodomite, i.e., the sodomite.

Arsometry . . . Sodomy and/or pederasty.

Arson, sexual gratification derived from . . . PYROLAGNIA.

Article . . . A girl conceived as *the* thing for the restless pudendum of the male.

Article, the . . . A woman's vulva conceived as her choicest part.

Artifact of the imagination whereby a male, in coitus with an unexciting female, conjures a quarry infinitely more desirable, to enhance the pleasure of the act and to coax a tardy orgasm . . . GENDOLOMA.

Artificial insemination . . . **Caprification**; ARTINSEMINATION.

Artificial insemination, seminal fluid used in . . . **Bottled beer.**

Artificial penis and testicles, used by females in masturbation and in tribadism . . . DILDO; GODEMICHE; OLISBOS.

Artificial penis, use of, by a woman, upon herself . . . DILDOISM.

Artificial penis, use of, by the "male" female in the act of tribadism . . . OLISBONISM.

ARTINSEMINATION . . . The implantation of semen into the vagina by artificial means.

Asexual love between persons unrelated by blood and capable of erotic love for each other . . . PLATONIC LOVE.

Asexual relations, alleged . . . **Avuncular relations.**

Asexual relations between persons of the opposite sexes unrelated to each other by blood . . . PLATONIC RELATIONS.

ASPERMIA . . . Absence or deficiency of semen. Also, failure to emit the semen. Ex *a* (without) & *sperma* (seed).

Ass . . . Female pudendal flesh as pacifier for a rampant male poker.

Ass . . . Satisfaction for the phallus derived from the underside of a girl.

Ass . . . The rowdy pleasure derived from the female pudendum, as interpreted, obviously, by the male.

Ass . . . A well-rounded, provocative, and usually semaphoric behind of a pretty girl. Also, the arse of any female, pretty or not.

Ass . . . Girldom; girls as so many female pudenda.

Ass . . . The pudendal gift or favor of the female.

Ass artist . . . A girl who has a beautiful response to the phallic crawl.

Ass-glosser . . . A female who tries to make up for intellectual or other shortcomings by pudendal offerings.

Ass merchant . . . 1. A female who sells pudendal privileges. 2. A pimp or procurer.

Ass pincher . . . A wife who is niggardly with her pudendal smile.

Asshole plugging . . . Sodomy or pederasty.

Assist the phallus to find its quarry; said of a female directing manually the groping sightless male sausage . . . **Plant.**

ASTHENOBLYSIS . . . A feeble seminal ejaculation. Ex *a* (without) *sthenos* (strength), & *blyzo* (spurt).

ASTYPHIA . . . Sexual impotence in the male, caused by lack of ability to erect. Ex *styphelizo* (to thrust).

ASTYSIA . . . The condition in the male marked by inability to raise a functional erection.

ASYNODIA . . . The condition of living without sexual intercourse, either by choice or necessity. Ex *a* (without) & *synodos* (a coming together).

ASYNODIA . . . Sexual impotence in the male, due to lack of ability to produce a functional rigidity of the phallus.

ATESTUS . . . A castrated male. Ex *a* (without) & *testis.*

Athanasian wench . . . A girl who is readily persuaded to grant pudendal privileges to a male. An allusion to *Quicumque vult* (whosoever will), the initial words of the Athanasian Creed.

ATICTIA . . . Sterility in the male. From *a* (not) & *tiktein* (beget).

ATOLMIA . . . Sexual impotence in the male caused by lack of confidence. Ex *a* (not) & *tolma* (daring).

Attacker of women who slashes their genitalia . . . **Ripper.**

Attic . . . The sexual trinket of the female, conceived as the classic source of sensual pleasure.

Attractive female with a receptive pudendum . . . **A bit of all right.**

Attractive young girl who yields enticingly to manual squeezing . . . **Peach.**

Aunt . . . 1. A procuress for a brothel. 2. A mistress. 3. A common whore.

Aunt Maria . . . The female pudendum conceived as a loving vehicle.

Auntie . . . An adult catamite, i.e., an adult male who continues to play the role of the recipient in rectal phallation.

AUTO-EROTISM . . . The condition in which the sexual desire is directed toward oneself.

AUTOFELLATIO . . . An act of fellatio in which the subject takes his own penis.

AUTOFELLATOR . . . A male who manages to take his own penis into the mouth.

Autofellator . . . **Automatic muzzle loader.**

Automatic muzzle loader . . . A male with a supple vertebral column who is his own fellator, i.e., who takes his own phallic suck.

Aversion for being touched amorously, esp. in the female . . . SARMASSOPHOBIA.

Aversion for girls and women . . . MISOGYNY.

Aversion for marriage or married life . . . GAMORESPIA; MISOGAMY.

Aversion for men; in a female . . . MISANDRY.

Aversion for necking or amorous digital contact . . . SARMASSORESPY.

Aversion for sexual intercourse, usually in the female . . . COITOPHOBIA.

Aversion for the male sex organ . . . MISOPHALLY.

AVESTAPHRENIA . . . The state of mind behind the eternal complaint of women, "I haven't a thing to wear." Ex *a* (without), *vestimenta* (clothes), & *phren* (mind).

AVIRGYNIA . . . Lack of sexual relations between a man and his wife. From *a* (not), *vir* (man), & *gyne* (wife).

Avuncular relations . . . Alleged platonic relations between an uncle and a niece. Also, alleged asexual relations between others who are eligible.

Awkward situation . . . A pregnancy, esp. one not accounted for by wedlock.

Awry, tread the shoe . . . Of a female, to walk the primrose path, pudendally.

Axe, give the . . . To give the female pudendum the accolade of the male cleaver.

Axe-grinding . . . The honing of the male genital blade on the female pudendal strop.

Axed . . . 1. Deflowered. 2. Phallated and impregnated.

Axilla, female, especially erotic about the . . . MASCHALOPHILOUS.

Axilla, female, licking of; as erotic expression . . . MASCHALINGUS.

Axilla, female, phallation in . . . MASCHALAGNIA.

Axillary hair of the female, especially erotic about . . . HIRCUSOPHILOUS.

Axle grease . . . A lubricant applied to the introitus vaginae to facilitate intromission.

AZOOSPERMIA . . . The absence of functionally adequate spermatozoa from the semen.

Azzle out . . . To withdraw the phallus before the seminal spurt.

B

Babe . . . 1. A girl who might not say no to a reasonable pudendal request. 2. A girl resplendent with feminine attractions.

Baby . . . A girl as a fucksome thing.

Baby . . . A male homosexual.

Baby beef . . . A small male organon, esp. in a man of ample stature.

Baby-bound . . . 1. Pregnant. 2. Liberal with the female pudendum.

Baby food . . . The phallic ejaculant deposited vaginally.

Baby-gallop . . . A spirited pudendal engagement without the usual precautions.

Baby grinder . . . A man phallating without a condom.

Baby herder . . . A male with a fecund phallus.

Baby owl . . . A junior miss in the profession of Mrs. Warren.

Baby porker . . . A man who marries a very young girl.

Baby-sitters, erotic interest of, in infants and babies of the opposite sex . . . NEPIOLAGNIA.

Baby snatcher . . . A man who marries a very young girl.

Baby-split . . . A thigh-spread by the female, for the usual genital invasion.

Baby up . . . 1. To give the female the phallic drip. 2. To make a woman enceinte.

Babyolatry . . . 1. The adoration of "babes." 2. Libido for excessively young females.

Bachelor bait . . . A girl endowed with feminine charms who constitutes a hazard to celibacy.

Bachelor's fare . . . Manual gratification.

Back, female, especially erotic about the . . . NOTOPHILOUS.

Back Parlor . . . The rectum of a female, conceived as the receiving chamber for the sodomite phallus.

Back yard . . . The anus and rectum; the buttocks.

Back yard prowler . . . A sodomite; phallator per rectum.

Backwoods fiddler . . . A sodomite or a pederast, i.e., a male who phallates an adult male or female, or a boy, per rectum.

Bacon . . . The fleshy parts of a female which, by exposure to the visual and/or tactile receptors, impose upon the male a sense of erotic urgency.

Baculum . . . A Latin figurative synonym for the penis, in allusion to a small rod.

Badger bait . . . Of a female, to stimulate the male genital staff by tantalizing it through the pants.

Bag . . . The testicular sac; scrotum.

Bag . . . 1. To beget or to sire. 2. Conceive in uterus.

Bag . . . A not-too-classy female underbelly inlet, with its usual adnexa, conceived as too capacious for phallic comfort.

Bag . . . 1. A female pudendally unattractive. 2. A well-worn prostitute one would not wish even on one's enemy.

Bag-filler . . . The phallus erectus, esp. one such of princely size.

Bag of fruit . . . The scrotum and testicles.

Bag-twister . . . A female who gets out of pudendal tight spots by squeezing or twisting the male pouch.

Bagpipe . . . The phallus as the drain pipe of the scrotum.

Bag-piper . . . A down-and-outer who is reduced to phallating slovenly whores.

Bags of mystery . . . The female breasts as conceived by those males who have no access to them.

Bald cocksucker . . . A toothless fellator or fellatrice.

Bald eagle . . . The male genitalia shaved or otherwise deprived of hair.

Bald journey . . . A phallic invasion without a condom.

Ball arranged by prostitutes for the purpose of drumming up business . . . **Buttock ball.**

Ball at which the guests go about naked . . . **Buff ball.**

Ball . . . See also under **Dance.**

Balls . . . The male gonads; the testicles.

Balls and bat . . . The phallus and the testes.

Ballum rancum . . . A dance, if such it can be called, at which the female members are confirmed whores.

Ballum rancum . . . A dance, sir-reverence, at which the participants are shed of their clothes, and the female upper bombosities as well as the male lower testosities bob up and down.

Baloney . . . The phallus as a shaft of pudendal sausage.

Banbury . . . A female with loose pudendal strings.

Bang . . . To give the female a dish of phallus erectus.

Bankside lady . . . A businesswoman whose stock in trade is her lipped underside.

Banquet at which there is considerable whoremongering . . . **Bawdy banquet.**

Banquet . . . See also under **Ball** and **Dance.**

Barber's chair . . . A harlot, esp. a busy one, in allusion to her pudendum which, like a barber's chair, is being "sat upon" before it has a chance to cool off from a previous engagement.

Bardotian . . . Of the nature of, pert. to, or somewhat reminiscent of, the ineffable feminine Gallician whose pauciloquent interpretation of youthful muliebrity evoked a unanimous and universal masculine bravo, even from those on whom a Voronoff transplant would have remained fruitless.

Bare brisket . . . A female with a low-slung décolletage.

Barge . . . A capacious vagina made ample by childbirth, phallation, or masturbation.

Barge pole . . . A phallus of better than adequate size, large enough to fit a **barge.**

Barkis is willing but the flesh is weak . . . the man is desirous but the phallic pendant is flaccid.

Basic literature . . . Writing which deals with sex.

Basin over which a female stands, with a leg on each side, while bathing her pudendum . . . Bidet.

Basket . . . The male external genitalia, esp. the scrotum.

Basket . . . The pleasurable underside of the female, conceived as a gift basket of goodies.

Basket of oranges . . . An attractive female; in allusion to a clump of gold nuggets in a gold field, known by the same name.

Bastard . . . **By-blow; By-chop; By-scape; By-slip.**

Bastard, bear a . . . **Break a leg.**

Bastard; conceived as product of coital mishap . . . **Come-by-chance.**

Bat . . . The male genital club.

Bat . . . A female with an accommodating pudendum.

Bat . . . A whore who, like the mouse-like animal with the membranous wings, works by night.

Bat . . . To phallate a female, in allusion to the membrum virile as the male genital bat.

Bat-foul . . . To deflower a virgin, by fouling her with the male bat, in allusion to batfowl.

Bat off . . . To rid oneself of phallic tension by manual assistance.

Bathysadism . . . A subconscious form of sadism. Ex *bathys* (deep) & *sadism.*

Baton . . . The male genital "Kapellmeister," conceived as a conductor of the pudendal orchestra, in coitus.

Battered . . . Of a recent virgin, deflowered.

Battered . . . 1. Of a female, subjected to the phallic invasion, esp. by an organon of no mean dimension. 2. Of a male, fond of pudendal indulgence.

Battered cow . . . A woman who has a thoroughly phallated pudendum.

Battle bag . . . The business end of a harlot, used in "battle" for a living.

Battledore . . . The male genital paddle.

Bawdy banquet . . . A feast in which the victuals are pudenda.

Bawdy basket . . . 1. A female whose gratifying end is promiscuous and mercenary. 2. A female peddler of obscene devices, as godemiches.

Be a cuckold; an allusion to the figurative horns of one . . . **Wear a forker.**

Be a . . . For other entries beginning with *Be a,* see under more significant part of the expression.

Be attractive to girls, enough to give them butterflies in the pudenda; said of an Adonis . . . **Lay the femmes.**

Be deflowered of one's virginity . . . **Break one's knee.**

Be deflowered . . . See also under *Deflower, Virgin,* etc.

Be denied the female pudendal privilege, and allowed only to kiss the arse, as it were . . . **Kiss behind and not before.**

Be deprived of pudendal privileges by one's wife . . . **Be in Jericho.**

Be deprived of pudendal privileges by one's wife, as a device of retaliation or coercion . . . **Get the key to the street.**

Be desirous for a female . . . LIBIDINATE.

Be desirous for a female, chronically . . . **Carry a bat.**

Be desirous for (in love with) a particular woman . . . **Carry a bat for.**

Be desirous for the female pudendum . . . **Yen for the hen.**

Be drenched with seminal ejaculation even before the male organ reaches its vaginal destination; said of the female . . . **Catch the ball before the bound.**

Be enticed into pudendal surrender . . . **Have a leg twisted.**

Be hit on the master vein . . . To be impaled by the eburnated phallus.

Be in coitus with a female . . . **Strap.**

Be in coitus . . . See also under *Phallate.*

Be in for the plate . . . To have a venereal infection.

Be in Jericho . . . Of a husband, to be deprived of pudendal privileges by the wife, to coerce a concession or to effect punishment.

Be in sexual concourse; said esp. of a woman . . . **See.**

Be in sexual concourse . . . See also under *Sexual concourse, Sexual intercourse, Phallation,* etc.

Be infected venereally; in allusion to burning urination . . . **Piss fire.**

Be knapped . . . To be pregnant; to be impregnated.

Be of slightly mixed blood . . . **Have at least two annas of dark blood.**

Be on all fours while phallating a woman . . . **Dog.**

Be on jack . . . Of a newly married female, to be well supplied with phallus.

Be on top in the pudendal mattress dance; said of the male or of the female . . . **Play the bear.**

Be on top of the coital partner . . . **Play the bear with.**

Be out christening . . . Of the male, to be out with one (or more) of Mrs. Warren's girls.

Be phallated . . . **Get a ride; Have a bit of gut-stick; Take beef; Taste the gut-stick.**

Be phallated and take the phallic ejaculant . . . **Take gruel.**

Be phallated . . . See also under *Phallate, Phallation, Sexual concourse,* etc.

Be with a whore . . . **See a sick friend.**

Beak . . . The business end of the male genitalia, in its functional pose.

Beak . . . To peck the female pudendum with the male beak.

Bean . . . 1. To phallate. 2. To deposit the seminal cream intravaginally.

Bean belly . . . The distended abdomen of pregnancy, in allusion to "beans."

Bean feast . . . A pudendal jamboree in which phallic fluid runs like water.

Bean pods . . . The testicles as containers of the "beans."

Bean pole . . . The genital plunging end of the male by which the "beans" are deposited.

Bean-spilling . . . A spilling of the seminal "beans." Also, the act of phallation leading to it.

Beano . . . A heterosexual interpudendal celebration.

Beans . . . The ejaculated seminal lava.

Beany . . . Of the male, desirous; because of too much unexpended "beans."

Bear-garden language . . . Obscene and/or vulgar language.

Bear play . . . The giving of phallus erectus to the lady, in the conventional manner and posture, with the giver as the top sawyer.

Bearskin robber . . . A male who likes his pudendal fare very, very young —almost off the bearskin.

Beastie . . . The silent but eloquent mouth of the female.

Beat black and blue . . . To suggillate the female flesh, by squeezing and pinching, during the ecstatic phases of phallation.

Beat it while the beating is good . . . To phallate an impregnated wife, conventionally, till the belly gets in the way.

Beat one's time . . . To make good time with the girl of another.

Beat the brains out . . . Phallate a female with tissue-damaging strokes, i.e., too vehemently.

Beat to it . . . To experience the erotic payoff, in the course of a pudendal engagement, before the sexual partner does.

Beat with the spit . . . to punish—not really—with the thrusts of the membrum virile erectum.

Bed, as a site for copulation . . . **Breeding cage.**

Bed bargain . . . A pretty good piece of female pudendum.

Bed bugs . . . The brownish spots of dried blood on the bed sheet of a virgin bride, observed after the initiation night and occasionally thereafter, during the breaking-in period.

Bed bunny . . . A girlie who can be persuaded to lie down.

Bed-staff . . . That part of the male which is most likely to become staff-like when "messing around" with a female, in bed or elsewhere.

Bed-weary . . . Sexhausted, after a night of vulvar carnage.

Bedding . . . A good bad girl to lie with.

Bedfellow, female; a female sexual partner in coitus . . . COITANTE; PARACOITA.

Bedfellow, male; a male sexual partner in coitus . . . COITANT; PARACOITUS.

Bedful of sin . . . A charming girl, and willing too.

Bedrock . . . That granite monolith of the male pudendum, as seen by the softer half of the phallating team.

Bedtime story . . . Sexual communion conceived with fairy tale innocence.

Bedventure . . . A safari in the female jungle, all done cozily in bed.

Bedwork . . . Heterosexual pudendal inosculation.

Beef . . . From the standpoint of a female, esp. of one pudendally contented, the fleshy genital satisfier of the male.

Beef . . . to reciprocate the male genital outlet in the female genital inlet.

Beef bags . . . The female breasts, queen size.

Beef eater . . . One, male or female, who takes the phallus orally.

Beef extract . . . The lactescent emanation of an orbiting phallus.

Beef in the can . . . The phallus immersed in the blissful forgetfulness of the female sheath.

Beef on the hoof . . . A male with a phallic uprising in search for a girl with an accessible pudendal Lethe.

Beef stick . . . The male genital plunger.

Beef trust . . . A pride of corpulent females, esp. such engaged in the same profession, as hoofing, whoring, etc.

Beef-tugging . . . The characteristic and, from time immemorial, almost indispensable fingering, pressing, kneading, tugging, squeezing, and what not—of the female goodies.

Beef up . . . To cause the pants philistine to fill its skin; said esp. of a female encouraging an unwilling or a partly disabled obturator.

Beefcake . . . A picture or photograph depicting a muscular Adonis, in his splendor.

Beefsteak and onions . . . With regard to a sexual engagement, the works.

Beget a child . . . **Knock out an apple.**

Beget children late in life . . . **Have January chickens.**

Beget children late in life, ability to . . . OPSIGENIA.

Behave clumsily in the act of lovemaking . . . BOUSTROPHATE.

Behind, the; conceived as a camera . . . **Camera obscura.**

Behind . . . See also under *Buttocks, Rump,* etc.

Belgravia . . . The pudendal cynosure of an exclusive harlot, the excluded being the moneyless "bums," in allusion to the fashionable district bearing this name, in London.

Bell polishing . . . Some lightweight necking in the hall between young lovers after a date.

Belly-bump . . . Do the pudendal mattress dance.

Belly bumper . . . A vigorous phallator, esp. one who fructifies.

Belly itch . . . That certain feeling, of a pudendum, for its mate.

Belly piece . . . Same as **Belly plaster,** female pudendum as an application to male counterpart.

Belly plaster . . . Anything warm and comforting applied to a man's belly and its restless pendant, like a young female's pudendum.

Belly plea . . . Pregnancy as an excuse or extenuation for a female accused of a crime.

Belly rub . . . A dance in which the couple is so closely juxtaposed that hisn squirms against hern, or her belly.

Belly seed . . . The fertilizing syrup ejected by the phallus at the pinnacle of its enthusiasm.

Belly timber . . . A female suitable, with regard to age and morality, for quenching the flame of the male's insatiable.

Bellyful . . . 1. A vaginal insertion of a substantial phallus. 2. A burgeoning income tax exemption, in utero.

Belonging to the blue squadron . . . Of mixed blood; begotten in a coital session between a white person and one not so white.

Bene mort . . . A refreshingly pretty female.

Benjamin . . . A condom, in allusion to "benjamin" the coat.

Best body cavity . . . The middle of the three openings at the lower end of the female.

BESTIALITY . . . Sexual intercourse between a human being and an animal.

Between you and me is the bed post . . . Of man and maid, united by the post that goes to bed hard and comes out soft.

Biddy . . . A female—esp. a young girl, esp. a cute chick, esp. a Brigitte.

Biddy . . . Same as BIDET, a basin used by females when bathing the pudendum.

BIDET . . . A bathroom accessory consisting of an elongated basin, supported on four legs thigh high, over which a female stands with a leg on each side while bathing her pudendum.

Big number . . . A brothel; in allusion to the large numerals on the doors of such pudendal establishments, in Paris, of yore.

BIGYNIST . . . A male who engages in sexual play and/or coitus with two women at the same time, or with one in the mere presence of another. From *bis* (twice) & *gyne* (woman).

Bilabial trump card . . . The lipped genital convincer of the female, down under.

Billy . . . A young and, as yet, unambitious male genital pendant.

Billy and doo . . . The penis and testicles of a small boy.

Billy-doo . . . Same as **Billy and doo,** the pudendum of a small boy.

Billy-goat . . . Of a male, to engage in extra-cardiac love affairs, via the pudendal route.

Bimbo . . . A girl who yields to phallic persuasion.

Birdie . . . A male homosexual.

Bishop . . . A large and stretched condom, generally used as a container for small articles.

Bit . . . A young female as pudendal timber.

Bit of all right, a . . . An attractive female with a pudendum that listens to phallic reason.

Bit of beef . . . 1. The male genital perpetrator. 2. From the viewpoint of the female, a partaking of the male pants worm.

Bit of cavalry . . . A fling at mounting the female.

Bit of ebony goodness . . . A not so bad at all colored female, at least from viewpoint of an Ethiop.

Bit of fat . . . A fat female, conceived as phallus fodder.

Bit of fat . . . A bout of pudendal conjugation with a fat female.

Bit of fat . . . The retrobrassierean tenants, in allusion to their being chiefly adipose tissue.

Bit of fluff . . . A young girl, or, at worst, just a female, with a very understanding pudendum, as far as the problems of the phallus erectus are concerned.

Bit of fork . . . The female sanctum of the crotch.

Bit of fork . . . A bit of female pudendum, i.e., a fling at it, phallically.

Bit of goods . . . A female, regarded with a lechered male eye, as an arena for manual, or, still better, phallic dexterity.

Bit of jam . . . 1. A "piece" of female pudendum, from the avid viewpoint of the male. 2. A physically attractive girl.

Bit of mutton . . . A woman with a fat and, presumably, especially warm pudendum.

Bit of raspberry . . . A young and attractive female conceived as a cut of savory pie.

Bit of skirt . . . A girl as a girl, not as a sibling.

Bit of stiff . . . 1. That without which virgins would so remain. 2. From the viewpoint of a female, a welcome visit by the genital opposite number.

Bit of stuff . . . A thoroughly feminine female regarded as a desirable coital companion.

Bitch . . . Go out whoremongering.

Bitch . . . 1. A woman with a commercially-minded underpart. 2. A male prostitute.

Bitch . . . A child, usually a boy, in whose anus and rectum a pederast relieves his sexual tension.

Bitched, buggered, and bewildered . . . Exhausted physically and/or mentally, as after a pudendal incursion.

Bite the brown . . . To lick or suckle the anus of, usually but not necessarily, a female.

Bite the dog-end . . . To lick or suck the lower, pudendal, end of the female torso.

Bite upon the phallus in fellatio . . . **Yorkshire bite.**

Bivirist . . . A female who enjoys sexual practices with two males at the same time, or with one in the presence of another. Ex *bis* (twice) & *vir* (man).

Black bagging . . . Vulvae of colored females, collectively.

Black joke . . . The female cleft conceived as a shady boscage which is the center of robust masculine jocundity.

Black Maria . . . 1. An ebonite whore. 2. The sump of an Ethiop courtesan into which the wallowing male organon disgorges its balm.

Black meat . . . The flesh of a colored girl which to a susceptible male, e.g., an Ethiop, is phallically specific.

Black mouth . . . The lower, speechless "mouth" of a negrine female.

Black pencil . . . The erotic shaft of a Negro.

Blackleg . . . The genital "leg" of a Negro.

Blacksmith's shop . . . A house of ill repute, from the understandable viewpoint of women, staffed by willin' females of the swarthy persuasion.

Blade . . . The male genital cleaver.

Blandishment of female legs, noncommercial, intended to elicit a legitimate (or even illegitimate) proposal from a sluggish male . . . **Leg show.**

Blandishments of female breast . . . **Titty-itty.**

Blandishments offered, usually by the female, to encourage love(making) . . . **House.**

Blanket . . . A sexual play partner, of either gender.

Blanket . . . See also under particular kind of blanket, as *Flesh blanket.*

Blanket drill . . . An act of sexercise, esp. when performed as an extra, not in the regular nocturnal routine, usually on—rather than under—the blanket.

Blanket hornpipe . . . The concourse of heterosexual pudendal chiefs of state, ending, after some jockeying, in a gratifying, though soggy, denouement.

Blanket ruffling . . . On the bed, and on the blanket, amorous mischief, between man and maid, usually restricted to tissue sampling, by digital exploration, of the pectoral bonbons, the interfemoral crotch, *et alii, et alibi,* and often terminating in a **blanket hornpipe,** *q.v.*

Blanket stiff . . . The phallus erectus, in allusion to **blanket ruffling** and the ensuing intumescence.

Blanket-stiff . . . Of the male animal's lower animal, rearing up on its "hind legs," because of **blanket ruffling,** or its equivalent; i.e., erected.

Blasted brimstone . . . A whore of something less than the desirable grade, esp. one who, supposedly, uses alum solution to compensate for vaginal relaxation.

BLASTOLAGNIA . . . Sexual desire for teen-age girls, esp. girls under sixteen. Ex *blastos* (a bud) & *lagneia* (lust).

Blaze the trail . . . To phallate a female for her first time.

Blazer . . . A male who unvirgins a virgin.

Bleeder . . . The hymen, in allusion to its hemorrhagic diathesis, when first unholied by the phallic desecrator.

Blessing . . . In the act of sexual intercourse with a paid harlot, any little amorous favor, beyond the underlying call of duty, contributed by the succubant.

Blind alley . . . The mute mouth of the female, below the pubic moustache.

Blind buckler . . . The urogenital pendant of the male, in its nonpendent posture, conceived as the plugger of the female hawsehole, in allusion to the blind eye of the organon and a nautical buckler.

Blind cheeks . . . The fleshy domes at the junction of the thighs with the trunk; the buttocks.

Blind love . . . The non-paternal, nonmaternal, non-fraternal, non-sororal, non-avuncular, non-nepotical type of love—sexlove.

Blinders . . . The areolated retrobrassiereans, in allusion to their, usually, spellbinding effect upon the oculars of the male, if round, firm, and fully packed.

Bloke . . .The recipient male in an act of sodomy.

Blondes, hyperlibidinosity for . . . **High blonde pressure.**

Blood escaping from a virgin's introitus during the phallic initiation in the post-nuptial period . . . **Christening wine.**

Blood spots on the bed sheet of a virgin bride, observed after the initiation night and occasionally thereafter, during the breaking-in period . . . **Bed bugs.**

Blood-stained vulva of a just phallated virgin, whether bride or whorelet . . . **Bloody Mary.**

Bloody Mary . . . The blood-stained pudendal decorations of a just unvirgined virgin (bride or not).

Bloss . . . A female whose pudendal crypt is rentable for short phallic engagements; a whore.

Blossom . . . A girl who has surrendered her pudendal flower.

Blow . . . To take the penis of another into one's mouth.

Blow . . . A whore, conceived as the recipient of the phallic aggressiveness.

Blow . . . 1. The prod that cheereth, i.e., the ingress of the membrum virile into the fleshy scabbard of the female. 2. A pudendal concourse of heterosexuals.

Blow-book . . . A book containing pictures of nudity and, esp., of males and females in the act of sexual concourse.

Blow off on the groundsels . . . To "lay" a woman on the ground, as in a park, or on the floor.

Blow off the loose corns . . . To get rid of excess seminal pressure by sporadic bouts with receptive women.

Blowen . . . A female who dispenses pudendal accommodations, freely but not for free.

Blower . . . A mistress who is a rung higher than a whore.

Blown safe . . . A female who has suffered the phallus to have his way.

Blubber . . . Female breasts of ample tonnage, esp. those that, naked, hang like flattened cheese bags or, confined, lose their identity in a fused mound of adiposity.

Blubbers . . . A woman's breasts, senior size. See also entry above.

Blue boar . . . A chancre, in allusion, possibly, to the Blue Boar Tavern of 19th century London, where chancres were a dime a dozen.

Blue board . . . A chancre. Variant of **blue boar.**

Blue boy . . . Same as **Blue boar** and **Blue board,** a chancre.

Blue skin . . . The offspring of coitus between a white malc and a Negress.

Blue squadron . . . Those persons, collectively, who are the offspring of coital engagements between whites and not-so-whites.

Blue squadron, belonging to the . . . Begotten in a coital coalition between a white person and one not quite or not at all white; of mixed blood.

Bluff the rat . . . Of the female, to withdraw forcibly from the vagino-phallic duet when the male is near the gratification point.

Blurt out . . . To blow the anal horn by an expulsion of flatus in "opening up" rectally for the phallus, in sodomy.

Bo . . . A male child in whose anus and rectum a pederast finds phallic comfort.

Board . . . Of an able and willing male, to mount a supine and willing female, for a course of "saber rattling."

Boast of successful invasions into the female pudendal roaster, with the phallus erectus . . . **Cry roast meat.**

Bobbles . . . A man's testicles, conceived, by females, as bobbing in his walk.

Bobstay . . . Frenulum of the prepuce, connecting the prepuce with the lower surface of the glans penis.

Bobtail . . . 1. An impotent male. 2. A castrated male. 3. A male whose "tail" is cut or shot off. Based on *bob* (to cut short) and *tail* (the phallus).

Bobtail . . . 1. A harlot, esp. one who, in the course of fulfilling her professional engagements, makes it more interesting for her patrons by imparting a cooperative rhythm to her crotch. 2. A girlie who walks with a monronian oscillation of her gluteal cheeks.

Body job, do a . . . To do an amorous palpatory reconnaissance on the female body.

Boil one's lobster . . . To infect the male's short arm by contact with a venereally tainted female cranny.

Bona roba . . . A well-dressed whore, in allusion to the literal meaning, "good stuff."

Bone . . . A phallus erectus as the personification of male libido.

Bone ache . . . A venereal disease, esp. gonorrheal arthritis.

Boneless appendage . . . The genital troublemaker of the male.

Boneless beef . . . The male genital sausage that manages to become firm, p.r.n., without the aid of an endoskeleton.

Boneless fish . . . The membrum virile conceived as a fillet doing quite well without an osseous framework.

Boneless stiff . . . The genital coupler of the male, in allusion to its anosseous structure.

Bone-on . . . Same as **Bone,** the libidinous phallus erectus.

Boodle . . . The amorous favors granted by the girl to her escort at the door, at their parting, as after a dance, to entice him to return.

Boodle-fever . . . The sexual excitation induced in the swain by the good-night kiss and the attendant amorous favors bestowed by the girl as they part at her door.

Boodle-pinching . . . Of a girl, parsimonious with the dispensation of amorous favors when parting with her escort at her door, after a date.

Book . . . To engage a female for a sexual nocturne.

Book containing pictures of nudity, esp. of males and females in the act of coitus . . . **Blow-book.**

Boot . . . The female gimcrack, conceived as a sheath for the male "foot."

Born on the wrong side of the blanket . . . Conceived and delivered without an imprimatur from the parson, i.e., illegitimate.

Bosom cheaters; falsies . . . COLPOMENTIORS; COLPOMIMS; SEINSEMBLERS.

Bosom reinforced to give a specious impression of enticing prominence . . . **Doublet.**

Bosom . . . See also under *Breasts, female.*

Boston Tea Party . . . A defecation in the presence of another, esp. such act by a female in the presence of a male who derives sexual pleasure or gratification from the sight of it.

Bottle . . . Vaginal embrace pressure upon the invading phallus.

Bottle and glass . . . The behind, considered as a single dome; a rhyming slangonym on *ass.*

Bottle-arse . . . A person, esp. a female, fat and broad in the posterior prominence.

Bottle-arse . . . A female whose lower posterior prominences are disproportionately larger than her upper anterior.

Bottle up . . . To protect the cervix uteri by means of a diaphragm, against impregnation.

Bottled beer . . . Seminal fluid used in artificial insemination.

Bottom drawer, get together the . . . Of a girl, esp. a bride, to collect her trousseau.

Bottom position in sexual intercourse, one in . . . SUCCUBUS.

Bottom sawyer . . . Of a pair engaged in orthodox sexual intercourse, the one who is in the succubous or bottom position, usually the female.

Bottomless pit . . . 1. The external genitalia of the female. 2. The middle of the three passages at the lower end of the female torso.

Botty . . . The buttocks of an infant or a child.

Bouguereau quality . . . Effeminacy verging on the risque, in allusion to Adolphe William Bouguereau whose nudes excelled in this quality.

BOULVERSANTE . . . Of a female, something she wears, or part of her, completely upsetting and bewitching to the observing male, sexually; as a revealing gown, or that which is revealed. Ex *boulverser* (to overturn).

BOUSTROPHATE . . . To behave clumsily in the act of lovemaking. Ex *bous* (ox) & *strephein* (turn).

Bowl for timber . . . Of a leg-minded male, to search for a female with attractive stocking frames.

Bowl for timber . . . To lasciviate (knead amorously) the lower timbers of a female, i.e., the legs.

Bowl for timber . . . Of the male, to aim for a meeting at the pudendal level, no less.

Bowsprit . . . The genital beak of the male, in allusion to its figurative resemblance, when "under sailing orders," to the tapered pole extending forward from the bow of a sailing vessel.

Bowsprit, have one's, in parentheses . . . To have one's phallus erectus well sunk in the female pudendal orifice and clasped by the parentheses-like labia.

Box out . . . Of a married man having access to his lawfully wedded pudendum, to **eat out** anyway.

Box the compass . . . To replace the male genital needle in its intratrouserian den, after it has been out, esp. on a hurried pudendal foray, as in a hallway, park, etc.

Box the compass . . . To soften up, by well-rehearsed talk, a non-whoring, but not necessarily virgin, female, for a pudendal concourse; in allusion to the naming of the thirty-two points of the compass in any given order, a feat requiring some rehearsing.

Box the Jesuit and get cockroaches . . . To masturbate successfully to a seminal finale.

Boy exploited in the act of pederasty, in allusion to posteriors . . . **Bum-boy.**

Boy in pederasty, search for a . . . **Climb a tier; Go to town; Rummage; Run a tier.**

Boy used in the act of pederasty . . . **Bum-boy; Ingle; Fairy; Child bride; Schwantz-kid.**

Boy used in act of pederasty . . . **Angelina; Bitch; Bo; Gonsel; Gunsil; Punk kid; Wife.**

Boy used in act of pederasty . . . **Arseduke; Bronc; Bronco; Gazook; Gazoony; Kid; Punk; Ringtail.**

Bracer . . . An exposed, usually unexposed, area or structure of the female, in allusion to the tonic effect on a virile but unsated male pendant.

BRACHIOPHILOUS . . . Of the male, especially erotic about the female's arms. From *brachion* (arm) & *philein* (to love).

BRADYCONTIA . . . In coitus, a slowing of the ejaculatory response, as in older males. From *bradys* (slow) & *anakontızo* (to spurt out).

Braille . . . To savor manually the palpable characters of a female.

Braille anatomy . . . A caressing session involving the distinguishing characteristics of the female body.

Braille fever . . . The genital pyrexia induced in a male palpating the sweets of a girl.

Braille fiend . . . A devout palpator.

Braille-shy . . . Of a girl, skittish about being palpated erotically.

Branch of medicine dealing with the diagnosis and treatment of syphilis . . . SYPHILOLOGY.

Branch of medicine dealing with the prevention and treatment of venereal disease . . . VENEREOLOGY.

Branch of medicine dealing with the prevention of conception . . . ACEPTIATRY.

Branch of medicine . . . See also under *Study*.

Brassiere busters . . . Opulent, eckbergian mammae.

Brassiere, conceived as the confiner of the breasts . . . **Bubby trap.**

Brassiere empties . . . Small bubbies which leave the brassiere cups discouragingly unfilled.

Brassiere honeys . . . A girl's bubbies of medium size but bardotian format.

Brassiere intended to give the breasts a speciously favorable form and magnitude . . . **Brummagem.**

Brassiere, padded; falsies . . . COLPOMENTIORS; COLPOMIMS; SEINSEMBLERS.

Brassiere snatcher . . . A male who collects, through snatching or stealing, slightly used brassieres.

Brassiere tenants . . . The female bubbies.

BRASSIEROLAGNIA . . . Erotic contemplation of brassieres; lust aroused by the sight of brassicres.

Brazen gift . . . The gift of the female pudendum.

Bread bags . . . The-once-by-milk-engorged-but-now-flattened female breasts.

Bread buttered on both sides . . . A female who takes the phallus both fore and aft, i.e., vaginally and rectally.

Break a crust . . . To deflower a young one, by breaking the virgin crust.

Break a lance with . . . Of a male, to soften a rigid phallus in (a particular woman).

Break a leg . . . To bear a bastard.

Break a peter on . . . Soften the phallus in, i.e., phallate.

Break in the balls . . . To have pudendal concourse with a girl; applied esp. to a young man in his sexual novitiate.

Break the knee . . . 1. Of a virgin, to lose it. 2. To become pregnant, in the old-fashioned way.

Breast, female, as a milk-producing organ . . . MAMMA.

Breast, female, French form for . . . **POITRINE; SEIN.**

Breast, female, Greek form for . . . **MASTOS; MAZOS.**

Breast, female, Latin form for . . . MAMMA; UBERA; MAMMILLA.

Breast, female, shriveling of; with age . . . MAZORHIKNOSIS.

Breast, female, when abnormally small . . . **Tom tit.**

Breast finger-exercise . . . Digital calisthenics involving the retrobrassiereans, also known as the bubbies.

Breast, male, esp. when abnormally large . . . **Tom tit.**

Breast pads worn by females having small mammaries . . . **Brummagem bubbies.**

Breast pads . . . See also under **Brassiere, padded.**

Breast work . . . an indulgence in a palpatory foray upon the female breasts.

Breasts and buttocks, having beautiful . . . CALLIMAMMAPYGIAN.

Breasts and buttocks of a female . . . **Fores and afts.**

Breasts, female, a caressing of the . . . **Breast work.**

Breasts, female, amorous manipulation of . . . **Beef-tugging.**

Breasts, female, amorous stimulation of; as with the lips or the fingers . . . **Tittiellation.**

Breasts, female, ample . . . **Blubber.**

Breasts, female, ample, to display partly . . . **Sport the blubber.**

Breasts, female, as occasionally referred to by zee xenoepic members of the 50 million who, proverbially, can't be wrong . . . **Zee titties.**

Breasts, female, as victuals . . . **Vittles.**

Breasts, female, beautiful . . . **Sweater dandies; Prize fagots.**

Breasts, female, beautiful, having . . . CALLIMAZONIAN; CALLICOLPIAN; CALLIMASTIAN.

Breasts, female, beautiful, one having . . . CALLIMAZONIAN.

Breasts, female, caress the, as opposed to meandering in netherland . . . **Play to the gallery.**

Breasts, female, centering erotic interest on . . . MAZOCENTRIC.

Breasts, female, characteristic deformity of, as seen in women who have borne children . . . PAREMASTIA.

Breasts, female, cleft or line of cleavage of . . . **The hotline; Sweet line.**

Breasts, female, cleft or space between . . . MESOSEINIA; INTERMAZIUM.

Breasts, female, conceived as dazzlers, with regard to the oculars of the male . . . **Blinders.**

Breasts, female, conceived as denizens of the brassierean cups . . . **Areolated retrobrassiereans.**

Breasts, female, conceived as mysteries by those without access to them . . . **Bags of mystery.**

Breasts, female, condition marked by involution of; in old age . . . GEROMASTIA.

Breasts, female, considered as the toys of Satan . . . **Devil's playthings.**

Breasts, female, development of, at puberty . . . MAZANTHOSIS; SORORIATION.

Breasts, female, especially erotic about . . . MAZOPHILOUS.

Breasts, female, get a handful of, by slithering inside the bosom hammock . . . **Get inside.**

Breasts, female having beautiful . . . CALLIMASTA; CALLIMAZONIAN.

Breasts, female, having beautiful . . . CALLIMAZONIAN; CALLIMASTIAN; CALLICOLPIAN.

Breasts, female, having more than ample . . . MEGAMASTOUS.

Breasts, female, having such large, that one could make two . . . **Double-diddied.**

Breasts, female; in allusion to the breast of an animal . . . **Briskets.**

Breasts, female, in allusion to their adipose structure . . . **Bit of fat.**

Breasts, female, inequality in size of . . . ANISOMASTIA.

Breasts, female, licking or suckling of, erotic . . . MAMMILINGUS.

Breasts, female, manipulation of, for figurative digital calisthenics . . . **Breast finger-exercise.**

Breasts, female, non-beautiful . . . **Dugs.**

Breasts, female, of a mulatto . . . **Brown creatures.**

Breasts, female, of excessive tonnage . . . **Blubber.**

Breasts, female, of the young and the beautiful . . . **Sweater dandies.**

Breasts, female, overdevelopment of . . . MAZAUXESIS.

Breasts, female, pendulosity of . . . MAZECTENIA.

Breasts, female, person having large . . . MACROMASTA.

Breasts, female, phallate between the approximated . . . MASTOPHALLATE.

Breasts, female, proud of her . . . **Tittyuppy.**

Breasts, female, regarded as . . . **Northern hemispheres.**

Breasts, female, regarded as "front posteriors" . . . **Fore-buttocks.**

Breasts, female, regarded as sweet little fellows . . . **Bubbies.**

Breasts, female, regarded as the best in the house . . . **Top of the shop.**

Breasts, female, small or underdeveloped . . . MASTUNCULI; MICROMASTAE; **Teacups; Pointers; Featherweights; Flyspecks; Half portions; Runts; Tom thumbs; Warts; Stubs; Smallies; Pips; Picayunes; Little drinks; Smudges; Midgies; Peanuts.**

Breasts, female, so exquisite as to defy description . . . **Ineffables.**

Breasts, female, space between . . . INTERMAZIUM; MESOSEINIA.

Breasts, female, squeeze amorously the . . . MAZMASSATE.

Breasts, female, the wearing of artificial . . . COLPOMIMESIS.

Breasts, female, young and beautiful . . . **Mimpins; Sweater dandies; Prize fagots.**

Breasts, female, young and exquisite . . . **Pretty sweet meat.**

Breasts, interior of a woman's garment over the . . . **Bubby hutch.**

Breasts, large, woman having . . . MACROMASTA.

Breasts, vulva, and an arse as a bride's dowry . . . **Tipperary fortune.**

Breech; conceived as a one-eyed specter with halitosis . . . **Douglas with one eye and a stinking breath.**

Breeding cage . . . The bed as a site of vagino-phallic inosculations.

Brevet-wife . . . A woman who is a man's wife in every way but the legal.

Brick defecatorium . . . A literary equivalent of the plebeian "brick shit-house," *q.v.*

Brick shit-house . . . A personification of something elegant and well constructed, in allusion and contrast to the jerry-built privies of yesteryear; used fondly by men to designate a female figure of the highest provocative caliber.

Bride, man who married an immature or child . . . **Baby porker; Kentucky cradle snatcher; Cradle snatcher; Bearskin robber; Kid walloper; Kid napper; Kidskin stretcher; Chicken thief; Chick fancier; Kindergarten butcher.**

Brim . . . Of a male, to phallate the female of the species, in allusion to the standard meaning of the term as applied to swine.

Bring down by hand . . . To soften a lusty induration of the male genital limb by manual effleurage.

Bring home a case of claps . . . **Come home with clap'em.**

Brisket-happy . . . Of a woman, making a not unwelcome display of titty.

Brisket swarmer . . . A male lover who, above all else, fusses amorously over his quarry's breasts, at the first opportunity.

Briskets . . . The sub-brassierean fleshy gibbosities.

Bristler . . . A young female who bristles with titty-appeal.

Broach claret . . . To draw blood from a virgin, in the course of defloration.

Broad . . . A girl who takes a dim view of the narrow path of morality.

Broad-gauge . . . Of a female, having a wide "seat." Also, the female having such.

Broad jumper . . A seducer or a raper of young females.

Broiler . . . A young girl with a lively pudendum.

Broken-kneed . . . Of a desirable female, seduced—but good!

Broken-legged above the knee . . . Once a virgin but so no more.

Bronc . . . A boy in whose anus and rectum the phallus of a pederast finds solace.

Bronco . . . Same as **Bronc,** the boy in pederasty.

Bronco buster . . . A pederast, esp. one with a big phallus.

Broom . . . The female pubic brush and its underlying toothless mouth.

Broomstick . . . The male stick that fits the female **broom.**

Broomstick wedding . . . A mock wedding in which the principals jump over a broom, then live as man and wife.

Broth of joy . . . The lactescent treacle ex-spurted from the gratified male organ at the end of its caper in the pudendum muliebre.

Brothel as an academy of Aphrodite's Roman equivalent . . . **School of Venus.**

Brothel; conceived as a shop where female arses may be bought for short-term use . . . **Bum-shop.**

Brothel, female manager of; as a mother-aster . . . **Mother damnable; Mother-inferior; Mother midnight; Mother abbess; Mother of the maids.**

Brothel for colored patrons, stocked with female recipients of the same tinge . . . **Blacksmith shop.**

Brothel; in allusion to large numeral on door of some . . . **Big number.**

Brothel; in allusion to lascivious males, the goats . . . **Goat-house.**

Brothel; in allusion to the typical male movement often observed there . . . **Up-and-down place.**

Brothel, licensed . . . **MAISON DE TOLÉRANCE.**

Brothel, where males go for "knocking" . . . **Knocking-house.**

Brother of the gusset . . . 1. A procurer of mercenary female pudenda for males with high seminal fluid pressure. 2. A pimp or go-between who brings together sexually eager males and economically desirous females. 3. A whoremaster general.

Brother, sexual desire for one's own . . . **FRATRILAGNIA.**

Brother starling . . . A man who bunks with another man's pigeon.

Brown cow . . . A mulattess whose genital introitus is available for one night stands.

Brown creatures . . . The pectoral eminences of a mulattess.

Brown eyes . . . The female breasts; the female nipples.

Brown family . . . Catamites collectively; the world of catamites.

Brown Joe . . . The genital walloper of a mulatto male.

Brown madam . . . The moustache and lips and mouth of a female, at the nether end.

Browning Sisters, the . . . Catamites collectively; the world of catamites.

Brownsward . . . The space between the buttocks.

Bruiser . . . The phallus colossus conceived as the bruiser of the vagina.

Brummagem . . . A garment or device intended to give the female breasts a speciously favorable form and magnitude. An allusion to Birmingham, England, where imitation jewelry was made.

Brummagem bubbies . . . Breast pads worn by females with small ones to give the impression of having big ones.

Brummagem buttons . . . Small buttons or tufts affixed to the apices of the brassiere cups to give the outer garment the impression of bulging nipples. Also, the imitation nipples so created.

Brummagem Joe . . . A condom-like device padded with sponge rubber and, often, reinforced with lateral and on-end "tickling" attachments, to give a potent but small phallus greater authority.

Brunser . . . A child, male or female, in whose anus and rectum the pederast finds his phallic mate.

Brutal breasting . . . A dance in which the couple is so close together that the male feels the "brutal" pressure of the female pectoral attractions.

Bubbied . . . Well appointed in the pectoral region; i.e., having a delightful pair of sweater dandies.

Bubbies . . . The nippled denizens of the brassiere.

Bubbies and cunt . . . A poor girl's trousseau or dowry.

Bubbies, huffed on the . . . Of a man, but more often of a courting swain, enamored of his girl's intrabrassiereans.

Bubbies, lay it on the . . . To play the phallus erectus between the pectoral lactogens.

Bubbies' uncle . . . A fornicator of a married woman who, in the absence of the legitimate phallator, pretends, for the benefit of the neighbors or the female's children, to be an uncle of the quarry.

Bubble . . . A famished soldier or sailor who is unaware, in his breathless hop on a female pudendum, that his phallus has been diverted from the proper entrance, by the trained hand of the paid coitante.

Bubbleable . . . Of a wench, not adverse to communion with the sex-emissary of a desirable male.

Bubbled . . . Of the female, phallated; in allusion to the phallic ejaculant.

Bubblejack . . . The manna discharged by the phallus in its moment of supreme happiness.

Bubbly Jack . . . A phallus which disgorges its lava before it enters the empyrean of the female crotch.

Bubbly Jock . . . A phallus which oozes a little when its bearer is engaged in digital exercise with a well-appointed female.

Bubby . . . One of the jutters of a girl's chest.

Bubby bube . . . A man so enamored of his girl's breasts that he is myopic about her shortcomings and is easily managed by her.

Bubby circus . . . An alluring display of titty by a girl well titapointed.

Bubby hammock . . . The unappreciative constant companion of the female pectoral sweetmeat—the brassiere.

Bubby heaters . . . The cupped hands of an amorous man applied snugly, often from behind, to the "pride and joy" of a female.

Bubby hutch . . . The interior of the front part of a girl's bodicc, where the bubbies are.

Bubby hutch, drop anchor in the . . . To let the hand slither down a girl's neckline.

Bubby smoocher . . . A man who befouls the female breasts with seminal jam.

Bubby trader . . . A female who, having no other attractions, exploits to the best of advantage her pectoral eminences.

Bubby trap . . . 1. A brassiere. 2. A low neckline exposing the swell of the breasts and the intervening Y-shaped or linear demarcation.

Bubby trifler . . . A male who contents himself with the more or less innocuous pleasures of "titty-shucking."

Buck . . . A husband whose wife receives vaginal douches from a phallus not his.

Buck . . . Pudendal conversations, i.e., vaginal dilatation by the ithyphallos or membrum virile erectum.

Buck face . . . Not only the face but all of a man whose wife is, or was, unfaithful; i.e., a cuckold.

Buck one's stumps . . . Of a female in coitus, to stir about in erotic restlessness.

Bucket . . . The female pudendum, esp. the vaginal corridor, in allusion to its serving as receptacle for the phallic seminal sputum.

Buckinger's boot . . . The female gewgaw, whither the phallus goeth. An allusion to one Matthew Buckinger, a limbless erast whose only "foot" was usually in his wife's **boot.**

Buckinger's foot . . . The male organon, in allusion to a character whose limbless torso had but this one foot. See preceding entry.

Buff ball . . . A bail, of sorts, at which the guests are naked of clothes.

Buff the dog . . . To induce phallic disgorgement by manual flirtation with the organ, esp. such serenading performed by the hand of a female.

Buffing stick . . . The phallus as the polisher of the vagina.

Buffinger . . . A male who insists on absolute nudity, for himself and his coital playmate, during the act of phallation.

Bugger . . . A sodomite or a pederast.

Bugger . . . To phallate per rectum; to sodomize.

Bugger (with) . . . Make intensely amorous contacts with the female body, manually, labially, etc., but not phallically.

Buggerage . . . The additional charge made by a whore for the privilege of rectal admission.

Bugger-arsed . . . Having a painful anus, because buggered by a bulky phallus.

Buggered and bewildered . . . Of the female, phallated and impregnated extramaritally.

Buggerling . . . A female who submits willingly to phallic intrusion by way of the rectum.

Buggershy . . . Unwilling to take the phallus per rectum.

Built like a brick shit-house . . . Of the female figure, nonpareil, crème de la crème, ne plus ultra, etc.

Bull . . . The male urogenital horn, conceived as a goring appendage.

Bull . . . To gore a female pudendally with the male genital horn.

Bull by the souse . . . In fellatio, of the one who gives, to hold by the ears the one who takes.

Bull dance . . . A dance without girls, i.e., a dance in which the couples are all male, as in a prison, on shipboard, etc.

Bull in a china shop, to . . . To phallate a young girl, or a girl having a small introitus, with a massive baton.

Bull money . . . The "price of meat," i.e., the amount paid a Mrs. Warren girlie for a pudendal "bull session."

Bull nurse . . . A passive male homosexual, in allusion to his nursing the desires of the other.

Bull party . . . A sexually festive gathering of male homosexuals.

Bull point . . . The point used in bulling, i.e., the phallus erectus.

Bull ring . . . The female perineal trifle, conceived as the arena for bull sessions or gratifying pudendal collisions.

Bull session . . . A session with the female pudendum during which it receives, from the male drumstick, a sound drubbing.

Bull twister . . . A fellator or fellatrice who controls the exuberance of the fellatrant by holding and, if necessary, squeezing or twisting his testicles.

Bulldiker . . . A female homosexual.

Bulling . . . Sexual concourse, esp. the male's part therein.

Bullish . . . Of a male's genital scepter, at attention.

Bullshit . . . Seminal fluid, conceived as the dross resulting from "bulling."

Bully . . . A *pimp*ereeno or harlot's go-between who protects his protege from the harms of others but who exploits her nonetheless.

Bully in the muzzle . . . To give suck of one's phallus; to practice fellatorism.

Bum . . . 1. The behind; the arse. 2. The buttocks, both of them, as a unit. 3. The "asshole."

Bum-boy . . . A boy whose rectum is utilized as a vagina by a "backwoods fiddler," i.e., a pederast.

Bum-brusher . . . A lecherous male who seeks the opportunity to rub against the buttocks of desirable females in crowded public places.

Bum-fiddle . . . The behind, esp. the anus, in allusion to its occasional cacophony or to its service as a receiving chamber for the phallus of a sodomite.

Bum fiddle . . . To phallate per rectum, in allusion to **bum** the arse.

Bum fiddler . . . A phallator per rectum, i.e., a sodomite or a pederast, in allusion to **bum.**

Bum-fighter . . . A whoremaster general, i.e., a habitué of brothels and a patron saint of Mrs. Warren.

Bum-fighting . . . 1. Sexual concourse. 2. A rubbing of posteriors between female lesbians.

Bum-shop . . . The female pudendal toy, in allusion to an arse shop.

Bum-shop . . . A female flesh-exchange where men may rent the use of a pudendum for the relief of seminal pressure; an allusion to **bum,** an arse.

Bum sucker . . . A male who enjoys licking the female arse, including the rectal bunghole.

Bumbo . . . The female sexual kickshaw, whither the phallus flyeth.

Bun . . . The soft, moist, and furry animalcule at the lower end of the female trunk which sailors touch for good luck—so they say—before going on a long voyage.

Bung . . . The male genital shaft, conceived as a "cork" for the female bunghole.

Bung . . . To relieve the urgency of an adamant phallus by a plunge into the exhaust gut.

Bung juice . . . Phallic fluid, either the amber or the lactescent, but usually the latter.

Bung upwards . . . Of a posture, with the buttocks up.

Bunghole . . . The anus of a female, conceived as an introitus for a sodomite. Also a male anus so used.

Bunker-shy . . . Of a male picked as subject by a sodomist or pederast, opposed to the act.

Bunny . . . Same as **Bun,** the female pudendal contrivance.

Burgle . . . To coit through the rectum.

Burgle . . . To intromit into the female pudendal property of another man.

Burgle . . . To obtain pudendal privileges from an attractive but youngish and naive female by Madison Ave. talk.

Burner . . . A venereal disease, usually gonorrhea.

Bury the hatchet where it won't rust . . . To sheathe the male genital cutlass with vaginal mucosa.

Bushel bubby . . . 1. A female breast which is too much of a good thing. 2. A woman who possesseth bushel-size mammaries.

Bushes . . . The barbigerous underbelly of the female.

Bushy Park . . . The pubic beard of a female. Also, her pudendal mansion house.

Business . . . The erotic business end of either the male or the female torso, i.e., the phallus or the vulva.

Business, the . . . Sexual concourse prosaically delineated.

Busk . . . To peddle erotic merchandise, as special condoms (ticklers), alleged aphrodisiacs, etc.

Buss-beggar . . . An elderly, almost completely impotentiated male whom even an ordinary whore will not suffer near her pudendal satisfier, who must, therefore, consort with beggar-women and frazzled-out harlots. Also, a slovenly woman or whore who cannot find pudendal patrons.

Buster . . . The phallus, regarded as the colossus of the male pudendum because of its "busting" effect on the female channel.

Bust-maker . . . A "wolf" who phallates many females, causing some of them to be "with child" and, consequently, with engorged mammae; hence the antonomasia "bust-maker."

Butcher . . . To give a female a hard time with the phallus, esp. when the introitus is no match for the magnitude of the male lever.

Butt . . . A buttock; the rump.

Butt . . . Sexual intercourse regarded as a presentation of the female's unclean end, the arse.

Butt in . . . To intromit the phallus erectus into the fold between the glutei of a female.

Butt smasher . . . A man very well developed pudendally, in allusion to his vulva-clastic powers.

Butt sniper . . . A male who seeks out opportunities to rub against the buttocks of females, as in crowded public places.

Butter . . . Established access to a favorite female pudendum.

Butter . . . To whip a boy who derives sexual pleasure from punishment by flagellation.

Butter and cheesecake . . . A liberal display of legs, augmented by an equally liberal décolletage.

Butter and dash . . . Have a hurried fling at coitus.

Butter and eggs . . . Sexual accommodations supplied with alacrity by a friendly female pudendum.

Butter box . . . The female pudendal inlet, esp. when juicy with ungation.

Butter churn . . . A girl's cleavage, between the thighs.

Butter fingers . . . Male fingers with an amatory bent, esp. for the female pudendal thesaurus.

Butter-mouth . . . A man who liquidates his passion by basiating the lower lips of a girl.

Butter the bacon . . . 1. To grease the vaginal corridor with seminal ejaculant. 2. To pay a harlot for her services.

Buttered bun . . . A mistress, esp. one kept happy with substantial rewards.

Buttered bun . . . A prostitute who receives several patrons of the art in rapid succession, so that her vaginal hallway is well buttered with seminal ejaculant.

Buttered bun . . . A woman whose pudendal introitus is still redolent of seminal treacle, from a previous phallic engagement, when she takes on a series of new thrusts.

Buttered finger . . . A male finger emerging from a palpatory exploration of the humid female interior, at the nether end.

Butterfly . . . The elongated labia minora extruding from the interlabial slit of the majora.

Buttock . . . A whore of the lower middle-class.

Buttock . . . The pudendum of either sex, but more often that of the female, in the sense of "a piece of ass."

Buttock and tongue . . . A prostitute who, in addition to the usual, sucks the male teat and/or licks the anus.

Buttock ball . . . A ball arranged by prostitutes for the purpose of lining up new customers.

Buttock-broker . . . The manager(ess) of a vulva brokerage or brothel.

Buttock-broker . . . A matchmaker for bouts between heterosexual pudenda, within wedlock, i.e., a marriage broker.

Buttock-broker . . . A procur*er* or *ess* of female pudenda for males with problems of phallic rigidity.

Buttock climber . . . A man who prefers to phallate per rectum. Also, sometimes, a male who is fond of coitus à la vache.

Buttock-clingers . . . Very tight and, on an attractive girl, provocative short shorts.

Buttock-mail . . . A contraceptive device, as a diaphragm or a condom, usually the latter.

Buttock-mail . . . A fine imposed upon fornicators for indulging in sexual pleasures outside the legal formula.

Buttock-mail . . . Tight and unyielding female panties which thwart phallic aggression, or ingression.

Buttocks and breasts, having beautiful . . . CALLIMAMMAPYGIAN.

Buttocks as a unit of rump . . . **Toby.**

Buttocks as rear guard . . . **Hinder end.**

Buttocks as the antipodes of the "northern hemispheres" . . . **Southern hemispheres.**

Buttocks as the posterior dome . . . **Flankey.**

Buttocks, centering erotic interest on female . . . CLUNICENTRIC.

Buttocks; conceived as spheres . . . SPHEROMATA.

Buttocks, conceived as the blind counterparts of the subocular cheeks . . . **Blind cheeks.**

Buttocks, esp. naked . . . **Seat of shame.**

Buttocks, esp. of a female charming . . . **Seat of honor.**

Buttocks, esp. the inner halves . . . **Hind boot.**

Buttocks, female and beautiful . . . CALLIPYGUS.

Buttocks, female, especially erotic about the . . . PYGOPHILOUS.

Buttocks, flattening of . . . SPHEROPLANIA.

Buttocks, groin formed by junction of . . . **Gusset of the arse.**

Buttocks, kissing of . . . PYGOPHILEMIA.

Buttocks of a female on the receiving end of the provoked phallus, in allusion to the enacted mattress jig . . . **Itch-buttocks.**

Buttocks of an infant or a child . . . **Botty.**

Buttocks, rubbing of, as a means of deriving or giving sexual pleasure . . . PYGOTRIPSIS.

Buttocks, rubbing of, between female homosexuals . . . **Bum-fighting.**

Button . . . The erectile fillet of the male pudendum.

Button buster . . . An oo-la-la female whose exuberant goodies, at mere sight, cause the male boom to go upsy-daisy—and "bust" the fly buttons, at least figuratively.

Button-loose . . . Of a male, having a desirous and active genital picket.

Button-short . . . Having a phallus of junior size.

Button up . . . To plug the female paradisiac adit with the male gluttonous bung.

Button your arse! . . . An unpolished admonition of a termagant wench to her fly-bulging swain, to keep his vulture in its cage.

Buttonhole . . . The female sexual inlet for the phallus.

Buttonhole work . . . The act of sewing the female pudendum with the male procreative needle, i.e., coitus orthodoxus.

Buttonhole worker . . , The genital sewing needle of the male.

Buttonhole worker . . . A male in the act of reducing a tumefied phallus in the dephlogisticating inlet of the female pudendum.

Buttons attached to brassiere cups to give the outer garment an imitation nipple bulge . . . **Brummagem buttons.**

Buy milk . . . Buy sexual accommodations from a whore.

By-blow . . . The human product of unlicensed impregnation; i.e., a bastard.

By-chop . . . An offspring begotten out of parson-approved coitus; i.e., an illegitimate child.

By-scape . . . A child born of extranuptial coitus; i.e., a scion sinistral.

By-slip . . . A bairn conceived in illegitimate sexual concourse; i.e., a bastard.

C

Cab . . . A stable of whores; a brothel.

CACAVALENCE . . . Sexual impotence resulting from a sense of guilt. Ex *kakon* (guilt), *a* (negative), & *valere* (to be able).

Calf of leg, female, especially erotic about the . . . SURAPHILOUS.

Calf of leg . . . See also under *Calves*.

Calf-sticking . . . Phallic forays into the pudendal arcana of young females, esp. teeners.

CALLIANDRUS . . . A handsome male with an intriguing sex organ. Ex *kallos* (beauty) & *andrus* (man as a male).

CALLICNEMIC . . . Of the female, usually, having beautiful legs. Ex *kallos* & *kneme* (leg).

CALLICOLPOS . . . A beautiful bosom. Ex *kallos* (beauty) & *kolpos* (bosom).

CALLIFEMORAL . . . Having beautiful thighs; said esp. of the female.

CALLIMAMMAPYGIAN . . . Embellished with beautiful buttocks and breasts. Ex *kallos* (beauty), *mamma* (breast), & *pyge* (rump).

CALLIMASTIAN . . . Having beautiful breasts. Ex *kallos* (beauty) & *mastos* (breast).

CALLINYMPH . . . A beauteous bride. Ex *kalos* (beautiful) & *nymphe* (a bride).

CALLINYMPHID . . . A girl with exquisite labia minora. Ex *kalos* (beautiful) & *nymphae* (labia minora).

CALLIPHALLIC . . . Pert. to or adorned with an elegant membrum virile.

CALLIPHALLUS . . . A handsome male organ. Ex *kallos* (beauty) & *phallos* (the male organon).

CALLIPOMATE . . . Having dainty labia majora. Ex *kallos* (beauty) & *pomas* (labia majora).

CALLIPYGIAN . . . Of a girl, usually, having beautiful buttocks. Ex *kallos* (beauty) & *pyge* (rump).

CALLIPYGUS . . . The female behind beautiful.

CALLISPHYROUS . . . Having beautiful ankles. Ex *kallos* (beauty) & *sphyron* (ankle).

CALLISURAL . . . Of the female, decorated with beautiful leg calves.

CALLITREMA . . . A girl with an allegedly beautiful pudendum. Also, such a pudendum. Ex *kalos* (beautiful) & *trema* (a hole).

CALLITREMATA . . . Beautiful vulvas, if there are such. Also, the possessors of such.

CALLITRICHOUS . . . Having beautiful hair. Ex *kalos* (beautiful) & *thrix* (hair).

Calorific mama . . . A red-hot mama in dire need for the phallic extinguisher.

Calves, having beautiful . . . CALLISURAL.

Calves, having fat . . . STEATOSURAL.

Camel complaint . . . A condition of the male marked by enlargement and stiffness of the genital shaft, usually responding to treatment by local application of vaginal mucosa, in situ. Based on the allusion to the pants hump created by the tumefied organ.

Camel night . . . A night spent in pudendal revelry; an allusion to "hump"–sexual concourse.

Camel night . . . An evening spent with an attractive girl, resulting in a humping of the fly with erected phallus.

Camera obscura . . . The seat of the trunk, in allusion to the anus (lens) and the darkness behind.

Can . . . A non-aristocratic concept of the female pubic delta as a canning place for the phallus.

Can . . . The rump, usually of a female.

Can . . . Privileges to the pudendum muliebre.

Can of brown polish . . . The genital slit of a mulattess.

Can pack . . . A menstrual pack or pad.

Canary . . . A young, sprightly girl, conceived as a likely pudendal dish.

Canned goods . . . 1. A young virgin. 2. The untried pudendal luxuries of an adolescent girl.

Canned tomato . . . The oozing vulva of a menstruating girl.

Cannery . . . A commercial establishment for the rental of female pudenda.

Cannibalism . . . Cunnilinction, medolingus, etc.

Cannibalism associated with erotic pleasure, esp. the consumption of characteristic female or male structures . . . ANTHROPOPHAGY.

Cannibalism combined with rape . . . ANTHROPOPHAGOLAGNIA.

Cannibalist . . . A male who licks or kisses the pudendum muliebre.

Canterbury tale . . . The excuse given by a philandering husband to his wife to account for his coming home late from the office.

Capricornified . . . Made a cuckold of by the faithlessness of the wife's cunnus.

Capricornus . . . The phallus which makes a man a cuckold.

Caprification . . . Artificial insemination.

Captain is at home, the . . . The menses are on.

Captain of the ship . . . The phallus conceived as the skipper of the female frigate.

Caress a female beyond the usual boundary lines, above the garter, etc. . . . **Get over the garter.**

Caress a female erotically, by stroking or kneading her characteristic tissues . . . SARMASSATE.

Caress a woman amorously, sometimes with the aid of the male genital oar . . . **Paddle.**

Caress a woman erotically . . . CONTRECTATE.

Caress a woman erotically, the desire to . . . CONTRECTATION.

Caress a woman lecherously . . . **Fumble.**

Caress a woman with the phallus . . . **Rifle; Riffle.**

Caress a woman's sexually lovable parts . . . **Fiddle.**

Caress a woman's vulva with tongue and lips . . . CUNNILINGUATE.

Caress the female body, esp. the breasts, with one's lips . . . **Chew the she-fat.**

Caress the female goodies . . . **Do a braille in anatomy.**

Caress the female unmentionables with zeal but without dexterity . . . **Muck.**

Caress the male organ . . . PHALLOHAPTATE.

Caress the pudendum of a male child in order to pacify him or to put him to sleep . . . **Play with billy.**

Caress the tantalizers of the female body . . . **Sexplore.**

Caressing of male genitalia . . . PHALLOHAPSIS.

Caressing of the light-arms variety, after little sis (or brother) has been dispatched with the usual bribe . . . **Romantricks.**

Caressing session in which the female characteristics are the subject of digital scrutiny . . . **Braille anatomy.**

Carry a bat . . . To hanker for a female, in allusion to the frequent erections.

Carry a bat for . . . To be desirous for (in love with) a particular woman.

Carry a bicycle seat . . . Of a female in menstruation, to have the crotch padded.

Carry a bundle . . . Of a woman, to possess a pair of billowing mammae.

Carry a load . . . Of the male, to be disturbed by a large inventory of unexpended semen.

Carry live ammunition . . . To have a rocket in the fly-pocket, i.e., to bear an erected phallus.

Carry-me-down . . . A bout of sexual self-gratification.

Cast an optic . . . To leer lecherously.

Cast-off . . . The rank clabber eructated by a sated phallus.

Cast-off . . . A mistress spurned in favor of another, esp. after a lengthy tenure.

Castrate . . . **Sheathe one's talons.**

Castrate a female . . . EXMULIEBRATE; SPAY; THELECTIZE.

Castrate a male . . . EMASCULATE; EVIRATE; EXTESTATE; GELD.

Castrate, and thus disable the phallic vaginal painter . . . **Cut the painter.**

Castrated female . . . SPADA.

Castrated male . . . ATESTUS; EUNUCH.

Castrated male, esp. one whose dick is cut off . . . **Bobtail.**

Cat . . . The vulva of a youngish female.

Cat . . . A girl, esp. one with a genital port free to phallic navigation.

Cat around . . . Of a girl, to put the pudendum in circulation.

Cat burglar . . . A man who talks a girl into pudendal submission, esp. if the girl is young and/or naive.

Cat-lapper . . . A cunnilinguist.

Cat rig . . . A menstrual pad and the belt supporting it.

Catamite; boy in pederasty . . . **Fairy; Ingle.**

Catamite; in allusion to the posteriors of one . . . **Bum-boy.**

Catamite, search for a . . . **Climb a tier; Go to town; Rummage; Run a tier.**

Catamite, to secure the availability of a . . . **Snare.**

Catamite who accompanies a tramp . . . **Road kid.**

Catamite . . . See also under *Boy used in act of pederasty.*

Catamites collectively; the world of catamites . . . **Angelina sorority; Brown family; The Browning Sisters; Preshen fraternity.**

Catamites, fond of . . . **Kid-simple.**

CATAPHILIST . . . A male who derives sexual pleasure from submitting himself to the domination of a woman, usually his wife. He differs from a masochist in deriving the stimulus from a spiritual rather than a physical subjugation. Ex *kata* (down) & *philein* (to love).

Catch . . . A girl who is a pudendal windfall.

Catch a Tartar . . . To be with a girl who seemed like an easy pudendal target but who turns out to be quite refractory.

Catch-fart . . . A male, esp. a husband, excessively submissive to the female.

Catch it . . . Of a female, to receive a thorough pudendal shellacking by a bouncing phallus.

Catch it . . . 1. To become infected with a venereal disease. 2. To become impregnated.

Catch the ball before the bound . . . Of a female about to be phallated, to receive the seminal drench before the phallus is even intromitted.

Catching harvest . . . The provocative growths on the chest of a girl.

CATELALIA . . . Obscene language imputing to an adversary the fanciful descent from a female canine. Ex *catella* (young bitch) & *lalein* (talk nonsense).

Catheads . . . Small female breasts. Also, the nipples.

Catskin . . . The superficies of the female body. Also, a vaginal diaphragm.

Caught with the spinnaker down . . . Of a male unexpectedly confronted with an unusually attractive female pudendal opportunity, unable to avail himself because of a just completed manually improvised ejaculation and the resulting phallic uncome-up-to-it-ness.

CAULIS . . . A Latin figurative synonym for the penis, in allusion to a stalk.

Cause a phallic erection, in allusion to the straight stance of the proud; said of the agential female . . . **Do proud.**

Cause of causes . . . The libido, esp. of the male.

Caw-handed . . . Of a male, gauche in lovemaking.

Centering of sex interest on coitus, rather than the foreplay . . . COITOCENTRIC.

Centering of sex interest on one's own body . . . IPSEROTIC; NARCISSISTIC.

Centering of sex interest on the coital foreplay . . . PAIZOCENTRIC.

Centering of sex interest . . . See also under name of object or part involved.

Centering one's interests on sexual subjects . . . GENOCENTRIC.

CERCUS . . . A Latin figurative synonym for the penis, in allusion to a tail.

Cervix of uterus . . . **Dog's nose.**

Chafer . . . Of man and maid, to form a pudendal coalition; i.e., to coit.

Chance taking a cold . . . To sleep with a woman; an allusion to her "crack" which, if situated in a wall or window, might cause a draft and bring on a cold.

Chancre . . . **Blue boar; Blue board; Blue boy.**

Characteristics of male and female, having both . . . GYNANDROMORPHOUS

Characteristics of male . . . See also under *Secondary sex characteristics.*

Charm, handful of . . . A handful of titty.

Charms . . . All the delightful embellishments of the female body, esp. the bubbies.

Charms, bunch of . . . An attractive girl; also, her luxuries.

Charver . . . 1. To phallate a female. 2. A bout of sexual concourse.

Charvered . . . Sexually exhausted; fucked out.

Chased but chaste . . . Of a girl, desirable but unavailable, pudendally.

Chasing the skirts, and the enclosed pudenda . . . **Cunt-struck.**

CHASMA . . . The vulvar space bounded by the labia majora and the floor of the vulva, containing the labia minora, clitoris, urethral opening, and introitus vaginae. Ex *chasma* (a yawning hollow).

Chat . . . The female pudendal trinket, under the pubic beard.

Chauvering . . . A sexual intercoursing.

Chauvering donna . . . A female who earns her living by lying under desirous males.

Cheat the census . . . 1. To induce phallic defecation by manual persuasion. 2. To phallate a woman behind the protection of a contraceptive.

Cheek-climber . . . A short skirt, in allusion to the hemline which "climbs" to the rump cheeks.

Cheek-clinger . . . A tight skirt which accentuates the positive of a girl's rump.

Cheek it . . . Of a girl, in walking, to circulate the gluteal spheroids.

Cheek-to-cheek . . . Of homosexual females enjoying gluteal attrition; juxtaposed rump to rump.

Cheeker . . . A girl with attractively prominent sitting domes.

Cheeks . . . The buttocks, conceived as the cheeks of the rump.

Cheeks of Cunnyborough . . . The buttocks of a female, in allusion to their being near the borough of *Cunnus* (the vulva).

Cheesecake . . . Pictorial art featuring the legs of a female in varying degrees of provocative display.

Cheesecake . . . A photograph or any form of picture on which the legs of a female are provocatively displayed.

Cheesecake . . . A girl who has attractive legs and is fond of showing more of them than is the custom.

CHEILOPHILOUS . . . Of the male, especially erotic about the female lips. Ex *cheilos* (lip) & *philein* (to love).

Cherries . . . Young virgins, collectively.

Cherry . . . What a virgin is deprived of when she is given phallus, i.e., the state of inviolacy of the female pudendum with regard to membrum virile.

Cherry . . . The phallically untried vulva of a young girl, or, less often, of a female of any age.

Cherry apron . . . The hymen, conceived as the protector of the vagina, from befoulment by the puking phallus.

Cherry birch . . . The copulating organ of the male, esp. such a one lucky enough to luxuriate in the innards of a previously inviolate vagina.

Cherry blossom . . . The inviolate membrane guarding the entrance to the vaginal sanctum of a young virgin girl.

Cherry-blossom tale . . . A rodomontade concerning real or alleged conquests of virgin pudenda.

Cherry-blossom time . . . The pubertal anthesis of a girl, when the mons veneris is clad in pubescence and the breasts are in sororiation.

Cherry-boning . . . The softening up of a virgin for seduction.

Cherry harvest . . . The seduction of a young virgin.

Cherry-merry . . . Of a girl previously chaste, suddenly prodigal with the pudendum.

Cherry petals . . . The unravished nymphae of a young virgin girl.

Cherry picker . . . A seducer of a virgin or virgins.

Cherry pit . . . The clitoris, not necessarily of a virgin.

Cherry plum . . . A pulchritudinous bride, and a virgin too.

Cherry pudding . . . The vulva of a young virgin.

Cherry-shy . . . Of a male, afeard of despoiling a virgin of her inexperience.

Cherry-stuffer . . . A seducer of virgins.

Cherry sucker . . . A licker of the female pudendum.

Cherry-tomato . . . A girl rightfully classified as a "tomato," and a virgin to boot.

Cherry wine . . . The sanguine ooze of a deflorated young virgin pudendum.

Cherub . . . A youth or a young man who has a virgin phallus.

Chest and bedding . . . The female chest adorned with breast, the latter conceived as the bedding.

Chest plaster . . . The female breasts as an excellent non-medical application to the male chest.

Chew the balls off . . . Of a fellator, to bite the shaft that feeds him.

Chew the she-fat . . . To indulge in lipping of the female body, esp. of the breasts.

CHEZOLAGNIA . . . Sexual excitation and/or gratification derived from the act of defecation. Ex *chezo* (defecate) & *lagneia* (lust).

Chick . . . An attractive girl, esp. one young and petite.

Chick fancier . . . A man who loves his female pudenda so young as to be unfledged or, at "worst," no more than pubescent. Also, a man who marries such a chick.

Chickabiddy . . . A young girl. Also, a teen-age flirt or coquette.

Chicken . . . A young and, inevitably, pretty girl.

Chicken . . . A young boy or girl whose anus and rectum are the vaginal haven for the phallus of a pederast.

Chicken dinner . . . A pretty young girl, esp. one who gives the male some house.

Chicken thief . . . The phallator of a very young chick; also, the husband of a child-bride.

Child, abnormal attachment of, to the parent of the opposite sex . . . OEDIPUS COMPLEX.

Child borne by a relatively old female or conceived by an older male . . . **January chicken.**

Child bride, in allusion to the numerosity of such in the Bluegrass State, at least proverbially . . . **Kentucky quail.**

Child-bride, male who marries a . . . **Baby porker; Kentucky cradle snatcher; Cradle snatcher; Bearskin robber; Kid walloper; Kid napper; Kidskin stretcher; Chicken thief; Chick fancier; Kindergarten butcher.**

Child, female, erotic touching of; as by a lecher . . . PEDIHAPSIS.

Child in utero . . . **Bellyful.**

Child marriages, as practiced among the Hindus . . . HARAMAITISM.

Child of a white person and a mulatto . . . QUADROON.

Child of a white person and a Negro or Negress . . . MULATTO.

Child of a white person and a quadroon . . . GRIFFADO; OCTOROON.

Child used in pederasty . . . **Angelina; Bronc; Gazook; Kid; Punk.**

Child used in pederasty . . . **Arseduke; Bronco; Gazoony; Lamb; Ringtail.**

Child used in pederasty . . . **Bitch; Brunser; Gonsel; Preshen; Wife.**

Child used in pederasty . . . **Bo; Chicken; Gunsil; Punk kid.**

Childer . . . A lecher fond of little girls.

Children, erotic affection for . . . PEDEROSIS.

Children, sexual molestation of . . . PEDIOCHLESIS; PEDEROSIS.

Chingus . . . The phallus as the Genghis Kahn of the male pudendum.

CHIROMANIA . . . Masturbation by the hand, esp. chronic and, usually, excessive. Ex *cheir* (hand) & *mania.*

Chivalry . . . A pudendal coalition with the female fringe on the top.

Chopping . . . Of a girl, desirous and forward.

Chorus girls, keep libidinous company with . . . **Play the ponies.**

Christen the yak . . . Of the male, to make the maiden phallic plunge; maiden for him, not necessarily for the maiden.

Christenable . . . 1. Of a non-whoring female, amenable to pudendal persuasion. 2. Of a female in general, fit for the phallus, as with regard to age.

Christened with a pump handle . . . Of the female, "had"; i.e., a virgin no more.

Christener . . . The male organon, conceived as a sprinkler.

Christener . . . The phallus of a bridegroom just married to a virgin.

Christening, be out . . . Of the male, to be out with a girl, phallating.

Christening night . . . The first, occasionally bloody, night of a honeymoon with a virgin bride.

Christening nosebleed . . . Hymeneal coital hemorrhage in the virgin.

Christening wine . . . The claret which escapes from a young thing's vaginal introitus when the male Philistine ravishes her temple during the breaking-in post-nuptial period.

Christian compliment . . . The omission of coitus on the wedding night, in allusion to the benevolence (if that it be) shown by the male.

Christmas . . . To indulge in pudendal revelry.

Christmas . . . To provide cheer, to a female, and to oneself, with the phallus erectus.

Christmas beef . . . The best of male beef, the phallus erectus, in allusion to the better grade of meat bought even by the proletariat during the holiday season.

Christmas box . . . The to-the-male delightful receptacle situated in the crotch of the female thighs, conceived so esp. when the thighs are abducted.

Christmas Eve . . . The eve before the night after the day of the wedding.

Christmas Eve, a . . . The female désireuse; i.e., not the female desirable but the desirous female.

Christmas meditations . . . The mood d'amour.

Christmas tree . . . The female pubic beard.

Christmassy . . . Of the male, désireux; of the female, désireuse; of both, pudendally desirous.

Chub . . . A short, stout phallus.

Chuck . . . To spurt the phallic lava.

Chuck a tread . . . To phallate a female.

Chunk of meat . . . A girl as handfuls of good palpable flesh.

Churn the butter . . . To dance the pudendal jig; to phallate vigorously.

Circumcised phallus . . . ACUCULLUS.

Circumcised phallus, condition of having . . . ACUCULLOPHALLIA.

Circumcised phallus, fondness for, on the part of a woman . . . ACUCULLOPHILIA.

Circumcised phallus, in allusion to the mandatory practice of posthetomy among the Hebrews . . . **Jew's lance.**

Circumcision . . . PERITOMY; POSTHETOMY.

Clap'em, come home with . . . To bring home, after being out with Mrs. Warren's girl, a case of claps, alias gonorrheal urethritis.

Clap-shouldered . . . Slapped down with gonorrhea.

Clapster . . . A chaser of female pudenda (and catcher, too!) esp. one who also quite frequently catches *Neisseria gonorrhoeae.*

CLAVA . . . A Latin figurative synonym for the penis, in allusion to a club or stick.

Cleavage, line of; between the female breasts . . . **Sweet line; The hotline.**

Cleave . . . Of a female, to open up the sacred gates, in amorous reception of the male.

Cleaver . . . A female who, extramaritally, is not averse to a thigh spread.

Cleft . . . In the female, the crevasse of the lower mouth.

Climb a tier . . . To search for a boy as a subject in pederasty.

Climb upon the supine female, for phallic insertion, in case of a male, or for pudendal manipulation, in case of a tribade . . . **Mount.**

Climb upon the supine female, saber first . . . **Board.**

CLINOVALENT . . . Potent sexually but able to have pudendal concourse in the lying position only. Ex *klino* (recline) & *valere* (to be able).

CLITORIDISM . . . The condition in which sexual excitation is centered in the clitoris, rather than the vagina.

CLITORILINGUS . . . The labial and/or lingual titillation of the clitoris, generally by a male.

CLITORIS . . . A small erotically sensitive, penislike, erectile organ of the female, homologous to the phallus, situated at the anterior part of the vulva and partly concealed by the labia minora. Ex *kleiein* (to shut up).

Clitoris, abnormal enlargement of . . . CLITORISM.

Clitoris as usher to the phallus . . . **Usher of the hall.**

Clitoris conceived as a homunculus in the pudendal navis . . . **Little man in the boat.**

Clitoris conceived as a little bird in the female pudendal cage . . . **Cockyolly bird.**

Clitoris, erection of, persistent . . . CLITORISM.

Clitoris; in allusion to the goalkeeper in soccer . . . **Goalie.**

Clitoris, labial and/or lingual titillation of; generally by a male . . . CLITORILINGUS.

Clitoris, lick or suck the . . . **Muzzle the little man in the boat.**

Clitoris, sexual excitement centered in; rather than in vagina . . . CLITORIDISM.

CLITORISM . . . Enlargement of the clitoris, as in gynandrism.

CLITORISM . . . Condition marked by a persistent erection of the clitoris.

CLITOROMANIA . . . Intense sexual desire in a female.

Cloak the captain . . .To sheathe the phallus erectus with condom.

Close hug . . . The act of coitus, esp. when performed outdoors, as in a public park.

Clothes appropriate to the opposite sex, practice of wearing; usually associated with sexual pleasure . . . CROSS DRESSING; EONISM; TRANSVESTISM; TRANSVESTITISM.

Club . . . The male genital sausage.

CLUNICENTRIC . . . Of the male, centering the erotic interest upon the female buttocks. Ex *clunis* (buttock).

Clyster . . . A phallic injection administered rectally.

Cock . . . The most popular, amongst men, moniker for the genital bat.

Cock . . . To give the female pudendum a dose of phallus erectus.

Cock alley . . . The female genitalia, esp. the inlet, conceived as a lane for phallic promenades.

Cock and breeches . . . A man of small stature having a phallus of surprising size and excellent potency.

Cock-and-hen . . . 1. Pert. to both sexes; hermaphroditic. 2. A hermaphrodite.

Cock bawd . . . The male manager of a brothel.

Cock buster . . . A male or a female who alleviates phallic turgescence by oral propitiation.

Cock buster . . . A girl with a stenotic introitus which, at least figuratively, fractures the aggressive phallus.

Cock-chafer . . . That which is between the thickest parts of a girl's thighs, esp. the vaginal fiord.

Cock-chafer . . . A girl who gives a man a hard time by partaking in all but the summit meeting.

Cock-hall . . . The palatial receiving chambers of the female pudendum, regarded as reserved for VIP phalli.

Cock Inn . . . The female pudendal drive-in conceived as a haven of comfort for a homeless and lust-weary male pendant.

Cock lane . . . The hiatus between the thighs of a female, esp. the vaginal corridor.

Cock one's beaver . . . To erect one's phallus.

Cock-smitten . . . Of a female, excessively enamored of phalli.

Cock suckstress . . . A female **cock-sucker.**

Cockshire . . . The female sexual inlet conceived as the county seat of the male genital viceroy.

Cocksucker . . . A male or a female who takes the phallus by mouth for oral gratification.

Cocksucker . . . A despicable character, esp. a toady.

Cocksucker, bald . . . A toothless fellator or fellatrice.

Cocksucker's behind . . . A very worthless female.

Cocksucker's delight . . . A male with a relatively small phallus and a pendulous scrotum.

Cocksucker's teeth . . . Something quite superfluous.

Cockyolly bird . . . The little bird in the female pudendal cage; the clitoris.

Cod . . . The scrotum, conceived as a pod or purse.

Coddy-moddy . . . A teen-age girl, in allusion to a young gull.

Cods . . . The testicles, in allusion to a pod.

Co-ed as vulva material . . . **Ivy bush.**

COHABITATION . . . Sexual intercourse without wedlock.

COIT . . . To do the man's part in sexual intercourse.

Coital pains of virgin newlyweds . . . NEOGAMALGIA.

Coital partner, mental picture of a more desirable; fabricated by one of the participants in sexual intercourse to enhance the pleasure of the act . . . EUGENICON.

COITANT . . . The active or male member in normal sexual intercourse.

COITANTE . . . The passive member in normal sexual intercourse, i.e., the female partner.

COITHESIS . . . The position assumed in the act of sexual intercourse. Ex *coitus* & *thesis* (position).

COITION . . . Sexual concourse between heterosexuals. Ex *co* (together) & *ire* (to go).

COITOCENTRIC . . . Centering one's erotic interest on the "play" or coitus, rather than on foreplay.

COITOLIMIA . . . Hunger for sexual intercourse. Ex *coitus* & *limos* (hunger).

COITOPHOBIA . . . Aversion for or fear of sexual intercourse, usually, naturally, in the female.

COITUS . . . Sexual intercourse conceived as the coming together of the male and female pudenda. Ex *coire* (to go together).

COITUS À LA VACHE . . . Sexual intercourse in which the female is in a knee-chest position and the phallus is reciprocated from behind. Ex *vache* (a cow).

Coitus conceived as a jovial engagement . . . **Merry bout.**

Coitus conceived as a pudendal hug . . . **Close hug.**

Coitus, engage in . . . **Play at horses and mares.**

Coitus, engaged in by the male, as a salubrious exercise for the pudendal apparatus . . . **Constitutional.**

Coitus, good at; of either sex . . . **Good at it.**

Coitus, have three flings of, in one love session . . . **Triple.**

Coitus, have two flings of, in one love session . . . **Double.**

Coitus, in allusion to the to-and-fro movement (jig) . . . **Moll Peatley's gig.**

COITUS INCOMPLETUS . . . Same as COITUS INTERRUPTUS.

COITUS INTERRUPTUS . . . Sexual intercourse in which the male withdraws the phallus from the vagina before ejaculation.

Coitus, male deriving sexual pleasure only from the act of; rather than from the foreplay . . . TELOPHILIST.

Coitus, partake in; said of the female . . . **Do the naughty.**

COITUS PROLONGATUS . . . Sexual intercourse in which the male withdraws the phallus before the act is completed and resumes after a short period of relaxation, thus delaying the orgasm for a long time or indefinitely.

Coitus regarded as work at (thigh) crossroads . . . **Dirty work at the crossroads.**

COITUS RESERVATUS . . . Sexual intercourse in which the male withholds ejaculation.

Coitus, to do what is done in . . . **Belly-bump.**

Coitus which does not end in seminal ejaculation . . . **Dry bob.**

Coitus . . . See also under *Sexual concourse, Sexual intercourse, Phallation,* etc.

Cold . . . Without precoital play; used with reference to sexual concourse so begun.

Cold-canvass . . . To palpate digitally the fleshpots of the female, but not in the flesh.

Cold coffee . . . A frigid or, at best, a lukewarm reward of a maid to her swain, in return for a patient and costly pitch on his part.

Cold four . . . A couple lying in bed dos-à-dos, in cold indifference; an allusion to four cold feet.

Cold, have a . . . 1. Of the female, to be totally unresponsive. 2. To have a leukorrheal ooze.

Cold, have a bad . . . Of either the male or the female, to have gonorrhea.

Cold, risk taking a . . . To sleep with a woman, in allusion to sleeping near a **crack,** which, if in a window or door, may bring on a cold.

Cold shoulder of mutton, to give a . . . Of a female, to give a negative response, without qualifications.

COLES . . . A Latin figurative synonym for the penis, in allusion to a quill.

College girl as a schooled vulva . . . **Ivy bush.**

College girls . . . Same as **College ladies,** harlots.

College ladies . . . Girls in Mrs. Warren's profession.

College, ladies' . . . A Mrs. Warren-operated "college."

College pudding . . . An "educated" female pudendum, not in Virgil, but in the niceties of vulvar co-operation in the act of acts.

COLOBOSIS . . . The amputation of the male sex organs as an act of jealous retaliation. Ex *koloboo (to shorten).*

COLPALGIA . . . Pain in and around the vagina. Ex *kolpos* (hollow, vagina) & *algos* (pain).

COLPECTASIA . . . Dilatation or enlargement of the vagina, as a result of masturbation, childbirth, etc. Ex *kolpos* & *ektasis* (distention).

Colpeurynter . . . The phallus erectus as a vaginal dilator, in allusion to the instrument known by this name.

Colpeurysis . . . Sexual intercourse, esp. with a ponderous phallus, in allusion to the vaginal dilatation involved in the act, and to the standard meaning of the term. Ex *kolpos* & *eurynein* (to distend).

COLPISMUS . . . A spastic contraction of the vagina, sometimes resulting from fear of or aversion for sexual intercourse.

COLPISMUS, MENTAL . . . A contraction of the vagina resulting from fear of or aversion to the sexual act.

COLPOCLEISIS . . . The closure or obliteration of the vaginal canal by surgical means. Ex *kolpos* & *kleisis* (closure).

COLPOMENTIORS . . . Bosom cheaters; falsies. Ex *kolpos* (bosom) & *mentior* (deceiver).

COLPOMIMESIS . . . The wearing of falsies. Ex *kolpos* (breast) & *mimesis* (an imitating).

COLPOPHRONATE . . . Think excessively about the vulva and its could-be pleasures.

COLPOPLASTY . . . Any form of plastic surgery on the vagina, as the formation of a snug canal from one distended by childbirth, phallation, etc.

COLPOPOIESIS . . . The construction of a vagina by surgical means.

COLPORRHEXIS . . . A laceration of the vagina, as by a dildo, a massive phallus, etc. Ex *kolpos* & *rhexis* (a tearing).

Colpotherm . . . The ardent phallus conceived as a vagina warmer. Ex *kolpos* (the vagina) & *therme* (heat).

COLPOXEROSIS . . . A condition marked by abnormal dryness of the interior of the vagina. Ex *kolpos* (vagina) & *xeros* (dry).

COLPYLE . . . The external opening of the vagina. Ex *kolpos* (vagina) & *pyle* (gate).

Colt's tooth . . . Sexual desire in the young, esp. in youths.

Colt's tooth, feel the . . . Of a young man or a boy, to feel the first twinges of sexual desire.

Colt's tooth, have a . . . Of young people, to have a "tooth" for sexual pleasures.

Columbine . . . A mistress or an out-and-out whore.

Comb the cat . . . With reference to an amorously palpating male, to comb, with the fingers, the pubic chevelure of the female quarry.

Come . . . In the act of sexual concourse, to feel the paroxysm of gratification, in the male coincident with the spurt of the semen.

Come-by-chance . . . A bastard as the product of a coital accident.

Come-down . . . A collapse of the erected penis at a time when it shouldn't happen to one's worst enemy.

Come home with clap'em . . . to bring home not the proverbial bacon but the case of claps, after a pudendal bout with a female carrier of the infamous *Neisseria gonorrhoeae.*

Come off . . . Same as **Come,** to convulse in the acme of orgastic relish.

Come over at . . . To provoke sexual desirousness in a person of the opposite sex.

Come to heel . . . Fall in love libidinously.

Comfortable importance . . . A wife, regarded as an important adjunct to a man's life, and a mighty comfortable belly plaster too!

Comfortable impudence . . . A mistress, esp. one well entrenched, having the insolence of a legal wife.

Commit acts of youthful folly or, less euphemistically, to phallate . . . **Sow wild oats.**

Common-law marriage . . . **Unholy bedlock.**

Concession of defeat . . . **Hell! said the duchess when she caught her tits in the mangle.**

Concubine; conceived as a belly comforter . . . **Belly plaster.**

Concubine . . . See also under *Prostitute, Whore,* etc.

Condition marked by the presence of both testicular and ovarian tissues and anomalous genital organs typical of both sexes . . . HERMAPHRODITISM.

Condition marked by the presence of gonads of one sex, as testes or ovaries, and malformed external genital organs resembling those of the opposite sex . . . PSEUDOHERMAPHRODITISM.

Condition of being attracted sexually to another person of the same sex . . . HOMOSEXUALITY.

Condition . . . For more entries beginning with *Condition,* see under other parts of the thought complex.

Condom; as a sheath for the phallus . . . **Jacket.**

Condom; conceived as a sheath for the rabbit . . . **Rabbit skin.**

Condom; conceived as armor against infection or impregnation . . . **Buttock-mail.**

Condom, for man's third leg . . . **Legging.**

Condom; in allusion to a coat . . . **Benjamin.**

Condom; in allusion to its "contra" functions . . . **Anti.**

Condom-like device reinforced with sponge rubber and "tickling" appendages, to give a potent but small phallus greater ophelimity . . . **Brummagem Joe.**

Condom provided with tongue-like attachments to enhance the stimulation upon a relaxed or well-phallated vagina . . . **Tickler.**

Condom, sheathe the phallus with a . . . **Cloak the captain.**

Condom, without; in allusion to nakedness, of the phallus . . . **In cuerpo.**

Condom, without, sexual intercourse performed . . . **A cappella.**

CONSANGUINE FAMILY . . . A form of family based on the intermarriage of brothers and sisters.

Constitutional . . . With reference to the male, a session of coitus undertaken, jocosely or in earnest, for the sake of one's pudendal and spiritual or mental well-being; in allusion to a walking exercise taken for the good of one's constitution.

Constitutionalize . . . Not to make it constitutional, but, of the phallus, to make it soft from hard, by quenching plunges into the female genital delta.

CONTEMPLATIVE . . . A person who derives sexual pleasure from vivid erotic fantasies.

Contour chase . . . 1. A palpatory adventure of a male involving the surfaces and the nothing-like-a-dame's masses of a girlie. 2. To braille said masses and surfaces with an erotic hand.

Contour-chasing . . . Of a gown, following the outline of the female figure curve-atim.

Contours . . . The phallo-erigentic curves of the female body.

Contraception, branch of medicine dealing with . . . ACEPTIATRY.

Contraception, study of . . . ACEPTOLOGY.

CONTRARIATION . . . The derivation of sexual pleasure by the male from tantalization by the female, as by unapproachable nakedness, manual stimulation of the phallus short of the orgasm, etc. Also, the action involved. Ex *contrarier* (to thwart).

CONTRARIATOR . . . A male whose sexual pleasure is derived chiefly from sexual stimulation, by a female, short of ejaculation, as by exposure and denial of feminine charms, manual titillation, etc.

CONTRECTATE . . . To sarmassate, i.e., to handle in the characteristic manly way the provocative organs and tissues of a female.

CONTRECTATION . . . Sarmassation, i.e., the fondling of the provocative organs or tissues of a female. Also, the urge therefor.

Convalescence . . . The relaxation of the erected phallus after the seminal eruption.

Conveniency . . . A wife, regarded as an always available source of pudendal comfort; also, sometimes, a mistress.

Convenient . . . A mistress, regarded as a good thing to have around or on the string, for the comfort of one's pudendum.

Conversion of sexual cravings into nonerotic desires . . . SUBLIMATION.

Convert . . . A prostitute who gives up whoring and starts working for her living.

Convert . . . A whore whose pudendum was converted to peaceful use, via wedlock.

Convert . . . Of a whore, to remove the pudendum from mercenary circulation and apply it to conventional use, in wedlock.

Convert a pudendally clean woman into a harlot . . . **Turn an honest penny.**

Cook the kettle . . . To titillate the female underpart manually, in preparation for phallic invasion.

Cop a phinney . . . Do to another's girl what one would not want another to do to one's.

Copious seminal ejaculation . . . PLEOBLYSIS.

COPROLAGNIA . . . The derivation of sexual pleasure from the handling, sight, or contemplation of human feces, esp. such voided by a person of the opposite sex. Ex *kopros* (dung) & *lagneia* (lust).

COPROSCOPIST . . . Person who derives sexual pleasure from watching others in the act of urination or/and defecation. From *kopros* (feces) & *skopeo* (view).

COPULATION . . . Sexual intercourse. Ex *co* (together) & *apere* (to join).

Copulation; conceived dispassionately . . . **Flesh session.**

Copulation; in allusion to the animal proverbially lusty . . . **Goat's gig.**

Copulation . . . See also under *Phallation, Sexual intercourse,* etc.

COREPHALLIA . . . The introduction of the phallus into the anus of a female child. Ex *kore* (female child) & *phallos* (penis).

CORIKANTHOSIS . . . The development of female characteristics in a young girl. Ex *korikos* (girlish) & *anthos* (bloom).

Corker . . . A phallus of corking size.

Corporation work . . . The phallovaginal pumping action.

Corps commander . . . The commander-in-chief of the male crotch.

Corpse . . . A "dead" male genital baton; i.e., one hanging instead of jutting, esp. one not juttable even on provocation.

Corpse, female, molestation of a . . . NECROCHLESIS.

Corpse, female, sexual attraction to . . . NECROPHILISM.

Corpse, female, sexual intercourse with . . . NECROCOITUS.

Corpse out . . . To suffer a collapse of the indurated male sexual beak before either of the bedmates has "come," or—shame of shames!—before insertion.

Corpse reviver . . . A monronian female whose contours and callipygian sign language can a dead man revive, judging by the reaction of those who are not dead.

Corpse reviver . . . A gesture of the female body beauteous, esp. of the callicolpos and/or the callipygus, which revives into rigidity a presumably "dead" male organ.

Corpse, sexual gratification derived from mutilating a . . . NECROSADISM.

Corsican . . . A small but ebullient and efficacious phallus, in allusion to *the* Corsican, of Elba fame.

Corybungus . . . The rump, in allusion to the anus as a bung.

Cosh-carrier . . . A pimp as the protector and exploiter of a whore, in allusion to *cosh,* a bludgeon.

Costume, female, worn by a male homosexual at a costume party . . . **Drag.**

Costume . . . See also under *Clothes.*

Couple . . . To do what one does in sexual intercourse.

Couple-house . . . A house in which female pudenda are available for genital coupling, for a price.

Couple of flats . . . A frigid wife and an impotent husband.

Couple of fornicators who rent a room for a brief period, to effect pudendal coupling . . . **Short timers.**

Coupler . . . The male genital shaft conceived, quite understandably, as a coupling device.

Coupling-house . . . Same as **Couple-house,** a brothel.

Course with . . . To have pudendal concourse with (a woman).

Court of assistants . . . The potent younger males to whom the wives of impotent older husbands turn for pudendal comforts.

Court the girl of a friend while the former and the latter are chilled by a tiff . . . **Scab.**

Courting cream . . . Seminal fluid escaping uncomfortingly into one's undergarments while one palpates the physical charms of a female.

Cousen . . . To administer phallus erectus vaginally.

Cousin . . . A female seller of pudendal conveniences.

Cousin Betty . . . A card-carrying member of Mrs. Warren's sorority.

Cousin Jake . . . The man's physical arm of love, under the pubic arch.

Cousin Jane . . . That part of a girl's crotch which rides the tapering end of a bicycle seat.

Cousin-to-cousin . . . Of the coital approach between female homosexuals, pudendally apposed.

Covent Garden . . . A pudendal studio under the auspices of Mrs. Warren. An allusion to Covent Garden, the district in London, so named because it is on the sight of a former monastery garden, once rank with bordels.

Covent Garden abbess . . . A procuress; a female manager of a bawdy-house.

Covent Garden ague . . . What you get as an unwelcome bonus when you visit a bordello; the claps, or worse.

Covent Garden lady . . . A lady who is no such thing.

Covent Garden quail . . . A young prostitute.

Covent Garden rail . . . The coital couch of a whore.

Cover . . . Of a man, to lie upon a woman, with the pudendal motor running.

Cow . . . 1. Female ass, not of the donkey family. 2. A female providing such ass. 3. Any female of the human species conceived as ass-carrier.

Cow baby . . . A teen-age prostitute.

Cow-climbing . . . Sexual intercourse between female homosexuals, in allusion to the habit of ruttish cows, who climb upon their female mates in the manner of bulls.

Cow cock . . . A gargantuan human phallus big enough, the lady thinks, for a cow.

Cow-cunted . . . Having a cunt the size of a cow's, as a result of repeated dilatations in childbirth, masturbation with artificial phalli, or concourse with a male having a cow cock.

Cow feed . . . The seminal spurt of a satisfied phallus.

Cow gun . . . A human phallus big enough for a cow.

Cow-hitch . . . Sexual intercourse à la vache, i.e., from behind, in the manner of a bull and his playmate.

Cow-pad . . . A menstrual pad, queen size; or one made of two.

Cow-uddered . . . Of the human female, having much too much of a good thing, i.e., magnitudinous mammae.

C.P. . . . A **cunt-pensioner,** i.e., a man who lives on the earnings of a whore's cunt.

Crab . . . An impotent husband who can't do it himself and won't let others.

Crab . . . To attempt sexual intercourse with a half-hearted erection.

Crab exchange . . . A dance in which the partners are so close to each other that hisn bumps against hern —pudendum, of course.

Crack . . . The interlabial hiatus of the lower, silent mouth of the female. Also, the vulva as a (w)hole.

Crack . . . A female who lives by the labor of her lower, toothless mouth; in allusion to the interlabial fissure.

Crack . . . The vulva in the light of its central feature, the interlabial slit, conceived as a dominating but unworthy obsession.

Crack a crib . . . To deflower a young girl. Also, to phallate a young prostitute.

Crack a crust . . . To open for phallic traffic the virgin introitus of a female, in allusion to breaking the crust of an intact pie.

Crack a Jane . . . Same as **Crack a Judy.**

Crack a Judy . . . To deprive a virgin of her perfection, in allusion to cracking an *objet d'art.*

Crack-bat . . . Of the female pudendal entrance, tight enough to break, at least figuratively, the male genital bat.

Crack-halter . . . 1. A sanitary pad for the vulva in its monthly ooze. 2. A sanitary belt for holding the pad against the silent but bleeding mouth of the menstruating pudendum.

Crack hunter . . . 1. The male sexual organon. 2. A whoremonger.

Crack the belly . . . To phallate, esp. to impregnate.

Cracking tool . . . The phallus as a tool for the female crack.

Cradle snatcher . . . A man who marries a child-bride.

Crash the breast fleet . . . To phallate a Roman Catholic girl out of wedlock.

Creeper . . . A male who phallates the wife of another.

CROSS DRESSING . . . The practice of wearing clothes appropriately worn by members of the opposite sex, as a means of deriving erotic pleasure.

Crotch; conceived as a one-eyed ugly duckling with halitosis . . . **Douglas with one eye and a stinking breath.**

Cruelty, person inflicting, in sadism . . . SADIST.

Cruelty, recipient of, in masochism . . . MASOCHIST.

Cruelty, sexual pleasure or gratification derived from the infliction of, esp. upon one of the opposite sex . . . SADISM.

Cruelty, sexual pleasure or gratification derived from the subjection to, esp. at the hands of one of the opposite sex . . . MASOCHISM.

Cruiser . . . A male or female homosexual in search for a partner or patron.

CRUROCENTRIC . . . Of the male, centering the erotic interest upon the female legs. Ex *crus* (leg).

CRUROFACT . . . The female leg as a sexual fetish.

CRUROPHILOUS . . . Of the male, especially erotic about the female's legs. Ex *crus* (leg) & *philein* (to love).

CRUROTRICHOSIS . . . Excessive growth of hair on the legs, esp. in women. Ex *crus* (leg) & *thrix* (hair).

Crust . . . The hymen, esp. the virgin membrane.

Cry roast meat . . . Of the male, to tell tales of vaginal invasions.

Cubitopolis . . . The metr*opolis* revealed by a woman in the de*cubit*al position. The vulva.

Cuckold, become a; in the usual way, by the loss of one's wife's pudendum to the phallic invasion of another man . . . **Get the bull's feather.**

Cuckold, make a husband into a, by the usual method . . . **Give the bull's feather.**

Cuckold the parson To cue-snap the parson (or priest or rabbi) by savoring the pudendum of one's wife-to-be before the ding-dong of the wedding bells.

Cuckold, to . . . **Take a leaf out of another's book.**

Cuckold, to; esp. when the husband is unable or away . . . **Pinch hit.**

Cuckold, to; in allusion to the figurative horns of one so treated . . . **Double Cape Horn.**

Cuckolded, by wife's genital smile upon another man . . . **Headmarked.**

Cue-snap . . . To ejaculate prematurely, at the first cuddle of the vagina. See also under **Cue snapper.**

Cue snapper . . . A male who, in copulation, discharges the pent-up semen at the first caress of the vagina, in allusion to a cue-snapping actor who speaks his lines too soon.

Culls . . . The testicles, in allusion to "cull," a woman's dupe, which these ovoids a man make.

Cully . . . A male who, however smart otherwise and elsewhere, is to a woman, because of phallic insistence, a dupe.

Cully-shangy . . . Sexual concourse, esp. the male's part therein, conceived as a **shangy** (shanghaiing) of a **cully** (a woman's dupe or helot).

Culty-gun . . . The male genital organ conceived as a "blade gun," on the basis of *cultellus,* a knife.

CUNNECTASIA . . . A condition of the vulva in which the labia majora are not approximated and present a gaping slit. From *cunnus* (vulva) & *ectasia* (dilatation).

CUNNILALIA . . . 1. Excessive talk about the vulva. 2. Obscene language involving the vulva.

CUNNILINCTION . . . The kissing, licking, and/or sucking of the vulva, usually by a male. Ex *cunnus* (vulva) & *lingere* (to lick).

Cunnilinction, a bout of . . . **Tongue-lash.**

Cunnilinction practiced by female homosexuals . . . SAPPHOLINCTION.

CUNNILINGANT . . . The female in the act of cunnilingus. From *cunnus* (vulva) & *lingua* (tongue).

Cunnilinguate . . . **Give a length of tongue.**

Cunnilinguate . . . **Lark; Play a cannibal; Suck the twat; Pout the diddly.**

Cunnilinguate; in allusion to one of the postures . . . **Have legs around the neck.**

Cunnilinguate; in allusion to the "bushy tail" of the female . . . **Grin at the bush.**

Cunnilinguate; in allusion to the cunnus as a musical instrument . . . **Play a mouth organ.**

Cunnilinguate; in allusion to the female fiddle . . . **Have one's face on the fiddle.**

Cunnilinguate; in allusion to the female phallus-warmer . . . **Muff.**

Cunnilinguate; in allusion to the "pearls" of dried mucus sometimes found in and around the vulva . . . **Dive for pearls.**

CUNNILINGUIST . . . A person, usually a male, who licks, kisses, and/or sucks the vulva. Ex *cunnus* (vulva) & *lingere* (lick).

Cunnilinguist . . . **Cunt-sucker; Key-hole whistler.**

Cunnilinguist . . . **Diddly-pouter; Twat-sucker; Tenant of Abraham's bosom; The lord of pillicock-hill.**

Cunnilinguist conceived as an eater of human flesh . . . **Cannibal.**

Cunnilinguist, female . . . HOMOPHAGIST; **Twatter.**

Cunnilinguist, male, having vulvar pie while kneeling between the abducted thighs of a female sprawling in a chair or on the edge of a bed . . . **Kneeler.**

Cunnilinguist, male or female . . . **Mouther.**

CUNNILINGUS . . . Same as CUNNILICTION, the oral caressing of the female genitalia.

Cunnilingus . . . **Cow-lick; French lick; Larking; Pearl diving.**

Cunnilingus, esp. the kissing, sucking, and/or licking of the labia minora, the vaginal introitus, and the clitoris . . . **Muff diving.**

Cunnilingus, female in the act of . . . CUNNILINGANT.

Cunnilingus, male in the act of . . . CUNNILINGUIST.

CUNNIPHILEMIA . . . Sexual perversion in which pleasure is derived from kissing the female genitalia. Ex *cunnus* (vulva) & *philema* (a kiss).

CUNNIPHRENIA . . . Preoccupation with thoughts of the pudendum muliebre.

CUNNUS . . . The latin form for the vulva, in allusion to something one keeps covered. See also under **Cunt.**

CUNNUS . . . A female freelancing with her pudendum. Ex *cunnus* (vulva).

Cunny . . . The female genital mouth, including the fur-piece, in allusion to a cony, a rabbit.

Cunny-haunted . . . Of the male, obsessed by desire for and thoughts of the female genital cynosure. See also under **Cunny**.

Cunny-hunter . . . A man who chases girls; a whoremonger. See also under **Cunny.**

Cunt . . . In the realm of slang the most venerable, almost ivied, and from the viewpoint of an amorous male the most popular, appellation of the decorative and functional centerpiece, the epergne, the cynosure, the ornamental dish, the golden fruit, the interfemoral sanctum of the female—the pussy. It is derived from the Latin *cunnus* (vulva), in allusion to *cuneus* (a wedge).

Cunt in velvet . . . A woman married to a rich man.

Cunt-itch . . . Not really an itching of the vulva, but a yearning for the membrum virile erectum, or the bearer thereof.

Cunt-pensioner . . . A man living on the earnings of a harlot's genital bread-winner.

Cunt-pie . . . The vulva as conceived by a cunnilinguist.

Cunt-stand . . . An erection of the membrum virile.

Cunt-struck . . . Smitten by the lure of the vulva; chasing the skirts; lascivious.

Cunt-sucker . . . The male counterpart of a fellatrice, i.e., a kisser, sucker, and/or licker of the female cleft underbelly.

Cunting . . . 1. Of a male, out hunting for pussy. 2. Of same male, having a dish of it.

Curtain taker . . . A phallator who does an encore without much of an intermission.

Curves of the female body of special interest to the male . . . **Contours.**

Cut the painter . . . To excise the male gonads and thus hamstring the phallus, here regarded as the seminal "painter" of the vagina.

Cuticle cutie . . . A pretty female nudist.

Cuts . . . The male gonads.

CYESOLAGNIA . . . Sexual lust for pregnant women.

CYESTHES . . . Maternity clothes. (From *kyesis* & *esthes,* pregnancy & clothes.)

CYMBALISM . . . Sexual play between two female homosexuals consisting of a rubbing and bumping of the approximated pudenda. Ex *kymbalon,* a hollow vessel, to which the female pudendum is here likened.

CYPRIDOPHOBIA . . . Fear of prostitutes. Ex *cyprian* (prostitute) & *phobos* (fear).

CYPRIEUNIA . . . Sexual intercourse with a harlot. From *cyprian* (whore) & *eune* (bed).

D

Dance arranged by prostitutes for the purpose of stimulating the pudendal business . . . **Buttock ball.**

Dance at which the female participants are inveterate whores . . . **Ballum rancum.**

Dance at which the participants are in the buff, with female upper bombosities and male lower testosities bobbing up and down . . . **Ballum rancum.**

Dance attended primarily by male homosexuals . . . **Pansy Ball.**

Dance, close, feeling of body contour that the male gets of his female partner during a . . . **Dancensation.**

Dance in which only males participate . . . **Bull dance.**

Dance in which participants rub buttocks with one another because of crowding . . . **Tribadance.**

Dance in which the male suffers a loss of ejaculant fluid, because of titillation by honorable partner's contour undulations . . . **Greased hop.**

Dance in which the partners are so close that her mammary mounds beat a not unpleasant rhythm upon his breast . . . **Brutal breasting.**

Dance in which the partners are so close that phallus meets vulva . . . **Crab exchange.**

Dance in which the pudenda and abdomens of the couple are close enough to "feel" each other . . . **Belly rub.**

Dancensation . . . "The "feel" of body contour that the male gets from his female partner during a close dance.

Dancing, feel the hard phallus in; said of the female partner . . . **Know it's there.**

Dangle parade . . . A group of nudists walking, in allusion to dangling phalli and mammae.

Dangle parade . . . An inspection of soldiers or inmates for signs of venereal disease, in allusion to the dangling phalli.

Dangler . . . A male who derives sexual pleasure from the act of exhibiting his genitalia to the view of others, esp. to females.

Dant . . . A woman free with pudendal gifts or sales.

Dark meat . . . Same as **Black meat,** intimate parts of a Negress.

Daughter, sexual intercourse with one's own . . . THYGATRIA.

Daughter, sexual love of a, for her father . . . PATROLAGNIA.

Daughter, sexual love of a, for her father; accompanied by hostility toward the mother . . . ELECTRA COMPLEX.

Daydreaming about sexual subjects . . . HEMEROTISM.

Dead rabbit . . . The flaccid membrum virile.

Dearest member . . . The male urogenital chief of state, so conceived by an interested female.

Decencies . . . Pads used by actors wearing tight breeches to soften the contour of the genital pound of flesh.

Décolletage party . . . A gathering or party of young people at which generous portions of titty are on display, mostly through tantalizingly décolleté bodices.

Decrease in sexual potency of the male . . . HYPOPOTENTIA.

Defecation in the presence of another, esp. the defecation by a female in the presence of a male who derives sexual pleasure or gratification from the sight of the act . . . **Boston Tea party.**

Defecation, person who derives sexual pleasure from watching another in the act of . . . COPROSCOPIST.

Defecation, sexual pleasure derived from the act of . . . DEFECOLAGNIA; ANAL EROTICISM.

DEFEMINATION . . . Loss of sexual characteristics in a female, as atrophy of the breasts.

Deflower a virgin . . . **Break a crust.**

Deflower a virgin; an allusion to the bare skin . . . **Trim the buff.**

Deflower a virgin, in allusion to the bat . . . **Bat-foul.**

Deflowered, be . . . **Break one's knee.**

Deformity of breasts resulting from childbearing . . . PAREMASTIA.

Delay the wedding, after partaking of the pudendal fruit of one's future wife . . . **Hang in the bellropes.**

Delightful frightfulness . . . A bout of coitus, from the woman's viewpoint.

DELINOLAGNIA . . . Afternoon lustfulness, esp. in men. Ex *deilinos* (in the afternoon) & *lagneia* (lust).

DEMASCULINIZATION . . . The loss of the male characteristics, as atrophy of the testicles, loss of beard, change in voice. etc.

DENDROPHILIA . . . The condition of being aroused sexually by trees; sexual interest in trees. Ex *dendron* (tree) & *philein* (to love).

Denial of vaginal privileges by the wife to her husband, to coerce or punish . . . **Jamaica discipline.**

Deny one's husband pudendal privileges, as for not loosening the financial purse strings . . . **Give the key to the street.**

Deny one's husband the sexual gratifier in order to force his surrender to a demand . . . **Hold out; Hold the market.**

Desirous, because overloaded with "beans" . . . **Beany.**

Desirous but unable, because impotent . . . **Barkis is willing but the flesh is weak.**

Desirous; said of the female, with, it is said, a horripilation of the escutcheon . . . **Hairy.**

Desirous; said of the male, with a bulging fly . . . **Higher than a cat's back.**

Desirousness in the pubic region, in either sex . . . **Squirrel fever.**

Desirousness, mood marked by . . . **Christmas meditations.**

Development of feminine characteristics in a young female . . . CORIKANTHOSIS.

Development of . . . See also under name of the part developed.

Device intended to give the female breasts a specious form and magnitude . . . COLPOMENTIORS; COLPOMIMS; SEINSEMBLERS; **Brummagem.**

Devil . . . A parsonage concept of the phallus, esp. species erectus.

Devil's playthings . . . The female breasts regarded as such.

Diaphragm, protect against impregnation by means of a . . . **Bottle up.**

Diaphragm, vaginal; conceived as armor against impregnation . . . **Buttock-mail.**

Diaphragm, without a; used with reference to a bout of phallation . . . **A cappella.**

Dick . . . One of the most popular euphemisms for the male genital organon.

Dick . . . To give a woman a taste of phallus erectus.

Dick money . . . The money paid a whore for her pudendal cooperation.

Dick swallower . . . A fellator or a fellatrice.

Dick up . . . To come up with an erection.

Dickey . . . 1. A dick junior size. 2. The phallus of a boy.

DILDO . . . Artificial sex organs of the male, used by females in tribadism and in masturbation. Also, the penis alone, real or artificial. Ex *diddle* (to move jerkily).

DILDOISM . . . The use of an artificial penis by a woman upon herself.

Dingbat . . . The male organ as a swab or as a throwing stick.

Dinge . . . The organum virile of an Ethiop, esp. of a North American E.

Dingle-dangle . . . The boneless appendage of the male, which, in its lethargic mood, dangles listlessly in either of the trouser legs.

Dingus . . . The male genital probe as the nameless thing.

Dining room . . . The labia majora and the intervening and underlying structures of the female pudendum, from the viewpoint of a male who derives pleasure and gratification from lip service to these parts.

Dip one's bill . . . To insinuate the membrum virile erectum into the sexual adit of the female crotch.

Direction of early interests and energies toward the sex organs . . . AMPHIMIXIS.

Dirt . . . Normal persons, unsympathetic to the homosexual "cause," who participate in homosexual social affairs.

Dirty work at the crossroads . . . A licit or illicit meeting of the male and female counterparts, at the summit of the thighs.

Discovert . . . Of a female, having no legal husband; applied to a widow, divorcée, or a spinster.

Display intimate parts, esp., of a female, to show mamma, via low décolletage . . . **Hang it out.**

Display one's breasts; said esp. of such that are ample . . . **Sport the blubber.**

Displaying nude parts of the body, practice of, as a means of deriving erotic pleasure . . . Exhibitionism.

Divination by observing a bull's phallus . . . Phallomancy.

Do a bedspread . . . Of the female, in bed with a functional male, to open the vaginal gates, by a leg-spread.

Do a bit of skirt . . . Phallate a woman.

Do a braille in anatomy . . . To savor the female goodies with the hands.

Do a double act . . . To phallate; an allusion to **double** (coit).

Do a double act . . . To phallate a woman both fore and aft, i.e., vaginally and rectally.

Do a double act . . . Phallate two females, in one love session, with one looking on, or adding a loving touch, while the other is receiving.

Do a grind . . . To work the female pudendal mortar with the male pestle.

Do a grouse . . . To go out in search for females with accessible pudenda.

Do a mount . . . To assume the male posture upon the female.

Do a rasp . . . To phallate a female conventionally.

Do a spread . . . Same as **Do a bedspread,** of the female, to open up for the invading phallus.

Do a star pitch . . . To "sleep" in the open with a female; i.e., to phallate under the stars.

Do gospel work . . . To propagate the species; to do the pudendal jig without contraceptives.

Do her wrong . . . To taste the female pudendal merchandise, then refuse to buy it matrimonially.

Do it twice in one love session, **it** being sexual concourse . . . **Double.**

Do one's balls on . . . To be slavishly enamored of a woman.

Do one's business . . . To phallate a woman, without too much enthusiasm, esp. one's own Weib.

Do proud . . . Of a female, to make the male's lower beak stand at attention.

Do the naughty . . . Of a woman, to open the genital portals and partake of phallus stiffus.

Do the trick . . . To phallate and impregnate, when impregnation is an undesirable consideration.

Do unto her . . . To give a young virgin what she never had before, and could very well do without.

Dodad . . . The phallus as a not easily namable genital ornament.

Dofunny . . . The phallus as a funny guy.

Dog . . . To phallate a woman while supporting oneself on all fours, in allusion to a dog, who really does not do that at all.

Dog-drawn . . . Of a woman in the act of sexual intercourse, left cold by the forcible removal of the phallating male, as by an inopportunely returning husband.

Dog-end . . . That end of the female trunk which is perforated by three channels.

Dog in a blanket . . . The phallus erectus ensconced hot-dog-like between the halves of the female bosom.

Dog's match . . . A bout of sexual concourse staged on the spur of desire by the wayside, as canines are apt to do.

Dog's nose . . . The cervix uteri.

Dog's rig . . . A bacchanalian orgy of sexual indulgence carried to prostration and followed by a dos-à-dos bored convalescence of the participants. Also, and esp., this spiritless book-ends posture assumed by the bushed worshipers of King Priapus.

Dohickey . . . The male genital coupler.

Dohicky . . . Same as **Dohickey,** the male genital mandrel.

Dojigger . . . The phallus as an organ with a reciprocating motion.

Dojohnnie . . . The male genital pendeloque regarded as a stage-door Johnnie of the female pudendum.

Do-little sword . . . A partly impotentiated male organ, in allusion to a midshipman's dirk seldom used in action.

DOLEROS . . . Pain as a source of erotic pleasure. Ex *dolor* (pain) & *eros* (sexual love).

Dolly . . . A mistress; a whore; an accessible pudendum.

Dolly-mop . . . 1. A girl who gives pudendally, but for the sport of it, not for money. 2. A run-of-the-mill harlot.

Dolly-mopper . . . A consort of whores, esp. a soldier-consort.

Dominated by husband . . . MARITOCRATIC.

Doodad . . . Same as **Dodad,** the phallus as a nameless genital ornament.

Doodle . . . The male genital organ as a pudendal trifler.

Doorkeeper . . . The hymen, in allusion to its strategic position.

Dose of finger, a . . . A caressing intimacy consisting of a digital plunge into the vagina.

Dose of phallus administered orally . . . **Tonsil swab.**

Dose of phallus administered rectally . . . **Clyster; Gut ream.**

Dose of phallus administered vaginally . . . **Anglican length.**

Double . . . To phallate, in allusion to the beast with two backs, male and female pudendally coalesced.

Double-arsed . . . Of a female, having too much of a fairly good thing, behind; i.e., having gluteal prominences of which one would make two lapable ones.

Double-banked . . . Of a man and his maid, usually in bed, stratified in a double layer, and not a bit sleepy.

Double-barrelled . . . Of a harlot, taking the phallus fore or aft, vaginally or rectally, as it pleases his lordship and in consideration of a few additional shekels.

Double Cape Horn . . . To do to another man's wife that which one would not suffer another to do to one's own, in allusion to the figurative sprouting of horns upon the calvaria of a husband whose wife is so done to.

Double-cunted . . . Having a vagina large enough to make two.

Double-diddied . . . Having large breasts, one of which would comfortably make two.

Double event . . . An infection with both syphilis and gonorrhea.

Double event . . . A sexual orgy with two females, each alternately partaking of and witnessing the act.

Double header . . . Two bouts of coitus during a single love fiesta, or during one night.

Double header . . . A sexual revelry of one female with two males, simultaneously, in allusion to the two glandes involved.

Double jug . . . A big behind, in allusion to its need of two chamber pots to sit on.

Double one's milt . . . To effect two sessions of coitus, complete with ejaculations, without an intervening rest period, on a single erection, without withdrawal.

Double-ribbed . . . Of a phallated female, wearing cyesthes or maternity clothes; i.e., pregnant.

Double-shanked . . . Having a brawny phallus, the size of two legs put together, figuratively.

Double-shung . . . Of the male, having ponderous sex equipment, esp. a massive phallus. A perversion of **Double-shanked.**

Double sucker . . . Large labia majora, regarded as a king-size sucker for a cunnilinguist.

Double-tide job . . . A bout of phallation in which one or both of the participants experience the spasm of gratification twice.

Double wedding . . . A variety of fellatio in which each participant gives phallus to and takes phallus from the other.

Doublet . . . The female bosom reinforced with sham.

Douglas with one eye and a stinking breath . . . The perineum, where the anus is the eye.

Down to buckle and bare thong . . . Undressed and nude down to the bare skin.

Down to the ears . . . Of a phallus in action, inserted as far as the "balls" will let it, as it were.

Dowry consisting of nothing more than the vulva . . . **Rochester portion; Whitechapel portion.**

Dowry consisting of nothing more than the vulva, the arse, and a pair of titties . . . **Tipperary fortune.**

Doxy . . . A girl who dispenses pudendal comfort.

Drag . . . A female costume worn by a male homosexual at a costume party.

Drag party . . . A costume party attended by male homosexuals at which the passive members wear female costumes.

Draw blood from a virgin, in deflowering her . . . **Broach claret.**

Dressing . . . The lava vesuviating from the phallus during the male orgasm, in allusion to the female "salad."

Dressing in the clothes appropriate to the opposite sex, practice of, as a means of deriving sexual pleasure . . . CROSS DRESSING; EONISM; TRANSVESTISM; TRANSVESTITISM.

Dripper . . . A venereally infected phallus which drips.

Droopers . . . The female breasts, variety pendulous.

Drop anchor in the bubby hutch . . . To slither a hand down a girl's neckline. See also under **Bubby hutch.**

Drumhead . . . The hymen, conceived as a membrane stretched across the open end of the vagina.

DRURY LANE . . . See under **Drury Lane district.**

Drury Lane ague . . . An unwelcome "extra" supplied by a Drury Lane pigeon to her unwary phallator, as a result of which he is likely to "piss fire" for some time after the engagement.

Drury Lane district . . . A theatrical district abounding in promenading harlots as well as nonprofessional dispensers of perineal diving slits, in allusion to the famous Drury Lane of London, England.

Dry bob . . . A go at coitus which, for any reason, does not end in seminal ejaculation.

D.S.O. . . . A non-medical but utilitarian initialgram for the lugubricomic condition of having one's *d*ick *s*hot *o*ff, also for the male so afflicted. Said to have originated during World War I, when such casualties were not uncommon.

Duffer out . . . Of a male in phallation, to peter out before reaching the peak; i.e., to come down with a case of phallomalacia while in the midst.

Dugout . . . The covered shelter of the female bosom, conceived as a haven for an erotic male hand not otherwise occupied.

Dugs . . . The female breasts, not too fondly conceived.

Duke . . . The organum virile as a sexual nobleman.

Duker . . . 1. A phallus of impressive magnitude. 2. A proprietor of a magnitudinous phallus.

DYSORGASMIA . . . The achievement of the sexual orgasm by the male after a prolonged effort and with the aid of mental machinations, as the visualization of erotic scenes, etc.

DYSPAREUNIA . . . Sexual intercourse attended by pain or other discomfort, esp. in the female. From *dys* (difficult), *para* (beside), & *eune* (bed).

DYSPHALLATION . . . Sexual intercourse attended by pain or other discomfort in the genital organs, esp. of the male. From *dys* (difficult) & *phallation.*

E

Early development of the body and genitalia in either a boy or a girl . . . MACROGENITOSOMIA.

Early development of the breasts in a girl . . . EOTERPSIS.

Early development of the genital system in the female . . . PROIOVARIA.

Early development of the genital system in the male . . . PROIORCHIDISM.

Early development of the sexual desire . . . EOPOTHESIS.

Early development of sexual power or organs, in either the male or the female . . . PROIOTIA.

Early growth of pubic hair . . . EOPUBESCENCE.

Early loss of sexual desire . . . EOPOTHOZEMIA.

Early onset of menstruation (menacme) . . . PROIOMENORRHEA.

Early sexual development in boys . . . HYPERTESTIA.

Early sexual development in girls, resulting from excessive secretion of the ovaries . . . HYPEROVARIA.

Early sexual intercourse, i.e., early in life . . . EOPAREUNIA.

Ease nature . . . Give the semen its natural outlet, with an assist from the vagina.

Eat out . . . To have sexual pleasures other than those provided by one's wife.

Eat the calf in the cow's belly . . . To invade the pudendum of one's future wife.

Eating out . . . Of a married man, having sexual concourse with a female not the spouse.

ECDYOSIS . . . A form of exhibitionism in which the subject derives sexual pleasure from disrobing in the view of others.

Eckbergian . . . With reference to the feminine breasts, beautiful but, especially, on the D-plus side of the brassiere-cup spectrum.

ECRON . . . The seminal fluid discharged during orgasm. Ex *ekreo* (flow out).

Effeminate breast(s) in a male . . . **Tom tit.**

Effeminate breasts in a male, condition of . . . GYNECOMASTIA.

Effeminate characteristics in a man . . . FEMANDRISM.

Effeminate hips in a man . . . GYNEPYGIA.

Effeminate male; also, a homosexual . . . **Molly.**

Effeminate manners in a male . . . GYNESYNCRASY.

Effeminate voice in a boy or in a man . . . GYNEPHONIA.

Effeminate walk (manner of walking) in a male . . . **Lesbie trot.**

Effeminate . . . See also under *Female.*

Ejaculant in the mouth of a fellator or fellatrice . . . **Ivory rinse; Mouth wash.**

Ejaculant, phallic . . . ECRON; SEMEN; SEMINAL FLUID.

Ejaculant, phallic . . . See also under *Semen* and *Seminal fluid.*

Ejaculate and "grease" the female pudendum . . . **Butter the bacon.**

Ejaculate between the female breasts . . . **Piss in the dugout.**

Ejaculate between the thighs of a woman . . . **Load in the sticks.**

Ejaculate copiously, in fellatio . . . **Say a mouthful.**

Ejaculate, esp. profusely . . . **Throw the hash.**

Ejaculate; in allusion to emesis . . . **Chuck.**

Ejaculate; in allusion to testicular "beans" . . . **Give beans.**

Ejaculate in the interlabial pudendal passage of the female . . . **Sprinkle.**

Ejaculate intravaginally . . . **Bean.**

Ejaculate meal for the vagina . . . **Give one's oatmeal.**

Ejaculate outside of vagina . . . **Fire in the air.**

Ejaculate outside of vagina, in pubic hair of female . . . **Shoot in the bush.**

Ejaculate prematurely, at the first insinuation into the vagina . . . **Cuesnap.**

Ejaculate twice, in a dicrotic coitus, without an intermitting flaccidity of the phallus, and without a withdrawal of the line . . . **Double one's milt.**

Ejaculation; conceived as phallic favor . . . **Genital blessing.**

Ejaculation, copious . . . PLEOBLYSIS.

Ejaculation, endow with an . . . **Anoint.**

Ejaculation, feeble . . . ASTHENOBLYSIS.

Ejaculation in fellatio . . . **Mouthful.**

Ejaculation, meager . . . OLIGOBLYSIS.

Ejaculation, receive the, before intromission of the phallus; said of the drenched female . . . **Catch the ball before the bound.**

Ejaculation, withhold, to prolong phallation . . . **Keep it up.**

Ejaculatory response in the male, a slowing of . . . BRADYCONTIA.

ELECTRA COMPLEX . . . Sexual love of a daughter for her father. Also, unconscious attachment of a daughter to her father accompanied by hostility toward the mother. Ex a character in Greek legend who was so disposed.

ELYTRON . . . The Greek form for a covering or sheath, hence, by extension, the covering for the phallus, the vagina.

ELYTROSTENOPLASTY . . . A plastic operation for the purpose of narrowing the vaginal canal. Ex *elytron* (sheath), *stenos* (narrow), & *plassein* (form).

Embrace and caress a woman, intimately . . . SARMASSATE.

Embrace pressure of the vagina upon the incoming phallus . . . **Bottle.**

Embracing and caressing, erotic act of, by a male . . . SARMASSATION; CONTRECTATION.

Embracing of a female against her will . . . ENSPASMATION.

E.M.F. . . . The *e*roto*m*otive *f*orce, i.e., the libidinal urge, in either a male or a female. An allusion to the E.M.F. (electromotive force) in electronics.

Enamored of a female, to be slavishly . . . **Do one's balls on.**

Enamored of the female genital slit . . . **Placket-stung.**

Enamored of . . . See also under names of the parts involved, as *Breasts, Legs,* etc.

Enclose in parentheses . . . To submit the phallus to the amorous clasp of the female pudendal labia by plunging it, head-on, into the labial hinterland.

Encouragement in lovemaking, receive . . . **Get some house.**

End of The Sentimental Journey . . . The female crotch where, no matter whence begun, the male's attention finds its quarry.

End-on . . . Of the phallus, erected.

END PLEASURE . . . In sexual intercourse, the pleasure enjoyed during the brief moments of the orgasm, as opposed to the less intense pleasure of the act preceding the acme.

ENDYTOLAGNIA . . . A variant of the sex urge in which the desire is greater for a fully clothed woman than for one undressed. From *endytos* (clothed) & *lagneia* (lust).

ENDYTOPHALLIST . . . A male who prefers to have sexual intercourse with a woman who is fully dressed. Ex *endytos* (clothed) & *phallos* (penis).

Engage a female for a bout of coitus, usually a nocturne . . . **Book.**

Engage in insincere lovemaking . . . **Billy-goat; Free-lance; Shake a loose leg.**

Enough broomstick to charm the ladies . . . Enough phallus, in reach and heft, to please even the most discriminating phallatae.

ENSPASMATION . . . The holding of a female in one's embrace, against her will. From *en* (in) & *aspazomai* (embrace).

Enter into more or less permanent sexual relations with a homosexual partner . . . **Marry.**

Entertainment provided by the phallus erectus . . . **Jack entertainment.**

Entice a female into coitus . . . **Twist a leg.**

Entice a female to do the spread eagle . . . **Take for a ride.**

Entice a virgin into submission . . . **Break a crust; Bat-foul; Trim the buff; Blaze the trail.**

ENTOMA . . . The vulvar interlabial slit. From *en* (in) & *temnein* (to cut).

Entracte . . . A period of rest and minor erotic skirmishes between bouts of coitus.

Entrance to the vagina . . . **Keyhole.**

Entrance to the vagina . . . INTROITUS; INTROITUS VAGINAE.

EONISM . . . The adoption of the mental attitude, habits, and, especially, the costume of the opposite sex. Also, sexual pleasure derived from wearing female clothes by a male. Ex Chevalier d'Eon, a French diplomat who for many years posed as a woman.

EOPAREUNIA . . . Sexual intercourse early in life.

EOPOTHESIS . . . The early development of the sexual urge. Ex *eos* (early) & *potheo* (desire).

EOPOTHOZEMIA . . . Early loss of sexual desire. Ex *eos* (early), *pothos* (desire), & *zemia* (loss).

EOPUBESCENCE . . . The early growth of pubic hair, in either sex.

EOTERPSIS . . . The early development of the breasts in a girl. Ex *eos* (dawn) & *terpsis* (delight).

EPROCTOLAGNIAC . . . A male sexual idiosyncrat who derives erotic pleasure from the fetor of flatus, esp. such as is expelled by a female. Ex *eproctation* (expulsion of flatus) & *lagneia* (lust).

EPROCTOPHILE . . . A person who derives sexual pleasure from the expulsion of flatus.

Equipment . . . The male external genitalia.

Equipment . . . The appurtenances of the female of special interest to the male, as the mammae.

ERAST . . . A libidinous male with semen on his brain.

Erect a massive phallus . . . **Raise the boom.**

Erect one's phallus . . . **Cock one's beaver.**

Erected phallus . . . ITHYPHALLUS.

Erected phallus, adoration or worship of . . . PHALLACISM.

Erected phallus, fear of, as experienced by a female . . . ITHYPHALLOPHOBIA.

Erected phallus, involving or pert. to . . . ITHYPHALLIC.

Erected phallus, painfulness of . . . ITHYPHALLALGIA.

Erected phallus, sucking of . . . PENOSUGIA.

Erected; said of the phallus . . . **End-on; Blanket-stiff.**

Erected; said of the phallus, in allusion to its readiness . . . **Under sailing orders.**

Erected; said of the phallus, in allusion to rising prices . . . **Bullish.**

Erection, achieve or suffer an; depending on the opportunity to assuage . . . **Put on Sunday clothes.**

Erection, bring up a functional . . . **Get one's name up.**

Erection, cause the male to have an; said of the female . . . **Jack up; Put steam in the bucket.**

Erection, causing an; applied to a visual stimulus, thought, etc. . . . ITHYFACIENT; ITHYGENIC.

Erection; conceived as a straightening of the phallus . . . PENORTHOSIS.

Erection; conceived as best garments . . . **Sunday clothes.**

Erection destined for pudendal satisfaction . . . **Merry go-up.**

Erection, encourage the creation of an; by the female . . . **Beef up.**

Erection, enjoy the creation of an . . . **Put on a tin hat.**

Erection, full and functional . . . TELOTISM.

Erection, have an inopportune and embarrassing . . . **Have a bone in the throat.**

Erection; in allusion to its "stand" before the vulva . . . **Cunt-stand.**

Erection; in allusion to the hump caused by it in the region of the fly . . . **Camel complaint.**

Erection in which the phallus is partially curved . . . PHALLOCAMPOSIS.

Erection in which the phallus is partially curved and painful, usually as a result of gonorrhea . . . CHORDEE.

Erection, inability of the male to produce; sexual impotence . . . ASTYPHIA; ASTYSIA; ASYNODIA; INVIRILITY.

Erection, incomplete or partial . . . ASTYSIA.

Erection, lose the, in the vagina, before ejaculation . . . **Duffer out.**

Erection, nerves associated with . . . NERVI ERIGENTES.

Erection, normal deflation of . . . DETUMESCENCE.

Erection occurring during the day . . . HEMERITHYSIS.

Erection occurring during the night . . . NOCTORTHOSIS.

Erection occurring in the morning as a result of fullness of the bladder . . . **Pride of the morning; Morning pride.**

Erection occurring in the morning, esp. one due to fullness of the bladder . . . MATUTORTHOSIS.

Erection of the nipples . . . THELORTHIA.

Erection, painful . . . ITHYPHALLALGIA.

Erection, partial or incomplete . . . HYPOPEGNYMIA.

Erection, persistent, usually not associated with sexual desire . . . PRIAPISM.

Erection, subsidence of . . . DETUMESCENCE.

Erection, to achieve or be presented with an . . . **Make a long arm.**

EROTAUXESIS . . . An increase in the sexual appetite. Ex *eros* (sex love) & *auxesis* (increase).

EROTIC . . . Pert. to sexual lust.

EROTIC . . . A person whose thoughts and activities are abnormally influenced by sexual desire.

Erotic about the female breasts, especially . . . MAZOPHILOUS.

Erotic about . . . See also under name of part involved, as *Buttocks*.

Erotic amputation of the female breast . . . MAZOPEROSIS.

Erotic affection for children . . . PEDEROSIS.

Erotic desire, arising from . . . EROGENOUS.

Erotic desire, arousing . . . EROTOGENIC.

Erotic desire for one's sister . . . SORORILAGNIA.

Erotic desire for . . . See also under name of particular person or object involved.

Erotic desire, having a calming effect on . . . ANAPHRODISIAC.

Erotic desire, having a stimulating effect on . . . APHRODISIAC.

Erotic desire, intense, in the female . . . ANDROMANIA; CLITOROMANIA; NYMPHOMANIA.

Erotic desire, intense, in the male . . . GYNECOMANIA; SATYRIASIS.

Erotic desire, person having no . . . ANAPHRODISIAC.

Erotic desire, substance which calms . . . ANAPHRODISIAC.

Erotic desire, substance which stimulates . . . APHRODISIAC.

Erotic, in allusion to pudendal good cheer . . . **Christmassy.**

Erotic interest in a person of the same sex . . . HOMOSEXUALITY; HOMOSEXUALISM; HOMOEROTICISM.

Erotic interest in a person of the same sex, esp. when sublimated . . . HOMOEROTISM.

Erotic interest in pictures depicting nudity, lechery, etc. . . . GRAPHELAGNIA.

Erotic interest in . . . See also under name of person or object involved, as *Trees.*

Erotic obsessions, state of mind marked by . . . LAGNOIA.

Erotic pleasure derived from looking at the genitalia of another, esp. of one of the opposite sex . . . SCOPOLAGNIA; SCOPOPHILIA.

Erotic pleasure derived from watching others in the act of sexual intercourse . . . MIXOSCOPIA.

Erotic pleasure derived from . . . See also under *Sexual pleasure.*

Erotic; said of humor, stories, body parts, etc. . . . **Anatomical.**

Erotic sensitivity of a part of the body not normally so sensitive . . . TOPERETHISM.

Erotic sensitivity of the anus . . . ANAL EROTICISM; ANOERETHISM.

Erotic sensitivity of the buttocks . . . PYGERETHISM.

Erotic sensitivity of the nipples . . . THELERETHISM.

Erotic sensitivity of the scalp . . . SCALPOLAGNIA.

Erotic sensitivity to odors . . . OSPHRESIOLAGNIA.

Erotic sensitivity . . . See also under name of part, substance, etc.

Erotic thought or idea . . . LAGNOEMA.

Erotica, esp. literature devoted to the sanctum muliebre . . . **Hilltop literature.**

Erotically charming or upsetting, as a part of a female . . . BOULVERSANTE.

EROTICISM . . . An abnormal sexual craving or instinct. Ex *eros* (sexual love) & *ism* (condition).

EROTISM . . . Sexual desire; a manifestation of the sexual desire.

EROTOGENESIS . . . The production or initiation of sexual lust.

EROTOGENIC . . . Inducing sexual lust.

EROTOGRAPHOMANIA . . . An abnormal urge to write ardent love letters. Ex *eros* (sexual love), *graphein* (to write), & *mania.*

EROTOLOGY . . . The science dealing with sexual love.

EROTOMANIA . . . 1. Excessive sexual desire. 2. An exaggerated reaction to sexual stimulation.

EROTOMANIAC . . . A person marked by exaggerated response to erotic stimulation. Also, a person having an excessive sexual urge.

EROTOMASTIA . . . Sexual excitation induced in a woman by manipulation of her breasts. Ex *eros* (sexual love) and *mastos* (breast).

EROTOPATH . . . A person having abnormal sexual desires. Ex *eros* (sexual love) & *pathos* (disease).

EROTOPATHY . . . Condition marked by abnormality of the sexual desire.

EROTOPHOBIA . . . Dislike of or fear of sexual love.

Eskimo pie . . . A frigid woman, esp. a psychrotic wife.

ESODOPHOBIA . . . The fear of the first act of sexual intercourse, by the woman. Ex *eisodos* (a coming in) & *phobos* (fear).

ESTRUM . . . Same as ESTRUS, the periodic sexual excitation in female mammals, not women.

ESTRUS . . . In female beasts, the recurrent period of sexual excitation during which the animal will accept the male. Ex *oistros* (a vehement desire).

EUGENICON . . . In sexual intercourse, the fabrication of a mental picture, by one of the participants, of a more exciting coital partner, to enhance the pleasure of the act. From *eu* (improved form), *genos* (sex), & *eikon* (image).

Evening before the nuptial night . . . **Christmas Eve.**

Evening spent in company of an attractive girl, resulting in a humping of the fly with erect phallic tissue . . . **Camel night.**

Excessive, but not necessarily unpleasant, development of the secondary sex characteristics in the female . . . HYPERCOSMOSIS.

Excessive growth of hair on the body of a woman . . . GYNETRICHOSIS.

Excessive growth of hair . . . See also under name of part involved, as *Legs.*

Excessive sexual desire . . . EROTOMANIA.

Excessive sexual desire in the female . . . ANDROMANIA; CLITOROMANIA; NYMPHOMANIA.

Excessive sexual desire in the male . . . GYNECOMANIA; SATYRIASIS.

Excesisve sexual desire . . . See also under *Sexual desire.*

Excessive sexual use of the phallus . . . PHALLACRASIA.

Excite sexually a person of the opposite sex . . . **Come over at.**

Exclamation of an underlying female, addressed to a tardy superimposed male, exhorting commencement of the exercise . . . **Jack me Robinson!**

Exhausted physically and/or mentally . . . **Bitched, buggered, and bewildered; Well fukked and far from home.**

EXHIBITIONISM . . . The practice of displaying nude parts of the body, esp. the genitalia, to members of the opposite sex, as a means of deriving erotic pleasure.

Exhibitionism, form of, in which the subject derives sexual pleasure from disrobing in the view of others . . . ECDYOSIS.

Exhibitionist, male . . . **Dangler.**

Expel rectal gas, in "opening up" for the phallus of a sodomite . . . **Blurt out.**

Exposed delectables of a colored wench . . . **Hot dark meat.**

Exposed delectables of a white girl . . . **White hot meat.**

Exposed female nudity, in allusion to its possible roborant effect on a potent phallus . . . **Bracer.**

Exposed female tissues which are potent enough to cause a phallic inflation in susceptible males . . . **Hot meat.**

Exposed parts of a female usually hidden from the view of underprivileged males . . . **Hot stuff.**

Exposure and denial of female desirables to the male . . . TANTALIZATION.

Expression of sexual impulses by means of nonsexual activities . . . SUBLIMATION.

External genitalia, female, regarded as a Serbonian bog . . . **Bottomless pit.**

External genitalia of the female . . . PUDENDA.

External genitalia of the male, i.e., the phallus and the testes . . . PUDENDUS.

External genitalia . . . See also under *Vulva, Pudendum muliebre, Phallus, Penis, Female genitalia, Male external genitalia,* etc.

F

Fabrics, sexual gratification derived from touching certain . . . HYPHEPHILIA.

Face . . . Proper exposure, for pudendal calisthenics, on the part of the recipient woman, esp. with regard to sufficient thigh-split.

Face-ache . . . The aftermath of fellatio in an inexperienced fellatrice, or in one experienced who has taken one bigger than she could chew.

Face-up . . . Of a woman, lying in the posture of an inverted Y, legs apart and pussy up.

Fad-cattle . . . Women not exactly whores but with accessible pudenda.

Fad, the . . . Sexual concourse, conceived, waggishly, as a mere fad.

Faddle . . . To caress amorously, esp. the unmentionable parts of a girl.

Faddle . . . Food for the flame of lust, esp. the incendiary parts of a woman.

Faddle . . . An effeminate boy or man; also, sometimes, a homosexual male.

Fadoodle . . . The sexual slit of a girl, with its appurtenances, conceived—jocosely, it is hoped—as a trifle, a mere nothing.

Fadoodle . . . To give the usual phallic accolade to the central pit of the tritrematous end of the female torso.

Fag . . . A male homosexual.

Fag . . . The male genital pendant, conceived as the coarser end of the male trunk.

Fag-ender . . . A male who prefers the posterior of the three lower female perforations; a sodomite.

Fag-ends . . . A girl's panties.

Fagot . . . A male homosexual.

Fagot . . . To phallate, or have sexual intercourse with, a female.

Fagot . . . To consort with whores.

Fagot . . . A woman, esp. an unworthy one, fit only to be phallated, if that.

Fagot-master . . . A notorious whoremaster.

Fagot-vote . . . The welcome pudendal assent of a girl, conceived as influenced by a positive vote of her desirous underpart.

Fair blanket . . . A pretty girlie, conceived as a comfy fleshy blanket to wrap oneself in or around, or both, by a desirous male.

Fair do's . . . Erotically pleasant responses from a subjacent woman, who is being supplied with phallic reciprocations.

Fair itch . . . Of a girl, a pretty good stimulator, and satisfier.

Fair roebuck . . . A female at her most attractive age or stage of physical development, from the viewpoint of the appraiser.

Fair-trader . . . A whore, or just a girl, who gives a man a fair return for his investment.

Fairy . . . A male homosexual.

Fairy . . . A boy whose rectum is used as a vagina, by a pederast.

Fairy-tale . . . A lame excuse offered by a girl for not submitting, when she usually does.

Faithfulness in marriage . . . HEREISM.

Fake a curtain . . . Of an unwilling girl, to ride a functionless menstrual pad, as a means of warding off phallic ingression.

Fake pie . . . A woman's pectoral bulge made attractive by padding.

Fake the sweetener . . . Of a girl, to pretend that she likes it, by adding welcome responses to the phallic intrusion.

Fake up . . . Of a male confronted with a juicy pudendal opportunity, but hamstrung by phallic inertness, to raise the boom with the aid of manual prodding.

Fall in love, lasciviously . . . **Come to heel.**

Falsies . . . COLPOMENTIORS; COLPOMIMS; SEINSEMBLERS.

Falsies, the wearing of . . . COLPOMIMESIS.

Family, form of, based on the intermarriage of brothers and sisters . . . THE CONSANGUINE FAMILY.

Family, form of, based on the intermarriage of several sisters with each others' husbands, or on the intermarriage of several brothers with each others' wives . . . THE PUNALUAN FAMILY.

Family, form of, based on marriage between single pairs of individuals, with exclusive rights to sexual intercourse . . . THE MONOGAMIAN FAMILY.

Family, form of, based on the marriage of one man with several wives, the wives being, generally, secluded . . . THE PATRIARCHAL FAMILY.

Family, form of, in which marriage does not restrict sexual intercourse of the pair to each other, and coitus can be terminated by either one of the couple . . . THE SYNDYASMIAN FAMILY.

Family, head of . . . The hatchet-man, as it were, of a man's lower end, esp. when his posture is functional.

Family hotel . . . A hotel in which a tired businessman can untie his lower knot with the aid of a female pudendum supplied on the premises by thoughtful management.

Family jewels . . . The male gonads.

Fancy . . . The sexual yen or prod, in either sex.

Fancy . . . 1. An uprising of the male genital arm. 2. Such an arm uprisen.

Fancy frigate . . . A patrician whore, i.e., one who caters to well-heeled phallus-bearers.

Fancy-girl . . . 1. A mistress. 2. A harlot who employs refreshing innovations in the old pudendal game.

Fancy import . . . A non-autochthonous harlot.

Fancy Joe . . . The favorite of a harlot.

Fancy Joseph . . . A man who is to another man's wife what Potiphar's wife wanted Joseph to be.

Fancy lay . . . 1. A bout of sexual concourse variegated by stimulating departures from the orthodox. 2. A prostitute who charges more for the pudendal pizza, because younger or fortified with better accessories.

Fancy lip-service . . . Fellatricial performance deserving of praise.

Fancy man . . . 1. The husband, lover, or protector of a whore. 2. A man who lives on the pudendal income of a whore.

Fancy plover . . . Youngish and well supplemented genital flesh of a mercenary female.

Fancy woman . . . 1. A man's favorite whore. 2. A man's temporary mistress. 3. A woman with a pudendal yen for phallus erectus.

Fart catcher . . . A male who phallates per rectum.

Fart-lover . . . A male idiosyncrat who derives libidinal stimulation from the malodor of flatus, esp. that discharged by a female.

Fart sucker . . . A person who licks the anus of another, esp. a male licking the anus of a female for his pleasure.

Fart taster . . . A male who labiates the anus of a female.

Fartberry-picker . . . 1. An uxorious husband. 2. A male whose erotic interest in a female is centered on her buttocks and anus. An allusion to **fartberries,** fecal crumbs attached to the hairs about the anus.

Fast fuck . . . In sexual intercourse, a quickie bout, esp. in the standing position, usually with a harlot, in a hallway, a park, etc.

Fastidious cave . . . The inaccessible, because chaste or prudish, pudendal receiving apparatus of a reluctant female.

Fat cock . . . A male of considerable corpulence.

Fat fancier . . . A male whose nervi erigentes are especially susceptible to the charms of corpulent females.

Fat female, sexual concourse with a . . . **Bit of fat.**

Fat females, male who has a penchant for . . . **Fat fancier.**

Fat flabs . . . Pendulous female breasts, contemptuously contemplated.

Fat in the fire, have the . . . To have ejaculated semen in the vagina of a female one is anxious not to impregnate, as through the accident of a ruptured condom.

Fat Jack but no dowry . . . A good dose of phallus, but no money, for a harlot.

Fat male, considered, non sequiturially, as a stout phallus . . . **Fat cock.**

Father, sexual fixation of a daughter to her; with hostility to mother . . . ELECTRA COMPLEX.

Father, sexual intercourse of a, with his own daughter . . . THYGATRIA.

Father, sexual love of a daughter for her . . . PATROLAGNIA.

Father, sexual love of a, for his own daughter . . . THYGATRILAGNIA.

Fear of sexual intercourse, usually in the female . . . COITOPHOBIA.

Fear of the first act of sexual intercourse, by the female . . . ESODOPHOBIA.

Fear of . . . See also under name of object, as *Phallus*.

Feast in which the celebrating is done pudendally . . . **Bawdy banquet.**

Featherweights . . . Female breasts of the junior-miss size.

Feces, derivation of sexual pleasure from the handling, sight, or contemplation of; esp. of feces voided by a person of the opposite sex . . . COPROLAGNIA.

Feeble seminal ejaculation . . . ASTHENOBLYSIS.

Feeble . . . See also under name of action involved, as *Erection*.

Feel hairy . . . Feel the sexual urge; said more often about the female.

Feel, non-medically, the distinguishing characteristics of a female, upper and lower . . . **Mess.**

Feel of the female anatomy gained by a grab and a run, in allusion to this technique in purse snatching . . . **Grab-gain.**

Feel one's oats . . . To be high spirited under the pressure of the seminal fluid, in allusion to the boisterousness of a horse feeding on oats.

Feel the body of a female sexerotically . . . **Finger.**

Feel the draft . . . To lie close to a woman's pudendum, conceived here as an airy chink.

Feel the exciting tissues and parts of a human female . . . SARMASSATE; CONTRECTATE.

Feel the female body and its peculiar embellishments with an amatory hand . . . **Do a body job.**

Feel the fleshy ornaments of a female, with fingers and palms . . . **Fiddle.**

Feel the impact of the hardened phallus, said of a girl dancing with a male bearing such . . . **Know it's there.**

Feel the oysters . . . To feel or squeeze a man's testicles.

Feel the sexual urge . . . **Feel hairy.**

FELLATIO . . . The taking of the penis into the mouth for the purpose of satisfying it by oral titillation. Ex *fellare* (to suck).

Fellatio, active member in; i.e., the giver of the phallus . . . FELLATRANT.

Fellatio, be the recipient in . . . **Blow.**

Fellatio duet in which each participant takes from the other and gives to the other, at the same time . . . **Double wedding; Live-and-let-live.**

Fellatio, in the act of, to hold the recipient of the phallus by his or her ears . . . **Bull by the souse.**

Fellatio in which the phallus is suckled by an animal . . . ZOOFELLATIO.

Fellatio in which the subject takes his own phallus . . . AUTOFELLATIO.

Fellatio, one who practices, upon oneself . . . **Automatic muzzle loader;** AUTOFELLATOR.

Fellatio, passive female member in; i.e., a female who takes the phallus . . . FELLATRICE.

Fellatio, passive male member in; i.e., a male who takes the phallus of another . . . FELLATOR.

FELLATIZE . . . To take the membrum virile orally.

FELLATOR . . . A male who takes the penis of another into his mouth to give it oral satisfaction.

Fellator . . . **Beef eater; Jaw artist; Mouther; Sword swallower; Cocksucker.**

Fellator, toothless . . . **Bald cocksucker.**

FELLATORISM . . . The introduction of the phallus into the mouth of another for the purpose of having it gratified by oral titillation.

Fellatorism, one who practices, as the active member . . . **Muzzle loader;** FELLATRANT.

Fellatorism, practice the active part of . . . **Bully into the muzzle.**

Fellatorism, practice the passive part in . . . FELLATIZE.

FELLATRANT . . . In fellatio, the male who introduces the penis.

FELLATRICE . . . A female who takes the penis into her mouth to give it oral satisfaction.

FELLATRICE . . . Of the female, to take the membrum virile orally.

Fellatrice . . . **Beef eater; Jaw artist; Mouther; Sword swallower; Cocksucker.**

Female appurtenances regarded as targets for male hands . . . **Good stuff; Handfuls.**

Female as a recaptacle for the phallus . . . **Keg.**

Female as an amorous tickling target . . . **Minikin.**

Female as bliss in a dish . . . **Pot of bliss.**

Female at her best age or state of development, which varies with the viewpoint of the appraiser . . . **Fair roebuck.**

Female, attractive, having a pudendum that is not insurmountable . . . **Hairy bit.**

Female, attractive, with a reasonable pudendum . . . **A bit of all right.**

Female, be desirous for a . . . **Carry a bat.**

Female bedfellow; female sexual partner . . . COITANTE; PARACOITA.

Female behind beautiful . . . CALLIPYGUS.

Female breast, large, like a bushel . . . **Bushel bubby.**

Female breasts conceived as . . . **Front bumpers.**

Female breasts, flattened, of a parous woman . . . **Bread bags.**

Female breasts . . . See also under *Breasts, female.*

Female buttocks, beautiful . . . CALLIPYGUS.

Female canal which receives the phallus in sexual intercourse . . . VAGINA.

Fellatrice, toothless . . . **Bald cocksucker.**

Female characteristics, assumption of, by a male . . . FEMINIZATION; MULIEBRATION; THELYZATION.

Female characteristics, collectively . . . MULIEBRITY.

Female characteristics, flowering of, in a young girl . . . FEMANTHOSIS; THELYFLORESCENCE.

Female characteristics in the male, presence of . . . THELYSISM.

Female characteristics, normal development of, in a girl . . . EUTHELYSITY.

Female characteristics, overdevelopment of . . . HYPERTHELYSITY.

Female characteristics, partial or complete loss of . . . DEFEMINATION; DEFEMINIZATION; EXTHELYZATION; GYNECOZEMIA.

Female characteristics, underdevelopment of, in a girl . . . HYPOTHELYSITY.

Female charms, think about . . . **Think about something to eat.**

Female child presented to a visiting male VIP for a night of pudendal entertainment, in accordance with a custom prevalent in some countries . . . **Moko.**

Female child used as catamite . . . **Preshen.**

Female child . . . See also under *Child, Children,* etc.

Female conceived as a comforting application to an indurated male underbelly . . . **Belly plaster.**

Female conceived as a piece of genital "tail" . . . **Quail.**

Female conceived as a sexual slit . . . **Placket.**

Female conceived as something better than welcome, pudendally . . . **Bit of stuff.**

Female corpse, beating and/or mutilation of . . . NECROSADISM.

Female corpse, molestation of . . . NECROCHLESIS.

Female corpse, sexual attraction to a . . . NECROPHILISM.

Female corpse, sexual intercourse with a . . . NECROCOITUS.

Female cunnilinguist, i.e., a female who licks the vulva of another . . . HOMOPHAGIST.

Female cylinder . . . The chamber in which the male piston reciprocates in pudendal coitus.

Female, desirable fleshy parts of a . . . **Bacon.**

Female desirous pudendally, for the phallic quencher . . . **A Christmas Eve.**

Female dispenser of pudendal privileges . . . **Jazzabelle.**

Female easily steered into pudendal surrender . . . **Light frigate.**

Female especially fond of men . . . ANDROPHILIST.

Female flesh of special interest to a male . . . **Meat.**

Female flesh of special interest to a male, colored . . . **Black meat; Dark meat.**

Female flesh of special interest to a male, exposed . . . **Hot meat; White hot meat.**

Female from whom the phallating male has been suddenly and by force removed, designating a . . . **Dog-drawn.**

Female genitalia and mammae as amatory messables . . . **Kittleables; Tickleables.**

Female genitalia as the accommodator of the phallus . . . **Jack Straw's castle.**

Female genitalia conceived as a hospitable inn for a lust-weary male organon . . . **Cock Inn.**

Female genitalia conceived as a loving vehicle of joy . . . **Aunt Maria.**

Female genitalia conceived as a "piece" of savory goody . . . **Bit of jam.**

Female genitalia conceived as a thesaurus of big and little amatory pleasures . . . **Almanac.**

Female genitalia conceived as hell consigners . . . **Hell-matter.**

Female genitalia conceived as located on the opposite end of the trunk, in allusion to Australia and New Zealand regarded as being on the opposite side of the earth . . . **Antipodes.**

Female genitalia conceived as the cylinder in which the male organ jigs . . . **Jigger.**

Female genitalia conceived as the feminine classic . . . **Attic.**

Female genitalia conceived as the grand receiving chambers of the female pudendum, reserved for VIP phalli . . . **Cock-hall.**

Female genitalia conceived as the indescribable fountain of carnal pleasure . . . **Ineffable.**

Female genitalia conceived as the "shire" of the male governor . . . **Cockshire.**

Female genitalia conceived as the wooded center of ribald jocundity . . . **Black joke.**

Female genitalia, erotic licking of . . . CUNNILINGUS; CUNNILINCTION; EDELINGUS; **Pearl diving; Biting the dog-end; Brushing with Miriam.**

Female genitalia, external and internal . . . MULIEBRIA.

Female genitalia, fanatically enamored of the . . . **Hell for leather.**

Female genitalia, figure of, serving as symbol in worship of Shakti . . . YONI.

Female genitalia, in allusion to mons veneris . . . **The Mount.**

Female genitalia, lubricating discharge of, during excitation . . . UNGATION; **Gravy; Cow juice.**

Female genitalia, lubricating secretion of, during quiescence . . . HUMEX.

Female genitalia . . . See also under *Vagina, Vulva, Pudendum muliebre,* etc.

Female grooved underbelly with its pubic clump . . . **Apostle's grove.**

Female having a liberally lubricated vulva . . . **Juicer.**

Female having an aversion for being touched amorously . . . SARMASSOPHOBE.

Female having an enlarged clitoris resembling a penis and a scrotum-like pouch formed by the fusion of the labia majora . . . GYNANDROID.

Female having attractive buttocks . . . **Altar maid.**

Female having attractive buttocks, designating a . . . CALLIPYGIAN.

Female having attractive legs . . . **Legger.**

Female having attractive . . . See also under name of the part or organ involved.

Female having beautiful breasts . . . CALLIMAZONIAN; CALLIMASTA.

Female having more than ample breasts . . . MEGAMASTA.

Female having such large breasts that one would make two . . . **Double-diddied.**

Female homosexual, in allusion to ancient Lesbos where female homosexualism was in flower, they say . . . LESBIAN.

Female homosexual, in allusion to the ancient poetess Sappho who versified erotically . . . SAPPHIST.

Female homosexual, in allusion to the reciprocal rubbing of the female genitalia by two such . . . TRIBADE.

Female homosexual who has a large clitoris which she uses penis-like upon another female . . . TRIBADE.

Female homosexual who, in the act of tribadism or the like, takes the part of the male or active member . . . **Mason;** TRIBADE.

Female homosexual who is also a masochist, esp. with regard to other female homosexuals . . . SAPPHOMASOCHIST.

Female homosexual who is also a sadist, esp. with regard to other female homosexuals . . . SAPPHOSADIST.

Female homosexuality . . . SAPPHISM.

Female homosexuality in which one female (usually having a large clitoris) plays the role of a male and rubs her genitalia against the genitalia of the sexual partner . . . TRIBADISM.

Female homosexuals, rubbing of posteriors between . . . **Bum-fighting.**

Female intimate part, exposed; in allusion to its rampant effect on a potent male ramrod . . . **Bracer.**

Female, luscious, or her soft underbelly . . . **Jammy bit of jam.**

Female lying between two males with spiked phalli . . . **Rose between two thorns.**

Female nudity, pleasure derived from contemplation of . . . GYNHEDONIA.

Female nudity . . . See also under *Naked, Nakedness, Nude,* etc.

Female of tender age but of extremely good development . . . **Young thing.**

Female parts which have an inflationary effect upon functional phalli . . . **Hot meat.**

Female perineum . . . **Dog-end.**

Female, provocative, whose charms cause the male pants captive to exert pressure against the fly, breaking, figuratively, the buttons or zipper . . . **Button buster; Zipper-snapper.**

Female pudenda as a commercial product . . . **Milt market.**

Female pudendal apparatus . . . **Bumbo.**

Female pudendal apparatus . . . See also under *Female pudendum, Pudendum muliebre, Vulva,* etc.

Female pudendal privilege, be denied the; and allowed only to kiss the butt; figuratively . . . **Kiss behind and not before.**

Female pudendal privilege . . . See also under *Denial* and *Deny.*

Female pudendally accessible at a tender age . . . **January chicken.**

Female pudendum; an allusion to a breeding place for cattle . . . **Hairyfordshire.**

Female pudendum as a girl's best face . . . **Sunday face.**

Female pudendum as soothing application to male counterpart . . . **Belly plaster.**

Female pudendum, conceived as a furry rabbit . . . **Cunny.**

Female pudendum conceived as the end of the search . . . **End of The Sentimental Journey.**

Female pudendum; conceived as the shortest route to hell . . . **Hell.**

Female pudendum, make advances to, manually or with the phallus . . . **Go south.**

Female pudendum; regarded as an applicator to the male counterpart . . . **Pudendal plaster.**

Female pudendum, slit of . . . **Placket;** ENTOMA.

Female pudendum stripped and spread for coital action, the frantic picture presented by a . . . **View of the land.**

Female pudendum, the nod of assent from the . . . **Brazen gift.**

Female receptacle . . . The female sheathing for the male organon, esp. the vagina.

Female recipient in the act of sodomy . . . SODOMEE; SODOMANTE.

Female regarded as the carrier of sexual pleasure . . . **Joy wagon.**

Female responding nimbly to the phallic chopper . . . **Nimble-hips.**

Female sadist . . . MASTIX.

Female sex organ homologous to the male penis . . . CLITORIS.

Female sex organs . . . MULIEBRIA.

Female sex organs, pleasure derived from contemplation of . . . GYNHEDONIA.

Female sex organs . . . See also under *Vagina, Vulva, Pudendum muliebre,* etc.

Female sex, peculiar to the . . . IDIOTHELIC.

Female, sexual desire in, excessive . . . ANDROMANIA; CLITOROMANIA; NYMPHOMANIA.

Female sexual flesh, esp. that of a harlot . . . **Keg.**

Female sexual partner in the reversed coital posture, i.e., impaled upon the up-pointed male spike . . . **Flesh blanket.**

Female, slovenly, having a filthy pudendum . . . **Trapes.**

Female, small but very attractive; conceived as pudendal heaven . . . **Quartern of bliss.**

Female so well stacked and stocked that she could revive a dead male, as judged by one who is living . . . **Corpse reviver.**

Female suitable for and accessible to the phallus . . . **Belly timber.**

Female tissues grade A, conceived with a little assist from the phallic centers . . . **White meat.**

Female too young for legal phallic intrusion, but not by much; designating such a . . . **Few pence short of a shilling.**

Female torso, lower end of . . . **Dog-end.**

Female undergarments, esp. those that cover the most interesting parts . . . **Angel's gear.**

Female undergarments . . . See also under name of particular garment, as *Brassiere.*

Female who has been phallated; a non-virgin . . . PHALLATA.

Female who is good to a man's pudendum . . . **Good girl.**

Female who is not averse to a thigh spread, extra-maritally . . . **Cleaver.**

Female who is still a virgin . . . APHALLATA.

Female who may be persuaded to submit to the phallus, designating a . . . **Christenable.**

Female who may be phallated with impunity, because of maturity, unattachment to another male, etc., designating a . . . **Christenable.**

Female who "moans and groans" when taking the thrusts of the male plunger . . . **Yelper.**

Female who mouths the genitalia of another female . . . HOMOPHAGIST.

Female who sucks the male genital teat . . . FELLATRICE; **Beef eater; Jaw artist; Mouther; Sword swallower; Cocksucker.**

Female who sucks the male genital teat and/or licks his anus . . . **Buttock and tongue.**

Female who takes the phallus both vaginally and rectally . . . **Bread buttered on both sides.**

Female whose buttocks are disproportionately larger than her pectoral prominences . . . **Bottle-arse.**

Female whose pudendal labia have been split by the incoming phallus; non-virgin . . . **Split mutton.**

Female whose sexual desire is abnormally intense . . . ANDROMANIAC; CLITOROMANIAC; NYMPHOMANIAC.

Female whose vaginal corridor is still wet with the seminal oil of a previous sexual injection when she takes the phallus again . . . **Wet blanket.**

Female, wife or mistress, as an alleviator of the indurated phallus . . . **Importance.**

Female with a keen sexual appetite . . . **Greedy arse.**

Female with charitable pudendum . . . **Molly.**

Female with fat buttocks who takes the phallus per rectum . . . **Yorkshire hog.**

Female with prominent breasts . . . **Bristler;** MACROMASTA.

Female with small breasts . . . MICROMSTA.

Female with small genital organs . . . MICROGENITALA.

Female with . . . See also under *Female having.*

Female, young and attractive, conceived as a phallically savory cut of pudendal pie . . . **Bit of raspberry.**

Female's best of all possible places, as conceived by a male bothered by an uprising . . . **Molly's place; Polly's place.**

Females, desirable, from the lecherous viewpoint of Eros . . . **Good stuff.**

Females, non-virgin . . . PHALLATAE.

Females, non-virgin, pert. to . . . PHALLATIC.

Females, scarcity of; as in a particular country or region . . . SPANOGYNY.

Females, strong desire for company of; as after a protracted deprivation . . . GYNELIMIA.

Females, unripe, sexual urge for . . . **Babyolatry.**

Females who are accessible pudendally . . . **Fad-cattle.**

Females, young, conceived as gratifiers of the sex urge in the male . . . **Young blood.**

Females . . . See also under *Girl, Girls, Woman,* etc.

FEMANDRISM . . . Effeminate characteristics in a man.

FEMANTHOSIS . . . The blossoming out of the female characteristics in a girl at puberty. Ex *femina* (woman) & *anthosis* (a flowering).

Feminine gender . . . A gentle concept of the cleft underside of a girl, which makes her a girl.

Feminine manners, adoption of, by a male . . . GYNEMIMISM.

FEMINIZATION . . . The assumption of female characteristics by a male.

FETISH . . . A nonsexual part of the body or an object, as a hand or a glove, which produces sexual pleasure or excitation in susceptible persons.

Fetish, person who derives sexual pleasure from a . . . FETISHIST.

Fetish which is a part of the body, as the female hair . . . ORGANOFACT.

Fetish which is a sexual part of the body . . . GENOFACT.

Fetish which is the female breast . . . MASTOFACT.

Fetish which is the female leg . . . CRUROFACT.

Fever . . . The yen for a hen.

Few pence short of a shilling . . . Of a female regarded as good phallic pudding, somewhat short, legally, in age, esp. for extramarital buckling.

Fiddle . . . To feel with the fingers and palms the fleshy interests of a female.

Fiddle . . . The female coital receiving chamber, in which the male bow fiddles.

Fiddle fare . . . 1. Phallus erectus as fodder for the female pudendum. 2. Seminal fluid as manna for the fiddle.

Fiddleback . . . A whore, in allusion to her spending much time in the dorsal recumbent position.

Fiddle-bow . . . The male sexual stick, in allusion to its role as bow to the female fiddle.

Fiddlestick . . . The membrum virile erectum or flaccidum.

Fiddlestick rosin . . . Vaginal secretion serving as lubricant for the male genital stick.

Fig . . . The lower cynosure of the female figure, i.e., the phallic haven.

Figure . . . The derrière and bubbies of a girl, esp. when built like a brick defecatorium, as men are wont to put it.

Figure fancier . . . 1. A male who has a "tooth" for women with prominent breasts and even more prominent buttocks. 2. A man who pays more attention to a girl's figure than to her face.

Figure-maker . . . A whoremaster general or inveterate phallator.

Figure of an erected phallus, as used in Bacchic festivals . . . ITHYPHALLOS.

File for future use . . . Of the male, to replace a frustrated and unappeased phallus in the fly den after a futile attempt at penetration of the female pudendal line.

File in the wrong box . . . To plunge the erected spermapositor into the rectum; to sodomize.

Filly . . . A young, and usually svelte, girl. Also, a young girl who gives of her lower end.

Filly at a price . . . A girl generally continent with her pudendal dispensations, but amenable to a bribe.

Filly-hunter . . . A man out looking for accessible female pudenda, accessible for love or money.

Fine imposed for illicit sexual concourse . . . **Buttock-mail.**

Finger . . . To feel a woman's body with the fingers, etc.

Finger and thumb work . . . The fingerdoodling of the female perineum in which the index finger of the male is in the female rectum and his thumb in her vagina.

Finger dosing . . . The insertion of the male finger into the vagina, for pleasure, of course, and also for the purpose of eroticizing the female.

Finger fuck . . . Of the female, to masturbate by titillation with a finger or the fingers.

Fingerdoodle . . . To play with the female perineum, esp. by inserting one or more fingers in the rectal and vaginal openings.

Finish caressing with the genital blessing . . . **Play the whole game.**

Finish with a bout of coitus, that which was begun as a palpatory foray . . . **Go the whole animal.**

Fire in the air . . . Of a phallating male, to withdraw the organum and ejaculate extravaginally.

Fire ship . . . A harlot who is a source of venereal infection to her patrons.

Fire-box . . . A passionate male with an ebullient phallus to match.

Fireplug . . . A male nursing a venereal infection, in allusion to the plug that is on fire.

Fires, sexual gratification derived from sight of . . . PYROLAGNIA.

Fireworks . . . Spirited pudendal concourse.

Fireworks, be out of . . . Of the male, to be exhausted seminally.

Fireworks on the brain . . . In a man, phallus erectus on the brain, i.e., seminal hypertension and the state of mind resulting therefrom.

First-chop . . . The first engagement in coitus, for the male.

Fish . . . The lipped treasure at the lower end of a woman's torso, without which she would have to work for a living.

Fish, bit of . . . Same as **Fish, dish of,** i.e., coitus in the usual manner.

Fish, dish of . . . A bout of intercommunication between the male giver and female receiver.

Fish flesh . . . The good flesh of a bad woman.

Fish gunner . . . A male with female pudendal pressure on his brain.

Fish pond . . . The female genital inlet and its external embellishments, conceived, obviously, as fishing waters.

Fish trader . . . A procurer (of pudenda), a pimp, or a manager of a bordello.

Fishiness . . . The "it" of Clara Bow.

Fishing fleet . . . A brace of hungry sailors, out looking for pudendal pie.

Fishing, gone . . . Out looking for a pudendum of a charitable or mercenary woman.

Fishing rod . . . The male membrum, esp. erectum, in allusion to its fishing habits in the female pudendal waters.

Fishy . . . Of a male, hot in the gonads.

Fit for marriage, as with regard to age; applied to girls . . . NUBILE.

Fitness for marriage, as with regard to age; applied to a girl . . . NUBILITY.

Flabbiness of the female breasts . . . MADAROMASTIA.

FLACCILATION . . . The waning of the sexual power in the male. Ex *flaccus* (flabby).

Flag-about . . . A prostitute with a "for hire" look in her eyes.

Flag chaser . . . A man on the lookout for a girl with that certain smile.

Flag down . . . To give a circulating whore the sign of engagement.

Flag-flier . . . A woman with an unmistakable "to let" mien.

Flag of distress . . . An open pants fly with an ear of shirttail herniating through it.

Flag waver . . . A woman who wards off ardent phalli by waving the red flag of menstruation, when the captain is not really at home.

Flagger . . . A peripatetic whore perambulating the streets of pudendal commerce.

Flagrant delight . . . The act of lovemaking in public. A jocose corruption of the legal *in flagrante delicto.*

Flankey . . . The buttocks regarded as the posterior dome.

Flash-man . . . 1. In a bordello, a bouncer who ejects troublesome patrons of the pudendal arts. 2. A prostitute's ten-percenter.

Flash one's gab . . . Of a female, to spread and thus display the promised land; an allusion to **gab,** the nether silent mouth of the female.

Flash one's stick . . . Of a desirous male, to draw the six-incher from its fly holster.

Flash-tail . . . 1. A girl who gives an eloquent English to her derrière. 2. A harlot who picks up patrons at night.

Flash the red flag . . . To give off the menstrual claret.

Flash the roe . . . Of the male, to give with the seminal fertilizer.

Flash the upright grin . . . Of a woman recumbent, to smile upon the man with the silent mouth, by doing the precoital split.

Flash the wedge . . . Of a ruttish male, to pull out the genital coupling hose, from its cramped hang-out.

Flash woman . . . A harlot who is the favorite "girl" of a bordello bouncer.

Flattening of the buttocks, as in old age . . . SPHEROPLANIA.

Flesh . . . 1. The phallus and adnexa. 2. The vulva. 3. The bubbies.

Flesh . . . The tissues of a female sexually exciting to the male.

Flesh bag . . . 1. An undergarment covering an intimate part of a woman's body. 2. A brassiere. 3. A flaccid tissue, esp. a pendulous breast.

Flesh blanket . . . 1. A male as a sexual coitant, in his usual supernatant position. 2. The female sexual coitante when superimposed upon the spike of the male.

Flesh broker . . . A procurer of female pudenda for spiked phalli.

Flesh broker, abominable . . . The phallus erectus, who insists on having its menu of flesh.

Flesh broker, legitimate . . . A marriage broker.

Flesh broker, spiritual . . . A parson, rabbi, etc.

Flesh it . . . 1. To sink the tempered male genital poniard into the vulvar flesh of the female. 2. To dig in manually into the upper or lower female *summum bonum.*

Flesh maggot . . . A small membrum virile, irrespective of how virile it is.

Flesh market . . . The commerce of Mrs. Warren. Also, a female pudendal stock exchange, i.e., a bordello.

Flesh one's sword . . . To insinuate the male genital sword into the female pudendal scabbard.

Flesh session . . . Sexual copulation conceived dispassionately.

Fleshing . . . A bout of sexual concourse.

Fleshing, be out . . . Be out whoring.

Fleshpots . . . Liberal and satisfying pudendal accommodations, for the male.

Fleshy part of the thigh . . . A euphemism for the gluteal dome or buttock.

Flimp . . . To take part in sexual intercourse.

Fling at female pudendum, phallic . . . **Bit of fork.**

Flit . . . A male homosexual.

Flog a dead horse . . . To try to arouse an impotent phallus by manual stimulation.

Flog a willing horse . . . Of a female, to tantalize a more than willing membrum virile.

Flog one's mutton . . . Of a male burdened with a persistent hardening of a generally soft part, to tenderize it with an educated mutton fist.

Flog the bishop . . . Of a male badgered by an inflexible phallus, to render it pliable by removing its starch, manually.

Flog the donkey . . . Of a male confronted with a bullheaded erection, to drain the stubbornness of the phallus with a not too stern hand.

Flog the old whipping-boy . . . 1. To give the phallus erectus a going over with the cupped hand. 2. To resort to masturbation as an escape from tensions not necessarily erotic.

Flogger . . . The genital organon of a robust phallator.

Flogging . . . The whipping of a masochist by a naked, no less, woman.

Flogging-cove . . . A sadist who whips a masochist.

Flogging-cully . . . A male masochist who enjoys being whipped by a woman.

Flop about . . . To be awkward and have difficulty in finding the opening for the phallus, in coitus.

Flop in . . . To succeed in plunging the phallus into the introitus vaginae, after some fumbling and flopping about.

Flourish . . . Of the male, to brandish the phallus adamantinus. Of the female, to uncover the sanctum.

Flourish, have a . . . Of a male, to have a hurried copulation, often in the statant posture.

Flourish it . . . Same as **Flourish,** to trot out the virilia or muliebria.

Flower . . . The thing that counts in the female crotch, as viewed across the sights of a stiffly starched male plunger.

Flower fancier . . . A male devotee of the female hiatus.

Flower of chivalry . . . The same as **Flower,** the female pudendal funnel, whither the semen goes.

Flower pot . . . A slightly used vulva.

Flowers . . . The cruentous percolate to which a woman refers when she says (the) captain is at home.

Flute . . . The male genital dispenser, esp., in allusion to the form, an erotically expanded one.

Flutter . . . 1. To have a sexual experience with a female. 2. To ejaculate.

Flutter a brown . . . To phallate a colored cyprian.

Flutter a Judy . . . To "know" a girl, in the Biblical sense.

Fly . . . The penis, in allusion to its normal habitat, behind the pants fly.

Fly-by-night . . . The silent mouth of the female, in the perineal region. An allusion to its being, generally, a creature of the night.

Fly cage . . . The vulva, regarded as the place of confinement for the male genital fly.

Fly-catcher . . . The female vulvar apparatus, conceived as the captor of the male pants fly.

Fly of a man's trousers bulging with tumefied phallus . . . **Hot fly.**

Fly of a man's trousers which is on the verge of being unzipped, to release the nudging inmate upon the female pudendum . . . **Red hot fly.**

Fly the flag . . . To have the monthly leak of claret from the female genitalia.

Fly-trap . . . The vulva, conceived, in allusion to the labia, as trap.

Flyspecks . . . A pair of very small female breasts, conceived with derision.

Fond of pundendal entertainment . . . **Battered.**

Fondness for being touched amorously or for so touching another . . . SARMASSOPHILIA.

Fool around . . . Of an erotic male, to palpate amorously certain intimate parts of the female body.

Fool-sticker . . . The genital tentacle of the male which ties him subserviently to the pudendal strings of the female, in allusion to his being made a fool by the demands of the phallus.

Fool-trap . . . The pudendum muliebre conceived as the maker of male cullies and uxorious husbands, by the insuperable magnetism it exerts on the thoroughly conditioned membrum virile.

Fool's paradise . . . The illusory feeling of freedom and importance enjoyed by uxorious husbands.

Foot . . . The male genital sinker, conceived as man's third foot.

Foraminate . . . To insinuate the male's shortest extremity into the female's central perineal orifice; to phallate.

Force a boy to submit to pederasty . . . **Highjack.**

Force meat . . . Force the male phallic meat into the vaginal casing; to phallate.

Fore and aft . . . To phallate, esp. to phallate both ways, into the vagina and into the rectum.

Fore-and-after . . . A female peddling her pudendum who will take the male bat either way, regulation manner, in the well-trodden vagina, or in the wind tunnel, i.e., rectally.

Fore-buttocks . . . The female breasts.

Forecastle . . . The female pudendal apparatus.

Foregather . . . Of man and maid, to meet in pudendal embrace.

Foreman . . . The male sexual organon.

FOREPLEASURE . . . The pleasure of sexual intercourse preceding the orgasm.

Fores and afts . . . The breasts and the buttocks of a female.

Foreskin hunter . . . 1. A mohel. 2. A prostitute on the prowl.

FORHYMEN . . . The hymen of a woman who has had sexual intercourse. From *forare* (to bore).

Form-fitting; said of a gown following the female undulations with blind and fanatical adherence . . . **Contour-chasing.**

FORNICATE . . . To engage in any form of illicit sexual intercourse.

Fornicate freely and well . . . **Play the jack.**

Fornicate . . . See also under *Phallate, Sexual intercourse,* etc.

Fornicating tool . . . The male sexual organon.

FORNICATOR . . . A person who takes part in illicit sexual intercourse.

Fornicator . . . The male genital club.

Fornicator of harlots . . . **Bum-fighter.**

Fornicator's hall . . . The interlabial sanctum muliebre.

Forty-twa . . . A bordello, in allusion to an Edinburgh public comfort station, reputed to "sit" forty-two.

Fossick . . . To "search" diligently the interior of the female panties, or her brassiere, in allusion to standard meaning of the term, to search for gold, in Australia.

Fossicker . . . From the viewpoint of the female quarry, a lecherous male whose restless hands are forever sliding down her décolletage, or up her thighs.

Foul a plate . . . To deflower a young lady.

Four F's . . . Find, fool, frig, and forget 'em, the girls, i.e.

Four-legged frolic . . . The pudendal mattress jig.

Four legs in bed . . . A couple of heterosexual normals shaking the bed to the pudendal rhythm.

Four-letter man . . . A male homosexual, in allusion to the four letters in "homo."

Four-wheeled kip . . . A taxicab used as a fornicating chamber by a homeless whore and her patron.

Fourpenny cannon . . . A phallus of good size and substantial hardness.

Fox paw, make a . . . Of a female, to err in strategy and find herself with her pants down. Ex *faux pas.*

FRATRILAGNIA . . . Sexual desire for one's own brother. Ex *frater* (brother) & *lagneia* (lust).

Free-lance . . . To use the phallic pencil promiscuously, without commitment to a particular inlet.

Free of her lips, free of her hips . . . A non-sequitur proverbial logic concatenating upper labial activity with lower labial laxity.

Freezer . . . 1. A short skirt, allowing, figuratively, the formation of icicles on the pudendal beard. 2. A thoroughly frigid female.

French article . . . A delightfully disturbing Gallic filly.

French fare . . . A rich and elaborate pudendal menu for the male.

Frencher . . . A male who prefers unorthodox varietism in sexual play and concourse.

Frenchery . . . A bordello catering to the variegated tastes of an esoteric clientele.

Frenulum of the prepuce . . . **Bobstay.**

Fresh bit . . . 1. A freshman harlot. 2. A new, but not necessarily unused, mistress.

Fresh bit . . . A new lover and, hence, a fresh phallus; in allusion to the bit in a brace.

Fresh hand . . . A new female teaser, for a man who likes to be titillated manually.

Fresh milk . . . A new mistress, esp. a new set of titties, for a male who thinks of females in terms of so much breast tissue.

Freshen the hawse . . . To "clean" the female pudendal hawsehole with the male cable.

Fret one's fiddle-strings . . . Of the female, to masturbate by manual stimulation.

Fried chicken . . . 1. The best in the featherless poultry line. 2. A girl with an erotically feverish pudendum.

Frig . . . 1. Of an erotic male, to fidget his midget in Bridget. 2. Sexual piston-in-cylinder work.

Frig off . . . Of the male, to soothe a frenetic phallus erectus by a gentle hand.

Frigate . . . A female who harlots for a living; also, a free soul who gives it away as a largess.

Frigate on fire . . . A woman pudendally hot and eager for the phallic quencher.

Frigate on fire . . . A harloteering female who is infected venereally and thus carries the torch of Venus.

Frigger . . . The male genital intruder. An allusion to *fricare,* to rub (the vagina).

Frigging . . . 1. Phallic digging in the feminine pudendal mine. 2. A bout of self-gratification.

Frigid, sexually . . . PSYCHROTIC.

Frigid wife . . . PSYCHROTREMA.

Frigid wife and impotent husband . . . **Couple of flats.**

Frigid wife, mistress, etc. . . . **Eskimo pie.**

Frigidity . . . PSYCHROLAGNIA.

Frigidity in the female . . . ALGORGYNIA; PSYCHROGYNIA.

Frigidity in the male . . . ALGORSENIA; PSYCHROSENIA.

Frigidity of newly married women . . . NEOGAMOSIS.

Frigo . . . The phallus of a dead male, in allusion to "frigo," chilled meat.

Front bumpers . . . The softest parts of a woman's torso serving, in part, as support for a strapless gown.

Front lawn . . . The pubic region of the female.

Front parlor . . . The anterior, more conventional, receiving chamber of the female, as opposed to the **back parlor,** the sodomite's entrance.

FROTTAGE . . . The practice of rubbing against another, as in a crowd, to obtain sexual pleasure.

FROTTEUR . . . A pudendally hungry male who seeks out opportunities to rub, ostensibly casually, against the buttocks, or any parts, of females, as in crowded places. Ex *frotter* (to rub).

Frotteur who rubs against the buttocks of desirable females in crowded public places . . . **Bum-rusher.**

Fruiter . . . A male homosexual.

Fruitery . . . The female genital pleasure orchard.

Fruitful vine . . . The bawdy cleft of the female.

Frustration of the male resulting from the failure to get pudendal privileges after an evening of anticipatory spending on a girl who seemed promising coital clay . . . **Lemoncholy.**

Fryer . . . A teen-age desirable.

Fuck . . . 1. Of the male, to do to the female pudendum what comes naturally, with the phallus. 2. Of the female, to take the phallic thrusts, vaginally.

Fuck . . . 1. Sexual gratification by way of normal pudendal intercourse. 2. Sexual concourse.

Fuck . . . The creamy fluid ejected by the phallus at the acme of gratification.

Fuck . . . The female, or her pudendum, regarded as fodder for the phallus.

Fuck . . . A full life, provided with all pudendal comforts.

Fuck . . . Standard procedure; custom; mores.

Fuck . . . 1. Luxury; luxurious living. 2. Excessive refinement.

Fuck a bearskin . . . To phallate a very young girl, in allusion to the bearskin upon which babies were formerly photographed.

Fuck a blister . . . To have sexual concourse with a busy whore, in allusion to her chafed vagina.

Fuck a brisket . . . To phallate between the female breasts.

Fuck a Hoosier . . . To phallate a stranger, in allusion to a slurred "who's there," the alleged derivation of "Hoosier."

Fuck a Jesuit . . . Of a female, to have sexual intercourse with a male who has never had it.

Fuck a wet blanket . . . 1. To phallate a frigid wife. 2. To phallate a well-buttered bun, i.e., a female still wet, vaginally, from previous injections.

Fuck-arm . . . The right arm, in allusion to its use in manustupration, by right-handed males and females.

Fuck at the altar . . . To phallate a woman from behind, in allusion to the kneeling involved.

Fuck-beggar . . . A disreputable and partly impotentiated male whom even a "reputable" harlot will not suffer near her pudendum, who must, therefore, depend on beggar-women and outcast whores for sexual gratification, often by means of manual titillation.

Fuck book . . . A novel dealing heavily with sex.

Fuck-brained . . . Lecherous; addicted to sexual concourse.

Fuck brazen . . . To engage in sexual intercourse in an open place, as in a park.

Fuck by the book . . . To engage in orthodox sexual intercourse.

Fuck-crazy . . . Of a female, nymphomaniac. Of a male, suffering from vulvolimia, insatiable hunger for the cunt.

Fuck-dry . . . Of the male, exhausted (esp. seminally) by repeated bouts of coitus, in a given session.

Fuck dry... Of a female, to drain the male of semen by repeated inductions of phallic spurts.

Fuck ebony... To phallate a colored girl.

Fuck 'em and leave 'em... The credo of a wencher.

Fuck-finger . . . A female who masturbates digitally.

Fuck-fist... A male who relieves his seminal pressure by reciprocating the phallus in the clenched hand.

Fuck for blood . . . To phallate a woman with the intention of impregnating her, in allusion to the hematopoiesis in the expected fetus.

Fuck for gravy . . . Of the female, to dispense pudendal accommodations for a price, not for love.

Fuck-free... Unmarried; pudendally a free soul.

Fuck free and fancy loose . . . Maritally and sentimentally unattached, and out to paint the town red.

Fuck-fudge . . . Thickened or dried seminal ejaculant adhering to the female thighs, etc.

Fuck-hole . . . 1. The vagina. 2. The vulva as a cavity.

Fuck hot and cold . . . Of a female, to have a baffling range of erotic responsiveness or aggressiveness, varying from arctic frigidity to elephantine must.

Fuck-hungry... 1. Starved for pudendal food. 2. Sexually desirous; of the male, adorned with a phallus erectus.

Fuck in... To effect a pudendal take, i.e., a pregnancy.

Fuck in absentia . . . To think of a desirable female while actually phallating one not half so provocative.

Fuck in absentia . . . To phallate a woman mentally.

Fuck in the brown . . . Have sexual concourse with a woman per rectum.

Fuck in the teeth... To intromit the phallus orally.

Fuck it! . . . Let it be! The hell with it!

Fuck legit... To phallate in the conventional manner. 2. To phallate one's own wife.

Fuck legs . . . 1. Provocative female legs. 2. Female legs not averse to spreading.

Fuck-luck . . . A pudendal payoff where none was really expected.

Fuck-luck... In a bordello, a prostitute assigned to a patron by the manager, usually one he would not choose.

Fuck-marlin . . . A once-in-a-lifetime pudendal find which got away because of some fluff on the part of the male, in allusion to the big fish that usually also gets away. Also, such a hunk of provocativeness and its escape fabricated in the mind of a male.

Fuck me straight to the point... Cut out the crap and come to the point (of the issue).

Fuck-mother . . . A female who gives of her pudendum to apparently needy males, out of commiseration.

Fuck naked . . . To be in sexual concourse without a condom or diaphragm.

Fuck off . . . To give a woman the phallic treatment.

Fuck off one's tonsils . . . To sow wild oats, with the phallus.

Fuck on the run . . . To phallate a female with a dripping (gonorrheal) phallus.

Fuck on the run . . . To phallate a female hurriedly, often in a standing posture.

Fuck oneself . . . To masturbate; applied usually to the male.

Fuck oneself blue in the face . . . Of a partially impotent male, to phallate to exhaustion without achieving the orgasm.

Fuck-talk . . . Pudendal gasconade, involving alleged invasions of female introiti.

Fuck the lady of the house . . . To phallate the madame of a brothel when all the "girls" are on the street or bedded with patrons.

Fuck the parson . . . To celebrate a marriage proposal and acceptance by a pudendal initiation, right there and then, in allusion to making a fool of the parson.

Fuck to kill . . . To phallate with excessive vigor.

Fuck up . . . To give with the phallic spurt.

Fuck up . . . To phallate a woman while lying under her.

Fuck up and down . . . To reciprocate, or at least place, the phallus in various parts of the female body, as between the mammae, in the axilla, etc.

Fuck where the devil fears to tread . . . To intromit the phallus rectally.

Fuckable . . . 1. Of a woman, sexually accessible. 2. Of same, pudendally desirable.

Fuckaby . . . A complete round of coitus.

Fuckaby baby . . . 1. A desirable young female. 2. A **baby** that is available for the mattress dance.

Fucked and far from home . . . Of a girl, esp. a young thing, screwed and abandoned; hence, depressed.

Fucked fore and aft . . . 1. Of a female, given the phallic gusto both ways, normatim (i.e., in the usual place) and rectatim (by way of the rectum). 2. Given a thorough pudendal shellacking by a hungry and rambunctious phallus. 3. Of the female pudendum, inundated by several waves of seminal ejaculant.

Fucker . . . 1. A lascivious lover. 2. A man conceived by a woman as a prospective phallator. 3. A whore's lover or husband.

Fuckhouse . . . A pudendal flesh exchange; a bordello.

Fuckinest dame . . . The best piece of female pudendum you ever saw.

Fucking . . . Sexual concourse, conceived as a fuckin' good thing.

Fucking bone . . . The junction of the pubic bones at the symphysis, forming a mound which annoys some phallators.

Fucking lotion . . . Lubricating jelly used in coitus, either upon the phallus or in the introitus.

Fucking plaster . . . The pudendum muliebre conceived as a comforting application to the male counterpart.

Fucking stick . . . The able and willing phallus.

Fucking tadpoles . . . Spermatozoa, in allusion, it seems, to the similarity in form and locomotion.

Fucking triangle . . . A sexual orgy involving two males and one female, or two females and one male.

Fuckish . . . 1. Lusty; desirous. 2 Of a man, with a rampant phallus, ready to intromit.

Fucksome . . . Of girls, pudendally appetitive.

Fuckster . . . 1. A male devotee of the pudendal game. 2. A man whose pudendal act is something to brag about.

Fuckstress . . . 1. A wanton female. 2. A woman whose performance in the phallatory act is embellished with erotic virtuosity.

Fucky-talky . . . A male who boasts about his alleged pudendal conquests.

Fud . . . The pubic hair, esp. of the male.

Fulham virgin . . . A professional dispenser of sexual comfort to males with uneasy phalli; also a charitable dispenser of same.

Fulke . . . To be in the act of pudendal concourse; also, to phallate.

Full fig . . . A phallic erection; a phallus in erection.

Full-fledged . . . Of a girl, old enough for the pudendal invasion, by phallus erectus.

Full in the belly . . . With fetus in utero.

Full of beans . . . Of the male, overstocked with seminal fluid; hence, desirous.

Fumble . . . To make sexual love to a woman, with the hands.

Fumbler . . . A man who caresses a woman lecherously.

Fumbler . . . A male unable, because of penile suppleness, to perform effectually as a phallator.

Fumbler's hall . . . The female sexual receptacle into which the phallus erectus is deposited for action; the vagina.

Fumblers' hall . . . A home for aged males, regarded as a repository for out-of-commission phallators.

Fundamental feature . . . The fundament or rump of a female.

Funny bit . . . The sexual inlet of the female.

Funny business . . . A pudendal get-together of the orthodox variety.

Funny feeling . . . The phallic prod, as felt by the recipient.

Fur . . . The pubic hair, esp. in the female.

Furbelow . . . The pubic hair of a girl.

Furze-bush . . . The escutcheon of the female pudendum.

G

Gab . . . In the woman, the end of the phallic sentimental journey; i.e., that part of her which is seen best when she is on her back, with the legs flexed on her thighs, and the thighs widely abducted.

GAMOPHOBIA . . . Fear of marriage, esp. on the part of the female, due to anxiety regarding coitus. Ex *gamos* (marriage) & *phobos* (fear).

Garment intended to give the female breasts a speciously favorable form and magnitude . . . COLPOMENTIORS; COLPOMIMS; SEINSEMBLERS; **Brummagem.**

Garnish . . . To deposit the seminal juice where it will do the most good, vaginally.

Gash . . . The female sexual sanctum, conceived as a slash for the admittance of the male philistine.

Gash hound . . . A male devoted to the female pudendum.

Gates of hell . . . The labia majora, from the parsonage viewpoint.

Gaze voraciously at a provocative female part . . . **York.**

Gazook . . . The boy who plays "wife" to a pederast.

Gazoony . . . A boy who is phallated rectally by a pederast.

GENASTHENIA . . . Lack of sexual vitality, in the male. From *genos* (sex) & *asthenia* (lack of vitality).

GENDOLOMA . . . In the course of sexual coitus, a play of the imagination by the male, involving erotic situations, intended to hasten the onset of the orgasm. Ex *genos* (sex) & *doloma* (trick).

Genital blessing . . . The phallic payoff in coitus.

Genital organs as a dowry . . . **Rochester portion.**

Genital organs, condition of having abnormally large . . . MACROGENITALISM.

Genital organs, condition of having abnormally small . . . MICROGENITALISM.

Genital organs . . . See also under *Sex organs, Penis, Phallus, Vulva, Pudendum muliebre,* etc.

Genital parts of luscious female . . . **Jammy bit of jam.**

Genital privilege, grant the, to a male . . . **Stab with a rose.**

Genitalia as the region of erotic pruritus . . . **Itchland.**

Genitalia of a prostitute . . . **Kegged meat.**

Genitalia of another, abnormal desire to see . . . SCOPOLAGNIA; SCOPOPHILIA.

GENOCENTRIC . . . Centering one's interests on sexual matters. Ex *genos* (sex) & *kentein* (to goad).

GENOCHLESIS . . . Molestation motivated by lechery. Ex *genos* (sex) & *ochleo* (molest).

GENOCOSMICS . . . Sex characteristics of either male or female. Ex *genos* (sex) & *kosmein* (adorn).

GENOFACT . . . Any sexual part of the body which is a fetish.

GENOGRAPHY . . . A treatise on sex. From *genos* (sex) & *graphein* (to write).

GENOLIMIA . . . Starvation of the pudendal appetites.

GENOPAST . . . A sexual pervert; a person who likes to indulge in variants of normal sexual procedures; a paraphiliac. Ex *genos* (sex) & *paizo* (play).

GENOSTHENIA . . . Sexual vitality or potency, in the male. From *genos* (sex) & *sthenos* (strong).

Gentle trap . . . The vulva, conceived as a leniently sophisticated but inescapable snare.

Gentleman of the road . . . A male who rubs elbows with harlots; a frequenter of brothels.

Gentleman's pleasure garden . . . The underpart of the female torso, including the pubic tuft.

GENUPHALLATION . . . Sexual perversion in which the penis is reciprocated between the adducted knees of the female, the knees being an erotic fetish to many males. Ex *genu* (knee) & *phallos* (penis).

GEROMASTIA . . . The condition marked by involution of the breasts in older women. From *geron* (old) & *mastos* (breast).

GERONTOLAGNIA . . . Lechery observed in some older men. Ex *geron* (old man) & *lagneia* (lust).

Gesture of female body, or part thereof, which imparts pristine rigidity to a sexually valetudinarian and presumably "dead" male baton . . . **Corpse reviver.**

Get a big head . . . Of a male groping digitally in the mysteries of the female anatomy, to suffer the swelling of the phallus and its head.

Get a leg in . . . Of the male, to insinuate his third and shortest leg where it goes naturally.

Get a monopoly on . . . To secure exclusive rights to a female pudendum by marrying the owner.

Get a permanent . . . To get perpetual tenure to a particular female genital ensemble by way of a parson's certificate; to marry.

Get a ride . . . Of the male, to get a bit of female pudding; of the female, to act the mare to the stallion of homo sapiens.

Get inside . . . 1. To administer the phallus erectus vaginally. 2. To make a manual foray down the décolletage.

Get into a mess . . . To phallate a to oneself unwedded female and, alas, to impregnate.

Get into a mess . . . To sully the phallus in the slatternly introitus of a vagabond whore.

Get Jack in the orchard . . . To succeed in introducing the male pants worm in the female genital fruitery.

Get on the old fork . . . To mount one's wife, for the enth time and without phallic enthusiasm.

Get one's name up . . . To raise a functional phallus.

Get over the garter . . . In caressing a female, to abrogate conventional boundary lines and let the digital feeler slither above the garter, pudendad.

Get some house . . . In love or lovemaking, to receive encouraging encouragement.

Get the bull's feather . . . To be crowned king cuckold, by the accolade of another man's phallus upon the muliebral sanctum of one's own wife.

Get the order of the scimitar . . . Of a female, to receive, in her private chamber, the soft-headed but hard-bodied commander-in-chief of the male's netherland.

Giblets . . . The external genital organs, of either sex.

Girl as a female . . . **Bit of skirt.**

Girl as a good couch partner . . . **Bed bargain.**

Girl as a pudendal target, in allusion to the splitting of her labia phallically . . . **Split mutton.**

Girl as amorous flesh . . . **Chunk of meat.**

Girl as disorganizer of bachelorhood . . . **Bachelor bait.**

Girl as the reliever of phallic induration . . . **Angel.**

Girl as the very thing the doctor ordered for the membrum virile . . . **Article.**

Girl conceived as pudendal timber . . . **Bit.**

Girl Friday who can also be counted on pudendally . . . **Good Friday.**

Girl friend, provided with the comforts derivable from . . . **Hooked up.**

Girl having sexual appeal and an appealable pudendum . . . **Tart.**

Girl, in allusion to one of her lower provocatives . . . **Ankle.**

Girl leaving a male wanting more . . . **Miss Moreish.**

Girl not resistant to phallic invasion **Athanasian wench.**

Girl of not too stout morals . . . **Light skirt.**

Girl, pretty, conceived as something warm to wrap oneself in or around, by a male . . . **Fair blanket.**

Girl pudendally reasonable . . . **Quicumque vult.**

Girl, the better parts of a . . . **Bacon.**

Girl too young to be phallated, but phallated nevertheless . . . **Moko.**

Girl who, after an evening of anticipatory maneuvering by the escort, proves, at the usual payoff time, quite refractory, with regard to pudendal privileges . . . **Lemon.**

Girl who is not narrow-minded pudendally . . . **Broad.**

Girl who walks with a characteristic alternating oscillation of the buttocks . . . **Bobtail.**

Girl who would as lief spread them as cross them . . . **Thorough good-natured wench.**

Girl whose strongest points are under her brassiere, i.e., a sweater girl . . . **Bristler.**

Girl with understanding pudendum, with regard to the burdens of the male's pound of flesh . . . **Bit of fluff.**

Girl with whom one goes on a pudendal joy ride . . . **Joy-wheeler.**

Girl, young and charming, and sweet as molasses . . . **Pennorth of treacle.**

Girl, young and cute . . . **Biddy.**

Girl, young, petite and pudendally yummy . . . **Chick.**

Girlhood, unviolated . . . PARTHENITY.

Girlhood . . . See also under *Virginity*.

Girlie show in which thigh-and-buttock exposition is extraordinary . . . **Leg show.**

Girls, fear of being in the company of; on the part of a male . . . PARTHENOPHOBIA.

Girls, reasonable, go out in search for . . . **Do a grouse.**

Girls, young, conceived as sexual targets . . . **Young blood.**

Girth . . . The circumference of the male genital trunk.

Give a frigging . . . To give a temale an injection of male beef, in the normal port of entry.

Give a girl a past . . . To part a girl's lower lips with the phallic cleaver.

Give a green gown . . . To press a woman sexually on the grass, as in a park.

Give a green gown . . . To give a virgin the phallic accolade under the stars, esp. on the greensward of a park, whence the chlorophyll-stained gown cometh.

Give a hosing . . . Let the female feel the ingress of the male genital hose, and the spurt thereof.

Give a hot house . . . Of a female, to give more than the lover expected.

Give a length of tongue . . . 1. To cunnilinguate. 2. To give the female pudendum a length of male obturator.

Give a screwing . . . To give the female gash a thorough going over with the phallic bulldozer.

Give beans . . . Discharge the male roe; ejaculate.

Give fireworks . . . To dish out phallic enthusiasm, by the vaginal route.

Give more erotic refreshments than the male lover expected . . . **Give a hot house.**

Give one's oatmeal . . . Disembogue phallic satisfaction; ejaculate.

Give pudendal pleasure, to oneself and her, with thrusts of the phallus erectus . . . **Christmas.**

Give the bedroom eye . . . To look at a female with a pudendally voracious eye.

Give the bubble and squeak . . . To give a supine female the thrusts of a petrific phallus, in allusion to the seminal bubbles and the sexual grunt.

Give the bull's feather . . . To make a husband into a cuckold, by playing a pudendal duet with his squaw.

Give the business . . . Of a male, to give the female a thorough going over, below, with a lithoid phallus.

Give the key to the street . . . To shut a husband out of the bedroom in order to punish or coerce, usually in response to tight economic purse strings.

Give the length of . . . To sink the male genital plumb into the female pudendal shaft.

Give the phallus a friendly vaginal reception . . . **Roast the meat.**

Give the phallus a warm vaginal reception . . . **Roast brown.**

Give the vaginal caress to a rampant phallus . . . **Take care of.**

Gladius . . . A Latin figurative synonym for the penis, in allusion to a sword.

Gleam in eye of a desirous male confronted with a pudendal opportunity . . . **Intention.**

Go down on . . . To intromit the phallus into the rectum, in the practice of sodomy.

Go fishing . . . To go angling, phallically, in pudendal waters.

Go Hollywood . . . To practice sodomy.

Go on a bat bender . . . To go out whoring.

Go on a batter . . . Of the male, to go on a pudendal spree.

Go on a fishing trip . . . To go wenching.

Go on a girl spree . . . To go on a diet of titty and twat.

Go on a hand diet . . . To turn from female pudenda to manual appeasement.

Go on a job . . . Of a harlot, to make a house call.

Go on a liedown strike . . . Of a woman, usually a wife, to refuse access, in order to punish or coerce.

Go on a must . . . Of a male, to go out for phallic succor.

Go on a pudendal spree; of the male . . . **Go on a batter.**

Go on a religious . . . After whoring about, to marry.

Go on a sexploring expedition . . . To go on an erotic spree.

Go on a starvation diet . . . Of a male, to keep the semen in the vesicles, i.e., to abstain pudendally.

Go on a tear . . . Of the male, to go out "tearing" vulvas, phallically.

Go on the batter . . . Of a harlot, to walk the streets or frequent public places in search for patrons of the rentable pudendum.

Go on the halves . . . To phallate a female from behind.

Go on the hook . . . Of a female, to descend upon the upturned male pointer.

Go on the legit . . . Of a loose woman, to marry and give it legally.

Go on the thumb . . . Of an erotic female, to take to manual gratification.

Go on three legs . . . Of a female, to mount the male, in allusion to his two legs and a half.

Go out in search of accessible pudenda . . . **Do a grouse.**

Go south . . . To advance amorously to the female pudendum, manually or phallically.

Go the limit . . . Of an amorously active male, to finish the evening with the phallic compote, down the vaginal drain.

Go the whole animal . . . In an amorous adventure, to finish with the penile spurt.

Go to buck . . . Of a female, to have, sir-reverence, a fuck.

Go to Hairyfordshire . . . To "go" phallically through the female genital portal. See also under **Hairyfordshire.**

Go to town . . . 1. Of a pederast, to look for a receptive boy. 2. Of an amorous male, to dive for the female pudendal goodies.

Go uncling . . . To go after, or make love to, a married woman, while the cat's away; in allusion to the appellation "uncle," given to such a Lothario by the children in the house.

Go under . . . Of a female in bed, to assume the position most practical for the beef injection.

Go with a man because he is well-heeled . . . **Twist pockets.**

Goalie . . . The little man in the female boat, i.e., the clitoris.

Goat-house . . . A house stocked with rentable female pudenda, whither males with unruly phalli go for appeasement.

Goat-milker . . . A whore, in allusion to her relieving lascivious males (goats) of their phallic milk.

Goat-milker . . . The female pudendum, regarded as the milker of phallic juice, from lecherous males (goats).

Goat's jig . . . A bout of sexual intromission.

GODEMICHE . . . An artificially contrived penis and scrotum, used by females in masturbation and in tribadism. Ex, it is said, *gaudet mihi* (it gives me pleasure).

Godemiches, peddler of; usually female . . . **Bawdy basket.**

Golden Fleece . . . Reddish pubic hair of a female.

Gonorrhea and syphilis, concurrent infection with . . . **Double event.**

Gonorrhea, come home with a "case" of, after a pudendal coalition with a Neisseriated harlot . . . **Come home with clap'em.**

Gonorrhea, harlot dispensing the infection of; along with her favor . . . **Frigate on fire.**

Gonorrhea, infected with . . . **Clap-shouldered.**

Gonorrheal female pudendum . . . **Tetbury portion.**

GONOS . . . A Greek synonym for the phallus, in allusion to an offspring.

Gonsel . . . A young boy whose rectum is to the pederast what the vagina is to the normal phallator.

Gonyphilous . . . Of the male, especially erotic about the knees of the female. Ex *gony* (knee) and *philein* (to love).

Good at it . . . Of a female, sometimes also of the male, adept in coital procedures.

Good fellow . . . A pudendal virtuoso, i.e., an artistic phallator.

Good Friday . . . A girl Friday who is also a pudendal chum.

Good girl . . . A girl who is good to a man's phallus.

Good stuff . . . 1. Genitally desirable females, or one of such. 2. The good parts, erotically thinking, of a girl, as her retrobrassiereans.

Good tune . . . A satisfying pudendal concourse.

Good tune on an old fiddle . . . A satisfying genital tête-à-tête with an older woman, from whom one would hardly expect a gratifying response.

Goonas . . . The female breasts, conceived disrespectfully.

Goose . . . To phallate from behind between the thighs.

Goose . . . To intromit the phallus into the rectum, in the practice of sodomy.

Goose . . . Of the male, to draw the finger suddenly and forcibly in the female perineal groin, from behind.

Goose . . . The female pudendal cubbyhole, with its labial gates and furry welcome mat.

Goose . . . Restrain a woman by a hold on her pubic hair.

Goose . . . To rape or ravish a young untouchable.

Gospel preacher . . . An eloquent male who "sells" the motto of live and let live, pudendally, to a naive female.

Gospel shop . . . A bordello run under some innocuous front.

Gospel work . . . The gentle persuasion leading to female surrender.

Gouvernante sleeping pills . . . The titillation of an infant's or child's pudendum in order to put him or her to sleep, in allusion to the practice by governesses.

Gown, form-fitting, designating an obediently . . . **Contour-chasing.**

Gown worn by the female during the nightly pudendal invasions . . . **Knocking-jacket.**

Grab-gain . . . A feel of the female anatomy accomplished by a grab and a run, in allusion to the same technique in purse snatching.

Graduate . . . A woman, esp. one never married, who knows how to be a good bed partner.

Grant the genital privilege to a male . . . **Stab with a rose.**

Grapefruits . . . The female breasts, average American size.

Grease one's duke . . . To immerse the male genital appendage in the mucus of the female receptacle, i.e., to phallate.

Greased hop . . . A dance in which the male, oscillating against the charming prominences of his female partner, suffers a non-regrettable, but often embarrassing, loss of phallic lava.

Greedy arse . . . A female with an insatiable pudendal appetite.

Green bananas . . . Youngish, but well-equipped, girls, conceived as savory pudendal fare by those who like them rare.

Green goose . . . A prostitute, esp. a novice at the pudendal trade.

Green-grocery . . . The lower, headless, end of the female torso, esp. its central passage and the appurtenances.

Green grove . . . The pubic hair, esp. that of the female.

Grope . . . Of a sodomist or a homosexual, to test verbally the attitude of a prospective subject.

Groper . . . A sexually clumsy male who fumbles with the phallic insertion at the female putting green.

Grouse . . . To have a pudendal coalition with a female.

Grousing . . . 1. Pudendal reciprocation, alias phallation. 2. A forage for girls with rentable pudenda.

Gunsil . . . Same as **Gonsel,** the boy in pederasty.

Gusset . . . The distaff; women as targets for the night.

Gusset of the arse . . . The groin formed at the junction of the buttocks.

Gusseteer . . . A male who is excessively fond of female pudenda.

Gut reaming . . . The act of satisfying the hornified phallus by introduction into the rectum of another; i.e., sodomy or pederasty.

Gut-stick . . . The male genital lever, esp. that of a pederast or a sodomite.

Gutter . . . 1. The female genital receiver, conceived, inelegantly, as a draining channel for the phallic ejaculant. 2. The inner, crotch end of the thigh.

GYMNOMASTIA . . . With reference to females, the practice of going around bare breasted, as in some primitive countries.

GYMNOPHALLATION . . . Sexual intercourse with a naked (condomless) male organ.

GYMNOPHALLIC . . . Involving or done with the naked phallus, as coitus.

GYMNOPHALLUS . . . The naked penis, i.e., the phallus erectus sine condom. Ex *gymnos* (bare) & *phallos* (penis).

GYMNOTHESAURIST . . . A male who collects pictures depicting females in various states of undress. Ex *gymnos* (naked) & *thesauros* (treasure).

GYNACME . . . The sexual orgasm in the female. From *gyne* (woman) & *akme* (top).

GYNANDER . . . A man-like or masculine woman.

GYNANDER . . . Male hermaphrodite.

GYNANDRIA . . . Hermaphroditism in the male.

GYNANDRISM . . . 1. Pseudohermaphroditism in the male. 2. A form of pseudohermaphroditism in the female marked by the presence of ovaries, a hypertrophied clitoris, and a scrotum-like pouch formed by the fusion of the labia majora. 3. Hermaphroditism.

GYNANDROID . . . A female having an enlarged clitoris and a scrotum-like pouch formed by the fusion of the labia majora.

GYNANDROMORPHISM . . . The condition of having both male and female secondary sex characteristics and qualities.

GYNANDROMORPHOUS . . . Having the characteristics and qualities of both the male and the female. Ex *gyne* (woman), *aner* (man), & *morphos* (form).

GYNANDRUS . . . Male pseudohermaphrodite.

GYNATRESIA . . . Blockage of a part of the female genital passage, esp. of the vagina. Ex *gyne* (woman), *a* (not), & *tresis* (perforation).

GYNECENTRIC . . . Holding women as the center of one's interest.

GYNECOGEN . . . A substance, as a hormone, which stimulates the development of the secondary sex characteristics in a female. Ex *gyne* (woman) & *gennao* (produce).

GYNECOID . . . Resembling a woman; like a woman. Ex *gyne* (woman) & *eidos* (form, figure).

GYNECOMANIA . . . Excessive sexual desire in the male; uncontrollable urge to possess a woman or women.

GYNECOSMICS . . . The secondary sex characteristics of females, as the breasts. Ex *gyne* (woman) & *kosmeo* (decorate).

GYNELIMIA . . . A hunger for the company of females, as after a protracted deprivation. From *gyne* (woman) & *limos* (hunger).

GYNELIMOUS . . . Hungry for females, their decorations, and their pudendal offerings. Ex *gyne* (woman) & *limos* (hunger).

GYNELOPH . . . The pubic hair of the female. Ex *gyne* (woman) & *lophos* (tuft).

GYNELOPHILOUS . . . Of the male, especially erotic about the pubic hair of the female. Ex *gyne* (woman), *lophos* (tuft), & *philein* (to love).

GYNELOPHISM . . . A criminal act of sexual perversion in which the pubic tuft of the female is "scalped" or excised with the underlying tissues, as a trophy.

GYNEMIMISM . . . The adoption of feminine manners by a male. From *gyne* (woman) & *mimesis* (an imitating).

GYNEPHOBIA . . . Aversion for or fear of women.

GYNEPHONIA . . . Effeminate voice in a boy or in a man. From *gyne* (woman) & *phone* (voice).

GYNEPHRONATE . . . Think about women, erotically. Ex *gyne* (woman) & *phroneo* (think).

GYNEPHRONESIS . . . Preoccupation with thoughts of women and sexual pleasures involving females. From *gyne* (woman) & *phroneo* (ruminate).

GYNEPYGIA . . . Effeminate hips in a man. Ex *gyne* (woman) & *pyge* (buttocks).

GYNESADISM . . . The condition in which sexual pleasure is derived from the infliction of cruelty upon females. Ex *gyne* (woman) and *sadism*.

GYNESYNCRASY . . . Effeminate manners in a male.

GYNETRESIA . . . The intromission of the phallus in the vagina, conceived as the consummation of the marital contract. Ex *gyne* & *tresis* (perforation).

GYNETRICHOSIS . . . Excessive growth of hair on the body of a woman. Ex *gyne* (woman) & *thrix* (hair).

GYNEZOON . . . An animal used by a man in the practice of zooerastia.

GYNHEDONIA . . . Pleasure derived from the contemplation of female nudity or female sex organs. From *gyne* (woman) & *hedone* (delight).

GYNOPHELIMITY . . . In the female, the ability to give sexual satisfaction.

H

Hair brush . . . An erected phallus forming a bulge at the side of the fly, in allusion to the answer given by an aroused beau to his provocative but naive girl, when asked to explain what he had in his pocket.

Hair butcher . . . A pervert who practices gynelophism, i.e., one who excises the pubic hair of a female, including the underlying tissues, as a sexual trophy.

Hair, excessive growth of, on body of a woman . . . GYNETRICHOSIS.

Hair, excessive growth of . . . See also under name of part, as *Legs*.

Hair of female, especially erotic about . . . TRICHOPHILOUS.

Hair on the chest . . . Virility; sexual potency.

Hair pounder . . . A male addicted to the pleasures derivable from the female gentle trap.

Hair raid . . . 1. The seduction of an innocent. 2. A whoring spree.

Hair-raiser . . . A tantalizing girl, or a part thereof, which causes horripilation in the pubic region of the male.

Hairatorium . . . 1. A place where women congregate. 2. A bordello.

Haired up . . . Sexually aroused; of the male, having a phallic erection.

Hairs growing around a nipple in the female . . . THELECOMAE.

Hairy . . . Of a female, sexually desirous.

Hairy bit . . . An attractive girl having an accessible pudendal slit.

Hairy dick . . . 1. A desirous man. 2. The phallus erectus.

Hairy oracle . . . The gentle trap of the female perineum.

Hairy ring . . . The partly by hair surrounded female sexual favor dispenser.

Hairyfordshire . . . The partly hair-surrounded lower mouth of the female, in allusion to Herefordshire, where an important breed of cattle originated.

Half-baked . . . Of a phallus, not standing up to the occasion with sufficient determination.

Half portions . . . Female breasts which are not up to snuff, volumewise.

Hallway necking between young lovers after a date . . . **Bell polishing.**

Halve the crack . . . To part the labia majora (and minora) with the phallic partitioner.

Hammer the sword into a plowshare . . . Of a harlot, to marry and thus convert the pudendum into a respectable dispenser of phallic appeasement.

Hammocks . . . The female breasts, glutton's size.

Handfuls . . . Female anatomical decorations regarded as targets for male lickerish hands.

Hand-minded . . . Of an amorous male, inclined to manual palpation.

Handshaker . . . A prostitute who relieves men of their lower burdens manually.

Hang in the bellropes . . . Of a male who has eaten of his future wife's pudendal tree, before the official aye, to delay meeting the parson.

Hang it on the arse . . . Intromit the phallus rectally.

Hang it on with . . . To engage in minor amative skirmishes with a woman in preparing her for the role of a paramour.

Hang it out . . . To display intimate parts, esp., of a female, to show titty.

Hang out the flag of distress . . . To practice the vocation of harlotry.

Hang up one's fiddle . . . Of a harlot, to give up the mercenary pudendal traffic in favor of marriage or retirement.

Hang up the ladle . . . Of a man about town with a busy boneless appendage, to marry.

HAPHEPHOBIA . . . Aversion for or fear of being touched. Ex *haphe* (touch) & *phobos.*

HAPTOSIS . . . An unlawful physical contact with the body of another, as forcible sarmassation.

HARAMAITISM . . . Marriage between children, as practiced among the Hindus.

Hardback . . . The temporarily hardened spermapositor of the human male, esp. one such borne by a dancing male and felt by the female partner.

Hard-on . . . 1. The male libido. 2. A temporarily petrified phallus.

Hard-soldered . . . Married; an allusion to the permanent union.

Harlot as a female with loose pudendal strings . . . **Banbury.**

Harlot as a jovial pudendal tool . . . **Merry bit.**

Harlot as the bearer of pudendal pie . . . **Rabbit pie.**

Harlot conceived as a demulcent application to the male pudendum . . . **Belly plaster.**

Harlot conceived as a female with a bawdy business end . . . **Bawdy basket.**

Harlot conceived as an inferior phallating target . . . **Palliasse.**

Harlot; in allusion to a warmer . . . **Chauvering donna.**

Harlot; in allusion to her splitting the labia for incoming phalli . . . **Split pilot.**

Harlot, well-dressed, considered "good stuff" . . . **Bona roba.**

Harlot who derives at least some pleasure from her work . . . **Merry-legs.**

Harlot who is being "sat upon" by a number of patrons seriatim, so that her pudendum does not get the chance to cool off between bouts . . . **Barber's chair.**

Harlot who is infected venereally . . . **Frigate on fire.**

Harlot who takes the male petard either by way of the well-trodden vagina, or, to please her phallic adventurers and to feather her nest, through the backdoor, the rectum; designating a . . . **Double-barrelled.**

Harlot who takes the male shillelah either through the conventional, but well attrited, vaginal route, or, for the more discriminating, who seek a firmer phallic embrace, through the exhaust pipe, the rectum . . . **Fore-and-after.**

Harlot who takes the phallus either in the vagina or in the rectum . . . **R.R.3.**

Harlot who takes the phallus in the rectum . . . **R.R.2.**

Harlot who takes the phallus in the vagina, in the time-honored manner . . . **R.R.1.**

Harlot . . . See also under *Prostitute* and *Whore.*

Harlotry as a business . . . **Leg business.**

Harlotry, engage in practice of . . . **Hang out the flag of distress.**

Harlots, keep company with; of the male . . . **Bitch.**

Harlots, one consorting with, esp. one such who is also a soldier . . . **Dolly-mopper.**

Harry Common . . . A patron of Mrs. Warren's profession; a harlotophile.

Hatch . . . The female pudendal gadget, esp. the space between the labia.

Have a banana . . . To have a swing at the female pudendum.

Have a bellyful . . . To nurture an incipient tax exemption, in the uterus.

Have a bellyful . . . Of a female in coitus, to have a vaginaful of bouncing phallus.

Have a bit of fun . . . Engage in sexual caressing and, usually, pudendal coalition.

Have a bit of giblet pie . . . Have a piece of female pudendum.

Have a bit of gut-stick . . . Of a female, to receive vaginally the male genital scout.

Have a blow-through . . . Of a male with seminal pressure, to clean the presumably clogged genital passages by a phallic sneeze in the female introitus.

Have a bone in the throat . . . To have an inopportune and embarrassing erection which is impossible to subdue or secrete, as while dancing.

Have a brush with . . . Of a male, to lie in pudendal comfort with (a woman).

Have a case of pursitus . . . To have an itch of the scrotum, esp. while in the presence of others.

Have a cold . . . Of a woman, to have the monthly claret ooze.

Have a flutter . . . Have a fling at coitus, more for the sport of it than for the relief of sexual tension.

Have a good luck round! . . . A wish addressed to a male who is pudendum-bound, esp. to a soldier or sailor headed home for lots of it, after a long period of unwelcome abstinence.

Have a leg twisted . . . Of a girl, to be enticed into pudendal surrender.

Have a male sexually ardent and hence not likely to get off the hook . . . **Have by the short hairs.**

Have a nice go at the female pudendum, with several gratifying emissions . . . **Have good innings.**

Have a poker itch . . . Have an itch of the phallus, esp. while one is in the presence of others.

Have a private party . . . Have an itch of the scrotum while one is in the company of others.

Have a private worry . . . To itch where one cannot scratch while in the presence of others, esp. such an itch affecting the vulva or the phallus, when one is not alone.

Have a pudendal soiree with an agreeable female . . . **Break a lance with.**

Have a ride . . . Of a male, to pound the female pudendum with the male pound of flesh; of the female, to take the pounding.

Have a venereal infection . . . **Be in for the plate.**

Have a wife, as opposed to buying the milk of pudendal kindness from a whore . . . **Keep a cow.**

Have an amorous urge . . . **Feel hairy.**

Have an erection . . . **Put on a tin hat.**

Have an erection . . . See also under *Erection.*

Have an oar in another's boat . . . To have one's phallus in another's wife.

Have anties in the panties . . . Of the female, to have an itch in a part that one cannot scratch in the presence of others, esp. in the region of the lipped underside.

Have ants in the pants . . . 1. Of the male, to feel the pangs of repeated genital uprisings. 2. Of a female, to yearn for the phallic scratcher, to allay that certain itch.

Have apartments to let . . . Of a female, to be in the whoring business.

Have at least two annas of dark blood . . . Of a predominantly white person, to have at least a touch of the tarred phallus, in the blood.

Have been around, to . . . To have had considerable intimate experience with the girls.

Have been hipped, to . . . Of a female, to have been had.

Have been there, to . . . To have had sexual concourse.

Have big ears . . . Have big testicles.

Have blood in the eye . . . To have a hot genital poker.

Have by the heels . . . To have a man by the balls, i.e., hopelessly enamored.

Have by the short hairs . . . Of the female, to have the male erotically ardent and hence on the hook, matrimonially or otherwise.

Have Cape Horn fever . . . Of a husband, to be tormented by the suspicion or knowledge of the wife's unfaithfulness.

Have cupid's itch . . . 1. To be venereally infected. 2. Of a female, to have a prurient vulva.

Have eyes for . . . To be desirous for the female pudendum, or, more often, for a particular one.

Have good innings . . . Have several satisfying seminal spurts during a pudendal session, not necessarily a nocturnal.

Have high-heeled shoes on . . . Of a female, to be receptive to persuasion, regarding surrender.

Have Jack out of doors . . . Live the life of a nudist; said of the male, obviously.

Have legs around the neck . . . 1. To partake orally of the vulvar fruit. 2. Of the female, to have a mouthful of phallus.

Have no beans in the pod . . . 1. To be fresh out of phallic ejaculant, because of heavy vaginal deposits. 2. To be sexually impotent.

Have one wrinkle more in one's arse . . . To add another item of information to one's store of knowledge, in allusion to wrinkled buttocks resulting from sitting on one's arse and studying.

Have one's bowsprit in parentheses . . . To have one's male genital probe in the female sheath and clasped by the parentheses-like labia.

Have one's face on the fiddle . . . To eat pudendal pie, i.e., to cunnilinguate.

Have sexual concourse with one not one's wife, when one has one . . . **Box out; Eat out.**

Have snap in the garter . . . To have a potent phallus.

Have sporadic bouts with receptive women, to rid oneself of excessive seminal pressure . . . **Blow off the loose corns.**

Have the curse of Venus . . . To have a venereal disease.

Have the phallus in the vagina and amorously clasped by the labia . . . **Have one's bowsprit in parentheses.**

Have two coital bouts in a single love session . . . **Double.**

Having a too roomy vagina, one having the capacity of two . . . **Double-cunted.**

Having beautiful breasts . . . CALLIMASTIAN.

Having beautiful breasts and hips or buttocks . . . CALLIMAMMAPYGIAN.

Having large breasts, one of which would suffice for two . . . **Double-diddied.**

Having . . . See also under the name of the part or condition involved.

Hawk one's brawn . . . Of an attractive male, to sell the manly act to well-heeled but not-so-well-formulated females, who have to pay for it. Also, to submit to an active homosexual, for pay.

Hawsehole . . . A naughtical concept of the female inlet for the male genital cable.

Hawsehole creep . . . A phallic invasion of the female hawsehole.

Hay bag . . . A female regarded as something to lie upon, but not of the best variety.

Hay lass . . . A farmer's daughter or her equivalent who, without a whale of a resistance, may be laid in the hay.

Haymaker . . . A male who partakes of another man's wife's pudendal orchard while the authorized gardener is away.

Haymaking . . . The gaining of illicit pudendal knowledge of a married woman, while her licensed phallator isn't around.

Haymarket ware . . . A harlot of the plebeian class.

Head-marked . . . Made a cuckold of, by the wife's pudendal largess to another man.

Hear the call . . . Of a male, to get the message from a rising phallus.

Heat wave . . . In the female, a period of unusual eagerness for the spurt that refreshes.

Heater . . . The female pudendal gun.

HEDRALINGUS . . . The erotic licking of the anus. From *hedra* (anus) & *lingere* (to lick).

Hell . . . The female apparatus conceived as a short cut to h.

Hell for leather . . . Zealously devoted to the female pudendum.

Hell! said the duchess when she caught her tits in the mangle . . . Ouch!

Hell-box . . . The labial and interlabial domain of the female perineum.

Hellfire dick . . . A pudendally aggressive male with an organon that satisfies; also, the organon.

Hell-hole . . . The genital pudding of the female, regarded as an introitus to h.

Hell-matter . . . The female genitalia conceived as demoralizers.

Helping foot . . . The third, erectile, foot of the male.

HEMEROTISM . . . Daydreaming involving erotic subjects, as nudity, coitus, etc. From *hemera* (day) & *erotism.*

Hemorrhage, coital, in the virgin or not-so-long-ago virgin . . . **Christening nosebleed.**

HEREISM . . . Marital faithfulness. Ex *Hera,* the Greek goddess of women and marriage.

Herm . . . Short for hermaphrodite.

HERMAPHRODITE . . . A person whose gonads are composed of both testicular and ovarian tissues and whose external genitalia resemble in part the organs of both sexes.

Hermaphrodite, female . . . ANDROGYNE.

Hermaphrodite, male . . . GYNANDER.

Hermaphrodite, or at least a markedly effeminate male . . . **Jenny Willocks.**

HERMAPHRODITISM . . . A condition marked by the presence of both testicular and ovarian tissues in the same person, and by the presence of anomalous external genitalia which resemble in part the organs of both sexes. Ex *Hermes* & *Aphrodite.*

Hermaphroditism in the female . . . ANDROGYNIA.

Hermaphroditism in the male . . . GYNANDRIA.

HETEROCOITUS . . . Sexual intercourse between members of the opposite sexes, i.e., between heterosexuals.

HETERO-EROTISM . . . The condition in which the sexual desire of an individual is directed toward another person, as opposed to oneself.

HETEROSEXUAL . . . A person whose sexual desire is directed toward the opposite sex. Also, pert. to or directed toward the opposite sex. Ex *heteros* (other) & *sexual.*

Heterosexual and homosexual . . . AMPHISEXUAL.

HETEROSEXUALITY . . . The quality or characteristic of being attracted erotically to the opposite sex.

Hicky . . . Same as **Dohicky,** the male genital coupler.

High blonde pressure . . . Hyperlibidinosity in the male directed toward the pudenda of auricomous females.

High on the bottle . . . Of the vagina, marked by good embrace pressure upon the incoming phallus, because virgin or only slightly used.

High voltage . . . In the female, high erotomotive force, the pudendal equivalent of electronic electromotive force.

Higher than a cat's back . . . Of the male, most desirous of cooling the hot petard in the female bucket, in allusion to the bulging fly which simulates the arched back of a bristling cat.

Highjack . . . To force a boy to submit to pederasty.

Hill topper . . . A phallator, i.e., the male overlying the "hilltop."

Hilltop . . . The "Mount of Venus," the fleshy pad overlying the symphysis pubis, forming the vanguard of the vulva.

Hilltop literature . . . Erotica, esp. literature dealing with the female interfemoral sanctum.

Hind boot . . . The buttocks, esp. the inner halves, conceived, from the viewpoint of a sodomite, as the counterpart of the female "boot."

Hind legs . . . The testicles, conceived as the legs upon which the phallus erectus stands when *en amour.*

Hinder end . . . The buttocks; the rump.

Hinder entrance . . . 1. The anus as a pederast's or sodomite's haven or heaven. 2. The rump.

Hindustani jig . . . A phallation from behind into the exhaust gut.

Hiposterior . . . The combined bulge of the hips and the buttocks.

Hips and buttocks, wide in the . . . **Wide in the bows.**

Hips and rump, having a provocative complex of . . . **Arse from elbow down.**

Hips, woman having large and wide; in allusion to railway tracks . . . **Broad-gauge.**

HIRCUSOPHILOUS . . . Of the male, especially erotic about the axillary hair of the female. Ex *hircus* (axillary hair) & *philein* (to love).

Hitch to the wrong side of the post . . . To phallate per rectum.

Hobbe's voyage . . . A phallic journey into the female pudendum.

Hog-eye . . . The pudendum muliebre conceived as a phallic target or/and an insatiable demander.

Hold a woman by her pubic hair . . . **Goose.**

Hold by the ears the recipient of the phallus, in fellatio . . . **Bull by the souse.**

Hold down . . . Of a female, to keep her man's phallus flaccid or down, i.e., satisfied.

Hold out . . . Same as **Hold the market.**

Hold the market . . . Of a wife, to withhold the pudendal alleviator from her husband, in order to force his surrender to a demand.

Holding women as the center of one's interest . . . GYNECENTRIC.

Hole . . . The introitus vaginae, or the entire female pudendal complex, as a despised but indispensable (the former because the latter) millstone.

Hole . . .To up-and-down the male genital reciprocator where it is meant to go in up and come out down.

Hole . . . A woman, regarded as the bearer of the genital pore.

Hole . . . Sexual concourse metaphorized.

Hole . . . The anus, esp. as a sodomite's target.

Holy ground . . . 1. The netherland sanctum of a thou-shalt-not-phallate-her female, as one under age. 2. Any such sanctum, including the unholy.

Holy Joe . . . The phallus of a male dedicated by vows, or otherwise, to total abstinence.

Home for aged male impotents . . . **Fumblers' hall.**

Homie . . . A homosexual, generally a male.

HOMINSEMINATION . . . Artificial insemination with semen taken from the husband.

HOMOCOITUS . . . Sexual intercourse between members of the same sex.

HOMOEROTICISM . . . Erotic interest in a member of the same sex.

HOMOEROTISM . . . Erotic interest in a person of the same sex, esp. when sublimated.

HOMOPHAGIST . . . A female cunnilinguist. Ex *homos* (same) & *phagein* (to eat).

HOMOSEXUAL . . . 1. A person whose sexual desires are directed toward individuals of his or her own sex. 2. Pert. to or directed toward the same sex.

Homosexual and heterosexual . . . AMPHISEXUAL.

Homosexual, female . . . **Bulldiker; Lesbie; Sapphie.**

Homosexual female . . . LESBIAN; SAPPHIST; TRIBADE; URNINDE.

Homosexual female who rubs her genitalia against the genitalia of her female partner . . . TRIBADE.

Homosexual, male . . . **Angel; Faggot; Fruiter; Molly; Painted Willie; Queen.**

Homosexual, male . . . **Baby; Fairy; Homie; Nance; Pansy; Queer.**

Homosexual, male . . . **Birdie; Flit; Lavender boy; Nancy; Pix; Sweet homo.**

Homosexual, male . . . **Agfay; Fag; Four-letter man; Man's man; Nola; Pogue; Undercover man.**

Homosexual male . . . TAUTANER; URNING.

Homosexual, male, active; i.e., one who takes the part of the male in normal coitus . . . **Turk.**

Homosexual, male, in search for a patron . . . **Salesman.**

Homosexual, male or female, in search for a patron or partner . . . **Cruiser; Prowler.**

Homosexual person of either sex . . . INVERT; URANIST.

Homosexual relations, enter into more or less permanent, with a particular partner . . . **Marry.**

Homosexual, submit to an active, for pay; said of a male . . . **Hawk one's brawn.**

Homosexual world of the male variety . . . **Pansyland.**

Homosexualism, in the male or the female . . . **Nameless crime.**

HOMOSEXUALITY . . . The condition of being attracted sexually to another person of the same sex. Ex *homos* (same).

Homosexuality between females in which one female plays the role of a male, rubbing her genitalia against the other's . . . TRIBADISM.

Homosexuality between females, practice of . . . LESBIANISM; SAPPHISM; TRIBADISM.

Homosexuality between men, practice of . . . COMMASCULATION.

Homosexuality in either sex . . . URANISM.

Homosexuals, male, costume party attended by . . . **Drag party.**

Homosexuals, normal persons unsympathetic to, who attend their social functions . . . **Dirt.**

Honest injun . . . A male who begets a child illicitly and admits it.

Honeyslot . . . The space between the labia of the female pudendum.

Hooked up . . . Of a male, provided with the creature comforts afforded by the female secondary sex characteristics, via a devoted girl friend, or with the ultimate pudendal payoff, via a mistress.

Hop . . . Of a man, to mount a woman and make a pudendal touchdown with the phallus rigidus.

Horniness . . . Prurience in the genital organ of the male, associated with partial erection.

Horny bastard . . . A male whose petard is more often that way than not.

Horny hussy . . . A woman low in morals but high in vulvar voltage.

Horse . . . To know a woman vaginally; to phallate.

Horse breaker . . . A woman who masturbates a stallion.

Horse-buss . . . A kiss in the category of a thunderclapper.

Horsecollar . . . The vulva, in allusion to the labia majora which resemble it.

Horse-godmother . . . A hulking, masculine-looking woman.

Horse kiss . . . A vigorous kiss, esp. one terminating in a bite.

Horse, male, woman who masturbates a . . . **Horse breaker.**

Horsechoker . . . A mastodonian (in size) phallus, from the viewpoint (quite understandable) of a fellator or a fellatrice.

Horseleech . . . A female trading with her underpart, esp. an aggressive one.

Horseshoe . . . The sexual underbelly of the female; an allusion to the labia majora which, in abduction, resembles the shoe.

Hortus . . . The female sexual garden.

Hose . . . To flush the pudendal arcanum of a girl with the seminal stream of the phallus contentus.

Hot chocolate . . . A Negress with a desirous pudendum.

Hot dish . . . A female who is an excellent pudendal prancer.

Hot fly . . . 1. The fly of an aroused man's trousers, which, from the viewpoint of the man's quarry, is on the verge of being unzipped. 2. The fly of a desirous man's trousers bulging before the rampant cyclopean beast. 3. A prurient male whose pants fly is under pressure from behind.

Hot lay . . . A girl who serves a hot pudendal course.

Hot lay . . . An especially attractive female pudendal opportunity.

Hot meat . . . Female delectables which trigger the erector mechanism of functional males. Also, such charming tissue exposed to view.

Hot nuts . . . Sexual urgency in the male.

Hotbox . . . The coital inlet of the female, in allusion, possibly, to an overheated bearing of an axle and to the similarity of this to the warm vaginal embrace of the male genital shaft.

Hotline, the . . . The line of cleavage between the female bubbies.

House . . . Blandishments offered, usually by the female, as encouragement in love(making).

Howitzer . . . The phallus, king size.

Huddle . . . Of an amorous couple, to rub pudenda.

HUMEX . . . The normal lubricating secretion of the vulva or chasma (*cf.* UNGATION). Ex *humere* (to moisten).

Humiliation, sexual pleasure or gratification derived from inflicting; esp. upon one of the opposite sex . . . **SADISM.**

Humiliation, sexual pleasure or gratification derived from subjection to; esp. at the hands of one of the opposite sex . . . **MASOCHISM.**

Hump . . . A mass of phallus erectus forming a bulge on either side of the fly.

Hump . . . Of a man having a humped fly, due to phallus induratus, to smooth it by mollification of the rigidity in the female introit.

Hung fiddle . . . The male sexual pusher retired from action, because no longer able to put up.

Hunger for sexual intercourse . . . COITOLIMIA.

Hunger for women, as after a prolonged deprivation . . . GYNELIMIA.

Hunger . . . See also under *Starvation.*

Hunk . . . Sexual concourse conceived as a good course of pudendum muliebre.

Hunk of meat . . . The male pound of flesh, esp. if it weighs more than a pound.

Hurry-whore . . . A harlot who hurries her patrons, urging them to get it over with. Also, one hired for a hurried pudendal performance.

Husband, dominated by . . . MARITOCRATIC.

Husband of an unfaithful wife, be the . . . **Play second fiddle.**

Husband whose wife is an adulteress . . . CUCKOLD.

Husband whose wife is "known" to another male, in the Biblical sense . . . **Buck; Buck face.**

Hustle . . . To busy oneself with one's pudendum; to phallate; to be phallated.

HYMEN . . . A thin, sometimes thick, mucous membrane or fold which in the virgin partially or, sometimes, wholly occludes the external entrance to the vagina. Ex *hymen* (skin, membrane).

Hymen . . . **Maiden seal; Maid's ring; Lucky sentry; Doorkeeper; Tail fence; Drumhead; Cherry apron; Bleeder; Pussy gate; Tail-gate.**

Hymen, esp. of a virgin . . . **Crust.**

Hymen of a virgin female . . . PARTHYMEN.

Hymen of a virgin, tear the; phallically . . . **Scalp.**

Hymen of a woman who has borne children, condition of . . . PAROHYMENIA.

Hymen of a woman who has had sexual intercourse . . . FORHYMEN.

Hymen, partial suturing of; as to assure phallic nonintervention . . . HYMENORRHAPHY.

Hymen, plastic operation on; to create an appearance of virginity . . . PARTHENOPLASTY.

Hymen, rupture of virgin; in sexual intercourse . . . DEFLORATION; HYMENORRHEXIS.

Hymen, stretch the, phallically; esp. in a virgin . . . **Blaze the trail.**

Hymen, thick, condition of having . . . PACHYHYMENIA.

Hymen, thick, having a . . . PACHYHYMENOUS.

Hymen, thin, condition of having . . . LEPTOHYMENIA.

Hymen, thin, having a . . . LEPTOHYMENOUS.

Hymen torn in sexual intercourse, condition of having . . . PHALLOHYMENIA.

Hymen, virgin, condition of having . . . PARTHYMENIA.

Hymen with a small opening which does not allow admission of the phallus erectus . . . STENOPYLE.

Hymen with a small opening which does not allow admission of the phallus erectus, condition of having a . . . HYMENOSTENIA.

HYMENOCLASIS . . . Surgical defloration of a virgin.

HYMENOPENTHY . . . Mental depression caused, in some women, by loss of virginity. Ex *hymen* & *pentheo* (to mourn for).

HYMENORRHAPHY . . . The partial suturing of the hymen, as to assure phallic nonaccess.

HYMENORRHEXIS . . . The rupture of the hymen, as in defloration. From *rhexis* (a rupture).

HYMENOSTENIA . . . The condition marked by the presence of a hymen with a small opening which does not allow admission of the phallus erectus.

HYPERCOSMOSIS . . . The condition marked by excessive, but not necessarily unpleasant, development of the secondary sex characteristics in the female. Ex *hyper* (excessive), *kosmeo* (decorate), & *osis* (a condition).

HYPERORCHIA . . . Early sexual development in boys, due to excessive secretion of the testes.

HYPEROVARIA . . . Early sexual development in girls, due to excessive secretion of the ovaries.

HYPHEPHILIA . . . The derivation of sexual gratification from the act of touching certain surfaces, esp. of fabrics, like velvet. Ex *hyphe* (a web) & *philein* (to love).

HYPOCOSMOSIS . . . The condition marked by an underdevelopment of the secondary sex characteristics in the female. From *hypo* (less), *kosmeo* (decorate), & *osis* (a condition).

HYPOLIBIDA . . . A female whose sexual desire is subnormal in intensity.

HYPOLIBIDUS . . . A male whose sexual desire is subnormal in intensity.

HYPOMEDIA . . . The condition of having an underdeveloped penis. Ex *hypo* (less than) & *medos* (penis).

HYPOMULIEBROSIS . . . Inadequate development of the genitalia and secondary sex characteristics in the female. Ex *hypo* (less than) & *muliebria* (female genitalia).

HYPOPEGNYMIA . . . A partial erection of the penis, insufficient to be functional but enough to be bothersome. Ex *hypo* & *pegnymi* (to stiffen).

HYPOPOTENTIA . . . A decrease in the sexual potency of a male. Ex *hypo* (under) & *posse* (be able).

HYPORCHIA . . . Delayed sexual development in boys due to deficient function of the testes.

HYPOVARIA . . . Delayed sexual development in girls due to deficient function of the ovaries.

I

I have friends to stay . . . An announcement by a female, to all concerned, that her pudendum is under the monthly red flag.

Ice the decision . . . Of a female, to nix the apparent rugged intentions of her fly-humped beau.

ICONOLAGNY . . . Sexual excitation aroused by pictures and statues of nude figures. Ex *eikon* (image) & *lagneia* (lust).

IDIORRHENIC . . . Peculiar to or characteristic of the male sex. From *idios* (one's own, peculiar to) & *arrhen* (male).

IDIOSYNCRAT . . . A person dominated by abnormal cravings, esp. those of the libido.

IDIOTHELIC . . . Peculiar to or characteristic of the female sex. Ex *idios* (one's own, peculiar to) & *thelys* (female).

If my aunt had been an uncle, she'd have had a pair of balls under her arse . . . An illustration of the absurdity inherent in iffing.

Ikey . . . The phallus of an Israelite.

I'll cut your cable if you foul my hawse . . . A naughtical threat of a female about to be spitchcocked by a phallus she suspects of carrying animalcules of the *Neisseria gonorrhoeae* type.

Illigetimate child, give birth to an . . . **Break a leg.**

Illegitimate child . . . See also under *Bastard.*

Illegitimate; conceived without the sanction of a parson or his equivalent, i.e., extramaritally . . . **Born on the wrong side of the blanket.**

Immature girl as a bride, in allusion to the Bluegrass State where young brideflesh is reputedly common . . . **Kentucky quail.**

Immature . . . See also under *Girl, Female, Young,* etc.

Impatiently waiting . . . Of the membrum virile, standing at attention.

Importance . . . A female, whether wife or mistress, as a comforter of the phallus desirous.

IMPOTENCE . . . The inability of the male to perform the sexual act, usually because of faulty erection.

Impotence, sexual, in the male . . . INVIRILITY.

Impotence, sexual, in the male, caused by lack of coital confidence . . . ATOLMIA.

Impotent . . . **Not a shot in the locker.**

Impotent husband and frigid wife . . . **Couple of flats.**

Impotent husband who can't satisfy his wife and won't, naturally, allow others who can . . . **Road hog.**

Impotent male and frigid woman, marriage of . . . **Yorkshire compromise.**

Impotent male, difficulty of a partially, in raising a coitally effective phallus durus . . . **Needle trouble.**

Impotent male, esp. one impotentiated by testicular excision or atrophy . . . **Bobtail.**

Impotent males, figurative hades for . . . **Fumblers' hall.**

Impotent phallus, present an, to a sizzling female pudendum . . . **Roast snow in a furnace.**

Impotent, sexually, under normal conditions or in the usual environment, as in one's own home (but often potent elsewhere, as in a motel cabin) . . . NOMAVALENT.

Impotent, sexually, with one's own wife, but potent with other, more exciting, females . . . UXORAVALENT.

Impregnate a female . . . **Sew up.**

Impregnate a female, esp. when phallation — not impregnation — is the aim . . . **Do the trick.**

Impregnate a female who is not the phallator's wife . . . **Get into a mess.**

Impregnate; seed with seminal fluid . . . INSEMINATE; **Kid.**

Impregnating ability of phallus . . . **Knock-upability.**

Impregnation, not capable of causing . . . IMPROCREANT; STERILE.

Impregnation of a woman who is already pregnant . . . SUPERFETATION.

Impregnation of the female egg by the male cell . . . CONCEPTION; FECUNDATION; FERTILIZATION.

Impregnation of the female egg by two or more male cells . . . POLYSPERMY.

Imprimatur . . . A properly executed marriage license, regarded as a permit for licit pudendal calisthentics.

Improve the breed . . . To phallate for the hell of it, without any regard for the breed, in facetious allusion to the time-honored justification of horse racing as a means for improving the equine breed.

In a minor key . . . With reference to a bout of phallation, (done) with a half-heartedly erected poker.

In aces with . . . In good pudendal relations with a desirable wench.

In-and-out jig . . . A bout of phallation, *en règle.*

In armor . . . 1. Of a phallus, in a condom. 2. Of same, in erection—with or without a condom.

In bad fig . . . Of a seducer, with a pregnant ex-virgin on his hands.

In bed with a moll . . . **Molled.**

In black ink . . . Of a whoremonger, in company with swarthy dispensers of phallic appeasement.

In cold storage . . . Of a man and his demanding organ, temporarily on a starvation diet, because wifie is indisposed, with child, etc.

In cuerpo . . . Of the phallus, in the flesh, sans condom; in allusion to *cuerpo,* the body, i.e., naked.

In dishybilly . . . Of a girlie, in an intimately interesting state of dishabille.

In flagrante delicto, caught in . . . Caught in the act of vaginal obturation, by the phallus erectus, in allusion to the more austere meaning of the phrase, "in the very act of committing the offense."

In for a trimming . . . Of a female, in for a thorough pudendal pillage.

In full feather . . . Of the phallus, bristling with erectile vigor.

In gear . . . Of the membrum virile, erectum.

In good trim . . . Of the female figure, well appointed.

In gravy . . . Of a male, well supplied with desirable and desirous female pudenda.

In heat . . . . Of a male, slavishly enamored of a female pudendum, because goaded by testicular messages.

In high . . . Of the phallus desirous, in the best possible state of induration.

In love with, i.e., lusty for, a particular woman; to be . . . **Carry a bat for.**

In mothballs . . . Of the phallus, retired pudendally, because no longer able to drain the semino-vesicular cream, for lack of stand-up-to-itness.

In mourning . . . Of the phallus, disconsolately droopy.

In quarantine . . . Of the phallus or the vulva, out of circulation, because venereally infected.

In red ink . . . Of a male, esp. of a young husband, phallating a recently deflowered virgin, up to the male gonads in hymeneal gore.

In reverse English . . . Of a man and maid in vulvo-phallic reciprocation, with the female providing the movement, from the top-sawyer position.

In sexual concourse, with the female in the top sawyer position . . . **Uphills.**

In shape . . . Of a woman readying for the act, on her back, with knees bent and thighs bifurcated.

In short pants . . . Of a girl, in provoking panties, and very little more.

In sight . . . Of a laboriously phallating mate, near, he hopes, the stage of phallic disemboguement.

In Sunday best . . . Of an obliging female, wearing Eve's pre-pomivorous vestimenta, i.e., nothing.

In the bushes . . . With regard to an ejaculation, (exploded) in the pubic hair of the female.

In the ditch . . . 1. Of a fumbling phallus having difficulty finding its way, (finally) in the grooved adit of the female indispensable. 2. With reference to the type of cavern into which the phallus is intromitted, in the normal one, in the vagina.

In the green goods business . . . Of a procurer or bordello manager, in the business of breaking in young and "green" harlots.

In there pitching . . . Of a partly impotentiated male, in there plunging, and trying his best.

In total eclipse . . . Of a male and his once puissant organum virile, completely and irrevocably out of the man-and-maid picture, due to loss of penile rise-ability.

Inability of a female to accept the male in coitus . . . ADECTIA.

Inability of a female to have sexual intercourse because of partial occlusion of the entrance to the vagina by hymeneal tissue . . . ANESODIA.

Inability of the male to perform the sexual act, usually because of faulty erection . . . IMPOTENCE.

Inability to satisfy sexually; said of the female . . . AGYNOPHELIMITY.

Inability to satisfy sexually; said of the male . . . ANOPHELIMITY.

Inadequate development of the genitalia and secondary sex characteristics in the female . . . HYPOMULIEBROSIS.

Inadequate development of . . . See also under name of condition or part.

Incandescent lamps . . . A pair of prize sweater fillers.

Incapable of bearing young . . . INTICTANT.

Incapable of . . . See also under name of function or action involved.

INCEST . . . Sexual intercourse between persons who are too closely related for legal marriage.

Inclined to amorous palpation; said of a concupiscent male . . . **Hand-minded.**

Incomplete or otherwise unsatisfactory orgasm in the male . . . SPHALORGASMY.

Increase in sexual desire . . . EROTAUXESIS.

Increase in the capacity of the vagina resulting from phallation, childbirth, etc. . . . COLPECTASIA.

INCUBOUS . . . Lying upon; said of the one who, in coitus, is on top of the other. From *incubare* (to lie upon).

INCUBUS . . . In sexual intercourse, the one who is on top.

INCUBUS . . . A spirit, conceived as male, once believed to lie upon women in their sleep, and to have sexual intercourse with the more desirable ones—by another version, with the more "needy" ones.

Indescribable, the . . . From the viewpoint of a male, the warm and moist cleft of the female underside; from the female's point of view, the cylindrical joy-dispenser of the male.

Indescribables . . . Intimate undergarments of the young female; the mazonian supporters and the brief pudendal pantalets.

India . . . The female pudendal desirables.

Indispensable, the . . . The lipped pudendal entree of the female.

Indorse . . . Practice sodomy or pederasty; phallate per rectum.

Indorser . . . A sodomite or a pederast.

Induce orgasm by labial or lingual stimulation of the phallus . . . **Kiss off.**

Induction of the sexual orgasm . . . ACMEGENESIS.

Indulge in palpation of the female embellishments but abstain from the ultimate privilege . . . **Keep off the grass.**

Indulge in pudendal revelries . . . **Christmas.**

Indulgence of one's sexual inclinations . . . VENERY.

Ineffable . . . The female genitalia, conceived as the indescribable garden of delight.

Ineffables . . . The finest of the best of the young mammae.

Ineffectual effort at coitus in which orgasm is not reached . . . XERONISUS.

Inexpressibles . . . Same as **Indescribables,** panties, mazonian supporters, etc.

Infants, attempted sexual intercourse with, usually with those of the opposite sex . . . NEPIPHTHEROSIS.

Infants, erotic interest in; of the opposite sex . . . NEPIOLAGNIA.

Infants, molestation of . . . NEPIOCHLESIS.

Infect the phallus by contact with a tainted female receptacle . . . **Boil one's lobster.**

Infected venereally; said of the female . . . **Shot between wind and water.**

Infected venereally; said of the male, in allusion to Judy, a cyprian . . . **Judy-bitten.**

Infected venereally . . . See also under *Venereal.*

Inferior desecration . . . The lower mouth of the female.

Infidel . . . The voracious pagan of the male crotch.

Inflated pigskin . . . A tumefied membrum virile.

Information, add another item of, by sedentary lucubration . . . **Have one wrinkle more in one's arse.**

Ingle . . . A catamite, i.e., the boy receiving the phallus in the act of pederasty.

Ingle-nook . . . The female genital underbelly.

Ingress of phallus into vaginal corridor . . . **Blow.**

INGRESSABILITY . . . Ability of the phallus to penetrate the introitus vaginae; used to evaluate hymeneal meability, penial rigidity, etc.

Inhibition of the sexual urge . . . LAGNOCOLYSIS.

Inlaid . . . Phallated and, usually, impregnated.

Inland metropolis . . . The niche at the bifurcation of the female thighs.

Inning . . . A bout of phallovaginal concourse.

Innominables . . . From the viewpoint of the female, the testicles.

INSEMINATION . . . The implantation of semen into the vagina.

Insemination . . . See also under *Semen, implantation of.*

Insert finger or fingers in rectal and vaginal openings of female perineum . . . **Fingerdoodle.**

Insert the phallus between the mammae . . . MAZOPHALLATE.

Insert the phallus in the vagina and thus ensconce it in the erotic embrace of the labia . . . **Enclose in parentheses.**

Insert the phallus into the mouth of another . . . IRRUMATE.

Insert the phallus into the rectum of a child . . . PEDERIZE.

Insert the phallus into the rectum of an adult . . . SODOMIZE.

Insert the phallus . . . See also under *Introduce the phallus,* and under IRRUMATE, PEDERIZE, SODOMIZE, etc.

Insertion of male finger into vagina, as a caressing intimacy . . . **A dose of finger.**

Insertion of male finger into vagina, to eroticize the female . . . **Finger dosing.**

Insertion of male index finger in female's rectum and of the thumb in her vagina; a form of sexual fingerdoodling . . . **Finger and thumb work.**

Inside job . . . A piece of work by the male interior decorator, where it does its best.

Inspection of soldiers for signs of venereal disease . . . **Short-arm inspection.**

Inspection of soldiers or inmates for signs of venereal disease, in allusion to the swinging phalli . . . **Dangle parade.**

INSPECTIONISM . . . The derivation of sexual gratification from watching others in the nude or in the act of sexual intercourse. Same as VOYEURISM.

Insurrection . . . An uprising in the male breeches.

Intellectual bulge . . . A prominent fanny, conceived as due to sedentary lucubration.

Intense sexual desire . . . TENTIGO.

Intense sexual desire, esp. in the male . . . LASCIVIA.

Intense sexual desire in the female . . . ANDROMANIA; CLITOROMANIA; NYMPHOMANIA.

Intense sexual desire in the male . . . GYNECOMANIA; SATYRIASIS.

Intention . . . The gleam in the eye of a male whose digital manipulation of the female peculiarities resulted in the ascendancy of his genital scepter.

Interest starter . . . An artfully exposed knee (and its circumjacencies) or a similarly viewable portion of the line of cleavage, offered by the female as an apéritif.

Interesting condition . . . The abdominosity of a pregnant woman; the pregnancy.

Interfemoral adit . . . The genital entrance between the thighs of the female.

Interior decorator . . . 1. A phallator, conceived as decorating the vaginal interior. 2. The male wand regarded as doing same.

Interior of front part of a girl's bodice, where the titties dwell . . . **Bubby hutch.**

Interlabial sanctum . . . What's behind the labia majora.

Interlabial slit of the vulva . . . ENTOMA; **Cleft.**

INTERMAZIUM . . . The space between the female breasts. Ex *inter* (between) & *mazos* (breast).

Interpolate . . . To insert the phallus between the non-mathematical values of a female, as the nether labia or the mazonians.

INTERSEX . . . A person in whom the characteristics of both sexes are manifested to a certain degree.

Interval of rest and junior erotic engagements between bouts of pudendal pounding . . . **Entracte.**

INTICTANT . . . Incapable of bearing young. From *tikto* (bear young).

Intimate scenes, excessive desire to look upon . . . PARASCOPISM.

Intimate . . . See also under *Sexual, Female,* etc.

Introduce the male genital "gardener" into the female pudendal fruitery . . . **Get Jack in the orchard.**

Introduce the phallus into "Molly's place" . . . **Plant.**

Introduce the phallus into the female slit . . . **Get a leg in.**

Introduce the phallus into the female tabernacle, in allusion to the mucus bath . . . **Grease one's duke.**

Introduce the phallus into the rectum of a child . . . PEDERIZE.

Introduce the phallus into the rectum of an adult . . . SODOMIZE; **Hang it on the arse.**

Introduce the phallus into the vagina . . . **Dip one's bill.**

Introduce the phallus into the vagina, in allusion to its scabbard-like action . . . **Sheathe the saber.**

Introduce the phallus . . . See also under *Insert,* and under IRRUMATE, PEDERIZE, SODOMIZE, etc.

Introduction of the phallus into the mouth of another, for the purpose of having it gratified by oral stimulation . . . FELLATORISM; IRRUMATION.

Introduction of the phallus . . . See also under *Phallate.*

Introitus to vagina . . . COLPYLE; **Keyhole.**

INVIRILITY . . . Sexual impotence in the male, due to faulty erective power.

IPSATION . . . Masturbation, conceived as a doing to oneself. Ex *ipse* (himself).

IPSEROTIC . . . Centering the sex interest on one's own body. From *ipse* (himself).

IPSISM . . . Masturbation, esp. chronic and excessive, conceived as a dominating habit. Ex *ipse* (himself).

Irish . . . Sexual temperament or fury.

Irish arms . . . Hefty female legs, in allusion to the proverbial heft of these parts in Hibernian females—of a past, more beefy century—who, the story tells, obtained a dispensation from Pope Benedictus XIV, allowing them to displace the thick ends of their thighs downward.

Irish assurance . . . Unfounded assurance of an impotent male that he can do it with the right kind of girl.

Irish clubhouse . . . A refined bordello.

Irish confetti . . . Seminal fluid spilled extravaginally.

Irish dip . . . 1. A cure for bashfulness with the girls. 2. A dip of the male shillelagh into the putting hole of an Irish—or other—wench.

Irish dividend . . . A harlot's largess in the act of coitus, esp. a scissors hold upon the phallator.

Irish draperies . . . The expansive, pendulous breasts of an adipose Irish matron, who even in her youth had a whale of a titty.

Irish evidence . . . In a legal suit of filiation, the usually persuasive imputation of the abdominous female, "He done it!".

Irish fortune . . . A woman's pudendal satisfier, and the bare behind.

Irish horse . . . A non-erectible membrum virile, in allusion to corned beef, so called.

Irish legs . . . Same as **Irish arms,** female legs of more than average beefiness.

Irish marathon . . . Six or more coital bouts in a single night.

Irish pasture . . . The pudendal grove revealed by a bifurcation of the female thighs.

Irish promotion . . . The denial of pudendum to a husband and his resort to manual softening of the adamantine member.

Irish rise . . . A collapse of the phallic inflation.

Irish root . . . The genital tuber of a functional male.

Irish toothache . . . 1. A persistent and, logically, disturbing erection. 2. Priapism.

Irish toothache . . . 1. An uprising of the male coupler. 2. The state of cyesis resulting from such an uprising, when subdued in the conventional manner.

Irish toothpick . . . The phallus erectus of a sodomite.

Irish wedding . . . A wedding which is intended to right a pudendal wrong, to a female.

Irish wedding . . . A peaceful manual settlement of the male uprising.

Irish whist . . . The pudendal game, in allusion to the card game in which the jack takes the ace.

Iron . . . A male prostitute; a vendor of the phallus.

Ironclad . . . The stiffly erected phallus.

Irreverend, the . . . The phallus as an organ undeserving of respect.

Irrumate; insert phallus into mouth of another . . . **Bully in the muzzle; Tickle the tonsils.**

IRRUMATION . . . The act of introducing the phallus into the mouth of another for the purpose of having it gratified by oral stimulation. Ex *irruo* (to rush into).

Irrumation, act of . . . **Muzzle loading.**

Irrumation . . . See also under *Fellatio.*

ISONOGAMIA . . . A mating or marriage involving spouses of nearly the same age, as opposed to a marriage in which one spouse is much younger than the other. Ex *isos* (equal), *aion* (age), & *gamos* (marriage).

Itch . . . To want the sexual gratification.

Itch affecting the female cleft, esp. when the proprietress cannot indulge in the pleasure of scratching, because of the presence of others . . . **Nurse a private worry; Wag a mute tongue; Have anties in the panties.**

Itch affecting the ninnies, esp. when the bearer cannot relieve it by scratching, because of the presence of others . . . **Titch.**

Itch-buttocks . . . The figuratively itching buttocks (behold their squirming!) of a female receiving phallic thrusts.

Itch in the belly . . . The sexual craving.

Itch of the phallus, have an . . . **Have a poker itch.**

Itch of the scrotum, have an; esp. when one is in the presence of others . . . **Have a private party; Wag a mute tongue; Have a case of pursitus.**

Itcher . . . The female cleft, conceived as the part which inspires that certain hankering.

Itching Jenny . . . The bilabial complex of the female netherland, conceived as prurient.

Itchland . . . The region of the body where either the male or the female feels the brunt of erotic pruritus; the genitalia.

ITHYALGIA . . . Apainful erection of the phallus. Ex *ithys* (straight) & *algos* (pain).

ITHYFACIENT . . . Causing erection of the penis. From *ithys* (straight) & *facere* (to make).

ITHYGENIC . . . Causing the erection of the phallus; said of a stimulus, etc. From *ithys* (straight) & *genic* (producing).

ITHYPHALLALGIA . . . A painful erection of the phallus. Ex *ithys* (straight), *phallos* (penis), & *algos* (pain).

ITHYPHALLIC . . . Pert. to or involving the erected phallus. Also, obscene.

ITHYPHALLOS . . . A figure of the membrum virile erectum carried in the Bacchic festivals. Also, such member live, in the flesh. Ex *ithys* (straight) & *phallos* (penis).

ITHYPHALLUS . . . The erotically rigid genital organ of the male.

Ivory rinse . . . The seminal spurt in the mouth of a fellator or a fellatrice, in allusion to *ivories,* the teeth.

Ivy bush . . . 1. The unlearned vulva of a learned female, i.e., the pudendal mouth of a bluestocking. 2. A college girl as pudendal fodder.

J

Jab . . . To sting with the phallus.

Jab artist . . . A daedal phallator; a virtuoso of the female fiddle.

Jab joint . . . A house in the Yoshiwara district in Tokyo; a bawdyhouse.

Jab off . . . 1. To "knock off" a woman, pudendally. 2. Of a male, to relieve oneself manually.

Jack . . . 1. The fleshy shaft with which the male expresses erotic love. 2. Of the shaft, to assume the consistency necessary to effectuate the erotic expression. 3. Of the male or the shaft, to express the amorous feeling by a fro-and-to motion in the vaginal corridor.

Jack entertainment . . . Pudendal entertainment provided by the phallus erectus.

Jack-hold-my-staff . . . A servant so humble he will literally or figuratively hold his employer's phallus.

Jack Johnson . . . A voluminous phallus, esp. one of an Ethiop.

Jack me Robinson! . . . An exclamation of an underlying female, to a lethargic superimposed male, indicating, in essence, "Go to it!".

Jack of all trades . . . A harlot who works vaginally, rectally, and orally.

Jack out of office . . . A phallus "retired" because of incompetency, with regard to the female crypt.

Jack Straw . . . The phallus as an inconsequential character.

Jack Straw's castle . . . The female underpart which accommodates the male genital pendant. See **Jack Straw.**

Jack the slipper . . . The male sex member, in allusion to its insinuation into the female slit.

Jack up . . . Of a female, to give the male phallus its standing vigor.

Jackanapes . . . That despicable character, the membrum virile, esp. the impotent variety.

Jackaroo . . . A young man's phallus, still inexperienced.

Jacket . . . A sheath for the phallus; a condom.

Jacket . . . The vagina, conceived as the sheath of the phallus.

Jack's delight . . . The soft female pudendal underbelly, as a phallic assuager.

Jacky . . . Of the male, easily aroused; of the phallus, erected at the drop of a female hat.

Jactitation . . . The boasting by a male that he has phallated a particular woman.

Jag . . . The vulva, esp. the interlabial slit, conceived as a pudendal tear.

Jail bait . . . A young attractive girl whose charms tempt the male libido and whose partakers of are foredoomed to incarceration, because of the immaturity of her fruit.

Jail fever . . . Sexual pyrexia of gaol inmates, due to forced abstinence.

Jake with the lever up . . . Of the male, sexually efficient, with the phallus jutting.

Jam . . . 1. The split underside of a girl. 2. A girl as a sweetheart or, better still, a mistress.

Jam . . . To impact the vagina with phallus induratus.

Jam-dandy . . . The phallus conceived as a pudendal fop, with a penchant for "jam."

Jam on both sides . . . To phallate a female vaginally and rectally.

Jam-pot . . . The fleshy sleeve of the female underside, as a potful of joy for the male jam-seeker.

Jam-seeker . . . The male organ which, in the virile, seeks the female genital fiord.

Jam-tart . . . A good, good female, i.e., a pudendally desirable one.

Jamaica discipline . . . The denial to one's husband of the pudendal privilege, to "learn him a lesson."

Jammy bit of jam . . . A luscious bit of female, or female underbelly.

January and May marriage . . . A marriage in which one of the spouses is much older than the other.

January chicken . . . 1. A child conceived by an older male or borne by a not-so-young woman. 2. A vaginally accessible female of tender age.

Jason's Fleece . . . Same as **Golden Fleece,** reddish pubic hair of a female.

Jaw . . . A fellator or a fellatrice conceived as the functional part in fellatio.

Jaw artist . . . A fellator or a fellatrice, conceived as an oistrach of the art.

Jawbreaker . . . In fellatio, a male with a gigantic, maxilloclastic organon.

Jawfest . . . A bout of fellatio, esp. a very gratifying one.

Jawsmith . . . A fellator or a fellatrice.

Jazz . . . Of the male, to give a female a pudendal syncopation, esp. extramaritally.

Jazz . . . Sexual concourse, conceived as a pudendal dance.

Jazz-ass . . . A female whose pudendum is readily available for extramarital syncopations.

Jazz-baby . . . A girl who gives, for love or for money.

Jazz bender . . . A whoring spree; an orgy of pudendal cymbal-pounding.

Jazz-dirt . . . A slovenly prostitute.

Jazz-fiddle . . . The instrument of copulation in the female.

Jazz insurance . . . A condom or a diaphragm.

Jazz joint . . . A house where a male with a taut genital bow may rent a female fiddle and play it on the premises.

Jazz stick . . . The male genital fiddlestick.

Jazzabelle . . . A female who dispenses genital privileges, for a consideration, to males in need of phallic alleviation.

Jehu . . . A reckless phallator, in allusion to the Biblical charioteer.

Jelly bath . . . A copious seminal ejaculation.

Jelly-belly . . . The relaxed abdominal wall of a multiparous woman.

Jelly cruse . . . The female receiving-nook in which the engorged male sausage unburdens itself in sexual concourse.

Jellyfish . . . An effete pudendal instrument of the male, no longer having erotic backbone.

Jemima . . . The female sex pudding, esp. that of an Ethiopess.

Jemmy . . . The male pudendal crowbar.

Jemmy . . . To pry the female sexual slit with the male pudendal crowbar.

Jenny Willocks . . . 1. A hermaphrodite. 2. An effeminate male.

Jerk . . . A male masturbator, regarded disdainfully as a failure with the women.

Jerk joint . . . A disreputable, even to men, bawdyhouse.

Jerk off . . . Of the male, to relieve a case of seminal hypertension, accompanied by phallic intumescence, by triggering the ejaculatory reflex with the gentle fist.

Jerk up . . . Of a female, to incite a phallic uprising.

Jerkster . . . A female who induces the phallic spurt manually.

Jewelry . . . The female genital ensemble.

Jew's lance . . . A circumcised phallus, in allusion to the universal practice of peritomy among the Jews.

Jigger . . . The female genital receptacle in which the male piston reciprocates.

Jigger . . . Same as **Dojigger,** the male organ with a built-in reciprocating action.

Jock . . . The male genital organon as jockey of the female pudendum.

Jockey . . . A man prone on a woman supine; a phallator.

Jockey . . . The short pudendal leg of the male, in allusion to its "riding" the female saddle, in coitus.

Jockey stick . . . The phallus, as the goad of the feminine crotch.

John . . . The male organon personified.

Johnny . . . The male pudendal cucumber, conceived with affection.

Johnny Hancock . . . A seminal autograph written with the male genital stylus in the female pudendum.

Johnny out of jail . . . The phallus jutting from the unzipped mouche, in readiness for an impromptu pudendal plunge.

Joies de Mariage . . . Literally, the joys of marriage; figuratively, ephemeral pleasures.

Join giblets . . . To fill the female pudendal hiatus with the male boneless appendage.

Join the stream . . . Of a female supine, to "open up" in acceptance of the male petard, by spreading the thighs.

Joy ride . . . A phallic gallop through the female perineal countryside.

Joy spot . . . The female perineal garden as the site of phallic festivities.

Joy stick . . . The male genital drumstick, as, obviously, the organon of pudendal joy.

Joy wagon . . . A female as the carrier of genital pleasure, for the male.

Joy-wheeler . . . A girl partaking in a joy ride, i.e., in sexual pleasures, esp. extramaritally.

Jude . . . A prostitute or, if not a mercenary pudendal dispenser, an art-for-art's-sake distributor of vaginal privileges.

Judy . . . A girl endowed with a pudendum sympathetic to the problems of the freedom-aspiring spermatozoa confined in the vesicular dungeons of the male.

Judy . . . The paradisiac adit of a girl.

Judy-bitten . . . Of a male, infected with a venereal disease, in allusion to Judy, the pigeon with a promiscuous pudendum.

Jug . . . The female genital container which in coitus contains the phallus; the vagina. Also, the entire vulvar complex.

Jug bag . . . An old prostitute having a bag where others have a jug.

Jug-bitten . . . 1. Of a man, to be hard-up for female pudendal alleviation. 2. To be enamored, up to the gonads, of a particular jug-bearer.

Jug-breaking . . . 1. Pudendal seduction of the innocent. 2. A whoremongering spree.

Jug gat . . . The phallus, esp. erectus.

Jug hack . . . A procurer, pimp, or bordello manager.

Jug-minded . . . In a mood for pudendal music.

Jug-pounding . . . A pounding of the female cleft with the phallic stiff.

Jug-stiff . . . Of the phallus, admirably hardened and fit for the vulvar invasion.

Jug up . . . To raise a functional membrum virile.

Jugful of joy . . . The genital underbelly of the female.

Juice . . . 1. The symbol of sexual desire. 2. Sexual gratification. 3. Ungation. 4. The seminal fluid.

Juice box . . . The vulva, esp. the vagina, in allusion to its own ungation and also the seminal deposit.

Juice, have some . . . To have a piece of female underside.

Juice jerker . . . A superannuated employée of a bordello.

Juice peddler . . . A procurer, pimp, or manager of a bawdyhouse.

Juice sucker . . . A male who makes love to the female pudendum with his mouth.

Juice up . . . 1. To bring up an erection. 2. To induce the phallic spurt. 3. To warm up a female with amorous affection and cause a liberal discharge of ungation.

Juicer . . . A female whose interlabial recess, of the lower mouth, is copious with secretion at the slightest provocation.

Juicy . . . Of a girl, piquant, nectareous, voluptuous, paradisiac, etc.

Jumbo . . . A pleasantly enormous phallus, from the viewpoint of females with spacious hiatuses.

Jump the besom . . . To go through the ceremony of a mock marriage by jumping over a broom—then live as man and wife.

Jump the broomstick . . . Same as **Jump the besom.**

Junior . . . The better part of a male, the boneless pudendal appendage.

K

Kangaroo droop . . . The abdominal droopiness of a multiparous woman.

Kate . . . A harlot described as "clean in and out," i.e., one of the better-than-average variety.

Kaulos . . . A greek figurative synonym for the penis, in allusion to a stem.

Kedavalence . . . Sexual impotence in the male resulting from worry. Ex *kedos* (concern), *a* (negative), & *valere* (to be able).

Keen . . . Sexually desirous; of the phallus, erectus.

Keen as mustard . . . Extremely keyed up sexually.

Keen-cutie . . . A young and quite appealing hetaera.

Keen-on . . . A phallic rigidification remediable by a vulvar caress.

Keen on . . . Phallically hard about.

Keen stuff . . . Desirable and desirous girls.

Keen up . . . To arouse sexually; to give the phallus the status erectus.

Keener . . . A desirous, and desirable, teener.

Keep a cow . . . To have a wife, as opposed to buying the "milk" from a pudendal-privilege dealer.

Keep a hold on the land . . . Hold a man by his phallus while kissing.

Keep a man sexually contented . . . **Hold down.**

Keep a stiff upper lip . . . To nurture a stiff lower pendant, but pretend not to be interested in the arouser's charms.

Keep from burning a hole in the pocket . . . To decompress an adamant phallus, manually.

Keep healthy . . . To give one's phallus the conventional calisthenics.

Keep hot . . . Of a female, to keep the male wanting, by the use of various amorous stratagems.

Keep in step . . . Of a female, to complement the phallic reciprocation with a matching vulvar rhythm.

Keep in the hugger . . . Of a female on the receiving end of manual love, to keep the titties in their twin hammock, i.e., to refuse to expose them to the hazards of direct digital palpation.

Keep it up . . . Withhold ejaculation to prolong phallation.

Keep off the grass . . . To indulge in palpation but abstain from phallation.

Keep off the grass . . . Of a sarmassating male, to refrain from trespassing on the female pudendal escutcheon.

Keep on the hump . . . Of a female, to keep her man's fly humped by recurrent uprisings.

Keep one hand for yourself! . . . An admonition of the female quarry to her inspired lover who, with one arm around her, aims with the other at her pudendum, to cease and desist from so doing.

Keep one's banana skinned . . . To keep one's phallus in vaginal comfort.

Keep open house . . . Of a female, to be pudendally reachable most of the time.

Keep the anchor on ice . . . Of a male, to be abstemious with regard to seminal expenditures.

Keep the phallus of an eager phallator performing outside of the vagina; said of a prostitute who misdirects the amblyopic organ to the cleft between her flattened gluteal mounds, or keeps it in her fist . . . **Mogue.**

Keep tight purse strings . . . Of a wife, or any pudendal dispenser, to keep a male on a starvation diet, vaginally.

Keep under wraps . . . To keep one's vulva out of reach of aspiring phalli.

Keep up an old queen . . . To patronize an older whore.

Keester . . . The lipped ornament on the underside of the female, regarded as a juicer.

Keg . . . Female pudendal flesh, esp. prostitutional.

Kegged meat . . . The genitalia of a prostitute.

Keister . . . Same as **Keester,** the female pudendal juicer.

Kelder . . . 1. The womb. 2. The vulva. 3. The abdomen, esp. the female abdomen conceived lecherously by the male.

Kelder seed . . . Seminal fluid, in allusion to **kelder,** the uterus.

Ken . . . The home of the phallus in the female pudendum; the vulva; the vagina.

Ken cracker . . . 1. The phallus, in allusion to its cracking the labial barrier to the ken. 2. One who deflowers a virgin.

KENORGASMY . . . A form of sexual orgasm in the male, yielding a measure of gratification but no perceptible seminal spurt. Ex *kenos* (empty, futile).

Kentucky bargain . . . A marriage agreement between a man and his wife-to-be, whereby the female child of the latter, by a previous marriage, is made part of the genital offering.

Kentucky colonel . . . An amorous male, not necessarily a native or resident of the Bluegrass State, who has a tooth for green bananas, i.e., youngish girls.

Kentucky cradle snatcher . . . A male married to a child, proverbially in Kentucky.

Kentucky dowry . . . The pudendum and sprouting mammae of a young girl who has nothing more to offer.

Kentucky horn . . . A phallus especially responsive to the charms of subripe girls.

Kentucky hunger . . . Lasciviousness directed toward early and sub teenagers.

Kentucky posture . . . The coital posture of a female whose buttocks are raised on a pillow.

Kentucky quail . . . Immature girls as brideflesh, in allusion to the proverbial youth of some Kentucky brides.

Kerkos . . . A Greek synonym for the phallus, in allusion to a tail.

Kettle . . . The female pudendal kettle of fish.

Keyhole . . . The female sexual introitus; the vulva.

Keyhole cocktail . . . A phallic spurt in the natural habitat, the vulva.

Keyhole whistler . . . A male who licks the female underpart; a cunnilinguist.

Kick for trade . . . Of a prostitute or a procurer, to solicit business.

Kid . . . To seed a woman with seminal fluid; to impregnate.

Kid . . . A boy in whose anus and rectum a pederast intromits his phallus.

Kid-leather . . . Teen-age prostitute.

Kid napper . . . Same as **Kid walloper,** the legal phallator of a child-bride.

Kid-simple . . . Fond of catamites; addicted to pederasty.

Kid-stretcher . . . A male attracted sexually to young females, esp. teen-age whores.

Kid-stuff . . . 1. Sexual concourse. 2. The seminal fertilizer.

Kid walloper . . . A man who marries a child-bride.

Kidded . . . With child; impregnated.

Kidskin stretcher . . . A man who phallates a very young girl; also, the husband of a child-bride.

Kindergarten butcher . . . A male who "butchers" young female pudenda, with the phallus. Also, the husband of an immature pudendum.

King-at-arms . . . A manually stimulated phallus.

King dick . . . A phallus of impressive size and enduring self-sustenance.

Kingsley's stand . . . A morning pudendal engagement, after a series of nocturnal skirmishes involving heavy seminal losses, in allusion to William Kingsley, British commander, whose regiment took up hazardous guard duty the morning after a day of severe losses.

Kip . . . Brothel as a pudendal exchange where bullish phalli are rendered bearish.

Kirk . . . Of young lovers, to exchange caresses while the cat's away, i.e., while the parents or other elders are out.

Kiss . . . To kiss, suck, or titillate lingually the genitalia or anus of another.

Kiss, applied with libidinous suction, which leaves an ecchymotic imprint on a non-mucous surface . . . **Monkey bite; Strawberry kiss.**

Kiss behind and not before . . . Be out of favor with regard to the sexual entree of the female, i.e., to get it not.

Kiss, intense desire to; esp. in the male . . . PHILEMAMANIA.

Kiss of the trunderclap variety . . . **Horse-buss.**

Kiss off . . . To introduce the phallus into the rectum.

Kiss off . . . To induce orgasm by labial or lingual stimulation of the phallus.

Kiss one where one sat on Saturday . . . To kiss one's arse, esp. that of a female.

Kiss the buttocks, of a female . . . PYGOPHILEMATE.

Kiss the genitalia or anus of another . . . **Kiss.**

Kiss the nipples of a female . . . THELEBASIATE.

Kiss, vigorous, esp. one terminating in a bite . . . **Horse kiss.**

Kissing, centering one's erotic expressions on . . . PHILEMACENTRIC.

Kissing of generally unkissable parts of the body . . . PARAPHILEMIA.

Kissing of the buttocks . . . PYGOPHILEMIA.

Kissing of . . . See also under name of particular part involved.

Kissing, person easily aroused by . . . PHILEMEROTIC.

Kissing, person who dislikes . . . PHILEMAPHOBE.

Kissing, person who is very fond of . . . PHILEMAPHILE.

Kittleables . . . The fleshy pectoral flourishes and the pudendal magnet of the female, so conceived by the male.

KLEPTOLAGNIA . . . Sexual excitation induced by stealing. Ex *kleptein* (to steal) & *lagneia* (lust).

Knead amorously the tissues of a woman, esp. those characteristic of her sex . . . SARMASSATE.

Kneader of female tissues, erotic . . . SARMASSOPHIL.

Knee drill . . . A bout of sexual concourse.

Knee-trembler . . . A bout of sexual coupling in the standing position, with the male flexing his knees.

Kneel at the altar . . . To phallate per rectum, with the recipient in the knee-chest position and the phallator on his knees.

Kneeler . . . A male cunnilinguist who takes his nourishment while kneeling between the abducted thighs of a female sprawling in a chair or on the edge of a bed.

Knees, female, especially erotic about the . . . GONYPHILOUS.

Knick-knack . . . The female crotch as a pleasurable trinket.

KNISMOLAGNIA . . . Sexual pleasure derived from tickling or from being tickled. Ex *knismos* (a tickling) & *lagneia* (lust).

Knock off . . . To give a virgin the first brazen thrust.

Knock off . . . To let a woman have the phallus erectus vaginally.

Knock out an apple . . . To beget an offspring of the old block.

Knock up . . . To phallate and impregnate.

Knocker . . . The middle of the three lower extremities of the male, in allusion to its ability to knock up a "knock-uppable" female.

Knocking . . . What a bridegroom and bride are most likely to engage in during the first postnuptial night.

Knocking-house . . . A house, as opposed to a home, where a man may bring down a rampant phallus pudendally, for a consideration; a brothel.

Knocking-jacket . . . The gown worn, usually, by a woman during the nightly "knocking" sessions; i.e., a nightgown.

Knocking-joint . . . Same as **Knocking-house.**

Knocking-shop . . . A house where males with phallic eburnation problems may engage an alleviating female pudendum for a bout of "knocking."

Knock-upability . . . The ability to "knock up" a female; said of the phallus and of its bearer.

Knock-upable . . . Of a female, pudendably not impenetrable; in fact, accessible.

Know . . . Of the male, to invade the female pudendum phallically.

Know it's there . . . Of a girl dancing with a willing and able, pudendally, partner, to feel the impact of his phlogisticated spermapositor.

Knowledge, add another item of, by sedentery study . . . **Have one wrinkle more in one's arse.**

Knuckle geld . . . Of a female resisting the advance of a determined phallus, to knuckle the male's testicles.

Koleos . . . The Greek form for sheath or vagina.

Kolpos . . . The Greek form for vagina, in allusion to a hollow, as that between the female breasts.

Koryne . . . A Greek synonym for the phallus, in allusion to a club.

Kysthos . . . The Greek form for a hollow and, hence, for the vagina.

L

La grande passion . . . Zee libido, the motive force of the male pudendum.

Labia Majora . . . The two rounded folds of skin or ridges which form the "lips" of the vulva, one on each side of the slit.

Labia majora . . . Pomas.

Labia majora, excessive size of . . . Macropomia.

Labia majora, in allusion to the cleft . . . **Split chums.**

Labia majora, large; regarded as a king-size portion for a hungry cunnilinguist . . . **Double sucker.**

Labia majora, space or region between . . . Interlabium.

Labia majora, spread the, by abducting the thighs, in order to create the climate of approval and posture of admission for the male coital sirdar . . . **Open up.**

Labia majora, surgical suturing of . . . Episiorrhaphy; Labiorrhaphy.

Labia majora, surgical suturing or clasping of, to prevent sexual intercourse . . . Infibulation.

Labia majora which are close together in the normal position of the thighs; such a condition . . . Synlabia.

Labia majora which are separated or gaping in the normal position of the thighs; such a condition . . . Chasmalabia.

Labia Minora . . . The two folds of mucous membrane on the inner aspects of the labia majora, one on each side of the introitus vaginae.

Labia minora . . . Nymphae.

Labia minora, excessive size of . . . Macrolabia.

Labia minora extruding through the slit between the majora . . . **Butterfly.**

Labia minora, partial closure of, with sutures . . . Nymphorrhaphy.

Labia minora, secretion found around . . . Humex; Smegma.

Labia of female pudendum, in allusion to their crescentric form, esp. when parted by the phallus . . . **Parentheses.**

Labia, to deliver the phallus erectus to the gentle embrace of the female . . . **Enclose in parentheses.**

Labia, to surround the phallus with the female pudendal . . . **Parenthesize; Enclose in parentheses.**

LABIUM MAJUS . . . POMA; **Parenthesis.**

LABIUM MINUS . . . NYMPHA; **Parenthesis.**

Lack of outlet for sexual urge, condition marked by . . . APHALLATIA.

Lack of response from the female sexual partner . . . ANAPOCRISIS.

Lack of sexual relations between a man and his wife . . . AVIRGYNIA.

LAGNEKINETIC . . . Designating movement of the female body which arouses desire in the male. Ex *lagneia* (lust) and *kinesis* (movement).

LAGNEPHRONESIS . . . Preoccupation with thoughts of lewdness. Ex *lagneia* (lust) & *phroneo* (ruminate).

LAGNESIS . . . Excessively strong sexual desire in either the male or the female. Ex *lagneia* (lust).

LAGNOCOLYSIS . . . Inhibition of the sexual urge. From *lagneia* (lust) & *kolyo* (inhibit).

LAGNOEMA . . . A lecherous or erotic thought. Ex *lagneia* (lust) & *noema* (thought).

LAGNOIA . . . A condition of the mind marked by obsessions with erotic thoughts. Ex *lagneia* (lust) & *nous* (mind).

LAGNOLALIA . . . The use of obscene language, esp. habitually. Ex *lagneia* (lust) & *lalein* (to speak).

LAGNOPATHIC . . . Pathologically lewd. Ex *lagneia* (lust) & *pathos* (disease).

LAGNOPATHY . . . Pathologic lewdness.

LAGNOSIS . . . Same as LAGNESIS, excessive sexual desire.

Laker-lady . . . The mistress of an actor.

Lamb . . . A male or female child used by a pederast for rectal phallic intromission.

Lame duck . . . A genitally non-functional male pendant.

LASCIVIA . . . Intense sexual desire, esp. in the male.

Lasciviate . . . To indulge in digital and manual exploration of the female charms.

Lasciviousness, inducing abnormal . . . TENTIGOGENIC.

Lavender boy . . . A male homosexual.

Lavender convention . . . A get-together of male homosexuals, for chit-chat and more serious conversation.

Lawful blanket . . . A lawfully wedded female spouse.

Lawful jam . . . Same as **Lawful blanket,** a wife.

Lay . . . A form of gavage in which the female is fed a rich protein diet by means of the phallic tube inserted into the lower mouth.

Lay . . . Of a man, to put his maid in the dorsal recumbent posture and perform a vaginal intubation with his phallus petrosus, for the purpose of administering a high protein injection.

Lay a fist on . . . To relieve phallic tension manually.

Lay a glove on . . . Of a male, to lay an erotic hand upon erotogenic parts of a female.

Lay a leg on . . . To phallate (a woman).

Lay away from . . . To lie with the back toward one's bedmate, in boredom or resentment.

Lay it in the black . . . To phallate a colored harlot.

Lay kid leather . . . To phallate young females.

Lay like a rug . . . . Of a girl, to have a most gratifying coital response.

Lay mitts on . . . To appreciate a girl's charms with the hands, by laying the latter on the former.

Lay of the land . . . The best lay love and/or money can secure.

Lay the femmes . . . Of an attractive male, to give the girls butterflies in their pudenda.

Lead apes in hell . . . To be a chaste old maid.

Lecherous; desirous; in allusion to the female furry pudendal "animal" . . . **Cunny-haunted.**

Lechery, leer with . . . **Cast an optic.**

Lécheur . . . A person who licks another's genitalia.

Leg act . . . A provocative but not indelicate display of female leg.

Leg art . . . Photography or other forms of pictorial presentation in which the legs of a female are the main feature.

Leg artist . . . A girl or woman skilled in making a display of her legs without appearing vulgar.

Leg bait . . . A alluring display of female legs.

Leg blandishment by a female, designed to precipitate a proposal by an itchy male . . . **Leg show.**

Leg business . . . Tantalizing display of female legs.

Leg business . . . 1. Phallic business in the interfemoral introitus. 2. The craft of harlotry.

Leg display, alluring . . . **Leg bait; Leg business; Leg show.**

Leg drama . . . Sexual concourse ending, unhappily for the unwed participants, in conception.

Leg joint . . . A branch office of the oldest profession.

Leg lifter . . . An unmarried male partaking of coitus.

Leg list . . . The little black book containing the names and phone numbers of girls with get-at-able pudenda.

Leg piece . . . The genital hollow in the female bifurcation of the thighs.

Leg show . . . 1. A blandishment of female leg tissue, intended to promote a cause, in favor of the female, as by way of nuptial bells. 2. A girlie stage show with plenty of thigh-and-buttock revelation.

Legged . . . Of the female, given the taste of the membrum virile erectum.

Legging . . . A rubber sheath for the phallus, serving the usual purpose.

Leggy . . . Of the female, distinguished by attractive, usually long, legs.

Legitimate show . . . The bowing of the female fiddle when done with the blessings of the parson, i.e., in wedlock.

Legitimate, the . . . The phallus assigned by nuptial vows to a particular female pudendal delta, when navigating in the assigned waters.

Legs around the neck, have . . . Of a male, to have a girl's thighs around the neck while brushing his teeth with her pubic tuft and vulvar juice; i.e., to cunnilinguate. Of the female, to suckle the membrum virile cupidum.

Legs, attractive, search for a girl with . . . **Bowl for timber.**

Legs, excessive growth of hair on; esp. in women . . . CRUROTRICHOSIS.

Legs, female, centering erotic interest on . . . CRUROCENTRIC.

Legs, female, especially erotic about the . . . CRUROPHILOUS.

Legs, female, knead amorously the . . . **Bowl for timber.**

Legs, female, make a display of . . . **Make with the Legs.**

Legs, female, tantalizing display of . . . **Leg business.**

Legs, long and attractive, distinguished by . . . **Leggy.**

Legs of female willing to spread for the male spermapositor . . . **Merry legs.**

Lemon . . . 1. An unattractive girl. 2. A girl, attractive or not, who, in the period of payoff, after an evening of monetary lavishments by the male, proves to be a pudendal tartar, i.e., shockingly inaccessible.

Lemoncholy . . . In the male, the melancholy resulting from a frustrating evening spent with a **lemon.**

Length . . . In re the phallus, the measurement of how long.

Length . . . A dose of phallus administered vaginally.

Length, having an effective and satisfying; said of the phallus . . . **Anglican length.**

Length of, give a . . . To administer vaginally a commendable length of phallus adamantinus.

LEPTOSADISM . . . 1. A sublimated form of sadism. 2. Mild or refined sadism. Ex *leptos* (refined).

LESBIAN . . . A female homosexual. Ex *Lesbos,* an ancient city in which female homosexualism is said to have been rampant.

Lesbie . . . A female homosexual. For etymology see LESBIAN.

Lesbie trot . . . An effeminate manner of walking in a male.

Let nature take its course . . . Of a man faced with a pudendal opportunity, to do what comes naturally.

Let out one's parlor . . . To engage in Mrs. Warren's profession.

Lewd; an allusion to a straight penis. . . . ITHYPHALLIC.

LIBIDO . . . 1. Sexual desire or urge. 2. The motive power of one's sex life.

Libido as the motive force of the male pudendum . . . **La grande passion.**

Libido, esp. of the male . . . **Cause of causes.**

LIBIDOCRATIA . . . The condition in which the sex urge is a person's dominating force. From *libido* & *kratos* (power).

LIBIDONEUROSIS . . . A form of frustration neurosis resulting from the failure to satisfy one's libido.

LIBIDOPATH . . . A person having pathologically abnormal sexual cravings, with regard to either their intensity or the manner of their gratification. Ex *libido* & *pathein* (to suffer).

LIBIDOPATHY . . . Any pathologic abnormality of the sex urge.

LIBIDOPHILE . . . A person, usually the male, devoted to libidinous pleasures. Ex *libido* (wantonness) & *philein* (to love).

Licensed brothel . . . **MAISON DE TOLÉRANCE.**

Licensed coitus; coitus in wedlock . . . **Legitimate show.**

Licensed to coit a given woman, by virtue of a wedding ceremony . . . . . . **Parsoned.**

Lich gate . . . The labia of the female pudendum, esp. the space between the labia.

Lick the anus, usually of a female . . . **Bite the brown.**

Lick the licorice stick . . . To take the phallus orally.

Lick the pudendum of the female, in allusion to a cigarette butt (dog-end) . . . **Bite the dog-end.**

Lick the . . . See also under the name of the part involved.

Lickbox . . . The pudendum muliebre as the target of a cunnilinguist.

Licking of female genitalia . . . CUNNILINGUS; CUNNILINCTION; EDELINGUS; **Pearl diving; Biting the dog-end; Brushing with Miriam.**

Licking of genitalia as practiced by female homosexuals . . . SAPPHOLINCTION.

Licking of male sex organs . . . MEDOLINGUS; VIRILINGUS.

Licking of penis, erotic . . . MEDOLINGUS.

Lie down to accept the male genital emissary . . . **Lie down for nourishment.**

Licking or suckling of the female breasts, erotic . . . MAMMILINGUS.

Licking of . . . See also under name of part, as *Anus.*

Licorice stick . . . The membrum virile in fellatio.

Lie back and enjoy it . . . Of a female confronted with an irresistible phallus and an inescapable situation, to assume the attitude that if you can't fight it, join it.

Lie down and take nourishment . . . Of the female, to recline for the interlabial phallic injection.

Lie in state . . . To rest comfortably in bed, with a female pudendum within phallic reach.

Lie in the act of phallation; of the female . . . **Pray with the knees upwards.**

Lie like a butcher's dog . . . Of a male who has pudendal privileges to a particular vulva, to lie near it in bored indifference; in allusion to a sated butcher's dog lazing indolently in a thesaurus of prime beef.

Lie on one's oars . . . To rest between bouts of pudendal intubation; applied to the male.

Lie under the male for the phallic prod of joy . . . **Go under.**

Lie with (a woman), to savor pudendal pleasures . . . **Have a brush with.**

Life in the raw . . . Nudism; life in a nudist colony.

Life without sexual intercourse, by choice or by necessity . . . ASYNODIA.

Lift a leg . . . Of a female, to partake of coitus.

Light frigate . . . A female who is easily steered away from the righteous.

Light skirt . . . A girl with an easily uplifted skirt, i.e., one who would rather take it off than have it wrinkled.

Like a cock on holy ground . . . Sexually excited, as a virile phallus on the putting green of the female.

Line of cleavage . . . **The hotline; Sweet line.**

Line the jacket . . . Of the female, to line the vaginal corridor with phallus erectus.

LINGA . . . A symbol of the phallus used in connection with the worship of Siva, the deity of reproductive power in Hinduism.

Lingerie conceived as undergarments sometimes worn by the female during her roasting of the phallus vaginally . . . **Roast meat clothes.**

Lip . . . To caress labially, esp. by sucking action.

Lip reading . . . A bout of cunnilinction between two female cunnilinguists.

Lip splitter . . . A male devotee of phallation.

Lip work . . . Pudendal basiation; cunnilinction.

Lippie chaser . . . An Ethiop who prefers Caucasian vulvas.

Lips, female, especially erotic about the . . . CHEILOPHILOUS.

Literature dealing considerably with the pudendal sanctum of the female . . . **Hilltop literature.**

Literature dealing with sex . . . **Basic literature.**

Little accident . . . The offspring of a phallation which was intended for pleasure, not for the census.

Little bit of all right . . . 1. A girl who is a whale of all right. 2. A lingeringly satisfying engagement in coitus.

Little bit on the go . . . Of a girl, not exactly squandering it, or selling it, but apportioning it judiciously to favorite males.

Little bitsy . . . A petite girl who makes up in quality what she lacks in size.

Little black book . . . The proverbially black-covered miniature notebook in which amative and unattached males list the names and phone numbers, as well as addresses, of the females they may (re)lie upon in case of pudendal need.

Little cat . . . A petite adult or a young girl with a, presumably, small vulvette.

Little drinks . . . Two small female breasts which, together, wouldn't fill one monronian cup.

Little finger . . . The male physical arm of love, down under.

Little man in the boat . . . The clitoris, conceived as a cute homunculus in the female pudendal ship.

Little misfortune . . . Same as **Little accident,** an addition to the census resulting from a coital engagement intended for pleasure alone.

Little monster . . . A small but adamantine and aggressive phallus.

Little nipper . . . A vulvette or small vulva, conceived as nipping the phallus with its toothless but firm "gums."

Little punkins . . . Small but, usually, well-formed ninnies.

Little sister . . . Big sister's pudendal pudding.

Little smack . . . A half-pint phallus.

Live-and-let-live . . . A game of fellatio, played by two, in which each participant receives from and gives to the other, simultaneously.

Live rabbit . . . The membrum virile, esp. with flexed muscles.

Live the life of a nudist; said of the male . . . **Have Jack out of doors.**

Living together of husband and wife without sexual relations, by mutual consent . . . AGENOBIOSIS.

Load in the sticks . . . Of a phallating male, to deposit the phallic cream between the thighs of the woman.

Lobster . . . The male organon regarded as a part likely to become infected. See under **Boil one's lobster.**

Long arm of love . . . The organum erectum of the male.

Long-balls . . . A male with an excessively pendulous scrotum, conceived by females as a vigorous phallator.

Long-cork . . . A male with a sizable phallus, esp. one remarkable for its length.

Long-eared chum . . . The phallus, in allusion to the pendulous pouch.

Long end of a short man . . . The phallus erectus.

Long eye . . . The vulva conceived as an eye placed vertically, in allusion to the resemblance of the labia to the eyelids and the introitus vaginae to the pupil.

Long-haired chum . . . A friendly female pudendum; also, the bearer thereof.

Long innings . . . Bouts of coitus prolongatus.

Long interest . . . An amative interest expressed by an elongation of the phallus.

Long lay . . . A leisurely bout of coitus, esp. such one with a harlot.

Long Meg . . . A tall woman, presumed, logically, to have a sesquipedalian pudendal slit.

Long nose, make a . . . To put up a substantial erection, or, of the female, to cause such an erection to materialize.

Look at a female with a hungry pudendal stare . . . **Give the bedroom eye.**

Look goats and monkeys . . . To look lasciviously, as at a female in dishabille or at exposed intimate parts, or at parts not exposed but suggestively bouffante.

Look hungrily at a provocative female part . . . **York.**

Look into the brown . . . To intromit the phallus into the rectum.

Look lustfully at provocative females, at what can be seen of their charms, or at the uncamouflaged contours of the latter . . . **Look goats and monkeys.**

Look with lechery in one's eye . . . **Cast an optic.**

Loose corns . . . Seminal fluid, esp. such excess of it that should be disgorged in sexual concourse.

Loose end . . . A female pudendum marked by laxity of the moral strings.

Loose-hung . . . Of female breasts, droopy.

Lose phallic rigidity while in the act, or even before the vaginal invasion . . . **Corpse out.**

Lose the match and pocket the stake . . . Of the female, to be phallated.

Loss of sexual characteristics in a female, as atrophy of the breasts . . . DEFEMINATION.

Loss of sexual characteristics in a male, as atrophy of the testicles, change in voice, etc. . . . DEMASCULINIZATION.

Loss of . . . See also under name of faculty, quality, etc. lost.

Love and beauty, Norse goddess of . . . FREYA; FREYJA.

Love and joy, Greek goddess of . . . HATHOR; ATHOR.

Love and wealth, Vedic god of . . . BHAGA.

Love apple . . . A girl endowed with all the embellishments necessary to qualify for the title "tomato."

Love, beauty, and life, Greek goddess of . . . APHRODITE.

Love, centering one's interest on . . . PHILOCENTRIC.

Love clinch . . . A pudendal coalition of normal heterosexuals.

Love feast . . . A thoroughly carnal engagement in lovemaking.

Love, Greek god of, regarded as the son of Aphrodite . . . EROS.

Love lane . . . The pudendum muliebre.

Love letters, abnormal urge to write . . . EROTOGRAPHOMANIA.

Love peddler . . . 1. A mercenary dispenser of the foremost female accommodation. 2. A procurer, pimp, etc.

Love pirate . . . 1. A seducer of the innocent. 2. A rapist.

Love, Roman god of, son of Venus . . . AMOR; CUPID.

Love, Roman goddess of; identified with Aphrodite . . . VENUS.

Love, sexual; as opposed to the paternal, maternal, fraternal, avuncular, etc. variety . . . **Blind love.**

Love stuff . . . The fertilizing fluid of the male.

Lovemaking, behave clumsily in the act of . . . BOUSTROPHATE.

Lovemaking in public places . . . **Flagrant delight.**

Lover of Aphrodite, Greek god and . . . ARES.

Lower the female pudendum upon a male lying spike-up . . . **Straddle the spike.**

Lubricate . . . To soften up a woman's underbelly, for the phallic intrusion, by wining and dining her.

Lubricate the phallus for ease of intromission . . . **Rosin the bow.**

Lubricating secretion of vulva during sexual excitation . . . UNGATION.

Lubricating secretion of vulva during sexual quiescence . . . HUMEX.

Lucky bag . . . The pudendum muliebre, conceived as a talisman of good luck, at least for the phallus immerging in it.

Lucky bags . . . The cups of the titty hammock.

Lucky piece . . . An illegitimate child borne by an unwedded woman to a wealthy sire, in allusion to the financial benefits usually derived by the mother.

Lucky sentry . . . The hymen, conceived in the light of its cynosural, but by it unappreciated, position.

Lullaby . . . The male genital piston.

Lust in older men . . . GERONTOLAGNIA.

Lust of a brother for his sister . . . SORORILAGNIA.

Lust of a father for his daughter . . . THYGATRILAGNIA.

Lust . . . See also under *Sexual love.*

Lustful; desirous; for the female sanctum . . . **Cunt-struck.**

M

Mace . . . The staff of virile authority dangling or jutting, in accordance with its functional mood, from the interfemoral angle of the male, in allusion to the heavy armor-breaking club with a metal head used in the Middle Ages and known by this name.

Mack . . .The protector, pimp, lover, or husband of a whore.

MACROGENITALISM . . . The condition of having abnormally large sex organs; said, usually, of the male.

MACROGENITOSOMIA . . . The early development of the body and genitalia in either a boy or a girl. Ex *makros* (large), *genere* (beget), & *soma* (body).

MACROMASTA . . . A woman with very large breasts.

MACROPHALLIA . . . The condition of having an unusually large phallus. From *makros* (large) & *phallos* (penis).

MADAROMASTIA . . . Flabbiness of the female breasts. Ex *madaros* (flabby) & *mastos* (breast).

Maiden gear . . . The intimate delicates of young females' apparel.

Maiden-hair . . . 1. The first hair sprouting on the intimate of a girl. 2. The pubic tuft of a female.

Maiden in . . . To intromit the phallus erectus in the usual place.

Maiden jock . . . 1. A phallus making its first invasion of the female interlabial Elysium. 2. A novice phallator.

Maiden jock . . . A case of sexual concourse in which one of the participants, usually the female, is virgin. Also, such get-together in which both are novices.

Maiden jockey . . . A male in his first fling at the female pudendal arena.

Maiden Lane . . . A street, or the like, where harlots promenade, in pursuit of their trade.

Maiden Lane . . . In the female, the narrow passage where the male fifth column has its seminal say.

Maiden-lips . . . The rounded fleshy folds which form the pillars of the pudendal temple of a female.

Maiden name . . . The real, or allegedly real, name of a harlot, working under a *nom de eune.*

Maiden pinks . . . The delicately hued nipples and areolae of a young girl, or of a woman who has had no pregnancies.

Maiden plum . . . The virginity of a female, esp. such virginity "saved" by the female as a reward for her lawfully wedded husband.

Maiden plume . . . The hairy tuft of the female pudendum.

Maiden plume . . . The virgin hymen, conceived as the ornament of maidenhood.

Maiden prayer . . . A phallus erectus of reasonable size.

Maiden seal . . . The hymen, conceived as something that affirms or refutes the virginal condition of a female.

Maiden splint . . . A virgin female's pudendal receiver, conceived as a tender but firm splint for the phallus induratus.

Maiden under . . . Of a maid, to slide under the male, with bifurcated thighs.

MAIDENHEAD . . . 1. The hymen. 2. Virginity.

Maid's ring . . . The hymen, conceived, because of its central opening, as a fleshy ring.

MAISON DE TOLÉRANCE . . . A licensed bordello, in a country where such are licensed and regulated.

Make . . . To soften up a female for a hard invasion.

Make a landing . . . Of the male, to land on the female pudendum.

Make a long arm . . . Of the male, to make his short arm longer, by erection.

Make a woman one's mistress . . . **Hang it on with.**

Make an honest woman of . . . To defecate a woman's reputation of the sully resulting from extramarital copulation, by marrying her.

Make bedroom eyes at . . . To look upon a female with pudendal murder in the eye.

Make bones . . . To phallate and impregnate.

Make ends meet . . . To mate hard (phallus) with soft (female underbelly).

Make faces . . . To phallate, or, if you will, to beget offspring.

Make good mileage with . . . To make palpatory progress with a female.

Make hay . . . Of a male in amorous embrace with another man's wife, to make genital hay while he's away.

Make horns . . . To phallate another man's wife, in allusion to the symbolic horns sprouting from the head of a cuckold.

Make insincere love to a female in order to set her up for seduction . . . **Promote.**

Make into a prostitute . . . **Turn an honest penny.**

Make it warm for . . . Of a female, to raise a man's phallic blood pressure.

Make leg music . . . To bump the pudendal cymbals.

Make love to a female without partaking of the vaginal privilege . . . **Keep off the grass.**

Make love while the parents are away; said of young lovers . . . **Kirk.**

Make love with the hands, to a woman . . . **Fumble.**

Make Mary . . . To deprive Mary of her cherry.

Make settlement in tail . . . 1. To neutralize the erotic charge of a phallus erectus by repeated contact with the pudendum muliebre. 2. Of a female, to settle an obligation, or repay a favor, by giving of the vulva.

Make the arm straight . . . To raise a functional phallic erection.

Make with the legs . . . Of a female, to expose the legs, esp. the knees and lower part of thighs.

Male amorous about very young girls . . . **Pullet squeezer.**

Male and female stacked in a double layer, and effecting a genital anastomosis, designating a . . . **Double-banked.**

Male and female stacked in a double layer, and in the process of pudendal coalition . . . **Double-layer cake.**

Male attracted to young females, esp. teen-age prostitutes . . . **Kid-stretcher.**

Male bedfellow or sexual partner . . . COITANT; PARACOITUS.

Male caressing a woman lecherously . . . **Fumbler.**

Male conversation . . . Sexual concourse, in allusion to the standard meaning of "conversation."

Male deriving erotic stimuli from the feeling of subjugation to a female . . . CATAPHILIST.

Male deriving sexual pleasure only from the act of coitus, not from foreplay . . . TELOPHILIST.

Male devoted to sexual pleasures . . . LIBIDOPHILE.

Male escort with a visible trouserian bulge, resulting from an unsatisfied phallic mind . . . **Angular party.**

Male external genitalia as pudendal rolling stock . . . **Equipment.**

Male external genitalia conceived as a complex device . . . **Apparatus.**

Male external genitalia conceived as "unbeautiful" by some females . . . **Uglies.**

Male external genitalia, esp. if weighing more than the proverbial pound of flesh . . . **Hunk of meat.**

Male external genitalia, esp. the scrotum . . . **Basket.**

Male external genitalia, in allusion to a demand in "The Merchant of Venice" . . . **Pound of flesh.**

Male genitally sterile . . . **Mule.**

Male having a bulky phallus . . . **Tommy buster; Tummy buster.**

Male homosexual, passive, in allusion to his caring for the desires of the other . . . **Bull nurse.**

Male homosexuals, a get-together of . . . **Lavender convention.**

Male homosexuals, gathering of, for sexual festivities . . . **Bull party.**

Male homosexuals . . . See also under *Homosexual.*

Male genital organ . . . See under *Penis, Phallus, Membrum virile,* etc.

Male impotent with his wife, but often potent with another woman . . . Uxoravalent.

Male infected venereally, in allusion to the fire in his petard . . . **Fire-plug.**

Male, lecherous, who fornicates with harlots . . . **Bum-fighter.**

Male phallating a female, in the prone upon supine position . . . **Jockey.**

Male possessing a phallus of impressive magnitude . . . **Duker.**

Male potent sexually, but not with his wife, designating a; also, such male . . . Uxoravalent.

Male potent sexually only with his wife . . . Uxorosthen.

Male prostitute; one who hawks his brawn . . . **Bitch; Iron.**

Male prostitute, to be in practice as a . . . **Hawk one's brawn.**

Male pudendal glutton . . . **Road hog.**

Male pudendally aggressive with a membrum appreciated by the distaff . . . **Hellfire dick.**

Male sex organ, in allusion to its lack of an endoskeleton . . . **Boneless fish; Boneless beef; Boneless stiff.**

Male sex organ, regarded as a dangler . . . **Dingle-dangle.**

Male sex organs . . . Virilia.

Male sex organs, conceived as so much flesh . . . **Pound of flesh.**

Male sex organs, external and internal . . . Arrhenidia.

Male sex organs, licking of . . . Medolingus; Virilingus.

Male sex organs . . . See also under *Penis, Phallus, Membrum virile,* etc.

Male sex, peculiar to or characteristic of the . . . Idiorrhenic.

Male sexual act, sell the; said of an attractive man who sells the favor to needy women . . . **Hawk one's brawn.**

Male sexual partner in his usual superimposed posture . . . **Flesh blanket.**

Male sexually impotent . . . **Mule.**

Male who achieves the seminal spurt through necking . . . Sarmassophil.

Male who derives sexual pleasure from the exhibition of his genitalia, esp. to members of the opposite sex . . . **Dangler;** Exhibitionist.

Male who discharges the semen at the first embrace of the vagina, in allusion to an actor who snaps his cues and speaks too soon . . . **Cue snapper.**

Male who engages in sexual play with two women at the same time, or with one in the presence of another . . . Bigynist.

Male who enjoys pretended resistance on the part of the female . . . Pseudorapist.

Male who falls short of being a satisfactory phallator because of, the usual, penile rubberiness . . . **Fumbler.**

Male who frequents brothels, loves whores, etc. . . . **Gentleman of the road.**

Male who has sexual contact with female children . . . **Bearskin robber.**

Male who has sexual intercourse with a female animal . . . **Sheepherder;** ZOOERAST.

Male who has sexual intercourse with a female corpse . . . NECROCOITANT; **Pork packer.**

Male who has sexual intercourse with a female per rectum . . . ANORAST.

Male who has sexual intercourse with an animal . . . ZOOPHALLIST.

Male who impregnates many females and, hence, causes their mammae to be large or "made" . . . **Bust maker.**

Male who insists on absolute nudity, for himself and his playmate, during sexual intercourse . . . **Buffinger.**

Male who introduces his phallus into the mouth of another . . . FELLATRANT.

Male who is a pudendal artist and satisfying phallator . . . **Good fellow.**

Male who is a woman's dupe, because of phallic demands . . . **Cully.**

Male who is clumsy with his phallus at the female putting hole . . . **Groper.**

Male who is especially erotic about females while they menstruate; one who phallates a menstruant . . . MENSOPHILIST.

Male who is in sexual concourse . . . **Up-and-downer;** COITANT; PARACOITUS.

Male who licks the anus of a female, for his own pleasure . . . **Fart sucker.**

Male who licks the female arse, including the anus . . . **Bum sucker.**

Male who marries a child-bride . . . **Kentucky cradle snatcher; Bearskin robber; Kid napper; Kid walloper; Kidskin stretcher; Chicken thief; Chick fancier; Kindergarten butcher; Baby porker.**

Male who phallates between the approximated breasts of a female . . . MASTOPHALLATOR; **Titty-bugger.**

Male who phallates out of wedlock . . . **Leg lifter.**

Male who pounces digitally upon his female's breasts, at the first, and any other, opportunity . . . **Brisket swarmer.**

Male who prefers to have sexual intercourse while standing . . . STASOPHALLIST.

Male who prefers to have sexual intercourse with a woman who is fully dressed . . . ENDYTOPHALLIST.

Male who repeats the coital act after a negligible intermission . . . **Curtain taker.**

Male who rubs against females, esp. against their jutting prominences, in crowded public places, as in a subway . . . FROTTEUR.

Male who rubs against the buttocks of desirable females in crowded public places . . . **Bum-brusher.**

Male who seeks, or actually has, sexual concourse with a girl who is under the age of menstruation . . . PREMENACMIST.

Male who sucks his own phallus . . . **Automatic muzzle loader;** AUTOFELLATOR.

Male who suffers frequent attacks of gonorrhea . . . **Clapster.**

Male who takes the penis of another into his mouth to give it oral satisfaction . . . FELLATOR.

Male whose phallus is cut off or shot off . . . **Bobtail.**

Male whose phallus is shorter than his scrotum . . . **Rantallion.**

Male whose phallus is shot off . . . **D.S.O.**

Male whose sexual pleasure is derived chiefly from sexual stimulation, by a female, short of the orgasm, as by exposure and denial of desirable feminine parts, manual teasing, etc. . . . CONTRARIATOR.

Male with an erected phallus . . . **Spiked male.**

Male with small genital organs . . . MICROGENITALUS.

Male . . . See also under *Man.*

Males, scarcity of; as in a particular region . . . SPANERIA.

Males . . . See also under *Men.*

MAMMA . . . The female breast; the milk-producing organ of the female.

MAMMALINGUS . . . The erotic titillation of the female breast with the lips and/or tongue; the erotic suckling of the female breast. (Ex *mamma* & *lingua.*)

Man and maid in bed beating the mattress with her buttocks . . . **Four legs in bed.**

Man living on the earnings of a harlot's pudendal bread-winner . . . **Cunt-pensioner.**

Man lying between two receptive females . . . **Sandwich.**

Man recently married to a provocative female . . . **All-night man.**

Man who begets a child outside of wedlock, and owns up to it . . . **Honest injun.**

Man who bunks with another man's mistress . . . **Brother starling.**

Man who has sexual intercourse with a female animal . . . **Sheepherder;** ZOOERAST.

Man who hates women . . . MISOGYNIST.

Man who likes his females fat . . . **Fat fancier.**

Man whose pants fly is under pressure from behind for the release of its menacing inmate upon the female interlabial sanctum . . . **Hot fly.**

Man with large phallus, regarded as a scourge of the vulva . . . **Butt smasher.**

Man . . . See also under *Male.*

Manager(ess) of a vulvar brokerage or brothel . . . **Buttock-broker.**

Maneuver a female into a genital spread eagle . . . **Take for a ride.**

Manifestation of sexual desire . . . EROTISM.

Man-like woman; masculine woman . . . GYNANDER.

Man's man . . . A male homosexual.

Manual excitation of the penis before normal coitus to enable a lethargic male to complete the act . . . **Warm-up.**

Manual induction of orgasm in the male, by the spouse; as in infirmity . . . TRIBORGASMIA.

MANUAL PREFERENCE . . . The inclination of a married man with pudendal privileges to resort to manual masturbation.

MANUSTUPRATION . . . Manual masturbation, usually in the male. Ex *manus* (hand) & *stuprare* (to defile).

MANUXORATE . . . Of the male, to make the hand serve as a wife. Ex *manus* (hand) & *uxor* (wife).

Marital life without sexual relations, by consent between husband and wife . . . AGENOBIOSIS.

MARITATE . . . Of the female, to masturbate by manual stimulation of the vulva. Ex *maritus* (husband), in allusion to the succedaneous role of the hand.

MARITOCRATIC . . . Dominated by the husband. Ex *maritus* (husband) & *kratein* (to rule).

Marriage between children, as practiced among the Hindus . . . HARAMAITISM.

Marriage between close relatives, who may not marry legally . . . INCEST.

Marriage between members of markedly different races . . . MISCEGENATION.

Marriage between Negroes and whites, esp. in the United States . . . MISCEGENATION.

Marriage broker, in allusion to the matching of pudenda . . . **Buttock-broker.**

Marriage, dislike or hatred of . . . MISOGAMY.

Marriage, faithfulness in . . . HEREISM.

Marriage, fear of, esp. on the part of a female, because of coital apprehension . . . GAMOPHOBIA.

Marriage involving spouses of markedly unequal ages, esp. one in which the female is much younger . . . ANISONOGAMIA.

Marriage involving spouses of nearly equal age . . . ISONOGAMIA.

Marriage, joys of . . . **JOIES DE MARIAGE.**

Marriage license, properly executed, as a permit for the pudendal symphony . . . **Imprimatur.**

Marriage, occurring after . . . POSTCONNUBIAL; POSTMARITAL.

Marriage, occurring before . . . PREMARITAL.

Marriage of a man to more than one woman at the same time, usually without the sanction of custom or law . . . POLYGAMY.

Marriage of a man to more than one woman at the same time, when sanctioned by law or custom . . . POLYGYNY.

Marriage of a woman to more than one man at the same time, usually without the sanction of custom or law . . . POLYGAMY.

Marriage of a woman to more than one man at the same time, when sanctioned by law . . . POLYANDRY.

Marriage, person who hates . . . MISOGAMIST.

Marriage with one spouse at a time, custom or practice of . . . MONOGAMY.

Marriageable, usually with regard to age; applied to a girl . . . NUBILE.

Marriageable, with regard to sexual maturity; said of a female . . . MULIPEPANTIC.

Married; in allusion to the relatively permanent union . . . **Hard-soldered.**

Married woman, go after or visit amorously a; when he's away . . . **Go uncling.**

Marry . . . **To tie a knot with the tongue that cannot be undone with the teeth.**

Marry . . . **Altar it; Merge; Drop anchor; Get exclusive rights to; Get parsoned; Get signed up; Pool interests; Take an option on; Sign a long term lease; Get a life sentence.**

Marry . . . To enter into more or less permanent sexual relations with a homosexual partner.

Marry a previously married woman . . . **Play second fiddle.**

Marry a woman whom one has phallated extramaritally . . . **Make an honest woman of.**

Marry; in allusion to the exclusive pudendal rights obtained thereby with reference to a particular female . . . **Get a monopoly on; Get a permanent.**

Marry; said of a wencher who kept his phallus busy before the marital tintinnabulation . . . **Hang up the ladle.**

MASCHALAGNIA . . . Lust aroused by the sight or contemplation of the female axilla; sexual desire for the female axilla. Ex *maschale* (armpit) & *lagneia* (lust).

MASCHALINGUS . . . The erotic licking of the axilla of a girl. From *maschale* (armpit) & *lingua* (tongue).

MASCHALOPHALLATION . . . Phallation in which the male organ is reciprocated in the female axilla.

MASCHALOPHILEMIA . . . The derivation of sexual pleasure from kissing the female axilla. Ex *maschale* (armpit) & *philema* (a kiss).

MASCHALOPHILOUS . . . Of the male, especially erotic about the female's armpits. Ex *maschale* (axilla) & *philein* (to love).

Masculine characteristics, deprive of . . . EMASCULATE; EVIRATE.

Masculine characteristics in a female, development of . . . MASCULINIZATION; VIRILIZATION.

Masculine characteristics in a female, presence of . . . MASCULINOSIS; VIRILISM.

Masculine manners, adoption of, by a woman . . . VIRIMIMISM.

Masculine type of homosexuality . . . COMMASCULATION.

Masculine woman . . . GYNANDER.

MASOCHISM . . . The derivation of sexual pleasure or gratification from subjection to humiliating or cruel treatment, esp. at the hands of one of the opposite sex. Ex the name of a novelist (Leopold von Sacher-*Masoch*) who described it.

Masochism, active member in . . . MASTIX.

Masochism, form of, in which the subject derives sexual pleasure from being rendered helpless by tying with a rope . . . MERINTHOLAGNIA.

Masochism, form of, in which the subject imagines himself to be a page or a servant of a beautiful woman . . . PAGEISM.

Masochism in a female homosexual, gratifiable by a sapphosadist . . . SAPPHOMASOCHISM.

Masochism, passive member in . . . MASOCHIST.

MASOCHIST . . . The recipient of the cruelty in masochism.

Masochist, female, who is also a homosexual . . . SAPPHOMASOCHIST.

Masochistic submissiveness to one's wife . . . UXORIOSIS.

Mason . . . A female homosexual who, in the act of tribadism or the like, takes the part of a male in normal coitus.

Master vein . . . The pudendum muliebre; the vagina.

Masterpiece . . . From the concupiscent viewpoint of the male, the interfemoral sanctum muliebre.

Masterpiece of night work . . . A very attractive whore.

MASTILAGNIA . . . The derivation of sexual pleasure from the act of being whipped; the desire to be whipped in order to enjoy erotic pleasure. From *mastizo* (whip) & *lagneia* (lust).

MASTIX . . . A female sadist. Ex *mastix* (whip).

MASTOFACT . . . The female breast as a sexual fetish.

MASTOPHALLATE . . . To reciprocate the phallus erectus between the approximated breasts of the female.

MASTOPHALLATOR . . . A male who prefers to, and does, phallate between the breasts of a woman.

MASTOPHRENIA . . . Preoccupation with thoughts of the female breasts.

MASTOS . . . The Greek form for the female breast.

MASTUNCULI . . . Small, underdeveloped breasts. Ex *mastos* (breast) & *unculus* (diminutive).

Masturbate . . . **Jerk off; Rub off; Pull oneself off; Whank off; Beat down; Milk off.**

Masturbate . . . **Frig off; Bring down by hand; Cheat the census; Spill one's beans.**

Masturbate . . . **Flog the donkey; Flog one's mutton; Flog the bishop; Flog the old whipping-boy.**

Masturbate a man's phallus manually; said of a manual prostitute . . . **Shake the hand of a stranger.**

Masturbate; an allusion to the waste of the jelly . . . **Sling one's jelly.**

Masturbate by directing a stream of water, as from a rubber hose, upon the clitoris, introitus vaginae, etc. . . . RHEOMIZ.

Masturbate by manual stimulation; of a female, in allusion to her "fiddle" . . . **Fret one's fiddle strings.**

Masturbate by rubbing the crossed thighs against each other in a motion resembling walking, to stimulate the compressed genitalia; said of females . . . SYNTRIBATE.

Masturbate by stimulating the phallus with the hand . . . MANUXORATE; MANUSTUPRATE.

Masturbate by stimulating the vulva with the hand . . . MARITATE.

Masturbate by using the fingers, or a finger, as a phallus . . . **Finger fuck.**

Masturbate, esp. by the hand of a female . . . **Buff the dog.**

Masturbate; in allusion to a piston-in-cylinder action . . . **Pump oneself off.**

Masturbate; in allusion to a reduction in phallic stature . . . **Take down.**

Masturbate; in allusion to monastics, to whom such diversions are proverbially attributed . . . **Box the Jesuit and get cockroaches.**

Masturbate; in allusion to the standard explanation offered by boys surprised in the act, that they were merely playing . . . **Play off; Play with oneself.**

Masturbate manually . . . **Wriggle off.**

Masturbate manually; of the male . . . **Bat off.**

Masturbate with the aid of an artificial phallus . . . OLISBONATE.

Masturbating device, used by women, composed of an improvised penis and, usually, testicles . . . DILDO; GODEMICHE; OLISBOS.

Masturbating with both hands . . . **With both sheets fore.**

Masturbation by the hand, esp. chronic and, usually, excessive . . . CHIROMANIA.

Masturbation, chronic . . . MASTURBISM.

Masturbation; conceived as a bachelor's lot . . . **Bachelor's fare.**

Masturbation; conceived as a doing to oneself . . . IPSATION.

Masturbation, disorder resulting from mental conflict and frustration incident to . . . MASTURBOSIS.

Masturbation, esp. chronic and excessive, conceived as a dominating habit . . . IPSISM.

Masturbation, frustration neurosis resulting from indulgence in . . . MASTURBOPHRENIA.

Masturbation; in allusion to the Latin *fricare,* to rub . . . **Frigging.**

Masturbation in the female effected by crossing the legs and rubbing the adducted thighs against each other, thus titillating the genitalia . . . SYNTRIBADISM.

Masturbation in the female effected by directing a stream of water, as from a rubber hose, upon the various parts of the vulva . . . RHEOMISM.

Masturbation in the female effected by rubbing the genitalia with the hand . . . MARITATION.

Masturbation in the female effected by the use of a device resembling a penis and scrotum . . . OLISBONISM.

Masturbation in the male . . . MENTULOMANIA; MANUXORISM; MANUSTUPRATION.

Masturbation in the male effected by having the genitalia rubbed and titillated by another person, usually a female . . . TRIBORGASMIA.

Masturbation in the male effected by stimulating the phallus with the hand, the hand being conceived as a "wife" . . . MANUXORISM.

Masturbation, preference for, by a married male with vaginal privileges . . . MANUAL PREFERENCE.

Masturbation prior to a normal session of intercourse, in order to prolong the coit and satisfy the female, by a male who is otherwise an ejaculator praecox . . . **Primer.**

Masturbation regarded as a waste of spermatozoa . . . **Slaughter of the innocent.**

Masturbator, female, who obtains gratification by directing a stream of water upon her genitalia . . . RHEOMIST.

MASTURBISM . . . Chronic masturbation, in either sex.

MASTURBOSIS . . . Disorder resulting from mental conflict and frustration incident to masturbation.

Maternity clothes . . . CYESTHES.

Matrimonial peacemaker . . . The unmitigated phallus erectus.

Matrimonial polka . . . Sexual concourse in the conventional manner and posture.

MATRINCEST . . . Sexual intercourse between a mother and her son. From *mater* (mother) & *incestus* (sinful).

MATROLAGNIA . . . Sexual love of a son for his mother. Ex *mater* (mother) & *lagneia* (lust).

MATRONORAPTUS . . . Rape by force involving a married woman. Ex *matrona* (married woman) & *raptus* (a violent attack).

MATRORAPTUS . . . Rape by force involving one's own mother. Ex *mater* (mother) & *raptus* (a violent attack).

Mattress jig . . . The pudendal duet resulting from a meeting of four bare feet in bed.

MATUTOLAGNIA . . . Morning lustiness. Ex *matutinus* (pert. to morning) & *lagneia* (lust).

MATUTORTHOSIS . . . A morning erection, usually due to fullness of the bladder. Ex *matutinus* (pert. to morning) & *orthosis* (a making straight).

Mawkes . . . A saleslady who sells short term leases to her own interlabial cranny.

MAZANTHOSIS . . . 1. The blossoming out of the female breasts at puberty. 2. Puberty in the female symbolized by the development of the breasts. Ex *mazos* (breast) & *anthos* (flower).

MAZAUXESIS . . . Overdevelopment of the female breasts. Ex *mazos* (breast) & *auxesis* (increase).

MAZECTENIA . . . Pendulosity of the female breasts. Ex *mazos* (breast) & *ekteino* (prolong).

MAZMASSATE . . . To do to the female breasts, with the male hands, what comes naturally. Ex *mazos* (breast) & *massein* (to knead).

MAZOCENTRIC . . . Of the male, centering the sex interest upon the female breasts. Ex *mazos* (breast).

Mazonian . . . A female superbly endowed with two, of which an Amazon had but one.

Mazonian . . . One of the titties.

Mazonian supporter . . . Bubby hammock, alias the brassiere.

Mazonians . . . The natives of the brassiere.

MAZOPEROSIS . . . The amputation of the female breast by a fiend, either as an expression of sadism or as an act of vengeance. Ex *mazos* (breast) & *peros* (maimed).

MAZOPHALLIST . . . A male who jiggles his phallus in the intermammary space.

MAZOPHILOUS . . . Of a male, especially erotic about the female breasts. Ex *mazos* (breast) & *philein* (to love).

MAZORHICNOSIS . . . The shriveling of the female breast with age. Ex *mazos* (breast) & *rhiknosis* (a shriveling).

Meager seminal ejaculation . . . OLIGOBLYSIS.

Meat . . . The male pound of flesh, esp. the shaft.

Meat . . . The erotically appetizing flesh of a female.

Meat pecker . . . The phallus as the pecker of the female pudendum.

MEDOLALIA . . . Obscene language involving the phallus. Ex *medos* (phallus) & *lalein* (babble).

MEDOLINGUS . . . The erotic licking of the penis. Ex *medos* (penis) & *lingo* (lick).

MEGAMASTOUS . . . Of a female, having more than ample breasts.

MEMBRUM VIRILE . . . The masculine genital limb.

Membrum virile, as a jovial sinker . . . **Merry-go-down.**

Membrum virile, conceived as conductor of the pudendal orchestra in coitus . . . **Baton.**

Membrum virile erectum . . . **Live rabbit.**

Membrum virile erectum, as an adorable rogue . . . **Bit of stiff.**

Membrum virile, in allusion to its "knock-upability" . . . **Knocker.**

Membrum virile prostratum . . . **Dead rabbit.**

Membrum virile . . . See also under *Penis, Phallus,* etc.

Men, dislike of, by a woman . . . APANDRY.

Men, fear of, by a woman . . . ANDROPHOBIA.

Men, hatred of, by a woman . . . MISANDRY.

Men, woman excessively fond of . . . PHILANDRIST.

Men, woman who dislikes or hates . . . MISANDRIST.

Men . . . See also under *Males.*

Menopausal hot flushes or "flashes" . . . MENOTHERMAE.

Menopause, artificially induced; as by surgery . . . MENOPHENIA.

Menopause, difficult or prolonged . . . DYSMENOTELIA.

Menopause, early onset of . . . PROMENOTELIA.

Menopause, easy and painless . . . EUMENOTELIA.

Menopause starting late in life . . . OPSIMENOTELIA.

Menses, fear of the onset of . . . MENOPHOBIA.

Menses, late onset of, during a particular month . . . OPSIMENIA.

Menses, male who is especially erotic about females during their . . . MENSOPHILIST.

MENSOPHILIST . . . A male who is especially erotic about, and wishes to phallate, females during their menstrual periods. Ex *menses* & *philein* (to love).

Menstrual activity, time of beginning of, at puberty . . . MENARCHE.

Menstrual activity, time of cessation; in middle age . . . CLIMACTERIC; MENOPAUSE; MENOTELIA.

Menstrual activity, years of a woman's life during which she exhibits . . . MENACME.

Menstrual bleeding from the mouth . . . STOMATOMENIA.

Menstrual flow, decrease in the quantity of . . . HYPOMENORRHEA.

Menstrual flow having an especially disagreeable odor . . . BROMOMENORRHEA.

Menstrual flow, increase in the quantity of . . . MENORRHAGIA.

Menstrual flow, medicine or procedure which stimulates . . . EMMENAGOGUE.

Menstrual flow prolonged beyond normal duration . . . MENOSTAXIS.

Menstrual odor, having the characteristic . . . MENOSMIAL.

Menstrual period marked by the usual symptoms but without a visible flow of blood . . . XEROMENIA; CRYPTOMENORRHEA; **Dry run.**

Menstruate; in allusion to the danger flag . . . **Fly the flag.**

Menstruate; in allusion to the inaccessibility . . . **Flash the red flag.**

Menstruation, absence of . . . AMENORRHEA.

Menstruation, announcement regarding onset of, by menstruant . . . **Captain is at home; I have friends to stay; My little friend has come.**

Menstruation, delay in start of; in a girl at puberty . . . EMANSIO MENSIUM; OPSIMENOPHANIA.

Menstruation, delay in start of, in a particular month . . . OPSIMENIA.

Menstruation, fear of, usually because of attendant pain . . . MENOPHOBIA.

Menstruation, medical term for . . . CATAMENIA.

Menstruation, period in woman's life during which she has . . . MENACME.

Mental depression resulting from loss of virginity . . . HYMENOPENTHY.

Mental disorder resulting from lack of association and/or intercourse with women . . . AMULIEROSIS.

Mental disorder resulting from lack of satisfaction in one's sex life . . . APHALLATOSIS.

Mental picture of a more exciting coital partner, fabricated by one of the participants in sexual concourse, to enhance the pleasure of the act . . . EUGENICON.

MENTULA . . . The membrum virile, in allusion to Mentu, the god of reproduction.

MENTULAGRA . . . A persistent and, usually, painful erection. Ex *mentula* (penis) & *agra* (seizure).

MENTULATE . . . Having a massive phallus. Ex *mentula* (penis) and a modicum of ignorance.

MENTULATE . . . Of the active female member in tribadism, provided with an artificial phallus. Ex *mentula* (penis) & *-ate* (suffix designating person having the part indicated).

MENTULOMANIA . . . Preoccupation with thoughts and manipulations of the penis; masturbation. Ex *mentula* (penis) & *mania*.

MENTULOMANIA . . . 1. Masturbation in the male. 2. Excessive sexual desire in a female. Ex *mentula* (penis) & *mania*.

MENTULOPHRENIA . . . Preoccupation with thoughts of the male organ, usually by a female. Ex *mentula* (penis) & *phren* (mind).

MENTULOPHRENIAC . . . A nymphomaniac with persistent thoughts of the membrum virile erectum.

MERINTHOLAGNIA . . . A form of masochism in which the subject derives sexual pleasure from being rendered helpless by tying with a rope. From *merinthos* (cord) & *lagneia* (lust).

MEROPHILOUS . . . Of the male, especially erotic about the female thigh. Ex *meros* (thigh) & *philein* (to love).

MERPHALLATE . . . To wigwag the phallus between the approximated thighs (of a female). Ex *meros* (thigh) & *phallate*.

MERPHALLATION . . . A form of sexual intercourse in which the phallus is reciprocated between the adducted thighs, usually of the female.

Merry bit . . . The jovial tool of a young female who lets it be used by favorite phalli, for art's sake, not directly for shekels, sugar, or brass. Also, the bearer of the mirthful nether orifice.

Merry bout . . . A bout between heterosexual pudenda.

Merry circle . . . The wide, wide open pudendum muliebre.

Merry go-down . . . The mirthful sinking of the male sinker. Also, the sinker.

Merry go, the . . . The jig of the male piston in the female cylinder.

Merry go-up . . . A phallic uprising that will be pudenally assuaged.

Merry legs . . . Female legs willing to spread for the male juggernaut.

Merry-legs . . . A prostitute who enjoys her work.

Merry Magdalen . . . 1. An amorous girl with a zest for the better things in life, and a matching pudendum. 2. A harlot.

Merry maker . . . The functional membrum virile.

Merry-arsed Christian . . . A female who, not of the goodness of heart, but for the benefit of her purse, loosens her pudendal strings, for paying phalli.

Mesopotamia . . . The region of the female between the urethra and the rectum, in allusion to the ancient country situated between the Tigris and the Euphrates.

MESOSEINIA . . . The region between the female breasts; line of cleavage. Ex *mesos* (middle) & *sein* (breast).

Mespot . . . The vulva of a slattern whore.

Mess . . . Of a male working over a female, to palpate the mammae and/or the pudendal messhall.

Messpot . . . Same as **Mespot,** a "messy" vulva.

MICROGENITALA . . . Female with small genital organs.

MICROGENITALUS . . . A male with small genital organs.

Midgies . . . A pair of gnatlike, in size, female breasts.

Milk . . . The kindness of the female pudendum; access to the cleft underside of the female; ass.

Milk of female kindness . . . The stare of assent emanating from the female pudendum.

Milk off . . . To relieve the male pudendal "udder" of its unexpended cream by the manual induction of the orgastic labor.

Milt . . . What the male parts with, phallically, at the height of the sexual paroxysm.

Milt market . . . 1. The female part that makes the male's milt flow. 2. Female pudenda regarded as a product in commerce.

Mimpins . . . Female breasts, the young and the beautiful.

Minge . . . 1. Women as female society. 2. The female bilabial trump card.

Minikin . . . 1. The female as a lush phallic tickling target. 2. The part most likely to be tickled.

MISANDRIST . . . A female hater of men.

MISANDRY . . . Hatred or dislike of men by a female. Ex *misein* (to hate) & *aner* (man).

MISCEGENATION . . . Marriage between members of markedly different races, as, in the United States, between Negroes and whites. Ex *miscere* (to mix) & *genus* (race).

MISOGAMIST . . . A person who hates marriage. From *misein* (to hate) & *gamos* (marriage).

MISOGAMY . . . Dislike or hatred of marriage. Ex *misein* (to hate) & *gamos* (marriage).

MISOGYNIST . . . A male who hates women. Ex *misein* (to hate) & *gyne* (woman).

MISOGYNY . . . Hatred of women, by a male. From *misein* (to hate) & *gyne* (woman).

Miss Moreish . . . A girl who, if tasted, or even if not, gives the male a more-of-her-ish feeling.

Mistake one's maid's bed for that of one's wife . . . **Stumble at the truckle bed.**

Mistress, conceived as a belly comfort . . . **Belly plaster.**

Mistress, conceived as a convenient pudendal appliance . . . **Conveniency; Convenient.**

Mistress, conceived as a financial dependent . . . **Kept woman; Keptive; Keptie.**

Mistress, conceived as a joy-mare . . . **Jomer.**

Mistress, conceived as a laying bird . . . **Laydybird; Ladybird.**

Mistress, conceived as a luxury . . . **Fancy woman.**

Mistress, conceived as a spouse of a celibate male . . . **Bachelor's wife.**

Mistress, conceived as a wife of sorts ... **Left-handed wife.**

Mistress, conceived as an added comfort ... **Side dish.**

Mistress, conceived as an impermanent wife ... **Wife in water colors.**

Mistress, conceived as an unorthodoxy ... **Doxy; Doxey.**

Mistress, entrenched, having the impudence of a lawfully wedded ... **Comfortable impudence.**

Mistress, esp. of a married man, conceived as a "just in case" accessory ... **Sparerib.**

Mistress, esp. one kept happy and in line by means of valuable rewards ... **Buttered bun.**

Mistress, in allusion to a common explanation ... **Niece.**

Mistress, man who sleeps with another man's ... **Brother starling.**

Mistress, provided with a; in allusion to the easily dissolvable union ... **Soft-soldered.**

Mistress, provided with the comforts of a ... **Hooked up.**

Mistress, share one's, with another man ... **Sail in the same boat.**

Mistress verging on a whore ... **Dolly.**

Mistress who is a shade whiter than a whore ... **Blower.**

Mixed blood, of ... **Belonging to the blue squadron.**

MIXOSCOPIA ... The derivation of sexual pleasure or gratification from watching others in the act of intercourse. Ex *mixis* (intercourse) & *skopein* (observe).

Mock wedding ceremony in which participants jump over a broom ... **Broomstick wedding.**

Mock wedding, go through ceremony of, by jumping over a broom ... **Jump the besom; Jump the broomstick.**

Modest quencher ... A small but not ineffective membrum virile.

Modicum ... The female genital suite.

Moey ... The female inlet for the male outlet.

Mogue ... Of a prostitute with a male on top, to keep the phallus oscillating outside of the labia, often in her fist.

Mohel; performer of ritual circumcision on Jewish infants ... **Foreskin hunter.**

Moko ... An unripe girl shot pudendally out of wedlock, in allusion to a pheasant shot out of season, known by this moniker.

Moko ... A female child presented by a tribal chief or a native potentate to a distinguished male visitor, as the best of all possible offerings for a night of pudendal entertainment, from the viewpoint of local tastes and customs.

Mole ... The genital burrowing organ of the male.

Mole catcher ... The female nether mouth whose warm, poultice-like interior is the catcher of the man's pants "mole."

Mole trap ... Same as **Mole catcher,** only worse.

Molestation motivated by lechery ... GENOCHLESIS.

Molestation of . . . See under the object of molestation, as *Corpse, Children, Infants,* etc.

Moll . . . A female who sells pudendal privileges at average prices, i.e., a run-of-the-mill whore.

Moll hunter . . . A male having whores on his brain; a whoremonger or womanizer.

Moll Peatley . . . A busy and not untalented whore.

Moll Peatley's gig . . . The pudendal mattress dance, in allusion to a storied whore with a phonetically similar (to Peatley) name.

Moll shop . . . A shop, of sorts, for distribution of boughten pudendal privileges, via moll carriers; a brothel.

Molled . . . Taken care of, pudendally, by a whore or by a female pudendal dilettante.

Molly . . . 1. An effeminate male; also, a homo. 2. A backside phallator; sodomite. 3. A female with a charitable pudendum; also, a whore.

Molly's hole . . . Molly's, sir-reverence, best body cavity, quoth the pants worm.

Molly's place . . . In Molly, or in Polly or Dolly, journey's end for the male pants worm.

Molrower . . . A lady's or ladies' man, esp. one who doesn't mind if the lady's a whore.

Money paid a prostitute for a pudendal bull session . . . **Bull money.**

Money paid a prostitute for the use of her pound of flesh . . . **Price of meat.**

Monkey . . . The pudendum muliebre as a funny animal capable of cute tricks.

Monkey bite . . . A libidinous, sucking kiss which leaves an ecchymotic spoor.

MONOGAMIAN FAMILY . . . A form of family based on marriage between single pairs of individuals with exclusive rights to sexual concourse.

MONOGAMY . . . The practice of being married to one spouse at a time; the custom or law which prohibits marriage to more than one spouse at the same time. Ex *monos* (one) & *gamos* (marriage).

Monosyllable . . . The vulva, in allusion to its fancy appellations usually expressed by monosyllables (puss, twat, cunt, etc.).

Monronian . . . Of a young female in the upper brackets of sexual bewitchery, contoured like, and speaking the gluteal sign language of, callimammapygian m.m.

Monronian hip doctrine . . . A nonpolitical theory which holds that the semaphoric oscillations of the posterior female tuberosities are more voluble, and valuable, than a heap of words.

MONS VENERIS . . . The mount of Venus, a rounded prominence anterior to the vulva formed by the symphysis pubis and the overlying pad of fatty tissue.

Mons veneris . . . **Hilltop.**

Mons veneris, undue prominence of . . . MONSEXIS.

Mons veneris; vulva . . . **Mount Pleasant.**

Monsexis . . . The condition marked by undue prominence of the mons veneris. Ex *mons* (mountain) & *existamai* (protrude).

Mood d'amour . . . **Christmas meditations.**

Morning erection, due to fullness of the bladder . . . Matutorthosis; **Pride of the morning.**

Morning lustiness . . . Matutolagnia.

Morning sexual engagement, after a night of sanguine pudendal skirmishes . . . **Kingsley's stand.**

Moses . . . A male bribed to take the blame of seduction actually committed by another.

Mother abbess . . . Female manager of a laying-in house; a bawd.

Mother-aster . . . A mother-inferior or bawd.

Mother damnable . . . The mother-inferior of a brothel.

Mother-inferior . . . The woman in charge of a pudendal exchange or bordello.

Mother midnight . . . The female overseer of a vulvatorium; a brothel manageress.

Mother of the maids . . . The woman in charge of a whoring establishment.

Mother, sexual love of a son for his . . . Matrolagnia; Oedipus Complex.

Mount . . . Of a male, and of a female tribade, to climb upon the female's mons veneris for vaginal intubation (in the former case) or trituration (in the latter).

Mount a female; an allusion to her crotch . . . **Get on the old fork.**

Mount a female for the pudendal jig . . . **Do a mount.**

Mount a female, with the male shillelagh foremost . . . **Slide home.**

Mount a supine female, saber first . . . **Board.**

Mount of Venus . . . **Hilltop.**

Mount Pleasant . . . The female pudendal ensemble, esp. the mount of Venus.

Mount, the . . . The female genital suite, in allusion to the mount of Venus.

Mount the red flag . . . To phallate a menstruating woman.

Mouse . . . The male hole crawler.

Mouse trap . . . The vulva as a trap for the male hole crawler.

Mouser . . . The pudendum muliebre conceived as the huntress of the male **mouse** or organum virile.

Mouth, erotic pleasure derived from activity of . . . Oral eroticism.

Mouth the female genitalia . . . Cunnilinguate; **Play a mouth organ.**

Mouth the female genitalia . . . See also under Cunnilinction; Cunnilinguate, etc.

Mouth wash . . . The phallic lava projected into the oral cavity of a fellator or a fellatrice.

Mouther . . . A person, of either sex, who takes the genitalia of another orally.

Mouth filler . . . A copious seminal spurt in fellatio.

Mouthful . . . A liberal dose of phallic ejaculant given orally, in fellatio.

Mouthpiece . . . The phallus as an oral dose in fellatio.

Mouthpiece . . . The female lower mouth, esp. the space between the labia.

Move legs and thighs in erotic restlessness; said of a female being phallated . . . **Buck one's stumps.**

Movement of female body which arouses sexual desire in the male . . . LAGNEKINESIS.

Muck . . . To caress the female intimates avidly but not well, from her point of view.

Muff . . . The pudendum muliebre and, principally, its warm inlet, in allusion to the sleeve-like covering used to keep the hands warm.

Muff diving . . . The act of kissing, sucking, or licking the feminine parts within the labia majora.

Mulatto whore or variant thereof . . . **Brown cow.**

Mule . . . A genitally sterile male; an impotent male.

MULIANTHIUM . . . A sexually desirable part of a girl. Ex *mulier* (woman) & *anthos* (flower).

MULIEBRATION . . . The assumption of female characteristics by a male. Ex *mulier* (woman).

MULIEBRIA . . . The female sex organs. Ex *mulier* (woman).

MULIEBRITY . . . 1. The state of being a woman. 2. Female sex characteristics, collectively.

MULIPEPANTIC . . . Sexually mature; said of the female. Ex *mulier* (woman) & *pepon* (ripe).

Mumble-peg . . . The coital ensemble of the female.

Muscle activity, sexual pleasure derived from or associated with . . . MUSCLE EROTICISM.

MUSCLE EROTICISM . . . Sexual pleasure derived from or associated with muscular activity.

MUST . . . Extreme sexual urgency, in allusion to the erotic frenzy of male elephants.

Mutilation of a female in jealous retaliation . . . PEROGYNIA.

Muzzle loading . . . The act of irrumation, i.e., the introduction of the phallus into the mouth of another, for oral stimulation and gratification.

Muzzle the little man in the boat . . . To titillate lingually or labially the "little man" in the forepart of the female navicula, i.e., the clitoris.

Muzzled bulldog . . . A rampant phallus erectus confined to quarters, behind the zippered safety of the fly, upon insistence of the would-be quarry.

My little friend has come . . . A declaration, to whom it may concern, of a menacmal female, to the effect that her crotch is stained with the monthly claret ooze.

N

Naf . . . 1. To move the phallus erectus to and fro in the female pudendal oubliette. Ex *naf*, to jiggle. 2. The pudendal oubliette.

Naggie . . . The pudendal magnet of the female, conceived with the appellative warmth evoked by most "cute" objects.

Naked, abnormal desire to go about . . . NUDOMANIA.

Naked, be or go about . . . **Air one's pores.**

Naked body, aversion for any . . . GYMNORESPIA.

Naked body, veneration of . . . NUDODULIA.

Naked breasts, practice of going about with; as observed among natives . . . GYMNOMASTIA.

Naked penis, i.e., without a condom . . . GYMNOPHALLUS.

Naked penis, sexual intercourse with a; i.e., without a condom . . . GYMNOPHALLATION.

Naked person, fear of any . . . GYMNOPHOBIA.

Naked, sexual pleasure derived from going about . . . NUDEROTISM.

Nakedness, abnormal interest in . . . GYMNOPHILY.

Nakedness, devotion to, as a cult . . . GYMNOSOPHY.

Nakedness, in allusion to the garb of angels . . . **Angel's suit.**

Nakedness of opposite sex, erotic pleasure derived from observing . . . GYMNOLAGNIA; GYMNOSCOPY.

Nakedness . . . See also under *Nude, Nudity*, etc.

Nameless crime . . . Sexual perversion of unspecified character, generally homosexualism in either the male or the female.

Nance . . . A male homosexual.

Nancy . . . Same as **Nance,** a male homosexual.

NAOSIPHILOUS . . . Especially erotic about the vulva; said of the male who regards the basic ornament of the female as her temple. Ex *naos* (temple) & *philein* (to love).

Nap the kid . . . To become pregnant.

NARCISSISM . . . 1. Sexual desire directed toward one's own body. 2. Erotic desire stimulated by contemplation of one's own body. Ex

Narkissos, a youth, in Greek mythology, who pined away loving his own reflection in a spring.

Natal fever . . . The ardent desire to go through the pudendal motions incident to procreation.

Naughty, the . . . That part of Jill which makes Jack lose his phallic decorum—her vulva.

Navis . . . The boat-shaped figure formed by the slightly abducted labia majora and the intervening chasm.

NEANILAGNIA . . . Sexual desire for young girls. Ex *neanikos* (youthful) & *lagneia* (lust).

NEANIROSIS . . . Sexual craving for young girls. From *neanias* (girl), *eros* (sexual love), & *osis* (condition).

Neck amorously by digital palpation of the female characteristics . . . SARMASSATE.

Neck, female, especially erotic about the . . . TRACHELOPHILOUS.

Necking, female having an aversion for . . . SARMASSOPHOBE.

Necking, fondness for; by either the male or the female . . . SARMASSOPHILIA.

Necking in the hallway after a date, by young people . . . **Bell polishing.**

Necking, male especially erotic about; more so than most of his fraters . . . SARMASSOPHIL.

Neckline, low, exposing the acclivity of the breasts and the intervening linear or Y-shaped demarcation . . . **Bubby trap.**

NECROCHLESIS . . . The molestation of a corpse, esp. that of a female. Ex *nekros (corpse)* & *ochleo* (molest).

NECROCOITANT . . . A male who has sexual intercourse with a female corpse. From *nekros* (dead) & *coitus.*

NECROPHILISM . . . Sexual attraction to a female corpse. Ex *nekros* (dead) & *philein* (to love).

NECROPHILIST . . . A male who is attracted sexually to a female corpse.

Necrophilist . . . **Pork packer.**

NECROSADISM . . . The derivation of sexual gratification from the act of beating or mutilating a female corpse. From *nekros* (dead body) & *sadism.*

Needle trouble . . . The difficulty experienced by a desirous but slightly impotentiated male in trying to put the needle in the groove.

Negress and white male, offspring of coitus between . . . **Blue skin.**

Negress, attractive, as pudendum . . . **Bit of ebony goodness.**

Negress, erotic tissues of a . . . **Black meat; Dark meat.**

NEOGAMALGIA . . . The coital pains experienced by virgin newlyweds, due to snugness of the introitus vaginae. Ex *neos* (new), *gamos* (marriage), & *algos* (pain).

NEOGAMOSIS . . . Frigidity of newly married women.

NEOLAGNIA . . . The first appearance of sexual desire in the female. Ex *neos* (new) & *lagneia* (lust).

NEOLAGNIUM . . . The nascence of sexual desire in the male. From *neos* (new) & *lagneia* (lust).

NEPIOCHLESIS . . . The molestation of infants. Ex *nepios* (infant) & *ochleo* (molest).

NEPIOLAGNIA . . . Erotic interest in infants of the opposite sex, as sometimes observed in so-called baby-sitters. Ex *nepios* (infant) & *lagneia* (lust).

NEPIPHTHEROSIS . . . Sexual violation of an infant, usually of the opposite sex, by attempted or modified phallic intromission. Ex *nepios* (infant) & *phtheiro* (violate).

NERVI ERIGENTES . . . The nerves proverbially associated with the erection of the phallus.

Nether mouth . . . In the female, the lower of her two mouths, the one which receives the phallus in orthodox sexual concourse.

Neurosis caused by sexual frustration . . . LIBIDONEUROSIS.

Never out, the . . . The female's most enticing cavity, in allusion to its cornucopial inventory of erotic pleasure.

Newlyweds, coital pains of virgin . . . NEOGAMALGIA.

Niggle . . . To pry open the pudendal fissure of a woman, with the phallic jimmy.

Night of the wedding, when a virgin is initiated phallically . . . **Christening night.**

Night spent in sexual concourse, in allusion to "hump," *q.v.* . . . **Camel night.**

Nightgown, as the gown worn by the female during the nocturnal phallic invasions . . . **Knocking-jacket.**

Nimble-hipped . . . Of a woman, with reference to her reaction to the chopping of the male cleaver, briskly responsive.

Nimrod . . . The male genital shooting iron, as a mighty hunter.

Ninnies . . . A girl's breasts, warmly conceived.

Ninny . . . One of the ninnies, conceived no less warmly than both.

Nipple chaser . . . 1. A whoremonger. 2. A male devoted to the adoration of the female nipples.

Nipple, growth of hair around; in the female . . . THELECOMOSIS.

Nipple, hairs growing around a; in the female . . . THELECOMAE.

Nipple of male or female . . . MAMMILLA.

Nipple, pigmented ring around . . . AREOLA.

Nipples, absence of; esp. in the female . . . ATHELIA.

Nipples, erection of . . . THELORTHIA.

Nipples, erection of, as expression of erotic excitation . . . THELERETHISM.

Nipples, esp. of the female . . . THELIA.

Nipples, female, erotic fingering of . . . THELEMASSATION.

Nipples, female, large and protruding . . . **Titty antlers.**

Nipples, female, licking of, in lovemaking . . . THELELINGUS.

Nipples, imitation, created by attaching small buttons or tufts to the apices of brassiere cups . . . **Brummagem buttons.**

Nipples, prominence of; esp. in the female . . . THELOTHISM.

Nipples, sexual excitation centered in . . . THELERETHISM.

NOCTORTHOSIS . . . Phallic erection occurring during the night.

Nocturne . . . A genital skirmish at night, conceived as a pudendal even song.

Nocturne . . . A female who sells pudendal privileges; a whore.

Nola . . . A male homosexual.

Nom de eune . . . The assumed name under which a harlot practices her profession, in allusion to the scene of the "crime," the bed.

NOMAVALENT . . . Of the male, sexually impotent in the usual environment or under normal conditions, as in one's home (but often potent elsewhere, as in a hotel). Ex *nomos* (law; the usual thing), *a* (not), & *valere* (to be able).

NONACCESS . . . Lack of opportunity for sexual intercourse, esp. between husband and wife.

Nookie . . . Sexual concourse as a cozy nuzzling of the pudenda.

Northern hemispheres . . . The pectoral prominences of the female.

Not a shot in the locker . . . 1. Phallated to complete exhaustion; said of the male. 2. No longer able to toughen the boneless appendage; impotent.

Not much bottle . . . Of the vagina, (having) little embrace pressure, because relaxed, as in a parous or well-phallated female.

NOTOPHILOUS . . . Of the male, especially erotic about the female's back. Ex *noton* (back) & *philein* (to love).

Novelty, the . . . The female's central orifice, of the three below, from viewpoint of a pudendal novice.

NUBILE . . . Fit for marriage, as with regard to age; applied to girls.

NUBILITY . . . Of females, fitness to marry, as with regard to age. Ex *nubere* (to marry).

Nude, completely, down to pubic feathers . . . **Down to buckle and bare thong.**

Nude, person who likes to watch others in the . . . VOYEUR.

Nude, sleeping in the; practice of or obsession with . . . HYPNUDISM.

Nudist, live the life of a; of the male . . . **Have Jack out of doors.**

Nudist, pretty female . . . **Cuticle cutie.**

Nudists' march . . . **Dangle parade.**

Nudity, female, exposed; in allusion to the encouraging effect it has on a potent male genital shaft . . . **Bracer.**

Nudity . . . See also under *Naked, Nakedness,* etc.

Nun . . . A woman who presses her pudendum into service, to make a living for her.

Nun . . . A female who limits her pudendal activities to urinating.

Nurse a private worry . . . Of the female, to have an itch in or around the vulva, esp. while in the company of others.

Nymphe du Pavé . . . A girl of the streets; a harlot.

Nymphet . . . A sub- or barely-teen-age girl whose nascent muliebral charms inflame the libido of mid-dle-aged males.

Nymphomania . . . An abnormally intense sexual desire as it occurs in the female.

Nymphomania, in allusion to a figurative itching of the vulva . . . **Cunt-itch.**

Nymphomaniac . . . A female whose sexual appetite is abnormally in-tense. Ex *nympha* (labium minus) & *mania* (madness).

Nymphomaniac with obsessive thoughts of the male genital orga-non, var. erectus . . . Mentulophreniac.

O

Oatbin . . . The female pudendal suite as a manger.

Oatmeal . . . Spurting phallic lava.

Oatmeal party . . . A party participated by two or more in which, eventually, there is a serving of phallic meal.

Obscene devices, peddler of; usually a female . . . **Bawdy basket.**

Obscene; in allusion to the spirit of a straight penis . . . ITHYPHALLIC.

Obscene language . . . LAGNOGLOSSY.

Obscene language, craving to use . . . COPROLALOMANIA.

Obscene language, habitual use of . . . LAGNOLALIA.

Obscene language imputing descent from a female canine . . . CATELALIA.

Obscene language involving sexual intercourse . . . COITOLALIA.

Obscene language involving the phallus . . . MEDOLALIA; PHALLOLALIA.

Obscene language involving the vulva . . . CUNNILALIA.

Obscene talk; vulgar language . . . **Bear-garden language.**

Obsessed by thoughts of the female pudendum . . . **Cunny-haunted.**

OBSOLAGNIUM . . . The period of waning sexual desire in males. Ex *obsolescere* (to go out of use) & *lagneia* (lust).

Odor of urine, person deriving sexual pleasure from; esp. from urine voided by one of the opposite sex . . . RENIFLEUR.

Odors, person who is aroused sexually by . . . OSPHRESIOLAGNIAC.

Odors, sexual excitation by . . . OSPHRESIOLAGNIA.

Odors, sexual excitation induced by certain . . . OSMOLAGNIA.

OEDIPUS COMPLEX . . . Sexual love of a son for his mother. Also, an unconscious attachment of a son to his mother accompanied by hostility toward the father. An allusion to a character in Greek legend who married his mother.

OENOLAGNIA . . . Sexual lust induced or enhanced by the drinking of alcoholic beverages, esp. wine. Ex *oinos* (wine) & *lagneia* (lust).

OENOSUGIA . . . The licking or suckling by an erotic male of wine deposited repeatedly by the female upon her nipples.

Offspring, ability to bear, relatively late in life . . . OPSIPROLIGERY.

Offspring, inability to produce . . . STERILITY.

Offspring of coitus between a white male and a Negress . . . **Blue skin.**

Offspring of coitus between white and colored persons collectively . . . **Blue squadron.**

Offspring of white person and mulatto . . . QUADROON.

Offspring of white person and Negro . . . MULATTO.

Offspring of white person and quadroon . . . GRIFFADO; OCTOROON.

Old Adam . . . The male sexual emissary, in allusion to the old sinner.

Old maid, be a chaste . . . **Lead apes in hell.**

Old maid, chaste . . . **Wasted blessing.**

Old maid who is skittish about pudendal subjects . . . **Quail.**

Old maid with, naturally, chaste underbelly . . . **Ape leader.**

Old women, sexual desire for . . . ANILILAGNIA.

OLESBEE . . . In tribadism, the active member who uses an artificial phallus. Ex the ancient Lesbos, where such practices are said to have been common.

OLIGOBLYSIS . . . A meager seminal ejaculation. Ex *oligos* (little) & *blyzo* (spurt out).

OLISBONISM . . . A form of tribadism in which two females rub their sexual organs against each other and the one who plays the role of the male is provided with an artificial penis. From *olisbos* (an artificial penis).

OLISBOS . . . An artificially contrived genital organ of the male, with or without an artifact scrotum, used by females in masturbation and in tribadism. Ex "O' Lesbos" (the ancient city where self-sufficient females are said to have been rampant).

Omission of coitus on the wedding night by a considerate male, to spare his virgin bride the (to her) ordeal . . . **Christian compliment.**

Omnibus . . . The female pleasure cavity, in allusion to its accommodating capacity. Also a whore, and for the same reason.

OMOPHILOUS . . . Of the male, especially erotic about the female's shoulders. Ex *omos* (shoulder) & *philein* (to love).

ONANISM . . . 1. Sexual intercourse in which the phallus is withdrawn from the vagina before ejaculation. 2. Masturbation.

One on top of the other, in a double layer, and doing what comes naturally; of man and maid . . . **Double-banked.**

ONEIROGMUS . . . A seminal ejaculation during one's sleep, resulting from the stimuli of erotic dreams. Ex *oneirogmos.*

Open up . . . Of a female supine in bed, with a male, to open the **gates of hell,** by a spread of the thighs, for the admission of the **devil.**

Open up for the male intrusion . . . **Cleave.**

Open up, refuse to, for the phallic intrusion; said of a recalcitrant or retaliatory female . . . **Say boo to the battledore.**

OPHELIMITY . . . Of the male, the ability to satisfy sexually. Ex *ophelos* (help).

Opposite sex, quality of being attracted to . . . HETEROSEXUALITY.

Opposite sex, the wearing of clothes appropriate for . . . CROSS DRESSING; EONISM; TRANSVESTISM; TRANSVESTITISM.

Oral dose of semen in fellatio . . . **Mouthful.**

ORAL EROTICISM . . . Erotic pleasure derived from or associated with activity of the mouth, as in eating.

ORCHIDOSIPHLATE . . . To sterilize a man by excision of the gonads. Ex *orchis* (testicle) & *siphloo* (cripple).

ORGANOFACT . . . A sexual fetish which is a part of the body, as the hair. Ex *organon* (an organ) & *facere* (make).

Organs of generation, pert. to . . . VENEREAL.

Organs of generation . . . See also under *Male external genitalia, Female genitalia,* etc.

Organum virile, esp. erectum . . . **Joy stick.**

Organum virile . . . See also under *Penis, Phallus,* etc.

ORGASM . . . The moment of paroxysmal gratification at the acme of the sexual act, in the male accompanied by ejaculation of the semen. Ex *orgao* (swell with lust).

Orgasm achieved by the male with the aid of a mental picture of a more desirable female than the one he is phallating . . . ALLORGASMIA.

Orgasm, achievement of, by either the male or the female, but more often the male, in quick time . . . TACHORGASMIA.

Orgasm, achievement of, by the male, after prolonged effort at phallation and with the aid of mental stimulants, as the vision of erotic scenes . . . DYSORGASMIA.

Orgasm, concentrated pleasure of the sexual . . . END PLEASURE.

Orgasm, experience the sexual . . . **Come; Come off.**

Orgasm in the male, incomplete or otherwise unsatisfactory . . . SPHALORGASMY.

Orgasm in the male, manual induction of, by spouse; as in cases of infirmity . . . TRIBORGASMIA.

Orgasm in the male without perceptible ejaculation, providing a measure of gratification less than complete . . . KENORGASMY.

Orgasm, inducing or producing . . . ORGASMOGENIC.

ORGASMOGENIC . . . Inducing or producing the sexual orgasm.

ORGASMOGENOUS . . . Induced by the sexual orgasm, as a pain.

OSMOLAGNIA . . . Sexual excitation induced by certain odors. Ex *osme* (odor) & *lagneia* (lust).

OSPHRESIOLAGNIA . . . The condition in which sexual excitation is produced by odors, as of perfume, perspiration, etc. Ex *osphresis* (sense of smell) & *lagneia* (lust).

OSPHRESIOLAGNIAC . . . A person who is aroused sexually by odors.

Ouch! . . . **Hell! said the duchess when she caught her tits in the mangle.**

Out with a girl . . . **Up in Annie's room.**

Overactivity of the libido . . . HYPERLIBIDINISM.

Overdevelopment of the buttocks . . . HYPERPYGIA.

Overdevelopment of the female breasts . . . HYPERMASTIA.

Overdevelopment of the sex organs, in either the male or the female . . . HYPERGENITALISM.

Own beauty, unfounded belief in one's . . . CALLOMANIA.

Own body, sexual interest directed toward . . . NARCISSISM.

P

PACHYHYMENIA . . . The condition of having a thick and tough hymen. Ex *pachys* (thick) & *hymen.*

Paddle . . . The male genital satisfier.

Paddle . . . Caress amorously, sometimes with the male paddle.

Pads used by actors wearing tight breeches to subdue the outline of the genital paraphernalia . . . **Decencies.**

Pagan . . . A woman who exploits her pudendum by the short lease method; a harlot.

PAGEISM . . . A form of sexual daydreaming in which a male derives sexual pleasure by imagining himself a servant of a beautiful woman.

Pain as a source of sexual pleasure . . . DOLEROS.

Pain, erotic pleasure derived from suffering or inflicting . . . ALGOLAGNIA.

Pain in a testicle, as after a knuckling by the female . . . ORCHIALGIA; **Stone ache.**

Pain in the anus, as after sodomy . . . ANALGIA.

Pain in the buttocks . . . PYGALGIA.

Pain in the clitoris, as after tribadic manipulation . . . CLITORIDALGIA.

Pain in the female breast . . . MASTALGIA.

Pain in the penis . . . PHALLALGIA.

Pain in the rectum, as after phallic intromission . . . RECTALGIA.

Pain in the sex organs, esp. of the female, as after coitus . . . PUDENDALGIA.

Pain in the vagina, as after accepting a prodigious male organon . . . VAGINALGIA.

Painful contraction of the vagina, as before a loathsome phallation . . . VAGINISMUS.

Painful erection of the penis . . . ITHYALGIA.

Painful menstruation . . . DYSMENORRHEA.

Painful sexual intercourse, esp. in a female . . . DYSPAREUNIA.

Painful sexual intercourse, esp. in the male . . . DYSPHALLATION.

Painful sexual intercourse in newlyweds, esp. in newlywed virgins . . . NEOGAMALGIA.

Painful sexual orgasm, in the male... ALGORGASMIA.

Painted Willie . . . A male homosexual.

Painter . . . The membrum virile conceived as a vaginal painter.

PAIZOCENTRIC . . . Centering one's sex interest on the coital foreplay. Ex *paizo* (play).

PAIZOGENY . . . The sexual foreplay. From *paizo* (play) & *genos* (sex).

PAIZOSIS . . . Sexual play involving acts of perversion. Ex *paizo* (play).

Pajamas as clothes worn when the phallus is roasted vaginally . . . **Roast meat clothes.**

Palliasse . . . A whore as an inferior phallating target, in allusion to paillasse, a cheap, straw-filled mattress.

Pan . . . The female avocal lower mouth.

Pansy . . . A male homosexual.

Pansy ball . . . A dance attended primarily by male homosexuals.

Pansyland . . . The world, real and imaginary, of male homosexuals.

Panties; conceived as innominate or innominable accouterments . . . **Indescribables; Inexpressibles.**

PARA . . . A woman who has borne a child, esp. one who has borne several children. Also, a woman who bears the anatomical stigmata of childbearing, as pendulous mammae, flaccid abdominal wall, etc.

PARACOITA . . . A female bedfellow or sexual partner. From *para* (beside) & *coeo* (come together).

PARACOITUS . . . A male bedfellow or sexual partner. From *para* (beside) & *coeo* (come together).

PARACOITUS . . . Any form of coitus in which the phallus is satisfied extravaginally, as in sodomy, phallation between the breasts, etc. Ex *para* (abnormal) & *coitus.*

PARAPHALLUS . . . An accessory penis. From *para* (beside) & *phallos* (penis)

PARAPHILEMIA . . . Erotic kissing of parts other than the mouth, esp. of the genitalia. Ex *para* (abnormal) & *philema* (kiss).

PARAPHILIATRY . . . The branch of psychiatry dealing with sexual aberrations, perversions, etc. From *paraphilia* (sexual aberration) & *iatreia* (medical treatment).

PARASCOPISM . . . An excessive desire to peep at sexually intimate scenes, as through a bedroom window. From *para* (abnormal) & *skopein* (to look).

PARAVALENT . . . Of the male, sexually potent only under unusual or special conditions, or in a particular environment, as in a hotel room. From *para* (abnormal) & *valere* (to be strong).

PAREMAMMAE . . . The pendulous and flabby breasts characteristic of women who have borne children.

PAREMASTIA . . . The condition of the female breasts resulting from the enlargement during pregnancy and the subsequent involution; the deformity of the breasts of women who have borne children. From *parere* (to bear) & *mastos* (breast).

PAREMASTOPHOBIA . . . A strong dislike, on the part of a male, for the female breasts that have undergone the changes incident to pregnancy and childbirth. Ex *parere* (to bear), *mastos* (breast), & *phobos.*

Parentheses . . . The female pudendal labia, in allusion to their form, esp. when clasping the phallus.

Parenthesize . . . 1. Of the male, to surround the phallus with female pudendal labia. 2. Of the female, to sheathe the incoming phallus with genital labia. 3. Of man and maid, to phallate.

PAREUNASTHENIA . . . Sexual impotence in the male.

PAREUNIA . . . Sexual intercourse. Ex *para* (on) & *eune* (couch, bed).

PAREUNOMANIA . . . A compelling need for sexual intercourse.

PAREUNOPHILIA . . . Fondness for sexual intercourse.

PAREUNOPHOBIA . . . Fear of sexual intercourse. Ex *para* (on), *eune* (couch, bed), & *phobos* (fear).

PAREUNOPHRENIA . . . A state of mind dominated by thoughts of or a craving for sexual intercourse.

PAREUNOSTHENIA . . . In the male, sexual vigor and ability to satisfy the female.

Paris as a favorite girlie center for American male tourists . . . **Yankee heaven.**

PAROHYMENIA . . . The condition of the hymen in a parous woman. Ex *parere* (to bear).

Parsley . . . The pubic hair, esp. that of the female.

Parsley-bed . . . The soft, slitted underbelly of the female.

Parson, cuckold the . . . To jump the gun on the parson by tasting the pudendum of one's wife-to-be before the official tie is tied.

Parsonage . . . Designating the moralistic viewpoint of a parson, minister, rabbi, priest, etc.

Parsoned . . . Licensed to phallate a particular woman, by virtue of a wedding ceremony.

PARTHENA . . . A virgin female.

PARTHENITY . . . Status of a virgin; virginity.

PARTHENOCLASIS . . . The defloration of a virgin. Ex *parthenos* (virgin) & *klasis* (a breaking).

PARTHENOCLEPT . . . A seducer of a virgin; a stealer of virginity. Ex *parthenos* (virgin) & *klepto* (steal).

PARTHENOCOLPIA . . . The condition of having a virgin vagina.

PARTHENOCOLPOS . . . A virgin vagina. Ex *parthenos* (maiden) & *kolpos* (vagina).

PARTHENOMASTA . . . A female breast that has not undergone the changes incident to pregnancy and childbirth. Ex *parthenos* (maiden) & *mastos* (breast).

PARTHENOMASTA . . . A girl or woman having unmilked breasts, i.e., breasts which have not undergone the changes occurring in pregnancy and after childbirth.

PARTHENOMASTIA . . . In the female, the condition of having unmilked breasts.

PARTHENOPHALLIC . . . Designating or pert. to male virginity; having a sexually untried phallus.

PARTHENOPHALLUS . . . A sexually untried phallus.

PARTHENOPHILE . . . A male who is attracted sexually only to girls who have not previously been defiled.

PARTHENOPHILIA . . . Veneration of virgins; erotic interest in virgins. From *parthenos* (virgin) & *philein* (love).

PARTHENOPLASTY . . . A plastic operation on the hymen to create an appearance of virginity.

PARTHENUS . . . A male sexually virgin.

PARTHYMEN . . . The hymen of an undeflowered female. Ex *parthenos* (virgin) & *hymen* (membrane).

PARTHYMENIA . . . Condition of having a virgin hymen.

PARTIALISM . . . The derivation of sexual pleasure by rubbing a part of one's body against the genitalia of another of the opposite sex.

Party . . . To toast the lipped underside of a girl with phallic accolades and seminal champagne.

Party at which generous portions of the female breasts are on display . . . **Décolletage party.**

Party at which seminal fluid is served vaginally . . . . **Oatmeal party.**

Party of male homosexuals, attended by sexual festivities . . . **Bull party.**

Pass through the fire . . . To phallate a venereally infected female.

Passionate male with a matching phallus . . . **Fire-box.**

Passionate . . . See also under *Sexual desire.*

PATHIC . . . A person who submits to the abnormal sexual desires of another.

PATHICANT . . . The active member in a bout of sexual intercourse with a boy per rectum; a pederast.

PATHICUS . . . The passive or recipient member in a bout of pederasty, i.e., the boy or catamite.

Pathologic abnormality of the sex urge . . . LIBIDOPATHY.

Pathologic lewdness . . . LAGNOPATHY.

PATRIARCHAL FAMILY . . . A form of family based on the marriage of one man with several wives.

PATRINCEST . . . Sexual intercourse between a father and his daughter. Ex *pater* (father) & *incestus* (sinful).

PATROLAGNIA . . . Sexual love of a daughter for her father. Ex *pater* (father) & *lagneia* (lust).

Pay a prostitute for services rendered or to be rendered . . . **Butter the bacon.**

Peach . . . An attractive young girl who, if squeezed, squeezes most delectably.

Peacherino . . . A young attractive girl even better than a **peach.**

Peanuts . . . A pair of despicable, goobersize female breasts.

Pearls . . . Bits of dried mucus or seminal fluid found in and around the vulva.

Pecker . . . Same as **Meat pecker,** the male pecker of the female underbelly.

Pederast, esp. one with a sizable phallus . . . **Bronco buster.**

Pederast or sodomite . . . **Backwoods fiddler; Indorser.**

Pederast or sodomite, in allusion to "bum" the posterior . . . **Bum fiddler.**

Pederasty . . . RECTAL SODOMY.

Pederasty, active member in bout of . . . PATHICANT.

Pederasty, addicted to . . . **Kid-simple.**

Pederasty; conceived as an enlarging of the intestine . . . **Gut reaming.**

Pederasty, male engaged in . . . PEDERAST.

Pederasty, not willing to submit to . . . **Bunker-shy.**

Pederasty, passive member in act of; a catamite . . . PARTHICUS.

PEDERIZE . . . To introduce the phallus into the rectum of a child; to practice pederasty.

PEDEROSIS . . . 1. Erotic love for children. 2. Sexual molestation of children. Ex *pais* (child).

PEDIHAPSIS . . . The amorous or erotic touching of the body of a child, as by a lecher. Ex *pais* (child) & *haptein* (make contact).

PEDIOCHLESIS . . . Sexual molestation of children. Ex *pais* (child) & *ochleo* (molest).

PEDIPHALLIA . . . Sexual intercourse with a female child. From *pais* (child) & *phallos.*

PEDIRAPTUS . . . Rape by force involving a child. Ex *pais* (child) & *raptus* (a violent attack).

Peenie . . . The penis, esp. of a small boy.

Peep at intimate scenes, excessive desire to . . . PARACIPITISM.

Peeping sickness . . . VOYEURISM.

Peeping Tom . . . VOYEUR.

Pencil . . . The male genital stylus.

Pencil and tassel . . . The penis and testicles, esp. of a child.

Pencil sharpener . . . A provocative girl who makes the male pendant sharp.

Pendulous and flabby breasts of women who have borne children . . . PAREMAMMAE.

PENIS . . . The male animal's sexual landing gear.

Penis, act of, in female lower sanctum . . . **Phalliloquence.**

Penis and testicles, esp. of a child . . . **Pencil and tassel.**

Penis and testicles of a child . . . **Twig and berries.**

Penis and testicles of a small boy . . . **Billy and doo; Billy-doo.**

Penis, artificial, use of; by the masculine female in the act of tribadism . . . OLISBONISM.

Penis, artificial, used by women in masturbation and in tribadism . . . DILDO; GODEMICHE; OLISBOS.

Penis as a burrowing organ . . . **Mole.**

Penis, as a crawler of holes . . . **Mouse.**

Penis as a male limb . . . MEMBRUM VIRILE.

Penis as a merryandrew . . . **Merry maker.**

Penis as a rod for the female trap . . . **Trap stick.**

Penis, cavorting of, in the female jelly cruse . . . **Phalliloquence.**

Penis conceived as a hunter of female pudenda . . . **Crack hunter.**

Penis, condition of having a very large . . . MACROPHALLIA.

Penis, construction or reconstruction of . . . PHALLOSYNTHESIS.

Penis dangling rather than standing, esp. one not capable of gelling for action . . . **Corpse.**

Penis, erotic licking of . . . MEDOLINGUS.

Penis, esp. of a small boy . . . **Peenie.**

Penis, esp. the erected, in allusion to a tubular instrument . . . **Flute.**

Penis, female who takes, into her mouth; to give it oral gratification . . . FELLATRICE.

Penis, having a pointed . . . ACULEOPHALLIC.

Penis, having a rough or spiny . . . ACANTHOPHALLIC.

Penis, having a round and smooth . . . TERETOPHALLIC.

Penis hugged in the fissure between the approximated female breasts, in allusion to a hot-dog in a cut roll . . . **Dog in a blanket.**

Penis; in allusion to its role as a stick for the female **broom** . . . **Broomstick.**

Penis; in allusion to Mentu, the god of reproduction . . . MENTULA.

Penis, introduction of, into the mouth of another, act of; for the purpose of having it gratified by oral stimulation . . . IRRUMATION.

Penis, introduction of, into the mouth of another; for the purpose of having it gratified by oral stimulation. . . . FELLATORISM.

Penis, Latin figurative synonym for; in allusion to a quill . . . **COLES.**

Penis, Latin figurative synonym for, in allusion to a shaft . . . **SCAPUS.**

Penis, Latin figurative synonym for; in allusion to a small rod . . . **BACULUM.**

Penis, Latin figurative synonym for; in allusion to a stalk . . . **CAULIS.**

Penis, Latin figurative synonym for; in allusion to a stick . . . **CLAVA.**

Penis, Latin figurative synonym for; in allusion to a sword . . . **GLADIUS.**

Penis, Latin figurative synonym for; in allusion to a tail . . . **CERCUS.**

Penis, male who takes, into his mouth; to give it oral gratification . . . FELLATOR.

Penis, malicious amputation or mutilation of . . . PHALLOPEROSIS.

Penis, marked deformity of . . . TERATOPHALLIA.

Penis, obscene language involving the . . . MEDOLALIA; PHALLOLALIA.

Penis of a Negro, in allusion to its duskiness . . . **Dinge.**

Penis, preoccupation with thoughts and manipulations of the . . . MENTULOMANIA.

Penis; regarded as a stick entering the female "guts" . . . **Gut-stick.**

Penis; regarded as the bow to the female fiddle . . . **Fiddle-bow.**

Penis; regarded as the commander-in-chief of the male netherland . . . **Corps commander.**

Penis, taking of, into the mouth; for the purpose of satisfying it by oral titillation . . . FELLATIO.

Penis, underdevelopment of . . . HYPOMEDIA.

Penis . . . See also under *Phallus, Membrum virile,* etc.

Pennorth of treacle . . . A mighty charming young wench whose kisses are treacle.

PENORTHOSIS . . . The erection of the phallus. Ex *penis* & *orthos* (straight).

Peos . . . A Greek synonym for the phallus.

PERCOLPAL . . . By way of the vagina. Ex *kolpos* (vagina).

Perineal atrium . . . The genial chamber of the female, playing scabbard to the male blade.

Perineal mouth . . . In the female, the lower mouth for which the phallus erectus hankereth.

PERINEUM . . . The region at the lower end of the trunk, between the thighs, occupied by the sex organs and the anus—in the female by the clitoris, the labia, the external opening of the vagina, and the anal canal.

Perineum; conceived as a one-eyed harridan with a foul breath . . . **Douglas with one eye and a stinking breath.**

Period of sexual recuperation between bouts of coitus; applied to the male, or to both partners, making a long run of it . . . **Retooling period.**

Period of time during which a husband is without access to his wife's pudendal inlet because of childbirth . . . **Stag month.**

PEROGYNIA . . . The mutilation of a female in jealous retaliation. Ex *peros* (maimed) & *gyne* (woman).

Person deriving sexual pleasure, and expressing it, by pinching the soft tissues of another; male or female . . . THLIPSOPHILIST.

Person devoted to sexual pleasures . . . LIBIDOPHILE.

Person dominated by anal eroticism . . . ANOCRAT; ANOCRATES.

Person, esp. a female, having a fat and broad posterior prominence . . . **Bottle-arse.**

Person having abnormal sexual cravings . . . EROTOPATH; LIBIDOPATH.

Person having an abnormally strong sexual urge . . . EROTOMANIAC.

Person having an exaggerated response to erotic stimulation . . . EROTOMANIAC.

Person having pathologically abnormal sexual cravings, either with regard to urgency or the manner of deriving gratification . . . LIBIDOPATH.

Person in whom the characters of both sexes are manifested to a certain extent . . . INTERSEX.

Person who derives sexual gratification from watching others in the nude or in the act of coitus . . . VOYEUR.

Person who derives sexual pleasure mostly from petting and necking . . . SARMASSOPHIL.

Person who dislikes kissing . . . PHILEMAPHOBE.

Person who enjoys, sexually, the wearing of clothes appropriate to the opposite sex . . . TRANSVESTITE.

Person who enjoys variations in and diversification of accepted sexual procedures . . . GENOPAST; PARAPHILIAC.

Person who has both ovarian and testicular gonadal tissues and whose external genitalia are partly male and female . . . HERMAPHRODITE.

Person who has gonads of one sex and malformed external genitalia resembling those of the opposite sex . . . PSEUDOHERMAPHRODITE.

Person who licks another's genitalia . . . LÉCHEUR.

Person who licks or labiates the vulva . . . CUNNILINGUIST.

Person who submits to the abnormal sexual desires of another . . . PATHIC.

Person whose sexual desire is directed toward oneself . . . NARCISSIST.

Person whose sexual desire is directed toward the opposite sex . . . HETEROSEXUAL.

Person whose sexual desire is directed toward the same sex . . . HOMOSEXUAL.

Person whose thoughts and activities are abnormally influenced by sexual desire . . . EROTIC.

Peter . . . Sexual concourse as a dish of phallus; a feminine concept.

Peter . . . The sexual arm of the male, regarded as a pudendal intruder, in allusion to a pete-breaker or safebreaker. Also conceived as an auxiliary of the male, in allusion to Pete, a substitute circus clown.

PHALLACRASIA . . . Excessive use of the phallus, sexually. Ex *phallos* (penis) & *akrasia* (incontinence).

PHALLALINGUS . . . The erotic licking of the phallus, usually by a female.

PHALLATA . . . A female who has had sexual intercourse. Ex *phallos* (penis).

Phallatable; that may be given the phallus erectus . . . **Christenable.**

PHALLATAE . . . Those females who are tasting, or have tasted, the sapor of the phallus erectus.

PHALLATE . . . Of the male, to subject the vagina to the thrusts of the phallus; i.e., to do the normal male part in sexual intercourse. Ex *phallos* (penis) & *ate* (a verbifying suffix).

Phallate a colored girl, generally a harlot . . . **Flutter a brown.**

Phallate a female . . . **Bull; Fagot; Grouse; See a man; Take a turn.**

Phallate a female; an allusion to mortar work . . . **Do a grind.**

Phallate a female; an allusion to the bare skin . . . **Trim the buff.**

Phallate a female; an allusion to the pubic hair . . . **Take a turn in the parsley-bed.**

Phallate a female; an allusion to the spreading of the labia in the process . . . **Halve the crack.**

Phallate a female by the light of the stars, in the open . . . **Do a star pitch.**

Phallate a female from behind . . . **Ride behind.**

Phallate a female; in allusion to a once popular name of a bull . . . **Roger.**

Phallate a female; in allusion to Biblical euphemism . . . **Know.**

Phallate a female; in allusion to man's third leg . . . **Lay a leg on.**

Phallate a female; in allusion to snuffing out her virginity, if she has it . . . **Snib.**

Phallate a female; in allusion to the attrition . . . **Do a rasp.**

Phallate a female; in allusion to the boar of swine . . . **Brim.**

Phallate a female; in allusion to the breed . . . **Improve the breed.**

Phallate a female; in allusion to the ejaculation and the sexual grunt . . . **Give the bubble and squeak.**

Phallate a female; in allusion to the figurative action . . **Pump.**

Phallate a female; in allusion to the impalement of the vulva on the male spit . . . **Spit-cock.**

Phallate a female; in allusion to the intromission . . . **Plant a man.**

Phallate a female; in allusion to the male shaft . . . **Rod.**

Phallate a female; in allusion to the phallic banana . . . **Have a banana.**

Phallate a female; in allusion to the pilose adit . . . **Work the hairy oracle.**

Phallate a female, in the sense of softening or "breaking" the rigidity of the male organ . . . **Break a lance with; Break a peter on.**

Phallate a female not one's wife, when one has one . . . **Box out; Eat out.**

Phallate a female on the grass, and tinge her clothes with green . . . **Give a green gown.**

Phallate a female on the ground or on the floor . . . **Blow off on the groundsels.**

Phallate a female, so as to "clean out" the male genital passages, conceived as clogged with seminal fluid . . . **Have a blow-through.**

Phallate a female vaginally and rectally . . . **Jam on both sides.**

Phallate a female whose pudendum is regarded as a hairy Herefordshire . . . **Go to Hairyfordshire.**

Phallate a female, with an ingredient of sadism . . . **Switchel.**

Phallate a female with excessive vehemence . . . **Beat the brains out.**

Phallate a female with her on top . . . **Ride rantipole; Ride St. George.**

Phallate a female without a preliminary warmup via her secondary embellishments . . . **Rush up the frills; Rush up the petticoats; Rush up the straight.**

Phallate a female . . . See also under *Phallate a woman.*

Phallate a girl for the lark of it . . . **Flutter a Jane.**

Phallate a menstruating woman . . . **Mount the red flag.**

Phallate a slatternly whore . . . **Get into a mess.**

Phallate a venereally infected female . . . **Pass through the fire.**

Phallate a virgin . . . **Blaze the trail.**

Phallate a virgin, in allusion to an intact pie crust . . . **Crack a crust.**

Phallate a virgin, in allusion to depriving an object of its perfection . . . **Crack a Jane; Crack a Judy.**

Phallate a woman . . . **Charver.**

Phallate a woman both vaginally and rectally . . . **Do a double act.**

Phallate a woman; in allusion to the pubic hair . . . **Take a turn in Bushy park.**

Phallate a woman; in allusion to the roborant effect on the male apparatus resulting from the exercise . . . **Constitutionalize.**

Phallate a woman while supporting oneself on all fours, in an inaccurate allusion to a dog's way . . . **Dog.**

Phallate a woman, with little enthusiasm, as one's own wife . . . **Do one's business.**

Phallate a woman . . . See also under *Phallate a female.*

Phallate a young female, or a female having a narrow corridor, with a massive organ . . . **To bull in a china shop.**

Phallate; an allusion to the female genital foramen . . . **Foraminate.**

Phallate; an allusion to the prying of the female slit with the male crowbar . . . **Jemmy.**

Phallate; an allusion to the stuffing of the vagina with masculine flesh . . . **Force meat.**

Phallate an impregnated wife conventionally till the belly gets in the way . . . **Beat it while the beating is good.**

Phallate and impregnate a to oneself unwedlocked female . . . **Get into a mess.**

Phallate another man's wife . . . **Have an oar in another's boat; Take a leaf out of another's book.**

Phallate another man's wife and thus make a cuckold out of a husband . . . **Give the bull's feather.**

Phallate another man's wife . . . See also under *Cuckold.*

Phallate, as if to prove one's love . . . **Tie the true lover's knot.**

Phallate, as if to punish thereby . . . **Switch.**

Phallate between the adducted thighs, usually of a female . . . MERPHALLATE.

Phallate between the breasts of a female . . . MASTOPHALLATE.

Phallate, esp. extramaritally . . . **Jazz.**

Phallate, esp. from the top position . . . **Play the bear with.**

Phallate for the first time . . . **Break in the balls; Christen the yack.**

Phallate from behind between the thighs . . . **Goose.**

Phallate; go the limit in lovemaking . . . **Play the jack.**

Phallate; in allusion to a duet . . . **Do a double act.**

Phallate; in allusion to a mount . . . **Ride.**

Phallate; in allusion to a stallion . . . **Horse.**

Phallate; in allusion to making a beast with two backs—male and female pudendally fused . . . **Double.**

Phallate; in allusion to "Peter Street" . . . **Take a turn at Cock Alley.**

Phallate; in allusion to pettiskirts . . . **Take a turn up one's petticoats.**

Phallate; in allusion to phallic "punishment" . . . **Beat with the spit.**

Phallate; in allusion to riding the female pudendum . . . **Have a ride.**

Phallate; in allusion to the bull . . . **Pizzle.**

Phallate; in allusion to the dipping action . . . **Dip one's bill.**

Phallate; in allusion to the embrace of the phallus by the pudendal labia . . . **Parenthesize.**

Phallate; in allusion to the female interfemoral "bosom" . . . **Take a turn in Abraham's bosom.**

Phallate; in allusion to the hairy "court" of the female . . . **Take a turn at Hair Court.**

Phallate; in allusion to the membrum virile as a baseball club . . . **Bat.**

Phallate; in allusion to the movement . . . **Swive.**

Phallate; in allusion to the mucus bath . . . **Grease one's duke.**

Phallate; in allusion to the penile fulmination . . . **Pump thunder.**

Phallate; in allusion to the phallic spurt . . . **Bean.**

Phallate; in allusion to the pubic stubble . . . **Take a turn through the stubble.**

Phallate; in allusion to the pudendal lane . . . **Take a turn in love lane.**

Phallate; in allusion to young man Cupid . . . **Take a turn at Cupid's Alley.**

Phallate; in the sense of giving cheer . . . **Christmas.**

Phallate; in the sense of sheathing the phallus with vagina . . . **Sheathe the saber.**

Phallate ineffectively to penile softness without the reward of ejaculation . . . **Strike out.**

Phallate into a female's vagina and rectum . . . **Fore and aft.**

Phallate or be phallated . . . **Hustle.**

Phallate per rectum . . . **Indorse; Shoot in the brown; Prowl in the back yard; Ride behind.**

Phallate per rectum, esp. a female . . . **Shoot in the back.**

Phallate per rectum, in allusion to the arse (bum) . . . **Bum fiddle.**

Phallate per rectum, in allusion to the rectum as the wrong coital compartment . . . **File in the wrong box.**

Phallate per rectum, in sense of making a wrong hitch . . . **Hitch to the wrong side of the post.**

Phallate per rectum with a female or male child . . . PEDERIZE.

Phallate per rectum . . . See also under *Pederasty* and *Sodomy*.

Phallate; said esp. of a young male . . . **Break in the balls.**

Phallate to beget offspring . . . **Make faces.**

Phallate two females, in one love session, with one of the participating females adding a caress or just looking on . . . **Do a double act.**

Phallate wife of another, while the another is unable or away . . . **Pinch hit.**

Phallate with a small and/or lethargically erected organon . . . **Strike with a feather.**

Phallate without contraceptives, and thus propagate the species . . . **Do gospel work.**

Phallated and pregnant . . . **Shot in the giblets.**

Phallated and, usually, with child . . . **Inlaid.**

Phallated, be . . . **Get the order of the scimitar.**

Phallated between anus and urethra . . . **Shot between wind and water.**

Phallated, esp. for the first time . . . **Christened with a pump handle.**

Phallated; in allusion to man's best leg of three . . . **Legged.**

Phallated; in allusion to the phallic syrup . . . **Bubbled.**

Phallated to exhaustion; said of the male . . . **Not a shot in the locker.**

Phallated, well and thoroughly . . . **Battered.**

Phallated; with a nuance of pudendal punishment . . . **Switched.**

Phallated without too much resistance; pudendally approachable . . . **Knock-upable.**

PHALLATEE . . . The passive member in normal sexual intercourse, i.e., the female partner.

PHALLATIC . . . Designating non-virgin females.

Phallating, to be out; of the male . . . **Be out christening.**

PHALLATION . . . Sexual intercourse, esp. the male's part in the act. Ex *phallos* (penis).

Phallation, a bout of . . . **Charver.**

Phallation, a bout of, involving a double orgasm on the part of one or both of the participants . . . **Double-tide job.**

Phallation, a fling at; in allusion to mounting the female . . . **Bit of cavalry.**

Phallation, act of, as a pleasure drive . . . **Joy ride.**

Phallation, act of, as the monologue of the penis . . . **Phallic sweet talk; Phalliloquence; Phalliloquy.**

Phallation as a cut from the arse pudding . . . **Piece of ass.**

Phallation as an act of insinuation . . . **Inside job.**

Phallation conceived as a measuring of the vagina . . . **Vaginometry.**

Phallation from the viewpoint of the phallated female . . . **Bit of beef.**

Phallation in the female axilla . . . MASCHALATION.

Phallation in which the phallus is reciprocated between the approximated thighs, usually of a female . . . MERPHALLATION.

Phallation per rectum . . . **Arsometry.**

Phallation per rectum with a boy . . . PEDERASTY.

Phallation per rectum with a female . . . ANOMEATIA; THELYSODOMY.

Phallation per rectum with an adult . . . SODOMY.

Phallation regarded as the incorporation of the male monolith and the female cavern . . . **Corporation work.**

Phallation with a condomed phallus . . . **Armored division.**

Phallation without tintinnabulation, of the wedding bells . . . **Unholy bedlock.**

PHALLATOR . . . The active or male member in normal sexual intercourse.

Phallator as a mounter . . . **Rider.**

Phallator; in allusion to his overlying the "hilltop" . . . **Hilltopper.**

Phallator; in allusion to the pubic hair . . . **Whisker-splitter.**

Phallator per rectum . . . **Molly.**

Phallator per rectum . . . See also under *Pederast, Pederasty, Sodomite,* etc.

Phallator, peristent and dedicated . . . **Road hog.**

Phallator, vigorous, esp. one who boosts the census . . . **Belly bumper.**

Phallator who is active frequently and/or vigorously . . . **Pot walloper.**

Phallic erection as expression of the libido . . . **Hard-on.**

Phallic erection . . . See also under *Erection.*

Phallic fling at female pudendum . . . **Bit of fork.**

Phallic intromission . . . **Plant.**

Phallic measurement, from end to root . . . **Length.**

Phallic prurience and partial erection . . . **Horniness.**

Phallic recuperation period between go's in a sexual orgy . . . **Retooling period.**

Phallic sweet talk . . . The doings of the phallus when, in its romantic mood, it does what comes naturally.

Phallic thickness or circumferential dimension . . . **Girth.**

Phalliloquence . . . Phallic sweet talk, i.e., a phallic cavorting in the female hopper or pudendal hiatus.

Phalliloquy . . . Same as **Phalliloquence,** which see.

PHALLITY . . . The status of a woman with regard to her having partaken in or not having partaken in sexual intercourse.

PHALLOHAPSIS . . . The caressing, usually by a female, of the male genitalia, esp. the phallus. Ex *phallos* (male organ) & *haptomai* (touch).

PHALLOHAPTATE . . . To caress the phallus.

PHALLOLALIA . . . Obscene language involving reference to the penis. Ex *phallos* (penis) & *lalein* (to speak).

PHALLOMANCY . . . Superstitious divination by the method of observing a bull's phallus.

PHALLOMANIAC . . . A woman who is excessively fond of the membrum virile erectum.

PHALLOPEROSIS . . . Malicious amputation or mutilation of the penis. Ex *phallos* (penis) & *perosis* (malicious mutilation).

PHALLOPHOBIA . . . Fear of the erected phallus, by a female.

PHALLOSUGIA . . . An erotic sucking of the phallus. Ex *phallos* & *sugo* (suck).

PHALLOSYNTHESIS . . . The plastic construction or reconstruction of a penis, as following mutilation. Ex *phallos* (penis) & *synthesis.*

PHALLUS . . . 1. The genital shaft of the male. 2. A symbol or figure of the penis used in primitive ceremonies, as in the Dionysiac mysteries, to represent the male power of generation. Ex Greek *phallos.*

Phallus . . . **Beef stick.**

Phallus and testes . . . PUDENDUS.

Phallus and testes . . . **Balls and bat.**

Phallus and testicles, as a triumvirate . . . **Rule of three.**

Phallus as a contemptible fellow good only for anal intrusions . . . **Arse worm.**

Phallus as a coupler . . . **Dohickey; Dohicky.**

Phallus as a dilator, of the vagina . . . **Reamer.**

Phallus as a funmaker . . . **Dofunny.**

Phallus as a hard to name genital ornament . . . **Dodad; Doodad.**

Phallus as a jockey of the female pudendum . . . **Jock.**

Phallus as a precious organon . . . **Dearest member.**

Phallus as a pudendal scribe . . . **Pencil.**

Phallus as a pudendal trifler . . . **Doodle.**

Phallus as a puncher . . . **Beef.**

Phallus as a rubbing device for the vagina . . . **Frigger.**

Phallus as a stage-door Johnnie of the female pudendum . . . **Dojohnnie.**

Phallus as a swab . . . **Dingbat.**

Phallus as a violin bow . . . **Fiddlestick.**

Phallus as a wriggler . . . **Wriggling pole.**

Phallus as an inconsequential character . . . **Jack Straw.**

Phallus as an intruder in the female ken . . . **Ken cracker.**

Phallus as an organ undeserving of respect . . . **The irreverend.**

Phallus as goad of "feminine gender" **Jockey stick.**

Phallus as pudendal intruder (peteor safe-breaker) . . . **Peter.**

Phallus as the business end of the male torso . . . **Business.**

Phallus as the coarser end of the male trunk . . . **Fag.**

Phallus as the drumstick of pudendal festivities . . . **Joy stick.**

Phallus as the finger of masculine love . . . **Little finger.**

Phallus as the nameless thing . . . **Dingus.**

Phallus as the partner of lower status in the male firm . . . **Junior.**

Phallus as the puncturer of the pudendum muliebre . . . **Prick.**

Phallus, be well supplied with; said of a recently married woman . . . **Be on jack.**

Phallus, big, having a; the size of two legs! . . . **Double-shanked; Double shung.**

Phallus, big, in allusion to its punishing effect on the introitus vaginae . . . **Bruiser.**

Phallus, circumcised, in allusion to the early practitioners of peritomy . . . **Jew's lance.**

Phallus; conceived as a baseball club . . . **Bat.**

Phallus; conceived as a begetter . . . GONOS.

Phallus; conceived as a Biblical hunter . . . **Nimrod.**

Phallus; conceived as a "blade gun" . . . **Culty-gun.**

Phallus; conceived as a club . . . **Bat.**

Phallus; conceived as a crowbar . . . **Jemmy.**

Phallus; conceived as a device for fishing in the pudendal waters of the female . . . **Fishing rod.**

Phallus; conceived as a Genghis Khan . . . **Chingus.**

Phallus; conceived as a genital forefoot . . . **Pud.**

Phallus; conceived as a gorer of female pudenda . . . **Bull.**

Phallus; conceived as a plum getter . . . **Plum-tree shaker.**

Phallus; conceived as a rammer of the seminal charge . . . **Ramrod.**

Phallus; conceived as a sexual nobleman . . . **Duke.**

Phallus; conceived as a shaft of lunch meat . . . **Baloney.**

Phallus; conceived as a short firearm or pistol . . . **Short arm.**

Phallus; conceived as a spirited pudendal invader . . . **Uhlan.**

Phallus; conceived as a staff used in bed . . . **Bed-staff.**

Phallus; conceived as a stopper . . . **Cock.**

Phallus; conceived as a tail . . . **CERCUS.**

Phallus; conceived as a transmitter of the "beans" . . . **Bean pole.**

Phallus; conceived as a vaginal dilator . . . **Colpeurynter.**

Phallus; conceived as an all right piece of meat . . . **Bit of beef.**

Phallus; conceived as an auger . . . TRYPAN.

Phallus; conceived as an auxiliary pes . . . **Helping foot.**

Phallus; conceived as an instrument of illicit sexual concourse, jocosely . . . **Fornicator; Fornicating tool.**

Phallus; conceived as an organ with a reciprocating motion . . . **Dojigger.**

Phallus; conceived as an untamed rascal . . . **Wild rogue.**

Phallus; conceived as "cork" for the female bunghole . . . **Bung.**

Phallus; conceived as staff of authority . . . **Mace.**

Phallus; conceived as the better grade of beef . . . **Christmas beef.**

Phallus; conceived as the commander-in-chief . . . **Sirdar.**

Phallus; conceived as the drain of the scrotum . . . **Bagpipe.**

Phallus; conceived as the entrant into the female scabbard . . . **Saber.**

Phallus; conceived as the maker of buttonholes . . . **Buttonhole worker.**

Phallus; conceived as the male's third lower limb . . . **Foot.**

Phallus; conceived as the original sinner . . . **Old Adam.**

Phallus; conceived as the plugger of the female hawsehole . . . **Blind buckler.**

Phallus; conceived as the rider of the female pudendal saddle . . . **Jockey.**

Phallus; conceived as the seminal decorator of the vagina . . . **Painter.**

Phallus, dimension of, around the trunk . . . **Girth.**

Phallus, dimension of, from root to end . . . **Length.**

Phallus *en amour,* i.e., erectus . . . **Blanket stiff.**

Phallus, entrance of, into vagina . . . **Blow.**

Phallus erected halfheartedly, designating a . . . **Half-baked.**

Phallus, erected, spasmodic twitching of, at the sight of its quarry, before the plunge in the abyss . . . **Saber rattling.**

Phallus erectus as fodder for the vulva . . . **Fiddle fare.**

Phallus erectus as the expression of the male libido . . . **Bone; Bone-on.**

Phallus erectus as the lower male proboscis . . . **Beak.**

Phallus erectus, conceived as the stylus used in the act of penial disk-jockeying . . . **Bull point.**

Phallus erectus confined to quarters behind the zipped fly . . . **Muzzled bulldog.**

Phallus erectus, fear of, by a female . . . PHALLOPHOBIA.

Phallus erectus; in allusion to its figure . . . **Rod.**

Phallus erectus; in allusion to its impaling function . . . **Spit-cock.**

Phallus erectus, lose rigidity of, while reciprocating, or while getting ready for the action . . . **Corpse out.**

Phallus erectus of a male dancing partner, esp. as felt by the closely approximated female, who made it thus . . . **Hardback.**

Phallus erectus of a sodomite . . . **Irish toothpick.**

Phallus erectus, unalleviated; as peacemaker between man and wife . . . **Matrimonial peacemaker.**

Phallus, esp. an impotent one; regarded as a "monkey" . . . **Jackanapes.**

Phallus, give, to suck . . . **Bully in the muzzle.**

Phallus, Greek figurative synonym for; in allusion to a schemer . . . **MEDOS.**

Phallus, Greek figurative synonym for; in allusion to a stem . . . **KAULOS.**

Phallus, Greek figurative synonym for; in allusion to a straight shaft . . . **THYRSOS.**

Phallus, Greek figurative synonym for; in allusion to offspring . . . **GONOS.**

Phallus, Greek metonym for; in allusion to a club . . . **Koryne.**

Phallus, Greek metonym for; in allusion to a tail . . . **Kerkos.**

Phallus, Greek metonym for; in allusion to a wooden nail used in shipbuilding . . . **Tylos.**

Phallus, Greek synonym for . . . **Peos.**

Phallus, have one's, ensconsed in the female pudendal chamber and amorously clasped by the labia . . . **Have one's bowsprit in parentheses.**

Phallus implanted in female pudendum . . . **Bellyful.**

Phallus, impotent, regarded as shut up because it cannot put up . . . **Shut-in.**

Phallus; in allusion to its form . . . **Club.**

Phallus; in allusion to its resemblance, when erected, to the tapered pole extending forward from the bow of a sailing vessel . . . **Bowsprit.**

Phallus; in allusion to the god of male generative power . . . **Priapus.**

Phallus in fellatio, as an oral dose . . . **Mouthpiece.**

Phallus in female vagina, introduced as far as "balls will let it" . . . **Down to the ears.**

Phallus in its higher moments of ambition . . . **Rattling saber.**

Phallus infected venereally and dripping . . **Dripper.**

Phallus initiating a virgin . . . **Christener.**

Phallus, introduce the, into the female accommodations . . . **Give the length of.**

Phallus, introduce the, into the female fruit garden . . . **Get Jack in the orchard.**

Phallus, introduce the, into the female sanctum . . . **Put the devil into hell.**

Phallus, introduce the, into the vaginal corridor . . . **Bury the hatchet where it won't rust.**

Phallus, intromit the, between the approximated female breasts . . . Mastophallate.

Phallus, intromit the, in the female dish . . . **Put in the pot.**

Phallus invalidated by flaccidity and regarded as hanged . . . **Hung fiddle.**

Phallus junior size . . . **Dickey.**

Phallus large enough to fit a "barge" . . . **Barge pole.**

Phallus, large, in allusion to a swimming mammal . . . **Whaler.**

Phallus, large, in allusion to its "busting" effect on the female pudendum . . . **Buster.**

Phallus, large; in fellatio . . . **Horsechoker.**

Phallus, large, or bearer thereof, in allusion to the punishment of the vulva . . . **Butt smasher.**

Phallus, Latin figurative synonym for; in allusion to a branch . . . **Ramus.**

Phallus, Latin figurative synonym for; in allusion to a plow . . . **Vomer.**

Phallus, Latin metonym for; in allusion to a root . . . **Radix.**

Phallus, long and hefty . . . **Enough broomstick to charm the ladies.**

Phallus, lose erection of, while in the act . . . **Corpse out.**

Phallus, lose erection of, while in the act, in allusion to an unproductive mine . . . **Duffer out.**

Phallus, lubricate the . . . **Rosin the bow.**

Phallus of a boy . . . **Dickey.**

Phallus of a bridegroom whose bride is a virgin . . . **Christener.**

Phallus of a corpse, in allusion to chilled meat . . . **Frigo.**

Phallus of a male dedicated by vows to total sexual abstinence . . . **Holy Joe.**

Phallus of a mulatto . . . **Brown Joe.**

Phallus of a Negro . . . **Blackleg; Black pencil.**

Phallus of a sodomite . . . **Arser.**

Phallus of a wedded male, with regard to his wife's genital valley . . . **The legitimate.**

Phallus of a young male, still learning the craft . . . **Jackaroo.**

Phallus of a youth . . . **Young strop.**

Phallus of an Israelite . . . **Ikey; Jew's lance; Yehudi.**

Phallus of dead male, female who, reputedly, can impart rigidity to; because of outstanding physical charms . . . **Corpse reviver.**

Phallus of good size and proper consistency . . . **Ace poker.**

Phallus of impressive bulk . . . **Duker.**

Phallus of impressive size and enduring rigidity . . . **King dick.**

Phallus of modest size . . . **Modest quencher.**

Phallus of the half-pint size . . . **Little smack.**

Phallus, partly impotentiated . . . **Dolittle sword.**

Phallus personified . . . **John.**

Phallus, preoccupation with thoughts of, by a female . . . MENTULOPHRENIA.

Phallus, regarded as a simpleton detective who likes to investigate the female pudendal mysteries . . . **Dick.**

Phallus; regarded as an insinuator into the female sex crypt . . . **Jack the slipper.**

Phallus; regarded as the pudendal head man . . . **Foreman.**

Phallus, replace the, within the fly slit; esp. after a hurried foray upon the female pudendum, as in a hallway, park, etc. . . . **Box the compass.**

Phallus "retired" because of impotence, esp. one formerly very dashing . . . **Antiquated rogue.**

Phallus "retired" because of inability to stand up to the pudendal occasion . . . **Jack out of office.**

Phallus satisfied vaginally . . . **Roast jack.**

Phallus sexually lamed . . . **Lame duck.**

Phallus sexually untried . . . PARTHENOPHALLUS.

Phallus, short and stout . . . **Chub.**

Phallus, sink the, in the vagina . . . **Hole.**

Phallus, small but efficacious; in allusion to the man who lost at Waterloo . . . **Corsican.**

Phallus, small caliber . . . **Antony pig.**

Phallus, small; in allusion to small printers' type . . . **Agate.**

Phallus, stiffly erected . . . **Ironclad.**

Phallus, stimulate the, by titillation through the intermediacy of the trousers; by a female, in course of caressing . . . **Badger bait.**

Phallus stimulated manually . . . **King-at-arms.**

Phallus, symbol of, used in connection with the worship of Siva . . . LINGA.

Phallus, take the, orally . . . FELLATIZE.

Phallus, take the, orally; in allusion to one of the postures . . . **Have legs around the neck.**

Phallus, voluminous, esp. of an Ethiop . . . **Jack Johnson.**

Phallus which makes a husband into a cuckold . . . **Capricornus.**

Phallus, young and, as yet, unaspiring . . . **Billy.**

Phallus . . . See also under *Penis, Membrum virile,* etc.

PHANERODAEDALY . . . Of a woman, the skill in displaying provocative parts of the body without appearing vulgar. Ex *phainein* (to show) & *daedaly* (skill).

Philander . . . **Billy-goat; Free-lance; Shake a loose leg.**

PHILEMACENTRIC . . . Centering one's erotic feelings on kissing. Ex *philema* (kiss).

PHILEMAGENIC . . . Inducing a desire to kiss.

PHILEMAGENOUS . . . Induced by kissing, as lust.

PHILEMAMANIA . . . An intense desire to kiss, esp. in the male. Ex *philema* (a kiss) & *mania.*

PHILEMAPHILE . . . A person very fond of kissing; a person deriving sexual pleasure from kissing.

PHILEMAPHOBE . . . A person who dislikes kissing.

PHILEMEROTIC . . . A person easily aroused by kissing.

PHILOCENTRIC . . . Centering interest on love or romantic aspects of life. Ex *philos* (loving).

PHRENAPISTIA . . . Spiritual or mental sexual unfaithfulness to one's spouse, expressed by erotic daydreaming and/or illusory engagements in amatory pleasures with another. From *phren* (mind) & *apistia* (unfaithfulness).

Phutz . . . To give a girl a length of "putz," the ebullient allantoid spermapositor of the male crotch.

Physician who specializes in contraception . . . ACEPTIATRIST.

Physician who specializes in the diagnosis and treatment of syphilis . . . SYPHILOLOGIST.

Physician who specializes in the problems of sex and sexual relations . . . SEXOLOGIST.

Physician who specializes in the treatment of diseases transmitted by sexual intercourse . . . VENEREOLOGIST.

Picayunes . . . A set of unimpressive female breasts, because they forgot to grow.

Pick a cherry . . . Incongruously, to take (virginity) by giving (phallus).

Pictures of nude figures, sexual excitation aroused by . . . ICONOLAGNY.

Piece of ass . . . 1. A hunk of female pudendum, of the best possible grade. 2. A dish of cunt, regardless of grade or quality. 3. A partaking of 1 or of 2, i.e., a honing of the phallus erectus in the female perineal cul-de-sac, as conceived with drooling concupiscence by a male who has recently had the pleasure, or by one who is, not without reason, anticipating.

Piece of Eve's flesh . . . A good girl to sin with.

Piece of tail . . . Sexual concourse conceived as a piece of the pudendally functional end of the female.

Pigeonhole . . . The space between the labia of the female pudendum.

Piggyback . . . A "game" played almost invariably by a pair of newlyweds on their wedding night, and thereafter too, it is said. Also, the same game varied slightly, with him serving from behind.

Pimp as protector of a harlot, in allusion to his carrying a bludgeon or cosh . . . **Cosh-carrier.**

Pimp who is a "schatchen" for seminally hypertensive phalli and mercenary vulvas . . . **Brother of the gusset.**

Pimp who protects his charge from others but not from himself . . . **Bully.**

Pinch hit . . . To cuckold; phallate the wife of another when the other is unable or away.

Pinching, derivation or expression of sexual pleasure by; applies to both the male and the female . . . THLIPSOPHILIST.

Pips . . . A pair of inconsequential female breasts, because not much bigger than radar pips.

Piss fire . . . To be infected venereally, in allusion to the burning urination.

Piss in the dugout . . . Of a male, to discharge the phallic enthusiasm between the breasts of a woman. See **dugout.**

Piston-in-cylinder work . . . The act of reciprocating the male genital piston in the female pudendal cylinder.

Pix . . . A male homosexual.

Pizzle . . . The soft, sometimes hard, coupling link of the human male animal, with which he expresses genital love.

Pizzle . . . To interject the membrum virile between the generally unkissable labia of the female.

Placket . . . A female as a sexual slit.

Placket . . . The genital slit of the female.

Placket racket . . . The traffic in prostitution.

Placket-racket . . . The membrum virile.

Placket-stung . . . 1. Enamored of the female slit. 2. Infected venereally.

Plant . . . To insinuate the male genital connector into the female socket.

Plant . . . Of a female receiving the male pudendally, to assist the amaurotic plunger to its quarry.

Plant a man . . . To phallate a woman.

Plant oats . . . To give a girl's pleasure cavity an instillation of testicular roe.

Plaster of warm guts . . . A non-medicinal but still salubrious application of warm female pudendum to where it will do the most good.

Platonic relations, alleged between uncle and niece . . . **Avuncular relations.**

Play a mouth organ . . . Of the male, and sometimes of the female, to mouth the female pudendal ensemble.

Play at horses and mares . . . To beat the pudendal cymbals, i.e., to engage in coitus.

Play at itch-buttocks . . . Of man and nymphette, to be in pudendal communion.

Play at pully-hauly . . . Of the male, to match pudendum with the female counterpart.

Play at rantum-scantum . . . Partake in sexual concourse, esp. exuberantly.

Play at uptails all . . . To make phallovaginal obturations, in a lively fashion.

Play first fiddle . . . To phallate a previously unperforated female.

Play house . . . To give and take the male gonadal fertilizer.

Play of the imagination on the part of the male during sexual intercourse, to hasten the orgasm . . . GENDOLOMA.

Play off . . . Of the male, to induce manually, or in some other manner, except vaginally, the climactic spurt of the seminal treacle.

Play second fiddle . . . To phallate by way of the rectum.

Play second fiddle . . . 1. Marry a previously married female. 2. Be the husband of an unfaithful wife.

Play the ace against the jack . . . Of the female, to give a soft reception to a hard approach.

Play the bear . . . Regardless of the sex, to be the top player in the pudendal mattress game.

Play the bear with . . . To give the phallus to (a woman) from the top position.

Play the bitch to . . . Of a female, to play the bottom sawyer to a male top sawyer.

Play the giddy goat . . . Of the male, to give the genital jack plenty of exercise.

Play the jack . . . 1. In lovemaking, to go to the summit. 2. To be a fornicator.

Play the ponies . . . To satisfy the libidinous yen with chorus girls.

Play the whole game . . . In a session of palpable lovemaking, to finish with the climactic seminal spurt.

Play to the gallery . . . Of a caressing male, to fondle the bubbies, rather than the lower attractions.

Play with billy . . . To titillate the "billy" and the "doo" of a child in order to pacify him or put him to sleep.

Play with oneself . . . Same as **Play off,** to masturbate.

Play with the fleshy characteristics of a female . . . **Fiddle.**

Pleasure cavity . . . The female pudendal inlet.

Pleasure garden . . . That part of a girl to which the menstrual pad is applied, p.r.n.

PLEOBLYSIS . . . A copious seminal ejaculation. Ex *pleion* (more) & *blyzo* (spurt out).

Plum tree . . . The inlet of pleasure in the female crotch.

Plum-tree shaker . . . The genital arm of the male which, for its bearer, loosens the plums of the female pudendum.

Plump in the rump . . . **Short and thick, like a Welshman's prick.**

Plush . . . The pubic hair, esp. of the female.

Pocketful . . . The mass of phallus erectus which forms a bulge in the region of the pants pocket of an aroused male.

PODOPHILEMIA . . . Sexual perversion in which pleasure is derived from kissing the feet of a woman. Ex *pous* (foot) & *phileo* (kiss).

Pogue . . . A male homosexual.

Poker fun . . . Fun with the male sex poker, stirring up female pudendal fire.

Poker-ripe . . . Of a girl, barely old enough to sapor the male red-hot.

Polly's place . . . Polly's (or Molly's) soft inlet for Tom's (or Dick's) hard outlet.

POLYANDRY . . . Marriage of a woman to more than one man at the same time, when sanctioned by custom or by law. Ex *polys* & *aner* (man).

POLYGAMY . . . The marriage of a man or a woman to more than one spouse at the same time, usually without the sanction of custom or law . . . Ex *polys* (many) & *gamos* (marriage).

POLYGYNY . . . The marriage of a man to more than one woman at the same time, when sanctioned by law or custom. Ex *polys* & *gyne,* (woman).

Ponce . . . A protector, exploiter, keeper, lover, or husband of a prostitute.

Pork packer . . . A male who desires or has sexual intercourse with a female corpse.

PORNEPHILIA . . . 1. A benevolent attitude toward prostitutes. 2. Fondness for or preoccupation with whores. Ex *porne* (prostitute).

Porte-cochere . . . The female genital inlet, esp. the space between the labia.

Position assumed in the act of coitus . . . COITHESIS.

POSTCONNUBIAL . . . After marriage; occurring after marriage. Ex *post* & *connubium* (marriage).

Posterior, fat and broad, person having . . . **Bottle-arse.**

Posterior; in rhyming allusion to ass . . . **Bottle and glass.**

POSTMARITAL . . . After marriage; occurring after marriage. Ex *post* & *maritus* (married).

POSTORGASMIA . . . The occurrence of the sexual orgasm in the male after the acme in the female.

Pot . . . A female as a dish, a pudendal dish.

Pot of bliss . . . A female tomato dish, a nymphet, or the pudendal pudding of either.

Pot walloper . . . A frequent and/or vigorous phallator.

Potency, gradual waning of; in the male . . . FLACCILATION.

Potent sexually and able to have pudendal intercourse in a lying position only . . . CLINOVALENT.

Potent sexually and able to have pudendal intercourse in a standing position only . . . STASIVALENT.

Potent sexually and able to have pudendal intercourse in the face-down or prone position only . . . PRONOVALENT.

Potent sexually and able to have pudendal intercourse in the supine posture only . . . SUPINOVALENT.

Pounce-spicer . . . A bully, keeper, protector, or lover of a harlot.

Pound of flesh . . . The external genitalia of the male, in allusion to a demand in "The Merchant of Venice."

Pound of flesh, early allusion to . . . "A man's a man the world around, But a boy's not a man till his parts weigh a pound."

Pray with knees upwards . . . Of the female, to be the recipient of the phallic nudge.

PREBLYSIS . . . A premature ejaculation. From *prae* (before) & *blyzo* (spurt out).

Precoital excitation of the phallus by the hand, to aid a lethargic organ in completing the action . . . **Warm-up.**

Preference for masturbation exhibited by a married male having easy vaginal access . . . MANUAL PREFERENCE.

Pregnancy as a plea for special consideration by a female convict or one accused of a crime . . . **Belly plea.**

Pregnancy occurring as result of coitus between unwed coitants . . . **Leg drama.**

Pregnant . . . **Kidded; Shot in the giblets.**

Pregnant, become, the old-fashioned way . . . **Break one's knee; Nap the kid.**

Pregnant, condition of being . . . **Interesting condition.**

Pregnant; in allusion to the uterine seeding . . . **Run to seed.**

Pregnant; in allusion to the young set of ribs forming . . . **Double-ribbed.**

Pregnant or impregnated, be . . . **Be knapped.**

PREMARITAL . . . Before marriage; occurring before marriage.

Premature ejaculation . . . PREBLYSIS.

Premature loss of sexual potency by the male . . . PROIMPOTENCE.

PREMENACMIST . . . A male who desires to have, or actually has, sexual intercourse with a girl before she has reached the age of menstruation. From *menacme* (the years of a woman's life during which she menstruates).

Premises . . . The realest possible estate of the female, from the biased view of the male genital pendant.

Preoccupation with thoughts of lewdness . . . LAGNEPHRONESIS.

Preoccupation with thoughts of the female breasts . . . MASTOPHRENIA.

Preoccupation with thoughts of the penis, by a female . . . MENTULOPHRENIA.

Preoccupation with thoughts of the vulva . . . CUNNIPHRENIA.

Preoccupation with thoughts of women and feminine pleasures . . . GYNEPHRONESIS.

PREORGASMIA . . . The occurrence of the sexual orgasm in the male prior to its occurrence in the female.

Preshen . . . A child in whose rectum a pederast finds phallic comfort.

Preshen fraternity . . . Catamites collectively; the world of catamites.

Pretty sweet meat . . . Prize mammae of a young female, confected with exquisiteness by a hand of Eros.

PRIAPISM . . . A persistent erection of the membrum virile, usually induced by some disorder rather than sexual desire. Ex *Priapos* (a Greek god personifying the male generative power).

PRIAPUS . . . The male copulative organ. Also, capitalized, a god personifying the male reproductive power.

Price of meat . . . The price of admission (of the pants worm) to the interlabial firth of a common-garden-variety harlot.

Prick . . . The organum virile as a perforator of the female pudendum.

Pride and joy . . . The left breast (pride) and the right breast (joy) of a tastefully endowed girl.

Pride of the morning . . . In a middle-aged or older male, having a willing but unable phallus, an eburnation of the petard observed in the morning, due, alas, not to a naturally regained virility, or even a successful Voronoff transplant, but to the utterly prosaic pressure of the ouron in the vesica.

Primer . . . The induction of ejaculation manually, prior to a normal sexual engagement, in order to prolong the coit and thus satisfy the female, by a male who is otherwise a sexual minute man.

PRIMESODIA . . . The first act of sexual intercourse by a female. Ex *primus* (first) & *eisodos* (a coming in).

PRIMESODIAL . . . Pert. to the first act of sexual intercourse partaken of by a female.

PRIMESODOPHOBIA . . . The fear of the first act of sexual intercourse, as experienced by the female.

Prize fagots . . . The female breasts beautiful.

Procreation of children . . . TECNOPOIESIS.

Procreative desire, esp. as felt periodically by animals . . . NISUS.

Procreative period in a man's life . . . GENNEON.

Procreative period in a woman's life . . . PROLEGERON.

Procreative power of the female . . . TECNODYNAMIA.

Procreative power of the male . . . VIRILITY.

Procurer . . . **Ass broker; Ass middleman; Brother-in-law; Butt broker; Butt middleman; Crack detail man; Eastman; Fish and shrimp; Macgimper; Shill; Skirt man; Sweet man; Squire of the placket; Pimp; Taxi steerer.**

Procurer of females for ruttish males . . . **Schatchen.**

Procurer of mercenary female pudenda for males with desirous genital pendants . . . **Brother of the gusset.**

Procuress . . . **Ass middlewoman; Sister-in-law; Crack detail woman; Skirt woman; She pimp.**

Procuress of mercenary vaginae for desirous phalli . . . **Buttock-broker.**

PROIMPOTENCE . . . The premature loss of sexual potency by the male. From *proios* (early) & *impotence.*

PROIOGENOCOSMIA . . . Precocious development of the secondary sex characteristics. From *proios* (early), *genos* (sex) & *kosmeo* (decorate).

PROIORCHIDISM . . . Early development of the genital system in the male. Ex *proios* (early) & *orchis* (testicle).

PROIOVARIA . . . Early development of the sexual organs and characteristics in the female.

Prolong phallation by withholding ejaculation . . . **Keep it up.**

Promote . . . Of a male, to make insincere love in order to set up the quarry for seduction.

PRONOVALENT . . . Potent sexually and able to have pudendal concourse in the face-down position. Ex *prone* (lying face downward) & *valere* (to be able).

Propagate the species . . . **Do gospel work.**

Proprietor(ess) of a vulvar exchange or brothel . . . **Buttock-broker.**

Prosser . . . A go-between, protector, exploiter, lover, or keeper of a whore.

Prostituette . . . A young and pudendally provocative whorelet.

Prostitute, as a pudendal merrymaker . . . **Merry-arsed Christian.**

Prostitute; conceived as a nymph of the pavement . . . **NYMPHE DU PAVÉ.**

Prostitute; conceived as an Australian "peach" . . . **Quandong.**

Prostitute; conceived as recipient of the phallic impact . . . **Blow.**

Prostitute; conceived as relieving men of their hypertensive phallic milk . . . **Goat-milker.**

Prostitute, engage a, for a pudendal nocturne . . . **Book.**

Prostitute, esp. a slovenly one . . . **Trug.**

Prostitute, esp. a young and/or inexperienced one . . . **Green goose.**

Prostitute, esp. an aggressive one . . . **Horseleech.**

Prostitute, give the sign to a; that she is wanted for a pudendal engagement . . . **Flag down.**

Prostitute; in allusion to her hiding behind a moniker . . . **Anonyma.**

Prostitute; in allusion to her rentable lower accommodation . . . **Apartment to let.**

Prostitute, in bed with a . . . **Molled.**

Prostitute of no special note . . . **Moll.**

Prostitute of proletarian class . . . **Buttock.**

Prostitute of proletarian class, esp. one who uses alum solution to shrink vaginal cavern . . . **Blasted brimstone.**

Prostitute on the prowl . . . **Foreskin hunter.**

Prostitute or a non-mercenary pudendal-privilege-giver . . . **Jude.**

Prostitute, short visit to, for one ejaculation . . . **Short time.**

Prostitute, to be out with a . . . **Be out christening.**

Prostitute, very attractive . . . **Masterpiece of night work.**

Prostitute who cooperates by imparting to her perineum a gratifying rhythm . . . **Bobtail.**

Prostitute who cooperates with a man in the act of blowing off his loose corns . . . **Blowen.**

Prostitute who hurries her patrons . . . **Hurry-whore.**

Prostitute who is also a fellatrice and anolinguist . . . **Buttock and tongue.**

Prostitute who is hired for a quick pudendal exchange, rather than for the night . . . **Hurry-whore.**

Prostitute who is infected venereally . . . **Fire ship; Frigate on fire.**

Prostitute who receives several patrons in rapid succession . . . **Buttered bun.**

Prostitute who softens men's hardships manually . . . **Handshaker.**

Prostitute who takes the phallus conventionally, rectally, and orally . . . **Jack of all trades.**

Prostitute who works mostly at night . . . **Bat.**

Prostitute . . . See also under *Harlot* and *Whore.*

Prostitutes as ladies . . . **St. John's Wood donas.**

Prostitutes, benevolent attitude toward . . . PORNEPHILIA.

Prostitutes, fear of . . . CYPRIDOPHOBIA.

Prostitutes, fondness for . . . PORNEPHILIA.

Prostitutes, patron of . . . **Harry Common.**

Prostitutes, young, in the teen-age class . . . **Kid-leather.**

Prostitutes . . . See also under *Harlot* and *Whore.*

Prostitution as a breadwinning procedure . . . **A way of life.**

Prostitution as a business . . . **Leg business.**

Protect against impregnation by clothing the phallus in a condom . . . **Put on a raincoat; Put on the diving suit.**

Protect against impregnation by insertion of a diaphragm . . . **Bottle up.**

Provocative; said of body parts, but also of humor stories, etc . . . **Anatomical.**

Prowl in the back yard . . . To phallate per rectum.

Prowl in the middle . . . Probe the female pudendum with the phallus, in allusion to the middle of the three openings of the female perineum.

Prowler . . . A male or female homosexual in search for a patron or partner.

Pseudohermaphrodite, female . . . ANDROGYNUS.

Pseudohermaphrodite, male . . . GYNANDRUS.

PSEUDOHERMAPHRODITISM . . . The condition in which a person has gonads of one sex, as ovaries or testes, and malformed external genitalia resembling those of the opposite sex.

PSEUDOHERMAPHRODITISM, FEMALE . . . A form of pseudohermaphroditism in which the individual's gonads are ovaries but the external genitalia and/or secondary sex characteristics resemble those of a male.

Pseudohermaphroditism in the female . . . ANDROGYNISM.

Pseudohermaphroditism in the female marked by the presence of ovaries, an enlarged clitoris, and a scrotum-like pouch formed by the fusion of the labia majora . . . ANDROGYNISM; GYNANDRISM.

Pseudohermaphroditism in the male . . . GYNANDRISM.

PSEUDOHERMAPHRODITISM, MALE . . . A form of pseudohermaphroditism in which the gonads of the subject are testes but the external genitalia and/or the secondary sex characteristics resemble those of a female.

PSEUDORAPIST . . . A male who enjoys pretended resistance on the part of the female.

Psychiatry dealing with sexual aberrations . . . PARAPHILIATRY.

PSYCHOLAGNY . . . Sexual excitation induced by thoughts of erotic matters.

Psychopathic lechery . . . TENTIGO.

Psychopathic lust, obsessed by . . . TENTIGINOUS.

PSYCHROGYNIA . . . Sexual frigidity in the female.

PSYCHROLAGNIA . . . Sexual frigidity. Ex *psychros* (cold) & *lagneia* (lust).

PSYCHROSENIA . . . Sexual frigidity in the male. Ex *psychros* (cold) & *arsen* (male).

PSYCHROTIC . . . Sexually frigid.

PSYCHROTREMA . . . A sexually frigid wife. Ex *psychros* (cold) & *trema* (vulva).

PUBEBLASTESIS . . . The appearance of pubic hair. Ex *pubes* (pubic hair) & *blastesis* (a sprouting).

Pubic hair, esp. of the female . . . **Green grove; Parsley.**

Pubic hair, esp. of the female, as rich fabric . . . **Plush.**

Pubic hair, first appearance of . . . PUBEBLASTESIS.

Pubic hair, first scattered, of a budding girl . . . **Schpritz.**

Pubic hair of the female . . . GYNELOPH; **Christmas tree.**

Pubic hair of the female, as conceived by a cunnilinguist . . . **Shaving brush.**

Pubic hair of the female, conceived as a "park" . . . **Bushy Park.**

Pubic hair of the female, especially erotic about . . . GYNELOPHILOUS.

Pubic hair, restrain a woman by a hold on her . . . **Goose.**

Pubic region of the female . . . **Front lawn.**

Pud . . . The organum virile as a genital forefoot.

PUDENDA . . . The external genitalia of the female. (Plural, PUDENDAE.)

PUDENDAL . . . Of the nature of, pert. to, or designating the sex organs of the male or the female. Also, genital, sexual, or erotic.

Pudendal artist; good phallator; virile fornicator . . . **Good fellow.**

Pudendal celebration marked by bean-spilling . . . **Beano.**

Pudendal delta . . . The genital entrance of the female; the lower mouth of the female.

Pudendal entertainment provided by the phallus erectus . . . **Jack entertainment.**

Pudendal feast marked by substantial spilling of seminal fluid . . . **Bean feast.**

Pudendal hiatus . . . In the female, the cavity between wind and water into which the male phallus without unusual cravings insinuates itself for erotic comfort.

Pudendal indulgence, given to; of the male . . . **Battered.**

Pudendal mouth . . . In the female, the silent mouth which accommodates the phallus in normal sexual concourse.

Pudendal plaster . . . The female coital apparatus, or the bearer thereof.

Pudendal privileges, bestow; to a more than willing jack . . . **Play the ace against the jack.**

Pudendal privileges, denial of, by a wife to her husband, as coercion or punishment . . . **Jamaica discipline.**

Pudendal spree, go on a; of the male . . . **Go on a batter.**

Pudendal telegraphy . . . A form of communication in which purely arbitrary gyrations of female body ornaments send a universal message to male observers.

Pudendalia . . . The various erotically disturbing components of the vulva, collectively, as conceived by a living male.

Pudendally approachable; said of a female . . . **Knock-upable.**

PUDENDUM . . . The external genital organs, esp. of the female. In the female it includes the mons pubis, labia majora, labia minora, clitoris, and introitus vaginae. Ex *pudere* (to be ashamed).

Pudendum, basin over which a female stands, with one leg on each side, while washing her . . . Bidet.

Pudendum muliebre as a loving arena . . . **Love lane.**

Pudendum muliebre as a phallic toaster . . . **Roaster; Toaster.**

Pudendum muliebre as a roaster for the phallus . . . **Roasting jack.**

Pudendum muliebre as a soothing application . . . **Plaster of warm guts.**

Pudendum muliebre as phallic pie . . . **Rabbit Pie.**

Pudendum muliebre, as seen by a novice . . . **The novelty.**

Pudendum muliebre, conceived as a furry cat . . . **Chat.**

Pudendum muliebre, esp. the vagina . . . **Hole.**

Pudendum muliebre . . . See also under *Vulva.*

Pudendus . . . The phallus and the testicles. (Plural, Pudendi.)

Pull oneself off . . . Of a man harassed by phallic inflation, to counter with a few well-chosen deflationary movements of the cupped hand.

Pullet . . . A young girl, pudendally speaking.

Pullet squeezer . . . An amorous male who has more than an average interest in fledgling girls.

Pump . . . To phallate a female.

Pump oneself off . . . To trigger the seminal spurt by manual stimulation.

Pump thunder . . . To phallate a female with a genitally famished organum virile.

Punaluan Family . . . A form of family based on the intermarriage of several sisters with each others' husbands, or on the intermarriage of several brothers with each others' wives.

Punk . . . A boy whose anus and rectum is a "vagina" for a pederast.

Punk kid . . . Same as **Punk,** the boy in pederasty.

Pursitus . . . An itching of the scrotum, esp. when one cannot relieve it by scratching, because of the presence of others.

Puss . . . The female's furry and warm animalcule, between the thickest parts of her thighs.

Pusse . . . Old spelling of **puss,** the irresistible entrance at the lower end of the female torso.

Pussy . . . A cuddlier form of **puss,** the fur-trimmed pudendal edifice of the female.

Pussy and pepper . . . A female pudendal offering served with the proper rhythm.

Pussy-bait . . . A substantial bank account, or its equivalent.

Pussy beard . . . The pubic hair of the female.

Pussy bumping . . . An act of sexual gratification in which two females rub their genitalia against each other.

Pussy cap . . . A contraceptive diaphragm.

Pussy-cat . . . An affectionate variant of **puss**, the phallically best part of a woman.

Pussy-driller . . . The membrum virile erectum.

Pussy-fishing . . . The endless search for accessible female introiti.

Pussy gate . . . The hymen, conceived as a framework swinging at the entrance to pussyland.

Pussy-grass . . . The hairy mat of the female pudendum.

Pussy guard . . . The menstrual pad as a red flag, in re coitus.

Pussy-hack . . . The manager of a bordello.

Pussy heater . . . The fervent phallus erectus.

Pussy lawyer . . . An attorney who specializes in breach-of-promise, heart-balm, mental cruelty, and similar female-favoring legal suits; esp. one who is eminently successful in obtaining favorable verdicts for his distaff clients.

Pussy-license . . . A marriage license, as a permit to join giblets.

Pussy lunch-counter . . . A commercial dispensary of female pudendal creature comforts; a bordello.

Pussy massage . . . Sexual concourse, conceived, not seriously, as a means for improving pudendal circulation.

Pussy paint . . . The rubicund effluent of the female slit, during one of the catamenia.

Pussy-queer . . . A female homosexual; also, a female heterosexual with aberrational tendencies.

Pussy rag . . . The pad which gags the lower mouth of the female during the monthly claret ooze.

Pussy smeller . . . A lecherous male who derives erotic pleasure from whiffing the aroma of used but unwashed female undies.

Pussy-whacker . . . A hungry and, therefore, vigorous phallator.

Pussy-whanker . . . A female masturbator, esp. one who uses a godemiche.

Put away . . . Replace the phallus in its normal hangout, after a futile plea for and frustrated attempt at interlabial intromission.

Put in the pot . . . To intromit the phallus in the conventional manner and place.

Put it in . . . Plunge the phallus into the female pudendal ravine.

Put on a raincoat . . . To invest the phallus with a condom.

Put on a tin hat . . . To give the phallus starch.

Put on Sunday clothes . . . To achieve or suffer an upthrust of the phallus.

Put on the diving suit . . . To sheathe the penis with a condom.

Put one's hand down a girl's neckline . . . **Drop anchor in the bubby hutch.**

Put steam in the bucket . . . To give the phallus cause for upstanding.

Put the boots to . . . To give the seminal injection to.

Put the devil into hell . . . To sink the male plumb into the female pudendal well.

Put the oar in . . . Invade the pudendal suite of the female with the fleshy oar of the male.

Putz . . . The male rhizome which has a natural pudendotropism for the female lower hawsehole.

PYGOPHILEMIA . . . Sexual perversion in which pleasure is derived from kissing the female buttocks. Ex *pyge* (rump) & *phileo* (kiss).

PYGOPHILOUS . . . Of a male, especially erotic about the female buttocks. From *pyge* (rump) & *philein* (to love).

PYGOTRIPSIS . . . A rubbing of the buttocks, between male and female or between females, as a means of deriving sexual pleasure. Ex *pyge* (rump) & *tribein* (rub).

PYROLAGNIA . . . Sexual gratification derived from the sight of fires or from arson. From *pyr* (fire) & *lagneia* (lust).

Q

Quaedam . . . 1. A female who is the monger of her pudendal favors. Ex the Latin, "a certain woman." 2. A homosexual.

Quail . . . A female regarded as "tail."

Quail . . . Female pudenda collectively.

Quail . . . An old maid, or any pudendally unsampled female, who is skittish or easily frightened by the very mention of amorous themes.

Quail hunting . . . A search for girls with get-at-able feminine charms.

Quaint . . . A girl's privy parts, known also, in Middle English, as the "cunte."

Quality of being attracted erotically toward another person, rather than to oneself . . . HETERO-EROTISM.

Quality of being attracted erotically toward oneself . . . AUTO-EROTISM.

Quality of being attracted erotically toward the opposite sex . . . HETEROSEXUALITY.

Quality of being attracted erotically toward the same sex . . . HOMOSEXUALITY.

Quality . . . See also under *Condition*.

Quandong . . . A practitioner of Mrs. Warren's profession, in allusion to the Australian fruit of the same name, easily corrupted.

Quarry . . . A female conceived as the target of the male libido.

Quarry . . . In a girl, the objet d'art, from the barbarian viewpoint of the phallus.

Quartern of bliss . . . A small but very attractive female, conceived as a concentrate of pudendal heaven.

Quean . . . A passive male homosexual.

Queen . . . A male homosexual.

Queen of swiveland . . . A girl fit to be queen in a Utopia devoted to sexual pleasures.

Queer . . . A homosexual, esp. a male with obvious effeminate manners.

Queer mort . . . A syphilitic whore; a pocky strumpet.

Quickie . . . A sexual bout with an ardent male who dispenses the seminal elixir before the succubant female has a chance to say "Jack me Robinson."

Quicumque vult . . . A girl pudendally really quite reasonable. From the opening words of the Athanasian Creed, *Quicumque vult,* whosoever will (be saved).

Quid . . . The pudendum muliebre, as something to chew on.

Quiff . . . A poor man's whore, in allusion to the cheap perfume used by same.

Quiver . . . The female pudendal case in which a desirous male loves to quiver his arrow.

Q.T. cutie . . . A girl or young woman, usually a pulchritudinous one, who gives pudendal privileges to needy males, for money.

R

Rabbit . . . The extensile pudendal organ of the male.

Rabbit pie . . . 1. The bilabial lower ornament of the female. 2. A woman whose pudendal inlet is available for short-term engagements.

Rabbit skin . . . A sheath for the phallus, used in coitus, for prophylaxis against infection and impregnation.

RADIX . . . A Latin figurative synonym for the penis, in allusion to a root.

Ramrod . . . The fleshy rod of the male used to ram down the seminal charge in the female pudendum.

RAMUS . . . A Latin figurative synonym for the penis, in allusion to a branch.

Rantallion . . . A male whose phallus is shorter than his scrotum.

Rantum-scantum . . . A bout of genital copulation, esp. a noisily exuberant one.

RAPE . . . Sexual intercourse or, in some states, mere pudendal contact with a female, not the wife of the male, against her will, by force or threats, or by deceit or stealth. Also called *rape of the first degree.*

Rape by force involving a child . . . PEDIRAPTUS.

Rape by force involving a married woman . . . MATRONORAPTUS.

Rape by force involving an elderly woman . . . ANORAPTUS.

Rape by force involving one's own mother . . . MATRORAPTUS.

Rape by force involving one's own sister . . . SORORIRAPTUS.

Rape combined with cannibalism . . . ANTHROPOPHAGOLAGNIA.

Rape, male committing . . . RAPTOR.

Rape of one's own wife . . . VAGINORAPTUS.

RAPE OF THE FIRST DEGREE . . . See under RAPE.

RAPE OF THE SECOND DEGREE . . . See under RAPE, STATUTORY.

RAPE, STATUTORY . . . Sexual intercourse with a female, not the phallator's wife, who is under the age of consent to the act, the age being fixed by the law of the state or the land where the rape is committed. Also called *rape of the second degree.*

Rape, victim of . . . RAPTEE.

Rapist, esp. one attacking immature females with small inlets . . . **Tommy buster.**

Rapist of old women . . . ANORAPT.

RAPTEE . . . A female upon whom rape was committed. Ex *rapto* (ravage).

RAPTOR . . . A male who commits rape.

Rasp . . . The female pudendal receptacle, in allusion to its attrition upon the incoming phallus.

Rattling saber . . . The male pudendal monolith in its saber-rattling mood.

Reaction, exaggerated, to sexual stimulation . . . EROTOMANIA.

Ream . . . To insinuate the phallus into the rectum.

Reamer . . . The male genital mandrel conceived as a dilator of the vaginal corridor or, in sodomy, of the rectum.

Receive the phallus from behind . . . **Say prayers backwards.**

Receiving set . . . The pudendum muliebre as the receiver of the membrum virile.

Rectum as a sodomite's haven . . . **Spice island.**

Rectum as the aberrant route for phallic invasion, usually applied to the rectum of the female, so used . . . **Rural Route No. 2.**

Rectum, phallating per . . . **Shooting into the brown.**

Rectum, phallation by, with a female . . . ANOMEATIA.

Recuperation period of the phallus between bouts of a sexual orgy . . . **Retooling period.**

Red comb . . . Ruttishness in the male, in allusion to the ruddiness of the comb in desirous birds.

Red-hot . . . A desirous, upstanding membrum virile.

Red hot fly . . . The fly of a man's trousers hotter than a hot fly.

Refuse phallic intromission . . . **Abstain from beans.**

Refuse to open up for the reception of the male organ; said of a retaliatory or simply recalcitrant female . . . **Say boo to the battledore.**

Rehabilitate . . . Of a harlot, to give up whoring, esp. in favor of marriage.

Relaxation of the erected phallus following the seminal vesuviation . . . **Convalescence.**

RENIFLEUR . . . A person who derives sexual pleasure from the odor of urine, esp. that voided by one of the opposite sex.

Replace the phallus in its natural hangout, after an ejaculatorywise futile attempt at action . . . **Put away.**

Replace the phallus within the fly slit, esp. after a hurried sexual foray, as in a hallway, park, etc. . . . **Box the compass.**

Response, lack of, from female sexual partner . . . ANAPOCRISIS.

Responsive, with motion, to the phallic lunges . . . **Nimble-hipped.**

Rest between bouts of coitus . . . **Rest upon the oars.**

Rest between bouts of coitus . . . **Retooling period.**

Rest upon the oars . . . To rest between coital activity.

Retire from whoring and apply pudendum to peaceful uses, in wedlock . . . **Convert.**

Retire from whoring, by way of marriage or otherwise . . . **Hang up one's fiddle.**

Retooling period . . . The period of sexual recuperation between two flings at coitus; said of a couple planning to make a night of it.

RHEOMISM . . . A form of masturbation practiced by females in which a stream of water, as from a rubber hose, is directed against the clitoris and introitus. Ex *rheo* (flow) & *mihi* (me).

RHEOMIST . . . Female masturbator who obtains erotic gratification by directing a stream of water upon her genitalia.

Ride . . . The act of genital copulation.

Ride . . . Of the male, to bob on the female pudendal saddle; to overlie the female in sexual concourse.

Ride behind . . . To intromit the male insinuator rectally. Also, to phallate vaginally from behind.

Ride rantipole . . . To phallate a female with her superimposed.

Ride St. George . . . Phallate a female with her on top.

Ride the deck . . . To phallate from behind, into the rectum.

Rider . . . The phallator of a woman, usually from the top position.

Riding St. George . . . A bout of sexual concourse in which the female is the rider and the male is the mount, in allusion to St. George and the dragon, and also to the belief, not current, that a child conceived in this fashion is likely to become a bishop.

Riffle . . . 1. To feel, digitally, the decorative parts of a girl. 2. To feel girl and phallate same.

Righteous bush . . . The hairy tuft, the nether labia, and, under all, the inclosed muliebral fascinallia of a female who avers never to have been, or alas never indeed was, spitcocked.

Ringtail . . . A boy phallated per rectum by a pederast.

Ripe for childbearing; said of a young girl . . . TOCOPEPANTIC.

Ripe for marriage; said of a girl just old enough . . . NUBILE.

Ripe for the phallus; said of a girl, with regard to age . . . **Poker-ripe.**

Ripper . . . A savage attacker of women who slashes their genitalia.

Road . . . 1. The female's soft sheath for the phallus. 2. A female who makes her sheath available on short term loans.

Road hog . . . An impotent husband; because of his dog-in-the-manger role.

Road hog . . . A male who seemingly never gets enough of the female pudding.

Road kid . . . A boy who accompanies a tramp and serves as his catamite.

Road-starved . . . Starved for the female **road** to pudendal gratification.

Roast beef dress . . . The interlabial sanctum muliebre, conceived as a fleshy dress for roasting the phallus amorously.

Roast brown . . . To give the phallus a hot reception, vaginally.

Roast jack . . . The membrum virile with a satisfied mind, 'cause he's had it.

Roast meat clothes . . . Night clothes as garments worn when phallic meat is roasted vaginally.

Roast snow in a furnace . . . To offer an impotent phallus to an ardent female pudendum.

Roast the meat . . . To give the phallic tissue a hot vaginal reception.

Roast the meat . . . Of the female, to let see and feel much of the desirables, but to remain to the phallus a *noli me tangere.*

Roaster . . . The female interlabial oven as a phallic cooker.

Roasting jack . . . Same as **Roaster,** the pudendal cooker of the female.

Rob-the-ruffian . . . The female genital appeaser that robs the male pudendal ruffian of his plethora.

Roby Douglas . . . The anus, in allusion to a sailor so named, who had but one eye and "a stinking breath."

Rochester portion . . . A meager dowry consisting of nothing more than the genitalia.

Rod . . . Same as **Ramrod,** the seminal rammer.

Rod . . . The male membrum erectum, in allusion, quite obviously, to its figure.

Rod . . . Tho phallate a female.

Rodger . . . Same as **Roger,** to give a female the taste of the membrum virile erectum.

Roger . . . To phallate a female, in allusion to a ruttish bull frequently, formerly, named Roger.

Rogue and pullet . . . A seducer and his seduced-to-be, or already seduced, young thing.

Roll in the hay . . . Bring to fruition, with a farmer's daughter or her equivalent, the glint in the eye of the proverbial salesman.

Rolling pin . . . The fleshy cudgel wherewith the male gives the female pudendum its seminal irrigation.

Roly-poly . . . The male pudendal rascal.

Roman Catholic girl, phallate a, out of wedlock . . . **Crash the breast fleet.**

Romantricks . . . What young lovers engage in after little brother, or sister, has been disposed of with the usual bribe.

Rose . . . The decorative doorway to the sexual reception chamber of the female.

Rose . . . The figurative symbol of girlish pudendal innocence.

Rose between two thorns . . . A female lying between two desirous and able males with spiked phalli.

Rose, pluck a . . . To take away the pride of a virgin female pudendum by giving it phallus erectus.

Rosin the bow . . . To lubricate the phallus prior to intromission.

Roughness of the vaginal mucosa . . . TRACHYCOLPIA.

R.R. 1 . . . A coded term designating a harlot of the conventional variety who takes the phallus in her well-polished vagina, as opposed to the rectum. See also under **Rural Route No. 1.**

R.R. 2 . . . An esoteric designation for a harlot who takes the membrum virile erectum per rectum. See also under **Rural Route No. 2.**

R.R. 3 . . . A recondite brand for a harlot of the fore-and-after variety, who takes the genital mandrel of the male either by the vaginal or by the rectal route. See also under **Rural Route No. 3.**

Rub off . . . Of a male haunted by phallic hunger, to substitute palmar skin for vaginal mucosa.

Rubbing against another, as in a crowd, to obtain sexual pleasure . . . FROTTAGE.

Rubbing of buttocks as a means of deriving or giving sexual pleasure . . . PYGOTRIPSIS.

Rubbing of buttocks between female homosexuals . . . **Bum-fighting.**

Rubbing of female genitalia against each other, in the act of tribadism . . . **Pussy bumping.**

Rubbing of genitalia against each other by two females . . . TRIBADISM.

Rufus . . . The lipped underside of the female, in allusion to the reddish mucosa.

Rule of three . . . The triumvirate of the penis and the testicles. Also, the genital union of these with the female inlet.

Rummage . . . To search for a catamite or for an adult subject in sodomy.

Rump, big, in allusion to the two chamberpots it would take to support it . . . **Double jug.**

Rump; conceived as the posterior feature . . . **Fundamental feature.**

Rump, esp. as the arena of a sodomite . . . **Seat of vengeance.**

Rump, female, especially erotic about the . . . PYGOPHILOUS.

Rump; in allusion to the anus as a bunghole . . . **Corybungus.**

Rump, mountainous, having a; of the female . . . **Double-arsed.**

Rump, too much of . . . **Too much Charley.**

Run a tier . . . To search for a catamite, the boy in pederasty.

Run to seed . . . Of the female, seeded with spermatozoa and "took," i.e., impregnated.

Runts . . . Female breasts that didn't quite make it, size-wise.

Rupture of the hymen, as in defloration . . . HYMENORRHEXIS.

Rural Route No. 1 . . . The vagina as the conventional route for the phallus erectus. Also, normal concourse between phallus and vagina.

Rural Route No. 2 . . . The rectum, usually of the female, as the extracurricular receptor of the male sexual probe. Also, sexual intercourse in which the rectum is the phallic receptor.

Rural Route No. 3 . . . A female perineum which receives the male visitor in either the front or the rear parlor, i.e., vaginally or rectally. See also under **R.R. 1, R.R. 2,** and **R.R. 3.**

Rush up the frills . . . Of a male presented with the smile of assent from the female pudendum, to take to the entree, without regard for the *hors d'oeuvres.*

Rush up the petticoats . . . Same as **Rush up the frills,** to jettison the *apéritif* in favor of the sexual *chef-d'oeuvre.*

Rush up the straight . . . Same as **Rush up the frills,** to dispense with the foreplay in favor of immediate pudendal action.

Rusty . . . Sexually impotent, or at least partly so.

S

Saber . . . That part of the male for which the vagina is a scabbard.

Saber rattling . . . 1. The spasmodic twitching of a tumefied phallus in its higher moments of ambition, usually at the sight of its quarry. 2. The act of assuaging an adamantine phallus by sheathing it with vagina.

SADISM . . . The derivation of sexual pleasure or gratification from the infliction of humiliation or physical cruelty upon another, esp. upon one of the opposite sex. Ex the name of an author (Count Donatien de *Sade)* who described the condition.

Sadism alternating with masochism . . . SADOMASOCHISM.

Sadism combined with some form of mania . . . SADOMANIA.

Sadism expressed in cruelty toward females . . . GYNESADISM.

Sadism expressed in cruelty toward men . . . ARSENOSADISM.

Sadism in a female homosexual, directed toward other females . . . SAPPHOSADISM.

Sadism, intense or maniacal form of . . . SADOMANIA.

Sadism practiced on a dead body, esp. on the corpse of a female . . . NECROSADISM.

Sadism practiced on an animal, esp. on an animal of the opposite sex from the subject . . . ZOOSADISM.

Sadism, subconscious . . . BATHYSADISM.

Sadism, sublimated or refined form of . . . LEPTOSADISM.

SADIST . . . The person inflicting the cruelty in sadism.

Sadist, female . . . MASTIX.

Sadist, female, who is also a homosexual . . . SAPPHOSADIST.

SADOMANIA . . . Sadism combined with some form of mania.

SADOMANIA . . . An intense, maniacal form of sadism.

SADOMASOCHISM . . . The coexistence of sadism and masochism, i.e., the condition in which the subject derives sexual pleasure from inflicting or suffering pain.

Sail in the same boat . . . To share one's mistress with another man.

Sail into the wind . . . To phallate per rectum, in allusion to the rectum as an exhaust for flatus.

Salad . . . The female pudendal dish.

Salad dressing . . . The phallic ejaculant, in allusion to its function as "dressing" upon the female "salad."

Salesman . . . A male homosexual who is looking for a patron.

Salute the hips . . . To tap the female crotch with the turgid mace.

Sanctum muliebre . . . The not always sacred genital appurtenances at the lower end of the female torso.

Sandwich . . . A man lying between two willing women.

Sanitary belt supporting the vulvar pad against the bleeding slit during menstruation . . . **Crack-halter.**

Sanitary pad applied to the vulva during its monthly claret ooze . . . **Crack-halter.**

Sapphie . . . A female homosexual.

SAPPHISM . . . The erotic desire of a woman for another woman. Also, the expression and/or gratification of such desires.

SAPPHISMOLAGNY . . . The derivation of sexual pleasure by a male from the contemplation of, reading about, or witnessing expressions of erotic love between females.

SAPPHIST . . . A female homosexual. Ex *Sappho,* an ancient poetess who wrote exquisitely about love.

SAPPHOLINCTION . . . The licking of genitalia as practiced by female homosexuals.

SAPPHOLOGY . . . The study of sexual love between females.

SAPPHOMASOCHISM . . . Masochism in a female homosexual, gratifiable by a sapphosadist.

SAPPHOMASOCHIST . . . A female homosexual who is also a masochist, with cravings for cruelty administered by other female homosexuals.

SAPPHOSADISM . . . Sadism in a female homosexual, directed toward other female homosexuals.

SAPPHOSADIST . . . A female homosexual who is a sadist, esp. with regard to other female homosexuals.

SARMASSANT . . . Pert. to or involving the desire for or the element of necking or kneading the female's tissues; as a *sarmassant* gesture, look, etc.

SARMASSATE . . . To knead amorously the tissues of a woman, esp. those which are characteristic of the female sex.

Sarmassation, forcible; against the subject's will . . . HAPTOSIS.

SARMASSOPHIL . . . A male who is especially, above most males, fond of kneading amorously the characteristically feminine tissues. Also, a male who is lukewarm about phallation but is able to derive sexual gratification from such kneading. (From *sarx,* flesh, & *massein,* to knead.)

SARMASSOPHOBE . . . A female who has an aversion for or fear of being touched amorously.

SARMASSOPHOBIA . . . An aversion for or fear of being touched amorously. (Ex *sarx,* flesh, *massein,* to knead, & *phobos,* fear.)

SARMASSORESPY . . . Aversion for necking or amorous digital contact. Ex *sarmassate* (touch amorously) & *respuo* (spit back).

Satyr . . . A male with a prodding libido.

Satyresque . . . Like a satyr, in lecherous merriment and lasciviousness.

Satyress . . . A female given to lasciviousness.

Satyriasis . . . Excessive sexual desire in the male; uncontrollable desire to possess a woman or women. Ex *satyros* (a woodland deity fond of lechery).

Satyrion . . . A plant, esp. an orchid, regarded as an aphrodisiac.

Satyrism . . . Indulgence in unrestrained sexual pleasures, by the male.

Satyromaniac . . . A male affected by satyriasis or excessive sexual lust.

Save one's fat . . . Of a male, to abstain from phallation until the wedding bell tintinnabulation.

Say a mouthful . . . In fellatio, to let go of a mouthfiller.

Say boo to the battledore . . . Of a woman in bed with a man, to refuse to "open up" for the eager beaver, in retaliation, usually, for his refusal to open the money purse.

Say prayers backwards . . . To receive the phallus from behind.

Scab . . . To court the girl of a friend while she is separated from him by a tiff.

Scabbard . . . That passage in the female which, above all other passages anywhere, is beloved by the male, because it provides the best known remedy, to date, for the, alas, too common affliction known as phallus induratus; in allusion to the sheathing it provides for the spavined organ during the course of treatment.

Scabbard-bound . . . Of a male, laid up in bed with a case of swelling involving the genital petard, and taking treatment for it by "soaking" the afflicted member in the mucus-lined sheath of a subjacent female.

Scabbard-bound . . . Of a male animal, coupled to the female partner by the phallic link, because unable to withdraw, after a bout of piggyback.

Scabbard hound . . . A male who cannot as much as pass a girl on the street without mentally measuring her warm interfemoral slit with his eager pudendal foot-stick.

Scabbarditis . . . Not an inflammation of the vagina, but, perversely, a feverish condition of the phallus for which the female quiver is a specific.

Scalp . . . To tear the virgin hymen, phallically, of a sexually intact female.

Scapus . . . A Latin figurative synonym for the penis, in allusion to a shaft.

Scarcity of men, as in a particular region . . . Spaneria.

Scarcity of women, as in a particular part of the world . . . Spanogyny.

Schatchen . . . A bringer-together of females with pudenda to let and males with phalli seeking solace.

School of Venus . . . A house where female pudenda may be rented, and used on the premises.

Schpritz . . . The first scattered pubic hair of a ripening girl.

Schwantz-kid . . . The boy used in the act of pederasty.

Science of sex and its biologic manifestations . . . SEXOLOGY.

Science of sexual love . . . EROTOLOGY.

Science of . . . See also under *Study of*.

SCOPOLAGNIA . . . 1. Erotic desire aroused by looking at the genitalia of another, esp. of one of the opposite sex. 2. The desire to see the genitalia of another, esp. the genitalia of a female. Ex *skopein* (to look, examine) & *lagneia* (lust).

SCOPOPHILIA . . . An abnormal desire to look at the genital organs of another, esp. of one of the opposite sex. Also, the pleasure derived from such observation. From *skopein* (to look, examine) & *philein* (love).

Screw . . . A bout of sexual concourse conceived as a screwing of the phallus erectus into the female *scrobis* or vulva.

Screw . . . To subject the female pudendum to the typical phallic thrusts which constitute sexual intercourse.

Screw in earnest . . . To phallate for posterity, i.e., with intent to impregnate.

Screw-Johnny . . . A condom.

Screw one coming and going . . . To phallate in the normal manner (vaginally) and also per rectum.

Screw pink elephants . . . To have dreams involving sexual concourse.

Screw sweetening . . . Erotic movements, utterances, etc., contributed by the female in coitus as a roborant to the act.

Screwballs . . . The testicles conceived as the organs which make pudendal screwing possible.

Scrotum as a sac . . . **Bag.**

Scrotum, conceived as a purse or a pod . . . **Cod.**

Scrotum, esp. of a child . . . **Tassel.**

Sear . . . The female genital inlet, in allusion to the vent by which fire was communicated to the powder in old-time cannons.

Search for a girl with attractive legs . . . **Bowl for timber.**

Search for girls with liberal pudenda . . . **Grouse.**

Seat of honor . . . The buttocks, esp. of a female.

Seat of majesty . . . The genital ensemble of the female.

Seat of shame . . . The buttocks, esp. in dishabille.

Seat of vengeance . . . The rump, esp. from a sodomite's point of view.

Secondary sex characteristics, early development of . . . PROIOGENOCOSMIA.

Secondary sex characteristics of female, substance which stimulates development of . . . GYNECOGEN.

Secondary sex characteristics of females, as the breasts . . . GYNECOSMICS.

Secondary sex characteristics of females, excessive development of . . . HYPERCOSMOSIS.

Secondary sex characteristics of females, underdevelopment of . . . HYPOCOSMOSIS.

Secondary sex characteristics of males, as the beard, quality of voice, etc. . . . VIROCOSMICS.

Secondary sex characteristics of males, hormone which stimulates development of . . . ANDROGEN.

Secure a catamite or a pathic . . . **Snare.**

Secure a . . . See also under name of particular object.

Seduced; no more a virgin . . . **Broken-legged above the knee.**

Seduced; said of a pretty thing who has been had, in depth . . . **Broken-kneed.**

Seducer and his to be or already seduced young chick . . . **Rogue and pullet.**

Seduction, set up for, by insincere lovemaking . . . **Promote.**

See . . . To be in sexual concourse; said esp. of a female.

See a man . . . Of a man, to see a woman, about pudendal matters.

See a sick friend . . . To visit a female pudendum.

Seeds . . . The male gonads.

SEIN . . . The female breast. Ex French.

SEMEN . . . The male generative fluid ejected during the orgasm.

Semen . . . **Man-roe; Balm of Gilead; Jack-saliva; Gravy; Tail-juice; Victoria Monk; Cream-stick juice.**

Semen . . . **Infant seed; Liquid fertilizer; Man oil; Cream; Papa grease; Baby formula; Sperm oil; Gism.**

Semen, absence of; also deficiency of . . . ASPERMIA.

Semen, absence of functionally adequate spermatozoa from the . . . AZOOSPERMIA.

Semen, decreased production of . . . SPERMATOSCHESIS.

Semen, discharge of, during one's sleep; not necessarily associated with erotic dreams . . . NOCTURNAL EMISSION.

Semen, ejaculation of, during one's sleep, as a result of erotic dream . . . ONEIROGMUS.

Semen, expulsion of, during the sexual orgasm . . . EJACULATION; SPERMOBLYSIS.

Semen, implantation of, into the vagina . . . INSEMINATION.

Semen, implantation of, into the vagina, by artificial means . . . ARTINSEMINATION.

Semen, implantation of, into the vagina, by artificial means; when semen is from male other than the husband . . . ALLINSEMINATION.

Semen, implantation of, into the vagina, by artificial means; when semen is taken from husband . . . HOMINSEMINATION.

Semen, involuntary discharge of, unaccompanied by sexual orgasm . . . SPERMATORRHEA.

Seminal fluid . . . **Salad dressing.**

Seminal fluid as seed for the uterus ... **Kelder seed.**

Seminal fluid as vaginal meal ... **Oatmeal.**

Seminal fluid conceived as the offal of a "bull session" ... **Bullshit.**

Seminal fluid conceived as vaginal manna ... **Fiddle fare.**

Seminal fluid, deposit the, in the vagina ... **Garnish.**

Seminal fluid, discharge, in sporadic bouts with receptive females ... **Blow off the loose corns.**

Seminal fluid discharged during orgasm ... ECRON.

Seminal fluid ejaculated into the oral cavity of a fellator or a fellatrice ... **Ivory rinse; Mouth wash.**

Seminal fluid, esp. the excess of such that should be ejaculated in sexual concourse ... **Loose corns.**

Seminal fluid; in allusion to fluid of male fishes ... **Milt.**

Seminal fluid; in allusion to the spermatozoa ... **Beans.**

Seminal fluid; overloaded with; hence, desirous ... **Full of beans.**

Seminal fluid regarded as ... **Bung juice.**

Seminal fluid, regarded as the essence of the coital brew ... **Broth of joy.**

Seminal fluid, scantiness of ... SPANECRONIA.

Seminal fluid used in artificial insemination ... **Bottled beer.**

Seminal spurt in fellatio ... **Mouthful.**

Seminal spurt in fellatio, copious ... **Mouthfiller.**

Semtone ... Seminal fluid conceived as vaginal paint.

Servant, humble, who literally or figuratively holds his employer's phallus ... **Jack-hold-my-staff.**

Servant of a beautiful woman, derivation of sexual pleasure from imagining oneself a; by a male ... PAGEISM.

Sew up ... To impregnate a woman in the conventional manner.

Sex characteristics of either the male or the female ... GENOCOSMICS.

Sex characteristics ... See also under *Secondary sex characteristics.*

Sex interest, centering of, on coitus; rather than on the foreplay ... COITOCENTRY.

Sex interest, centering of, on one's own body; designating a ... IPSEROTIC; NARCISSISTIC.

Sex interest, centering, on coital foreplay ... PAIZOCENTRIC.

Sex interest, centering, on coitus; rather than on the foreplay ... COITOCENTRIC.

Sex organ of the male ... COLES; MEDOS; PENIS; PHALLUS.

Sex organ of the male, a sucking of ... PHALLOSUGIA; **Cocksucking; Mouth-diving.**

Sex organ of the male, excessive size of ... MACROPHALLIA.

Sex organ of the male, excessive smallness of ... MICROPHALLIA.

Sex organ of the male . . . See also under *Penis, Phallus, Membrum virile,* etc.

Sex organs, act of exposing, to view of others, esp. to members of the opposite sex . . . EXHIBITIONISM.

Sex organs and body, early and excessive development of, in a boy or a girl . . . MACROGENITOSOMIA.

Sex organs, centering one's erotic urge upon . . . GONADOCENTRIC.

Sex organs, direction of early interests and energies toward . . . AMPHIMIXIS.

Sex organs, erotic desire to see; esp. those of the opposite sex . . . GENITOPHILIA; SCOPOLAGNIA; SCOPOPHILIA.

Sex organs, excessive size of . . . MACROGENITALISM.

Sex organs, external, male deprived of . . . EUNUCH.

Sex organs, external, of a female . . . PUDENDUM MULIEBRE; VULVA.

Sex organs, external of a male . . . VIRILIA.

Sex organs, male and female, condition marked by presence of both . . . HERMAPHRODITISM.

Sex organs, male and female, person having both . . . HERMAPHRODITE.

Sex organs of a female . . . MULIEBRIA.

Sex organs of a female . . . See also under *Vagina, Vulva, Pudendum muliebre,* etc.

Sex organs of a male . . . ARRHENIDIA.

Sex organs of a male . . . See also under *Penis, Phallus, Membrum virile, Testicles,* etc.

Sex organs of female, erotic licking of . . . CUNNILINGUS; CUNNILINCTION; EDELINGUS; **Pearl diving; Biting the dog-end; Brushing with Miriam.**

Sex organs of male, artificial, used by females as an instrument of masturbation or tribadism . . . DILDO; GODEMICHE; OLISBOS.

Sex organs of male, erotic licking of . . . MEDOLINGUS; VIRILINGUS.

Sex organs, person who licks . . . LÉCHEUR.

Sex organs, smallness of . . . MICROGENITALISM.

Sex organs, underdevelopment of . . . HYPOGENITALISM.

Sex subjects, centering one's interest on . . . GONOCENTRIC.

Sex, treatise on . . . GENOGRAPHY.

Sex urge, dominance of . . . LIBIDOCRATIA.

Sex urge, pathologic abnormality of the . . . LIBIDOPATHY.

Sexlove, as opposed to the paternal, maternal, fraternal, sororal, avuncular, or nepotic type . . . **Blind love.**

SEXOLOGY . . . The science dealing with sex and its biologic manifestations.

Sexplore . . . To explore manually the arcana of the female body.

Sexual aberration in which a female defecates in the presence of a male who derives pleasure or gratification therefrom . . . **Boston Tea Party.**

Sexual aberration . . . See also under *Sexual perversion.*

Sexual aberrations, psychiatry dealing with . . . PARAPHILIATRY.

Sexual abstainer, to be a . . . **Abstain from beans.**

Sexual appetite, keen, female having . . . **Greedy arse.**

Sexual appetite, keen, female having . . . NYMPHOMANIAC; CLITOROMANIAC; ANDROMANIAC; PHALLOMANIAC.

Sexual attraction to a female corpse . . . NECROPHILISM.

Sexual bout in which the participants perform fellatio and cunnilingus upon each other, simultaneously . . . **Sixty-nine.**

Sexual concourse . . . **Business; Turn; What Harry gave Doll.**

Sexual concourse, amorous contribution to the, by a liberal harlot . . . **Blessing.**

Sexual concourse as a journey on the female pudendum . . . **Ride.**

Sexual concourse, as a jovial sinking of the membrum . . . **Merry go-down.**

Sexual concourse, as a pounding on the gates of the female pudendal heaven . . . **Knocking.**

Sexual concourse as clinical work . . . **Bedwork.**

Sexual concourse as knee exercise . . . **Knee drill.**

Sexual concourse as the domination of the female pudendum by the male triumvirate . . . **Rule of three.**

Sexual concourse as the "talk" of males . . . **Male conversation.**

Sexual concourse, be in; in a lively fashion . . . **Play at uptails all.**

Sexual concourse, be in; in allusion to a rodent . . . **Skin a live rabbit.**

Sexual concourse, be in; in allusion to the movement . . . **Swive.**

Sexual concourse, be in; in allusion to the parting of the labia, in the act . . . **Split.**

Sexual concourse, be in; in allusion to the umbilical cicatrices . . . **Wriggle navels.**

Sexual concourse, be on top in; of either the male or the female . . . **Play the bear.**

Sexual concourse between a married man and a female not the spouse . . . **Eating out.**

Sexual concourse between unwed coitants ending in unwelcome impregnation . . . **Leg drama.**

Sexual concourse; conceived as a boisterous adventure . . . **Joy ride.**

Sexual concourse; conceived as a coalition of button and hole . . . **Buttonhole work.**

Sexual concourse; conceived as a form of direct pudendal communication . . . **Tick-tack.**

Sexual concourse; conceived as a meeting of "bums" . . . **Bum-fighting.**

Sexual concourse; conceived as a meeting of the pudendal characters . . . **Bull session.**

Sexual concourse; conceived as a portion of the sexually functional end of the female . . . **Piece of tail.**

Sexual concourse; conceived as a pudendal dance . . . **Jazz.**

Sexual concourse; conceived as a pudendal fidget . . . **Frig.**

Sexual concourse; conceived as a pudendal menu of phallus, from the feminine viewpoint . . . **Peter.**

Sexual concourse; conceived as a romantic cuddling of the pudenda . . . **Nookie.**

Sexual concourse; conceived as a rattling of the phallus in the female sheath . . . **Saber rattling.**

Sexual concourse; conceived as a stirring with the male genital poker . . . **Poker fun.**

Sexual concourse; conceived as an ample dose of female pudendum . . . **Hunk.**

Sexual concourse; conceived as an insertion of the phallic shaft in the *scrobis,* vulva . . . **Screw.**

Sexual concourse; conceived as the action involved in a "bull session," esp. the male's part in it . . . **Bulling.**

Sexual concourse; conceived as the shanghaiing of the man's will which makes him a **cully** (dupe) . . . **Cully-shangy.**

Sexual concourse; conceived, earthily, by the male, as a sanguine dose of mundane pleasure . . . **Ass.**

Sexual concourse; conceived, romantically, as a pudendal tale . . . **Bedtime story.**

Sexual concourse, ending, after some jockeying, in mutual, though soaking, appeasement . . . **Blanket hornpipe.**

Sexual concourse, esp. the phallating action of the male . . . **Blow.**

Sexual concourse, exuberant bout of . . . **Rantum-scantum.**

Sexual concourse in a standing position . . . **Knee-trembler.**

Sexual concourse; in allusion to a storied character who, to assuage his wife, pretended to go on sea voyages while actually disappearing in the catacombs of whoredom . . . **Hobbe's voyage.**

Sexual concourse, in allusion to the "beating" given the female pudendum . . . **Strapping.**

Sexual concourse, in allusion to the bed . . . PAREUNIA.

Sexual concourse, in allusion to Venus . . . VENERY.

Sexual concourse in the conventional posture and manner . . . **Matrimonial polka.**

Sexual concourse in the morning, after a night of heavy seminal losses . . . **Kingsley's stand.**

Sexual concourse in wedlock . . . **Legitimate show.**

Sexual concourse in which the female is on top . . . **Riding St. George; Riding the dragon upon St George.**

Sexual concourse, join in . . . **Join giblets.**

Sexual concourse metaphorized . . . **Hole.**

Sexual concourse, normal, between heterosexuals . . . COITUS; COITION; PAREUNIA.

Sexual concourse, partake of; said of the female . . . **Lift a leg.**

Sexual concourse, play the game of . . . **Play at itch-buttocks.**

Sexual concourse prosaically conceived . . . **The business.**

Sexual concourse, regarded, by the female, as a pretty stiff dose . . . **Bit of stiff.**

Sexual concourse, regarded, by the woman, as both delightful and frightful . . . **Delightful frightfulness.**

Sexual concourse, talk a non-whoring girl into a . . . **Box the compass.**

Sexual concourse, to be in . . . **Chafer.**

Sexual concourse, to live it up in . . . **Take and give.**

Sexual concourse with a seminally overflowing male who dispenses the elixir before the female has a chance to say "Jack me Robinson" . . . **Quickie.**

Sexual concourse with the female on the top . . . **Riding St. George; Riding the dragon upon St. George.**

Sexual concourse with the male as the top man . . . **Bear play.**

Sexual craving, abnormal . . . EROTICISM; PARAPHILIA.

Sexual craving, abnormal . . . See also under *Sexual perversion.*

Sexual craving; conceived as abdominal pruritus . . . **Itch in the belly.**

Sexual cravings, conversion of, into nonerotic desires . . . SUBLIMATION.

Sexual daydreaming . . . HEMEROTISM.

Sexual desire, abnormally strong, in older men . . . GERONTOLAGNIA.

Sexual desire aroused by tantalization . . . TANTALOLAGNIA.

Sexual desire aroused by the aroma and/or sight of flowers . . . ANTHOLAGNIA.

Sexual desire as an instinct . . . EROTISM; LIBIDO; EROTICISM.

Sexual desire as an offshoot of procreative pyrexia . . . **Natal fever.**

Sexual desire, excessive . . . EROTOMANIA.

Sexual desire, excessive, in the female . . . ANDROMANIA; CLITOROMANIA; NYMPHOMANIA; PHALLOMANIA.

Sexual desire, excessive, in the male . . . GYNECOMANIA; SATYRIASIS.

Sexual desire, first appearance of, in the female . . . NEOLAGNIA.

Sexual desire, first appearance of, in the male . . . NEOLAGNIUM.

Sexual desire for a dead body . . . NECROPHILISM.

Sexual desire for a female child . . . PEDILAGNIA.

Sexual desire for animals . . . ZOOLAGNIA.

Sexual desire for children . . . PEDEROSIS.

Sexual desire for old women . . . ANILILAGNIA.

Sexual desire for one's own brother . . . FRATRILAGNIA.

Sexual desire for one's own father . . . PATROLAGNIA.

Sexual desire for one's own mother . . . MATROLAGNIA.

Sexual desire for one's own sister . . . SORORILAGNIA.

Sexual desire for young teen-age girls . . . NEANIROSIS; NEANILAGNIA;

BLASTOLAGNIA; LOLITALAGNIA; LOLITAPHRENIA.

Sexual desire in male . . . **Red comb.**

Sexual desire in male, excessive . . . GYNECOMANIA; SATYRIASIS.

Sexual desire in women, in allusion to a vulvar itch . . . **Cunt itch.**

Sexual desire, increase of, in the spring . . . VERNOREXIA.

Sexual desire induced or enhanced by the drinking of wine or similar beverages . . . OENOLAGNIA.

Sexual desire, intense; verging on the psychopathic . . . TENTIGO.

Sexual desire, intense . . . See also under *Sexual desire, excessive.*

Sexual desire, period of recurrent, in female beasts . . . ESTRUS.

Sexual desire, subnormal, female having . . . HYPOLIBIDA.

Sexual desire, subnormal, male having . . . HYPOLIBIDUS.

Sexual desire, substance which arouses . . . APHRODISIAC.

Sexual desire, substance which calms . . . ANAPHRODISIAC.

Sexual desire, waning of, in the male . . . OBSOLAGNIUM.

Sexual desire which is greater for a fully dressed woman than for one undressed . . . ENDYTOLAGNIA.

Sexual development, delayed, in boys; due to deficient function of the testes . . . HYPORCHIA.

Sexual development, delayed, in girls; due to deficient function of the ovaries . . . HYPOVARIA.

Sexual development, early, in boys; due to excessive secretion of the testicles . . . HYPERORCHIA.

Sexual development, early, in girls; due to excessive secretion of the ovaries . . . HYPEROVARIA.

Sexual excitation aroused by pictures and statues of nude figures . . . ICONOLAGNY.

Sexual excitation aroused by the sight of another in the act of urination, or by the sight of urine . . . UROLAGNIA.

Sexual excitation aroused by the sight of water or the thoughts of water nymphs . . . UNDINISM.

Sexual excitation in the female centered in the clitoris . . . CLITORIDISM.

Sexual excitation induced by certain odors . . . OSMOLAGNIA.

Sexual excitation induced by stealing . . . KLEPTOLAGNIA.

Sexual excitation induced by thoughts of erotic matters . . . PSYCHOLAGNY.

Sexual excitation induced in a woman by manipulation of her breasts . . . EROTOMASTIA.

Sexual excitation induced in the male by the good-night kiss and the accompanying amorous gratuities of his girl, as they part at her door . . . **Boodle fever.**

Sexual excitation or gratification induced by tickling nonsexual parts of the body . . . TITILLAGNIA.

Sexual excitation produced by odors, as of perfume, perspiration, etc . . . OSPHRESIOLAGNIA.

Sexual excitation produced . . . See also under *Sexual excitation induced.*

Sexual excitement, esp. when urgent . . . APHRODISIA.

Sexual foreplay . . . PAIZOGENY.

Sexual frigidity . . . PSYCHROLAGNIA.

Sexual frolic upon the blanket-covered bed, between man and maid, usually restricted to warmup sexercise, not including *it* . . . **Blanket ruffling.**

Sexual frustration, neurosis resulting from . . . LIBIDONEUROSIS.

Sexual gratification conditioned by a basic instinct, as hunger . . . ANACLISIS.

Sexual gratification derived from beating or mutilating a female corpse . . . NECROSADISM.

Sexual gratification derived from defecation . . . CHEZOLAGNIA.

Sexual gratification derived from sight of fires or from arson . . . PYROLAGNIA.

Sexual gratification derived from stimulation of the anus . . . ANAL EROTICISM.

Sexual gratification derived from watching others in the nude or in the act of sexual intercourse . . . VOYEURISM; INSPECTIONISM; SCOPOLAGNIA; SCOPOPHILIA.

Sexual gratification, desire for . . . **Itch.**

Sexual gratification without perceptible ejaculation . . . KENORGASMY.

Sexual gratuity contributed by a harlot, beyond the call of duty, to enhance the enjoyment of the act by the patron . . . **Blessing.**

Sexual impotence in the male, caused by lack of ability to stiffen the phallus . . . ASTYPHIA.

Sexual impotence in the male caused by lack of confidence . . . ATOLMIA.

Sexual impotence resulting from a sense of guilt . . . CACAVALENCE.

Sexual impotence resulting from disorder of erection . . . ASTYPHIA; ASTYSIA; ASYNODIA; INVIRILITY.

Sexual impotence resulting from worry . . . KEDAVALENCE.

Sexual impotence with one's own wife . . . UXORAVALENCE.

Sexual impotence with one's own wife in the usual environment, i.e., at home . . . NOMAVALENCE.

Sexual impulses, expression of, by means of nonsexual activities . . . SUBLIMATION.

Sexual intercourse, a fling at, as an extracurricular adventure, usually between man and wife, but not necessarily so . . . **A little conversation.**

Sexual intercourse, able to have, in a face down position only . . . PRONOVALENT.

Sexual intercourse, able to have, in a lying position only . . . CLINOVALENT.

Sexual intercourse, able to have, in a standing position only . . . STASIVALENT.

Sexual intercourse, able to have, in the supine posture only . . . SUPINOVALENT.

Sexual intercourse, active or male member in normal . . . COITANT; PHALLATOR.

Sexual intercourse as a function involving the interfemoral space . . . . . . **Leg business.**

Sexual intercourse, as a shaking of the mattress . . . **Mattress jig.**

Sexual intercourse attended by pain or other discomfort, esp. in the female . . . DYSPAREUNIA.

Sexual intercourse attended by pain or other discomfort in the genital organs, esp. of the male . . . DYSPHALLATION.

Sexual intercourse, be in; in allusion to the labial embrace of the phallus . . . **Parenthesize.**

Sexual intercourse between a father and his daughter . . . PATRINCEST.

Sexual intercourse between a human being and an animal . . . BESTIALITY.

Sexual intercourse between a human male and a female beast . . . BESTIAL SODOMY.

Sexual intercourse between a mother and her son . . . MATRINCEST.

Sexual intercourse between brother and sister . . . SORORINCEST.

Sexual intercourse between man and wife . . . VIRGYNATION.

Sexual intercourse between members of the opposite sexes, i.e., intercourse between heterosexuals . . . HETEROCOITUS.

Sexual intercourse between members of the same sex . . . HOMOCOITUS.

Sexual intercourse between persons who are too closely related for legal marriage . . . INCEST.

Sexual intercourse between two females, expressed, usually, by a rubbing of the approximated pudenda . . . CYMBALISM; TRIBADISM.

Sexual intercourse between two females in which the member playing the role of the male is provided with an artificial penis . . . OLISBONISM.

Sexual intercourse by way of the vagina and the rectum, have . . . **Fore and aft.**

Sexual intercourse; conceived as a dilatation of the vagina . . . **Colpeurysis.**

Sexual intercourse; conceived as the unworthy contribution of the female's inferior end . . . **Butt.**

Sexual intercourse conceived as vaginal dilatation . . . **Buck.**

Sexual intercourse continued to prostration and followed by a bored convalescence of the participants, dos-à-dos . . . **Dog's rig.**

Sexual intercourse, derivation of erotic pleasure or gratification from the act of observing others in . . . MIXOSCOPIA.

Sexual intercourse, designating bottom position in . . . SUCCUBOUS.

Sexual intercourse, designating top position in . . . INCUBOUS.

Sexual intercourse engaged in by three persons, either by two females and one male, or by two males and one female . . . TROILISM.

Sexual intercourse, entice a female into . . . **Twist a leg.**

Sexual intercourse, esp. such act enjoyed as an "extra," outside the nocturnal menu, as in the afternoon . . . **Blanket drill.**

Sexual intercourse, esp. the man's part in the act . . . PHALLATION.

Sexual intercourse, fast bout of, esp. in a hurried standing position, when time does not permit the luxury of recumbency in a bed, usually with a whore, in a park, a hallway, etc. . . . **Fast fuck.**

Sexual intercourse, fear of or aversion for, by the female . . . COITOPHOBIA.

Sexual intercourse, female or passive member in normal . . . COITANTE; PHALLATEE.

Sexual intercourse, first act of, by the female . . . PRIMESODIA.

Sexual intercourse from behind, with the woman in the knee-chest posture . . . COITUS À LA VACHE.

Sexual intercourse, from the viewpoint of the turgid phallus . . . **Phallic sweet talk; Phalliloquence; Phalliloquy.**

Sexual intercourse, have, more for the sport than for the relief of erotic tension . . . **Have a flutter.**

Sexual intercourse, illicit, any form of . . . FORNICATION.

Sexual intercourse, illicit, engage in any form of . . . FORNICATE.

Sexual intercourse, illicit, fine imposed for . . . **Buttock-mail.**

Sexual intercourse in which one or both participants experience the orgasm twice . . . **Double-tide job.**

Sexual intercourse in which the male withholds ejaculation . . . COITUS RESERVATUS.

Sexual intercourse in which the phallus is satisfied extravaginally, as in sodomy, phallation between the breasts, etc. . . . PARACOITUS.

Sexual intercourse in which the phallus is withdrawn from the vagina before ejaculation . . . COITUS INCOMPLETUS; COITUS INTERRUPTUS; ONANISM.

Sexual intercourse indulged in by the wayside, on the spur of the mood, in the manner of canines . . . **Dog's match.**

Sexual intercourse, lack of opportunity for; esp. between husband and wife . . . NONACCESS.

Sexual intercourse, one who is on bottom in . . . SUCCUBUS.

Sexual intercourse, one who is on top in . . . INCUBUS.

Sexual intercourse, painful, esp. in a female . . . DYSPAREUNIA.

Sexual intercourse, pleasure of, preceding the orgasm . . . FOREPLEASURE.

Sexual intercourse, position assumed in the act of . . . COITHESIS.

Sexual intercourse, think about . . . **Think about something to eat.**

Sexual intercourse, to withdraw oneself forcibly from, when the male is near the gratification point; said of the female . . . **Bluff the rat.**

Sexual intercourse, transmitted by . . . VENEREAL.

Sexual intercourse while standing, male who prefers . . . STASOPHALLIST.

Sexual intercourse with a fat female . . . **Bit of fat.**

Sexual intercourse with a female child . . . PEDIPHALLIA.

Sexual intercourse with a fully clothed woman, male who prefers . . . ENDYTOPHALLIST.

Sexual intercourse with a whore . . . CYPRIEUNIA.

Sexual intercourse with another man's wife, have . . . **Take a leaf out of another's book; Have an oar in another's boat.**

Sexual intercourse with, have . . . **Have a brush with.**

Sexual intercourse with one's wife against her will . . . VAGINORAPTUS.

Sexual intercoursing . . . **Chauvering.**

Sexual love, fear of or strong dislike for . . . EROTOPHOBIA.

Sexual love of a brother for his sister . . . SORORILAGNIA.

Sexual love of a daughter for her father . . . PATROLAGNIA; ELECTRA COMPLEX.

Sexual love of a father for his daughter . . . THYGATRILAGNIA.

Sexual love of a sister for her brother . . . FRATRILAGNIA.

Sexual love of a son for his mother . . . MATROLAGNIA; OEDIPUS COMPLEX.

Sexual love of one's own body . . . NARCISSISM.

Sexual love, science dealing with . . . EROTOLOGY.

Sexual lust, inducing . . . EROTOGENIC.

Sexual lust, initiation or production of . . . EROTOGENESIS.

Sexual lust, pert. to . . . CARNAL; SENSUAL; VOLUPTUOUS; EROTIC; LIBIDINOUS; LECHEROUS; LASCIVIOUS; LEWD; LICKERISH; PRURIENT; SALACIOUS; CONCUPISCENT; LUSTFUL; SATYRIC; GOATISH; LUBRICOUS; MUSTY; RUTTISH.

Sexual neurosis, induced by frustration . . . LIBIDONEUROSIS.

Sexual orgasm, concentrated pleasure of . . . END PLEASURE.

Sexual orgasm in the female . . . GYNACME.

Sexual orgasm in the male . . . VIRACME.

Sexual orgasm in the male, occurrence of, after its occurrence in the female . . . POSTORGASMIA.

Sexual orgasm in the male, occurrence of, before its occurrence in the female . . . PREORGASMIA.

Sexual orgasm, occurrence of, at the same time in both partners . . . SYNORGASMIA.

Sexual orgasm, pleasure accompanying . . . END PLEASURE.

Sexual orgasm, pleasure accompanying stage of excitation preceding . . . FOREPLEASURE.

Sexual orgy with two females, each alternately partaking in or witnessing the act . . . **Double event.**

Sexual ornament of a female . . . MULIANTHIUM.

Sexual perversion, branch of medicine dealing with . . . PARAPHILIATRY.

Sexual perversion in which a female uses a phallic substitute, as a dildo . . . OLISBONISM.

Sexual perversion in which intercourse is had between two females, as by approximating and rubbing the vulvae, by the use of an artificial penis attached to one of the participants, etc. . . . INTERGYNIA; LESBIANISM; TRIBADISM.

Sexual perversion in which intercourse is had between two males, in any of several ways . . . INTERANDRIA.

Sexual perversion in which intercourse is had with a dead body . . . NECROCOITUS; NECROPHILISM.

Sexual perversion in which intercourse is had with a female animal . . . ZOOERASTIA.

Sexual perversion in which intercourse is had with a female child . . . PEDIPHALLIA.

Sexual perversion in which intercourse with a female is more exciting when the recipient is fully dressed, esp. in street clothes . . . ENDYTOLAGNIA.

Sexual perversion in which pleasure is derived from beating or mutilating a dead body . . . NECROSADISM.

Sexual perversion in which pleasure is derived from being teased but not satisfied . . . TANTALOLAGNIA.

Sexual perversion in which pleasure is derived from being treated cruelly or from personal humiliation . . . MASOCHISM.

Sexual perversion in which pleasure is derived from eating the cooked genital parts of a member of the opposite sex . . . ANTHROPOPHAGOLAGNIA.

Sexual perversion in which pleasure is derived from exposing naked parts of one's body, including the genitalia, to the view of members of the opposite sex . . . EXHIBITIONISM.

Sexual perversion in which pleasure is derived from handling, viewing, or contemplating human feces, esp. those voided by one of the opposite sex . . . COPROLAGNIA.

Sexual perversion in which pleasure is derived from imagining oneself a servant or page of a beautiful woman . . . PAGEISM.

Sexual perversion in which pleasure is derived from inflicting pain or cruelty or humiliation . . . SADISM.

Sexual perversion in which pleasure is derived from kissing the anus of a female . . . ANOPHILEMIA.

Sexual perversion in which pleasure is derived from kissing the female armpit . . . MASCHALOPHILEMIA.

Sexual perversion in which pleasure is derived from kissing the female buttocks . . . PYGOPHILEMIA.

Sexual perversion in which pleasure is derived from kissing the female feet . . . PODOPHILEMIA.

Sexual perversion in which pleasure is derived from kissing the female genitalia . . . CUNNIPHILEMIA.

Sexual perversion in which pleasure is derived from licking the anus of another . . . ANOLINGUS.

Sexual perversion in which pleasure is derived from licking the female axilla . . . MASCHALINGUS.

Sexual perversion in which pleasure is derived from licking the nipples . . . THELELINGUS.

Sexual perversion in which pleasure is derived from licking the phallus . . . MEDOLINGUS.

Sexual perversion in which pleasure is derived from licking the vulva . . . CUNNILINGUS.

Sexual perversion in which pleasure is derived from rubbing against another, of the opposite sex, as in a crowd . . . FROTTAGE.

Sexual perversion in which pleasure is derived from submitting to the abnormal erotic desires of another . . . PASSIVISM.

Sexual perversion in which pleasure is derived from suffering or from inflicting pain . . . ALGOLAGNIA; SADOMASOCHISM.

Sexual perversion in which pleasure is derived from suffering pain and/or humiliation, esp. when inflicted by a person of the opposite sex . . . MASOCHISM.

Sexual perversion in which the female repeatedly moistens her nipples with wine which the male licks or suckles from her flesh . . . OENOSUGIA.

Sexual perversion in which the penis is introduced into one's own mouth . . . AUTOFELLATIO.

Sexual perversion in which the penis is introduced into the anus of a child, usually of a boy . . . PEDERASTY.

Sexual perversion in which the penis is introduced into the anus of a female child . . . COREPHALLIA.

Sexual perversion in which the penis is introduced into the anus of an adult . . . PROCTOLAGNY; SODOMY.

Sexual perversion in which the penis is introduced into the mouth of another . . . FELLATORISM; IRRUMATION.

Sexual perversion in which the penis is taken into the mouth . . . FELLATIO.

Sexual perversion in which the penis is reciprocated between the adducted knees of the female . . . GENUPHALLATION.

Sexual perversion in which the penis is reciprocated between the adducted thighs of the female . . . MERPHALLATION.

Sexual perversion in which the penis is reciprocated between the female breasts . . . MAZOPHALLATION.

Sexual perversion in which the penis is reciprocated in the armpit of a woman . . . MASCHALOPHALLATION.

Sexual perversion of any kind . . . PARAPHILIA.

Sexual perversion of unspecified character, generally homosexualism . . . **Nameless crime.**

Sexual perversion practiced by three persons, two men and a woman or two women and one male . . . TROILISM.

Sexual perversion . . . See also under *Masturbation.*

Sexual pervert; a person enjoying unorthodox sexual procedures . . . GENOPAST; PARAPHILIAC.

Sexual pervert, female homosexual . . . INTERGYNEE.

Sexual pervert, female, who allows her vulva to be licked . . . CUNNILINGANT.

Sexual pervert, female, who derives gratification by rubbing her genitalia against those of another female . . . TRIBADE.

Sexual pervert, female, who submits to sodomy . . . SODOMEE.

Sexual pervert, female, who takes the penis into her mouth . . . FELLATRICE.

Sexual pervert, male homosexual . . . INTERANDRIUM.

Sexual pervert, male, who submits to sodomy . . . SODOMANT.

Sexual pervert, male, who takes penis of another into his mouth . . . FELLATOR.

Sexual pervert who collects pictures depicting females in various states of undress . . . GYMNOTHESAURIST.

Sexual pervert who derives pleasure from beating or mutilating a dead body . . . NECROSADIST.

Sexual pervert who derives pleasure from being humiliated or treated cruelly . . . MASOCHIST.

Sexual pervert who derives pleasure from being teased but not satisfied . . . TANTALOLAGNIAC.

Sexual pervert who derives pleasure from exposing naked parts of the body, including the genitalia, to the view of others, esp. members of the opposite sex . . . EXHIBITIONIST.

Sexual pervert who derives pleasure from handling, viewing, or contemplating human feces, esp. those voided by a member of the opposite sex . . . COPROLAGNIAC.

Sexual pervert who derives pleasure from inflicting cruelty or humiliation upon others . . . SADIST.

Sexual pervert who derives pleasure from pretended resistance on the part of the female . . . PSEUDORAPIST.

Sexual pervert who derives pleasure from rubbing against others, of the opposite sex, as in a crowded public place . . . FROTTEUR.

Sexual pervert who derives pleasure from the odor of flatus, esp. the flatus of a female . . . EPROCTOLAGNIAC; **Fart-lover.**

Sexual pervert who derives pleasure from vivid, erotic fantasies . . . CONTEMPLATIVE.

Sexual pervert who derives pleasure from watching others in the act of coitus . . . VOYEUR.

Sexual pervert who enjoys sexual intercourse more or only when performed in the standing posture . . . ORTHOLAGNIAC.

Sexual pervert who enjoys sexual intercourse more or only when performed with a woman who is fully dressed, esp. in street clothes . . . ENDYTOLAGNIAC.

Sexual pervert who enjoys sexual practices more or only in the presence of a third person as observer . . . TROILIST.

Sexual pervert who enjoys sexual practices with two female partners . . . BIGYNIST.

Sexual pervert who enjoys sexual practices with two male partners . . . BIVIRIST.

Sexual pervert who has sexual intercourse with a boy, by the anus . . . PEDERAST.

Sexual pervert who has sexual intercourse with a female child by the anus . . . COREPHALLIST.

Sexual pervert who has sexual intercourse with a female child, vaginally . . . PEDIPHALLIST.

Sexual pervert who has sexual intercourse with a female corpse . . . NECROCOITANT.

Sexual pervert who has sexual intercourse with an animal . . . ZOOERAST.

Sexual pervert who introduces his penis between the female breasts . . . MAZOPHALLATOR.

Sexual pervert who introduces his penis in the armpit of a female . . . MASCHALOPHALLATOR.

Sexual pervert who introduces his penis into the anus of a child, usually a boy . . . PEDERAST.

Sexual pervert who introduces his penis into the anus of a female child . . . COREPHALLIST.

Sexual pervert who introduces his penis into the anus of an adult, male or female . . . PROCTOPHALLIST; SODOMIST.

Sexual pervert who introduces his penis into the mouth of another . . . FELLATRANT.

Sexual pervert who submits to the abnormal sexual acts of another pervert . . . PATHIC.

Sexual pervert who takes own penis into his mouth . . . AUTOFELLATOR.

Sexual pervert who uses an artificial phallus in masturbation . . . OLESBEE.

Sexual play before intercourse . . . FOREPLAY; PAIZOGONY.

Sexual play involving acts of perversion . . . PAIZOSIS.

Sexual pleasure accompanying orgasm . . . END PLEASURE.

Sexual pleasure, derivation of, from suffering or inflicting pain . . . ALGOLAGNIA; SADOMASOCHISM.

Sexual pleasure derived by a male from tantalization by a female, as by unapproachable nakedness, manual stimulation of the phallus short of ejaculation, and other appetizers . . . CONTRARIATION.

Sexual pleasure derived by a male from the contemplation of, reading about, or witnessing expressions of erotic love between females . . . SAPPHISMOLAGNY.

Sexual pleasure derived by rubbing a part of one's body against the genitalia of another of the opposite sex . . . PARTIALISM.

Sexual pleasure derived from being rendered helpless by tying with a rope . . . MERINTHOLAGNIA.

Sexual pleasure derived from contemplating erotic matters . . . PSYCHOLAGNY.

Sexual pleasure derived from exposing naked parts of one's body, including the genitalia, to the view of others, esp. to members of the opposite sex . . . EXHIBITIONISM.

Sexual pleasure derived from foreplay . . . FOREPLEASURE.

Sexual pleasure derived from handling, viewing, or contemplating human feces, esp. those voided by a member of the opposite sex . . . COPROLAGNIA.

Sexual pleasure derived from inflicting humiliation or cruelty upon another . . . SADISM.

Sexual pleasure derived from inflicting pain or from suffering pain at the hands of another . . . ALGOLAGNIA; SADOMASOCHISM.

Sexual pleasure derived from looking at the genitalia or related parts of another, esp. of a member of the opposite sex . . . INSPECTIONISM.

Sexual pleasure derived from or associated with activity of the mouth, as in eating . . . ORAL EROTICISM.

Sexual pleasure derived from or associated with muscular activity . . . MUSCLE EROTICISM.

Sexual pleasure derived from the act of being whipped . . . MASTILAGNIA.

Sexual pleasure derived from tickling or from being tickled . . . KNISMOLAGNIA.

Sexual pleasure derived from touching or rubbing against certain fabrics, as velvet . . . HYPHEPHILIA.

Sexual pleasure derived from viewing nakedness in the opposite sex . . . GYMNOSCOPY.

Sexual pleasure derived from watching others in the act of coitus . . . MIXOSCOPIA.

Sexual pleasure of phallation preceding the orgasm . . . FOREPLEASURE.

Sexual pleasure or gratification derived from inflicting humiliation or physical cruelty upon another, esp. upon one of the opposite sex . . . SADISM.

Sexual pleasure or gratification derived from subjection to humiliation or cruel treatment, esp. at the hands of one of the opposite sex . . . MASOCHISM.

Sexual pleasures may be had with some older women . . . **There's many a good tune played on an old fiddle.**

Sexual potency, absence or lack of, in the male . . . IMPOTENCE; INVIRILITY.

Sexual potency, decrease in . . . HYPOPOTENTIA.

Sexual potency, fear of losing . . . APHANISIS.

Sexual potency, impairment of, due to deficiency in testicular secretion . . . EUNUCHOIDISM.

Sexual potency, premature loss of . . . PROIMPOTENCE.

Sexual potency, restoration of . . . REJUVENESCENCE.

Sexual potency, waning of; in the male . . . FLACCILATION.

Sexual potency with certain selected women and impotency with others . . . IDIOGAMY.

Sexual potency with most women but not with one's wife . . . UXORAVALENCE.

Sexual potency with one's own wife, but not with other women . . . UXOROVALENCE.

Sexual practice or rubbing buttocks, between male and female or between females . . . PYGOTRIPSIS.

Sexual practice . . . See also under *Masturbation, Sexual perversion,* etc.

Sexual precocity . . . PROIOTIA.

Sexual precocity in females resulting from excessive activity of the ovaries . . . HYPEROVARIA.

Sexual precocity in males resulting from excessive activity of the testes . . . HYPERORCHIA.

Sexual privilege, buy the, from a harlot . . . **Buy milk.**

Sexual privileges with a woman . . . **Milk.**

Sexual promiscuity . . . PANMIXIA.

Sexual receptivity in female beasts, recurrent period of . . . ESTRUS.

Sexual relations . . . See under *Sexual intercourse.*

Sexual revelry of one female with three males, the latter taking turns, in the presence of the others . . . **Triple header.**

Sexual revelry of one female with two males, the latter taking alternate action, in allusion to the two glandes (of the two phalli) involved . . . **Double header.**

Sexual satisfaction, ability to give, by the female . . . GYNOPHELIMITY.

Sexual satisfaction, ability to give, by the male . . . OPHELIMITY.

Sexual satisfaction, inability to give, by the female . . . AGYNOPHELIMITY.

Sexual satisfaction, inability to give, by the male . . . ANOPHELIMITY.

Sexual self-admiration . . . AUTOEROTICISM; NARCISSISM.

Sexual stimulation, exaggerated reaction to . . . EROTOMANIA.

Sexual subjects, centering one's interests on . . . GENOCENTRIC.

Sexual urge, lack of outlet for . . . APHALLATIA.

Sexual urgency in the male . . . **Hot nuts.**

Sexual vitality in the male . . . GENOSTHENIA.

Sexual vitality, lack of, in the male . . . GENASTHENIA.

Sexually desirous, in allusion to pudendal good cheer . . . **Christmassy.**

Sexually efficient; with the phallus jutting . . . **Jake with the lever up.**

Sexually excited, as a virile phallus on a young female pudendum . . . **Like a cock on holy ground.**

Sexually excited; said of a male with a bulging fly . . . **Higher than a cat's back.**

Sexually exhausted . . . **Charvered.**

Sexually impotent under the usual coital conditions . . . NOMAVALENT.

Sexually mature; said of a female . . . MULIPEPANTIC.

Sexually mature; said of a male . . . VIRIPOTENT.

Sexually potent only under unusual or special conditions, or in a particular environment . . . PARAVALENT.

Sexually potent with other women but not with one's wife . . . ALLOVALENT.

Shack up . . . To bunk for the night with one of the opposite sex.

Shag . . . To reduce phallic pyrexia by a plunge in the female bucket of comfort.

Shake a loose leg . . . Of a male, to use the third and shortest leg with a philandering promiscuity.

Shake the hand of a stranger . . . Of a prosti, to relieve the obdurate phallus manually.

Share cropper . . . A girl who believes in sharing the goodness of her pudendal crop with more than one male.

Share one's mistress with another man . . . **Sail in the same boat.**

Sharp . . . Of the penis, erected.

Shaving brush . . . The pubic hair of the female, esp. as seen by a cunnilinguist.

She sat in the garden with the gate unlocked . . . She was pudendally careless and got herself knocked up.

Sheathe one's talons . . . To deprive of sexual potency and aggressiveness by excision of the male gonads, the hind legs of the phallus.

Sheathe the phallus with vagina . . . **Hole.**

Sheathe the saber . . . To sink the male bayonet into the female pudendal scabbard; to phallate.

Sheepherder . . . 1. A male who phallates per rectum, either a sodomist or a pederast. 2. A male who phallates a female animal, as a sheep.

She-kindness . . . Vaginal privileges to the phallus desirous.

Shiksa . . . Same as **Shikseh**, an ambisemantic handle for a non-Judaic wench.

Shikseh . . . A popular, among the progeny of Abraham, moniker for a non-Jewish, especially Christian, young unmarried female; conceived with varying degrees of amativeness by the male species of said progeny, because, it is assumed, of an instinctive inclination for allogenic females, fortified by the lure of the, to them, forbidden fruit; and with equally varying degrees of sour disapproval by the daughters of Isaac, because of their forgivable urge for self-preservation, expressed, in a transubstantiated form, by the understandable "I don't understand what they see in them," "they" being the amative young male Israelites with an eye on the "shiksehs."

Shoot between the fagots . . . To reciprocate the phallus between the approximated breasts of the female.

Shoot in the back . . . To insinuate the phallus erectus into the rectum, esp. of a female.

Shoot in the brown . . . Give it to the female per rectum. Also, do same to a male.

Shoot in the bush . . . Of a phallating male, to withdraw the baton and ejaculate extravaginally, usually into the pubic bush.

Shoot one's wad . . . To rid oneself of a seminal backlog by depositing the excess in the female pudendal bank.

Short and thick, like a Welshman's prick . . . Of a short person, usually a male, plump in the rump.

Short arm . . . The phallus as a short firearm or pistol.

Short-arm inspection . . . An inspection, esp. of soldiers, involving a scrutiny of the genitalia, to detect signs of venereal disease.

Short time . . . A quickie engagement with a whore, for one ejaculation.

Short timers . . . A couple of heterosexual fornicators who rent a room for a brief period, to effect the pudendal union.

Shot between wind and water . . . Of a female, nipped by the male missile between the anus (wind) and the urethra (water), i.e., in the vaginal bull's eye. Also, infected venereally.

Shot in the giblets . . . Phallated and pregnant.

Shot in the tail . . . Same as **Shot in the giblets.**

Shoulders, female, especially erotic about the . . . OMOPHILOUS.

Shriveling of the female breast with age . . . MAZORHIKNOSIS.

Shriveling of the penis with age . . . PHALLORHIKNOSIS.

Shut husband out of the bedroom, as a punitive measure, for tight purse strings, etc. . . . **Give the key to the street.**

Shut-in . . . Phallus invalidus, regarded as shut up because it can't put up.

Sirdar . . . The chief of the urogenital state, in the male, in allusion to the standard English meaning, commander-in-chief.

Sit before a fireplace with skirt high . . . **Warm the husband's supper.**

Six-o-six; 606 . . . 1. Arsphenamine, the first specific medication for the treatment of syphilis; so called because it was in the 606th experimental attempt that Ehrlich and Hata made the discovery. 2. Syphilis.

Sixty-nine . . . A bout of sexual entertainment partaken in by a male and a female so situated that they can perform cunnilingus and fellatio upon each other, simultaneously.

Skill in displaying provocative parts of the body by a female, without appearing vulgar . . . PHANERODAEDALY.

Skin a live rabbit . . . To sheathe the membrum virile cupidum with vaginal mucosa.

Skirt . . . A woman as a female.

Skirt chaser; whoremonger . . . **Cunny-hunter.**

Skirt, the . . . The distaff; women collectively.

Slack puller . . . A female who causes the membrum virile to take up its slack skin.

Slasher of female genitalia . . . **Ripper.**

Slaughter of the innocent . . . A masturbatory waste of semen.

Sleep with a girlie under the canopy of the stars . . . **Do a star pitch.**

Sleep with a woman, in allusion to sleeping near a crack, which, if elsewhere, might cause a draft . . . **Risk taking a cold; Chance taking a cold.**

Slide home . . . To mount the female with a functional phallus foremost.

Sling one's jelly . . . Of the male, to induce the seminal spurt manually.

Slit of the vulva . . . **Placket;** ENTOMA.

Slit of the vulva, gaping . . . CUNNECTASIA.

Slot . . . The interlabial slit as the personification of the vulva.

Smallies . . . A couple of female breasts not exactly of the eckbergian stable, magnitude-wise.

Smitten with lust; of the male . . . **Cunt-struck.**

Smudges . . . Two ridiculously small female breasts which are discernible only as smudges of nipple pigment.

Snag . . . To phallate per rectum.

Snare . . . Of a sodomite or a pederast, to secure a subject.

Snib . . . To phallate a woman, in allusion to "snib," a bolt.

SODOMANT . . . The passive or recipient member in the act of sodomy, esp. a male.

SODOMANTE . . . The passive female member in the act of sodomy.

SODOMEE . . . The female recipient in the act of sodomy.

Sodomite . . . **Bunker; Fluter; Backgammon player; Usher of the back door; Gentleman of the back door.**

Sodomite . . . **Gut reamer; Gut stuffer; Reamer; Lapper; Jesuit.**

Sodomite as an anal borer . . . **Arser.**

Sodomite as invader of hinterland . . . **Back yard prowler.**

Sodomite, do as a . . . **Indorse.**

Sodomite; pederast . . . **Backwoods fiddler; Bum fiddler; Indorser; Sheepherder.**

Sodomize; phallate per rectum . . . **Bung; Go down on; Goose; Kneel at the altar; Ream; Sail into the wind; Worship at the back altar.**

Sodomize; phallate per rectum . . . **Bugger; Burgle; Go Hollywood; Kiss off; Play second fiddle; Ride the deck; Snag; Yodel; Shoot in the brown.**

Sodomize; phallate per rectum, esp. a female . . . **Shoot in the back.**

Sodomize; phallate per rectum, in allusion to the rectum as the wrong coital passage . . . **File in the wrong box.**

SODOMY . . . Phallation per rectum, usually with an adult male.

Sodomy, active member in the act of . . . SODOMITE; SODOMIST.

SODOMY, BESTIAL . . . Sexual intercourse between a human male and a female beast.

Sodomy; conceived as an enlarging of the lower intestine . . . **Gut reaming.**

Sodomy, female member in act of . . . SODOMANTE; SODOMEE.

Sodomy, male member in act of . . . SODOMANT.

SODOMY, ORAL . . . Same as FELLATIO, the taking of the phallus into the mouth, for gratification.

Sodomy, passive male member in act of . . . SODOMANT.

Sodomy, passive member in the act of . . . SODOMANT.

Sodomy, passive member in the act of, regarded with contempt . . . **Bloke.**

Sodomy practiced upon a female . . . THELYSODOMY.

Sodomy practiced upon a male . . . ANDROSODOMY.

SODOMY, RECTAL . . . Phallation per rectum with an adult male or female, or with a child.

Sodomy, unwilling to submit to . . . **Bunker-shy.**

Softening of the male sexual shaft before the coital climax, to suffer a . . . **Corpse out.**

Soft-soldered . . . Provided with a mistress, in allusion to the non-permanent union.

Soldier who consorts with harlots . . . **Dolly-mopper.**

Solicit pudendal business; said of a procurer or a prostitute . . . **Kick for trade.**

Son-of-a-bitch, habitual utterance of the imputation . . . CATELALIA.

SORORIATION . . . The development of the young breasts in a girl at puberty. Ex *soror* (sister).

SORORILAGNIA . . . Sexual love of a brother for his sister. From *soror* (sister) & *lagneia* (lust).

SORORINCEST . . . Sexual intercourse between a brother and a sister. From *soror* (sister) & *incestus* (sinful).

SORORIRAPTUS . . . Rape by force involving one's own sister. Ex *soror* (sister) & *raptus* (a violent attack).

Southern hemispheres . . . The gluteal spheroids of the rump.

Sow wild oats . . . To relieve seminal pressure by appropriate acts of what some call dissolution.

Space between the buttocks . . . **Brownsward**; INTERGLUTIUM.

Space between the female breasts, often a phallator's haven . . . INTERMAZIUM; MESOSEINIA; **Titfuck.**

Space between the labia majora and the floor of the vulva . . . CHASMA.

Space between the labia of the female pudendum . . . INTERLABIUM; ENTOMA; **Mouthpiece; Lich gate; Hatch; Porte-cochere; Crack; Vomitory; Honeyslot; Keyhole; Mousehole; Placket hole; Pigeonhole.**

Space between the thighs, esp. as a phallating area . . . INTERFEMINIUM.

SPANECRONIA . . . The condition marked by scantiness of the seminal fluid in the male; a meager ejaculation. From *spanos* (scarce) & *ecron* (seminal fluid).

SPANERIA . . . Scarcity of men, as in a particular part of a country. Ex *spanos* (scarce) & *aner* (man).

SPANOGYNY . . . Scarcity of women, as in a particular part of the world. Ex *spanos* (scarce) & *gyne* (woman).

Spasmodic twitching of the erected phallus, usually at the site of its quarry . . . **Saber rattling.**

Spend a night with one of the opposite sex . . . **Shack up.**

SPERMATORRHEA . . . Involuntary discharge of semen, unaccompanied by sexual orgasm.

SPERMATOSCHESIS . . . Decreased production of semen. Ex *sperma* (seed of animals) & *schesis* (suppression).

Spew alley . . . The female genital inlet.

SPHALMORGASMY . . . An incomplete or otherwise unsatisfactory orgasm in the male. From *sphalma* (frustration).

SPHEROMATA . . . The buttocks, conceived as spheres. Ex *sphairomata* (buttocks).

SPHEROPLANIA . . . The flattening of the buttocks, as in old age. From *sphairomata* (buttocks) & *planus* (flat).

Spice island . . . The rectum as an odoriferous haven of the sodomite's and pederast's phallus.

Spiked male . . . A desirous male whose urogenital pendant is not pendent.

Spill one's beans . . . To deflate an overpressurized phallus by a manual coaxing of the seminal spurt.

Spinsters, frustrated state of mind characteristic of . . . VIRGOPHRENIA.

Spiritual unfaithfulness to one's spouse, expressed by wishful or illusory engagements in amatory pleasures with another . . . PHRENAPISTIA.

Spit-cock . . . The blood-engorged male organon in its procreative mood.

Spit-cock . . . To mollify the indurated male genital petard by a series of plunges into the female pudendal bucket.

Split . . . To cause the pudendal labia of the female to part, if not already parted, by the phallic wedge.

Split-arse mechanic . . . A whore, in allusion to the labial split involved in the act.

Split-arsing . . . Whoring about, in allusion to the splitting of the labial gates, incident to the action.

Split chums . . . The labia majora.

Split crow . . . The female pudendum in the buff, as presented by a female about to receive the phallus erectus, lying supine, with thighs and labia abducted, simulating, with the pubic hair as the head of a crow, a split bird.

Split mutton . . . 1. A girl as a target for splitting with the phallus. 2. A girl that has been split pudendally by the phallus. 3. The phallus as the mutton-splitting organ.

Split pilot . . . A woman who does pudendal splits, for incoming phalli, on a commercial basis.

Sport the blubber . . . Of a female with ample bubbies, to let the swell of them be seen, via a dipping neckline.

Spread in bed for a vaginal invasion and lubrication job . . . **Do a bedspread; Do a spread.**

Spread the pudendal labia of the female with the phallic wedge; to phallate . . . **Split.**

Spread the thighs and the labia majora, for the receipt of the phallus erectus; said of a female supine in bed or elsewhere . . . **Join the stream; Open up.**

Spread wide open for the male . . . **Cleave.**

Spring fever; increase of romantosexual appetite in spring . . . VERNOREXIA.

Sprinkle . . . To discharge the seminal cream in the interlabial pudendal passage of the female.

Squirrel fever . . . That certain feeling, in the pubic region; in either sex.

St. John's Wood donnas . . . Women who earn a living by selling sexual privileges to their pudenda.

Stab with a rose . . . Of a female, to grant the genital privilege.

Stag month . . . The period during which a husband is deprived of his wife's pudendum because of childbirth.

Stallion, woman who masturbates a . . . **Horse breaker.**

Stand bitch to . . . To play the female part to a male with a pudendal urge.

Starvation, pudendal . . . GENOLIMIA.

Starvation . . . See also under *Hunger*.

Starved for pudendal pie; of the male . . . **Road-starved.**

Starved for women . . . GYNELIMOUS.

STASIVALENT . . . Potent sexually and able to have pudendal concourse in the standing position only. Ex *statis* (a standing) & *valere* (to be able).

STASOPHALLIST . . . A male who prefers to have sexual intercourse while standing. Ex *stasimos* (standing) & *phallos* (penis).

Statues of nude figures, sexual excitation aroused by . . . ICONOLAGNY.

Status of a virgin; virginity . . . PARTHENITY.

Status of a woman with regard to sexual intercourse . . . PHALLITY.

Stealing, sexual excitation induced by . . . KLEPTOLAGNIA.

STEATOFEMORAL . . . Having fat thighs. Ex *stear* (fat) & *femur* (thigh).

STEATOSURAL . . . Having fat leg calves. Ex *stear* (fat) & *sura* (calf).

STENOPYLE . . . A hymen with a small opening which does not allow admission of the phallus. Ex *stenos* (narrow) & *pyle* (a gate).

Sterility in the female . . . ACYESIS; ATOCIA.

Sterility in the male . . . ATICTIA.

Sterilize a female by excision of the ovaries . . . OVARIECTOMIZE; SPAY.

Sterilize a female by operating on the oviducts . . . SIPHOSIPHLATE.

Sterilize a human being or an animal by operating on the reproductive system . . . CASTRATE; GENOSIPHLATE.

Sterilize a male by excision of the gonads . . . CASTRATE; EMASCULATE; EVIRATE; GELD; ORCHIDOSIPHLATE.

Sterilize a male by operating on the vasa deferentia . . . VASOSIPHLATE.

Stimulate the female pudendal gates, prior to phallic invasion . . . **Cook the kettle.**

Stimulate the phallus through the pants; said of a female so doing in the course of caressing . . . **Badger bait.**

Stimulate . . . See also under name of part stimulated.

Stir about in erotic restlessness; said of a female already perforated by the phallus, i.e., in coitus . . . **Buck one's stumps.**

Straddle the spike . . . Of an enterprising and/or ruttish female about to engage in sexual concourse, to mount a supine male and lower the pudendal vault upon the eager male spike, which is anything but supine.

Strap . . . To be in coitus with a woman.

Strapping . . . The act of phallation.

Strawberry kiss . . . A lasciviously sucking kiss which, applied to the non-mucous parts of the body, leaves a strawberry-like ecchymotic imprint.

Strike out . . . Phallate ineffectively to phallic collapse, without wetting the female bed, i.e., coit to a softening of the membrum virile, without achieving the orgasm.

Strike with a feather . . . To phallate with a small and/or half-heartedly erected phallus.

Stubs . . . Female breasts of the lesser magnitude, allotted to a woman after all the better, monronian sets had been exhausted.

Study of contraception . . . ACEPTOLOGY.

Study of diseases of women, esp. of disorders affecting the genitourinary organs . . . GYNECOLOGY.

Study of genital organs . . . EDEOLOGY.

Study of limitation of offspring . . . OLIGOGENICS.

Study of reproduction . . . GENESIOLOGY.

Study of sex and sexual relations . . . SEXOLOGY.

Study of sexual love between females . . . SAPPHOLOGY.

Study of syphilis . . . SYPHILOLOGY.

Study of venereal diseases . . . VENEREOLOGY.

Study of virginity and of virgins . . . PARTHENOLOGY.

Stumble at the truckle bed . . . Of a man having an upstairs maid, to "mistake" her bed for that of his wife.

STUPRATOR . . . A defiler of virgins. Ex *stupro* (defile).

SUBLIMATION . . . The expression of sexual impulses by means of nonsexual activities. Also, the conversion of a sexual craving into a nonerotic desire.

Submit to phallation, in allusion to giving the phallus the necessary care . . . **Take care of.**

Submit to the male pudendally . . . **Play the bitch to; Stand bitch to.**

Substance which calms sexual desire . . . ANAPHRODISIAC.

Substance which stimulates the development of the secondary sex characteristics in a female . . . GYNECOGEN.

Substance which stimulates the development of the secondary sex characteristics in a male . . . ANDROGEN.

Substance which stimulates the sexual desire . . . APHRODISIAC.

Suck in an amorous way, esp. female appurtenances . . . **Lip.**

Suck the anus, usually of a female . . . **Bite the brown.**

Sucking of the penis by a human being, to give sexual gratification . . . FELLATIO.

Sucking of the penis by an animal, to give sexual gratification . . . ZOOFELLATIO.

Suck; sucking . . . See also under name of anatomical part involved.

SUCCUBOUS . . . Lying under; said of one in the bottom coital position.

SUCCUBUS . . . In sexual intercourse, the one in the lower position. Ex *succubare* (to lie under).

Sunday clothes . . . The elevation of the phallus for, or as if for, pudendal action.

Sunday face . . . 1. The buttocks. 2. In a girl, the upper anterior bulges.

Sunny south . . . A girl's lower mouth.

SUPINOVALENT . . . Potent sexually and able to have pudendal intercourse in the face-up position only. Ex *supine* (lying face upward) & *valere* (to be able).

SURAPHILOUS . . . Of the male, especially erotic about the calves of the female. Ex *sura* (calf) & *philein* (to love).

Sweat for a sugar report from one's gadget . . . To await impatiently a favorable menstrual report from the girl one has phallated without, or with inadequate, contraceptive auxiliaries.

Sweater dandies . . . Prize pectoral bunnies of a young female.

Sweet homo . . . A male homosexual.

Sweet line . . . The line of cleavage between the mammae.

Sweeteners . . . The lips of an attractive mouth of an attractive girl.

Sweeteners . . . Accessory movements or blandishments offered by a real good wench in the course of pudendal coalition.

Sweetening . . . Same as **Sweeteners,** coital spice offered by a girl in phallation.

Sweets . . . The good things to savor—visually, digitally, or organically—in a resplendent girl.

Switch . . . To "punish" the female pudendum with the male genital knout.

Switched . . . Of the female, "punished" pudendally by the phallus erectus.

Switchel . . . To phallate a female, esp. with sadistic vengeance.

Swive . . . 1. To be in the act of genital copulation. 2. To phallate a female.

Swiveland . . . The mythical land where one engages in nothing more strenuous than pudendal fiddling.

Swiver . . . A male in the act of copulation.

Sword swallower . . . A female prostitute who takes suck of the male genital teat.

SYNDYASMIAN FAMILY . . . A form of family in which marriage does not restrict sexual intercourse of the pair to each other, and coitus can be terminated by either one of the couple.

SYNORGASMIA . . . The occurrence of the sexual orgasm in both coitants at the same time.

SYNTRIBADISM . . . A form of masturbation practiced by females in which the legs are crossed and the adducted thighs are rubbed against each other. Ex *syn* (together) & *tribein* (rub).

Syphilis . . . **Grincomes; Jack in the box.**

Syphilis . . . **Arsphenaminitis; Bismuthitis.**

Syphilis . . . **Wasserman's disease; Six-o-six.**

Syphilis . . . **Sigma Phi; Sororitosis; Warrenitis.**

Syphilis . . . **Chancre disease; Pox; Bubonitis.**

Syphilis . . . **Fracastorosis; Morbus Gallicus; Gallic disease.**

Syphilis . . . **Neapolitan disease; Polish disease; Spanish pox; Turkish disease.**

Syphilis . . . **French aches; French crown; French disease; French goods; French gout; French marbles; French measles; French mole; French pox.**

Syphilis, abnormal fear of becoming infected with . . . SYPHILOPHOBIA.

Syphilis and gonorrhea, double infection with . . . **Double event; Full hand; Full house.**

Syphilis, course of injections for the treatment of . . . **A fling at cactus.**

Syphilis, euphemistic synonym for . . . LUES.

Syphilis, infect with . . . SYPHILIZE.

Syphilis, medicine used in the treatment of; general term . . . ANTILUETIC; ANTISYPHILITIC.

Syphilis, medicine used in the treatment of; old specific . . . **606.**

Syphilis, patient having . . . **Louie.**

Syphilis, physician specializing in the diagnosis and treatment of . . . SYPHILOLOGIST.

Syphilis, prostitute infected with . . . **Louise.**

Syphilis, science of . . . SYPHILOLOGY.

Syphilis, take injections for the treatment of . . . **Ride a steel steed.**

T

TACHORGASMIA . . . The achievement of the sexual orgasm by either the male or the female, but more often the male, in a shorter than normal time. In the male, the seminal spurt may occur before intromission.

Tail . . . The sexually functional end of the female torso; more specifically, the lipped gadget.

Tail . . . The invertebrate pudendal column of the male.

Tail . . . The buttocks of the female as sexual flesh.

Tail . . . 1. Of maid and man, to join giblets. 2. Of the male, to administer the phallic thrusts, in the usual place.

Tail anchor . . . That which a man is fond of dropping in the female interfemoral shelter.

Tail around . . . Of a female, to put the pudendum to work, now and then, on a semi-professional basis.

Tail-biz . . . The commercial traffic in female pudendal succor to famished phalli.

Tail box . . . The business end of the female, esp. the vagina conceived as a receptacle for the incoming male probe.

Tail cattle . . . Common harlots, collectively.

Tail chicken . . . A pretty girl who is not beyond approach, pudendally.

Tail duds . . . Such intimate garments as are worn by the female to cover and/or reform her pelvic contours.

Tail dynamite . . . A sexually provocative girl, in the megaton class.

Tail-femme . . . A girl who gives extramaritally.

Tail fence . . . The hymen, conceived as the barrier to the passage d'amour.

Tail frock . . . 1. A pair of sassy panties. 2. A lingerie garment worn by the female during the beef injection.

Tail-gap . . . 1. The slit of the vulva. 2. The external opening of the vagina, of interest to the phallus.

Tail-gate . . . The hymen, conceived as a barrier to the external opening of the most intimate female corridor.

Tail-gate . . . 1. The fleshy lips of the female pudendum, esp. the labia majora. 2. The labia majora and the structures which lie within their bailiwick.

Tail gone to seed . . . A phallus retired from the pudendal arena, because of chronic flaccidity.

Tail high, with . . . Of the male, brandishing an adamantine organon.

Tail-job . . . A case of pudendal coitus.

Tail-line . . . The fleshy, tubular link which connects the man to his maid, in coition; the membrum virile.

Tail music . . . Tintinnabulation of the wedding bells, conceived, cynically, as the necessary preludial formality to be dispensed with before getting to the gist of the matter, *q.e.,* the joining of giblets.

Tail oil . . . The spirited fluid erupting from the phallus in the spasm of erotic felicity.

Tail one's guts out . . . Usually of the male, to screw one's head off.

Tail over the dashboard, with . . . With the membrum virile erectum jutting from the open fly.

Tail security . . . The caoutchouc scabbard for a phallus erectus.

Tail sister . . . A girl with whom a man is intimate on the pudendal level.

Tail stew . . . The pudendum muliebre in the welcome posture of assent.

Tail-sweet . . . Of a girl, endowed with enticing hips and buttocks.

Tailfoul . . . To acquaint the virgin female pudendum with the phallic aspergillum.

Take a leaf out of another's book . . . To make a cuckold, i.e., to sink the phaliic sinker in the pudendal slit of another man's wife.

Take a turn . . . To obturate phallically the female pudendal canalis.

Take a turn among the cabbages . . . To take a swing at the interlabium of a girl, with a phallus risen to the occasion.

Take a turn at Cock Alley . . . To do a stint, with the phallus, in the female pudendal lane.

Take a turn at Cupid's Alley . . . To "know" with the phallus the secrets of the female pudendal inlet.

Take a turn at Hair Court . . . To work with the spermapositor in the hairy environs of the female unmentionable.

Take a turn in Abraham's bosom . . . Take a phallic plunge in the nether muliebral mouth.

Take a turn in Bushy Park . . . To make the right kind of turn, for the plethoric phallus, down the pudendal bush of the female.

Take a turn in love lane . . . To give the phallus a ride in the female's loving hiatus.

Take a turn in the parsley-bed . . . Have a go at the female's lower kisser, phallically.

Take a turn through the stubble . . . To bushwhack, phallically, through the female pubic stubble, slitward.

Take a turn up the petticoats . . . To explore, phallically, the soft underbelly of a female.

Take and give . . . Of man and maid, to be in genital copulation; to live it up pudendally.

Take beef . . . Of the female, to take phallic beef pudendally.

Take care of . . . To assuage the desirous phallus by a vaginal caress.

Take down . . . To reduce the stature of the warm phallus by manual trituration.

Take for a ride . . . To maneuver a female into surrender.

Take gruel . . . Of a female, to take the phallus and its broth.

Take it out in trade . . . To accept female pudendal accommodations as payment or reward.

Take on . . . Of the female, to accept the male spike pudendally.

Take the phallus into the vagina . . . **Line the jacket.**

Take the phallus of another into one's mouth . . . **Blow; Take a drink;** FELLATIZE.

Take the phallus of another into one's mouth; an allusion to one of the postures . . . **Have legs around the neck.**

Talk a girl into a pudendal concession . . . **Box the compass.**

TALOPHILOUS . . . Of the male, especially erotic about the ankles of the female. From *talus* (ankle) & *philein* (to love).

TANTALIZATION . . . The act of arousing a male by exposure and denial of the female desirables.

TANTALOLAGNIA . . . A manifestation of the libido in which the male is sufficiently aroused for coitus only by tantalization. Ex *Tantalus* & *lagneia* (lust).

Tart . . . A girl, esp. one with sexual tang, and one who is not pudendally insurmountable.

Tassel . . . The scrotum of a child. Also, the penis of a small boy.

Taste the gut-stick . . . Of the female, to savor a plunge of the male creamstick.

TAUTANER . . . A homosexual male. Ex *to auto* (the same) & *aner* (man).

TAUTANERISM . . . Homosexuality in males.

Teacups . . . Female breasts, size junior miss.

Tear off a piece . . . Of the male, to treat oneself to a gratifying portion of the female underpudding.

Tear off a piece of tail . . . To avail oneself of a thoroughly satisfying hunk of twat.

Tease but not appease . . . **Roast the meat.**

Teasement without appeasement . . . **A roast.**

TECNODYNAMIA . . . The procreative power of the female. From *teknon* (child) & *dynamis* (ability).

Teen-age girl, in allusion to a young gull . . . **Coddy-moddy.**

Teenager . . . **Fryer; Chicken dinner.**

Teenager, breasts of a . . . **Young apples.**

Teenager, defloration of a . . . **Teenicide.**

Teenager, junior grade . . . **Nymphet.**

Teenager, pudendal liberties with a . . . **Teentabulation.**

Teenager, young, sexual desire for, by a middle-aged or older male . . . LOLITALAGNIA; LOLITAPHRENIA.

Teenagers, sexual desire for . . . BLASTOLAGNIA.

Tell tales of vaginal conquests . . . **Cry roast meat.**

TELOPHILE . . . A male who derives sexual pleasure only from coitus, not from erotic foreplay. Ex *telos* (end) & *philein* (to love).

Tender trap . . . Same as **Gentle trap,** the mink-trimmed, inescapable lariat of the female perineum.

TENTIGINOUS . . . Obsessed by intense or psychopathic lust.

TENTIGO . . . 1. Intense sexual desire. 2. Psychopathic lechery.

TENTIGOGENIC . . . Inducing abnormal lasciviousness. From *tentigo* (lasciviousness) & *genic* (inducing).

Tenuc . . . The female sexual receiving set; a serutanian spelling of **cun**(e)**t.**

TERATOPHALLIA . . . A marked deformity of the penis. From *teras* (monstrosity) & *phallos* (penis).

TERATOPHALLIC . . . Pert. to or having a deformed penis; having a penis of monstrous size.

TERETOPHALLIC . . . Having a round and smooth phallus, as man. From *teres* (round, smooth) & *phallos* (penis).

Testicles . . . **Balls; Nuts; Twins; Berries; Ballocks; Creamballs; Fries.**

Testicles . . . **Seed factory; The pills; The nutmegs; Razoos; Rollies; Tommy Rollocks; Oysters.**

Testicles, as unmentionable parts . . . **Innominables.**

Testicles conceived as bobbing with the bearer's walk . . . **Bobbles.**

Testicles, conceived as the inhabitants of a pod . . . **Cods; Bean pods.**

Testicles, in allusion to their effect in making a man a woman's dupe . . . **Culls.**

Testosities . . . The male gonads; the testicles.

Tetbury portion . . . A dose of gonorrhea served on female pudendum.

That may be phallated, without too much resistance . . . **Knock-upable.**

THELECOMAE . . . The hairs growing around a nipple, in the female.

THELECOMOSIS . . . The growth of hair around a nipple, in the female. Ex *thele* (nipple) & *comae* (hairs).

THELELINGUS . . . The erotic licking of the female nipples.

THELEMASSATION . . . The erotic fingering of the female nipples.

THELERETHISM . . . 1. Sexual excitation centered in the nipples, in the female. 2. Erection of the nipples as expression of erotic excitation. Ex *thele* (nipple) & *erethizo* (to excite).

THELIUM . . . A nipple.

THELORTHIA . . . The erection of a nipple or the nipples. Ex *thele* (nipple) & *orthosis* (a making straight).

THELYFLORESCENCE . . . The flowering of the feminine characteristics in a young girl. Ex *thelys* (female) & *florescence* (a flowering).

THELYSISM . . . The presence of female characteristics in the male. From *thelys* (female).

THELYSODOMY . . . Sodomy performed on a female. From *thelys* (female) & *sodomy*.

THELYZATION . . . The assumption of female characteristics by a male. From *thelys* (female).

There's many a good tune played on an old fiddle . . . There are many gratifying sexual experiences to be had with some older females.

Thigh, inner surface of; often exploited in extravaginal phallation . . . INTERFEMINIUM.

Thighs, between; applied to phallation . . . INTERFEMORAL.

Thighs, female, especially erotic about the . . . MEROPHILOUS.

Thighs, having beautiful . . . CALLIFEMORAL.

Thighs, having fat . . . STEATOFEMORAL.

Thighs, having well-developed . . . MEROSTHENIC.

Thighs, phallate between the female . . . MERPHALLATE; MEROPHALLATE.

Thighs, phallation between the female . . . MEROPHALLATION.

Thighs, spread the, and the labia majora, to create the posture of pudendal assent; said, obviously, of the female supine in bed with a spiked male . . . **Open up.**

Think about female charms, pudendal engagements, etc. . . . **Think about something to eat.**

Think about girls' legs . . . CRUROPHRENATE.

Think about something to eat . . . To think of female charms, sexual concourses, etc.

Think about the female breasts . . . MASTOPHRONATE.

Think about the vulva . . . COLPOPHRONATE.

Think about women . . . GYNEPHRONATE.

THLIPSOPHILIST . . . A person, male or female, deriving sexual pleasure from, and expressing it by, pinching. (From *thlipsis*—pinching.)

THLIPSOSIS . . . A condition in which sexual pleasure is derived from and expressed by pinching the soft tissues of another, esp. one beloved; a form of sadism.

Thorough good-natured wench . . . A girl with easily abductable thighs, or, as one wag put it, a girl who lies down when she is asked to sit down.

Three bouts of coitus during a night, or during a single love fiesta . . . **Triple header.**

Three coital bouts in one love session, have . . . **Triple.**

Three males, sexual engagement of, with one female, the males taking turns in the presence of the others . . . **Triple header.**

Three persons partaking in mutual sexual entertainment . . . TROILISTS.

Throw the hash . . . To eject the seminal fluid, esp. copiously.

THYGATRIA . . . Sexual intercourse with one's own daughter. Ex *thygater* (a daughter).

THYGATRILAGNIA . . . Sexual love of a father for his daughter. Ex *thygater* (daughter) & *lagneia* (lust).

Thyrsos . . . A Greek synonym for the phallus, in allusion to a straight shaft.

Tickle the minikin . . . To tickle, amorously, the female tickleables.

Tickle the toby . . . 1. To thrash the buttocks. 2. To titillate the pudendum muliebre, usually with the male honey stick.

Tickle the tonsils . . . To irrumate; give suck of the phallus erectus.

Tickleables . . . The female genitalia and mammae as titillatory targets.

Tickling of nonsexual parts of body, erotic excitation or gratification induced by . . . TITILLAGNIA.

Tickling, sexual desire derived from; or from being tickled . . . KNISMOLAGNIA.

Tick-tack . . . Sexual concourse as a form of direct pudendal communication.

Tie a knot with the tongue that cannot be undone with the teeth . . . To marry.

Tie the true lover's knot . . . To seal the lover's pledge with seminal fluid; to phallate.

Tight vaginal entrance, in allusion to its breaking the male genital bat . . . **Crack-bat.**

Tipperary fortune . . . An arse, a cunt, and a pair of bubbies, regarded as a dowry of a penniless bride.

Tit . . . The female breast nipple.

Tit . . . A teat or, in the human female, a titty.

Tit . . . A girl, esp. a petite tit.

Tit . . . A female who dispenses pudendal cheer without the boundaries of wedlock, for shekels.

Tit . . . The female genital slit with its warm interior and ornamental exterior, including the tuft.

Tit bait . . . That irrepressible line of cleavage.

Tit-bit . . . The phallus erectus as a drill bit for the female tit (interfemoral adit).

Tit-bit . . . The female passage which receives the male erotic bit, in the pudendal mattress jig.

Tit-bit . . . A girl with a good bit of tit, i.e., with prize fagots, alias retrobrassiereans.

Tit-bits . . . Small female pectoral fagots, as in a teen-ager of the lower teens.

Tit-bits . . . The nipples of the female breasts.

Tit puller . . . 1. A male who likes to milk a woman's lactiferous breasts. 2. A male who likes to milk a woman's breasts, lactiferous or any other kind.

Tit smacker . . . A male who likes to slither his phallus in the line of cleavage.

Tit sucker . . . A male who has an erotic desire to suckle the milk of a woman's lactiferous breasts.

Tit willow . . . A willowy girl with attractive pectoral fruit.

Tit willow . . . A pillow of girl breast tissue, for an erotically weary head.

Titch . . . A pruritus affecting the retrobrassiereans, or one of them, esp. when bearer of same cannot scratch.

Titfuck . . . To reciprocate the phallus between the breasts of a female.

Titfuck . . . A sexual bout in which the phallus is moved between the approximated breasts of the female.

Titfuck . . . A woman who accepts the phallus between her breasts.

Titfuck . . . The space between the female breasts, conceived as a delightful den for phallic intromission.

Titfucker . . . A mastophallator or mazophallist, i.e., a male who jiggles his penis between the breasts of a female.

Tither . . . To make free with a girl's bunnies.

TITILLAGNIA . . . Sexual excitation or gratification induced by tickling nonsexual parts. From *titillare* (to tickle) & *lagneia* (lust).

Titillate amorously the female kittleables . . . **Tickle the minikin.**

Titillate the pudendum of a male child in order to pacify him and, often, put him to sleep . . . **Play with billy.**

Titillate with the lips or tongue the genitalia or anus of another . . . **Kiss.**

Titillation of a child's or infant's pudendum in order to put him to sleep . . . **Gouvernante sleeping pills.**

Titmouse . . . The groin-like dip between the upper parts of the female breasts.

Titmouse . . . A pad designed to give the female breast an illusory prominence.

Titmouse . . . That lush, warm animalcule between the thighs of a girl.

Tits . . . A non-patrician nickname contrived by men for the female milkers, conceived as quarries for pulling, etc.

Tittens . . . Girl's bubbies cute as kittens.

Titter . . . A man who begets only, it seems, girls.

Titter . . . A young girl with burgeoning bunnies.

Titter . . . A girl who's got it where it counts, up front.

Titter . . . A male who likes to lay it on the line, on the line of cleavage.

Tittery . . . A household in which there are several daughters.

Tittery . . . A family the female members of which are prominently buxom; a covey of such sisters.

Tittery . . . A commercial house, under the management of a Mrs. Warren, for the dispensation of sensual pleasures; in allusion to the, usually, well-displayed mammae.

Tittery . . . A girl with such fine pectoral quail as to justify the synecdochial appellation, in which the whole of her is named for the (prominent) part of her.

Tittie . . . The fleshy filler of the brassiere cup.

Tittie . . . To titillate, manually or labially, the titties.

Tittiebat . . . To phallate between the pectoral sisters; i.e., to reciprocate the male bat between the titties.

Tittie-bat . . . The phallus desirous, esp. one which likes to wallow in the fleshy gutter between the female breasts.

Tittiellation . . . The amorous stimulation of the female breasts, as with the lips or the fingers. Ex **tittie** & (titi)**llation.**

Titties . . . The paired lovelies of the female chest.

Titties, arse, and cunt as a girl's dowry or trousseau . . . **Tipperary fortune.**

Tittivate . . . To activate a male with blandishments of tittie.

Tittivated . . . Of a girl, well supplied with brassiere filler, of the natural variety.

Tittivated . . . Of a male, thoroughly aroused to the situation by blandishments of, or fooling around with, zee titties.

Tittuppity . . . In a girl, real or imagined uppity based on the possession of a ravishing "what's up front."

Titty . . . A girl, as the bearer of pectoral handfuls.

Titty . . . One of the two softies in a girl, up front.

Titty . . . Female erotic goodness, metamorphized.

Titty . . . Erotic stimulation or gratification derived in one way or another by way of the female bubbies.

Titty antlers . . . Large, protruding female nipples.

Titty bag . . . The double-domed hammock which covers and supports the pectoral mounds of the female.

Titty bugger . . . A male who reciprocates his phallus between the female breasts.

Titty high . . . Of the desirous phallus, jutting horizontally.

Titty-itty . . . Girl blandishments consisting of titty.

Titty masher . . . A male who manages to "bump" or rub against female bubbies, "accidentally," as in crowded places.

Titty-shucking . . . In living-room lovemaking, the exposure of the girl's breasts by shucking the covering garments.

Titty-uppy . . . Of a girl, seemingly proud of her retrobrassiereans, because carried high and uppity.

Titup . . . To carry the pectoral ninnies in an uplifting brassiere.

To have had a flutter . . . 1. To have had sexual concourse. 2. To have parted with the maidenhead.

To sit in the garden with the gate unlocked . . . To expose desirables and thus invite seduction.

To . . . For other entries beginning with *To,* see under more significant part of the concept.

Toaster . . . The warm pudendal cavern of the female.

Toby . . . The two gluteal prominences as a unit, esp. in the female.

Toby . . . The external genital formations of the female.

TOCOMORPHY . . . The condition marked by the inevitable figure changes resulting from childbearing, as discoloration of the nipples, flaccidity of the abdomen, etc.

TOCOPEPANTIC . . . Of a girl, ripe for childbearing. From *tokos* (childbirth) & *pepansis* (a ripening).

Tom thumbs . . . A pair of female breasts which are barely in the running as such, because of their Lilliputian size.

Tom tit . . . The breast of a male, esp. when abnormally large. Also, the breast of a female when abnormally small.

Tomato dish . . . A girl who is regarded as a good tomato.

Tommy buster . . . 1. A male with a massive phallus. 2. A rapist, esp. one attacking immature females.

Tongue twister . . . A bout of medolinction involving a mouthfilling and active phallus.

Tonguelash . . . A bout of cunnilinction.

Too much Charley . . . Too much of a good thing, behind; of a female.

Too young for the phallus erectus, legally, but not too young to be by said phallus wanted, because anatomically exuberant . . . **Few pence short of a shilling.**

Tooth . . . Desire, esp. sexual lust.

Toothless fellator or fellatrice . . . **Yorkshire muff.**

Top of the shop . . . The paired softies of the female chest.

Top position in sexual intercourse, one in . . . INCUBUS.

Top sawyer . . . Of a pair engaged in orthodox sexual intercourse, the one in the incubous or top position, usually the male.

TOPERETHISM . . . Erotic sensitivity of a part of the body not normally so sensitive. Ex *topos* (region) & *erethizo* (excite).

Torch of Venus . . . A venereal infection conceived as a firebrand passed from one bearer to the other, in sexual concourse.

Touch the bun for luck . . . To touch the pudendum muliebre for good luck before embarking on an adventure, a practice once—and still—popular among sailors.

TRACHELOPHILOUS . . . Of the male, especially erotic about the female's neck. Ex *trachelos* (neck) & *philein* (to love).

TRACHYCOLPIA . . . A condition of the vagina marked by roughness of the mucosa. Ex *trachys* (rough) and *kolpos* (vagina).

Trail blazer . . . A male who has scalped a virgin, with the erectile masculine tomahawk.

TRANSVESTISM . . . The derivation of sexual pleasure from the act of wearing clothes appropriate for the opposite sex; the wearing of such clothes, usually by a male. Ex *trans* (across) & *vestire* (to clothe).

TRANSVESTITE . . . A person who enjoys, sexually, the wearing of clothes appropriate for the opposite sex, generally a man.

TRANSVESTITISM . . . Same as TRANSVESTISM.

Trap stick . . . The male genital obturator of the vagina.

Trapes . . . A slovenly female with a foul introitus.

Trees, sexual excitation derived from observing . . . DENDROPHILIA.

TRIBADA . . . The passive member in the act of tribadism.

Tribadance . . . A dance in which the participants rub buttocks with one another because of the crowded conditions.

TRIBADE . . . 1. A female homosexual. 2. A female homosexual with a large clitoris (or one provided with a dildo) who rubs her genitalia against those of another female. Ex *tribein* (to rub).

TRIBADISM . . . A sexual bout between two females in which the participants approximate their genitalia and rub them against each other.

Tribadism, active member in the act of . . . TRIBADUS; TRIBADE.

Tribadism, active member in, using an artificial phallus . . . OLESBEE.

Tribadism, passive member in the act of . . . TRIBADA.

TRIBADUS . . . In tribadism, the female who acts the part of the male.

TRIBORGASMIA . . . The manual induction of the sex orgasm in the male, by the spouse; as in infirmity. Ex *tribo* (rub) & *orgao* (swell).

TRICHOPHILOUS . . . Of a male, especially fond, erotically, of the female's hair. Ex *thrix* (hair) & *philein* (to love).

Trick of the imagination by which a male in coitus pretends that his sexual partner is another woman, whom he would like to phallate . . . ALLOGYNIA.

Trick of the imagination whereby a woman in coitus pretends that her phallator is another, more desirable, man . . . ALLOANDRISM.

Trim the buff . . . To phallate a female. Also to deflower a virgin.

Triple header . . . Sexual revelry involving one female and three males, the latter taking turns, in the presence of the others.

Triple header . . . A fiesta of sexual pleasure in which there are three coital engagements; three phallic sallies into the female pudendum in a single night.

TROILISM . . . A sexual bout engaged in by two women and one man, or by two men and one woman. Ex *trois* (three).

Trousseau consisting of nothing more than vulva . . . **Rochester portion; Whitechapel portion.**

Trousseau consisting of nothing more than vulva, arse, and titty . . . **Tipperary fortune.**

Trousseau, to collect a . . . **Get together the bottom drawer.**

Trug . . . A harlot, esp. a slovenly one.

Trugging-house . . . A house where Mrs. Warren's girls labor pudendally.

TRYPAN . . . The male genital auger. Ex *trypanon* (a borer).

Tufts attached to brassiere cups to give the outer garment an imitation nipple bulge . . . **Brummagem buttons.**

Turk . . . A male homosexual, esp. one who takes the "male" part in the act of homosexualism.

Turn . . . A bout of sexual copulation.

Turn an honest penny . . . To make a living as a pimp.

Turn an honest penny . . . To convert a chaste female to the phallic faith.

Turn-round pudding . . . A well worked-over female pudendum.

Twat . . . The entire pudendal complex of the female, including the labia, the slit, and, especially, the entrance to the vagina, regarded by the male as a gap to be mended with phallic tissue, or as an opening with a toothless bite, and, at times, as a despised master from whose power there is no escape.

Twat-brushing . . . Phallation regarded as a brushing of the female pudendum with the pubic brush of the male.

Twat-crazy . . . Fanatically enamored of female pudenda.

Twat-faithful . . . Of a wife, pudendally faithful.

Twat-happy . . . Of the male, indulging in and constantly thinking about sexual pleasures with a responsive twat.

Twathopper . . . A husband not faithful to his wedded twat.

Twat-hungry . . . Of the male, famished for the homely but savory item.

Twat peddler . . . A female whose pudendal accommodations are available for short term engagements.

Twat reflex . . . The erectile response of the phallus to the charms of the twat.

Twat-sucker . . . A licker of the female pudendum. Also, an uxorious husband not necessarily a cunnilinguist.

Twatter . . . A female cunnilinguist.

Twatty . . . Of a girl, sexy, provocative, tantalizing, seductive, etc.

Twig and berries . . . The penis and testicles of a child.

Twins . . . The male gonads.

Twins . . . The pectoral adorables of a girl.

Twist a leg . . . To inveigle into sexual concourse; the female, of course.

Twist pockets . . . Of a girl gold-digger,, to gold-dig, with an assist from her pudendum.

Two bouts of coitus during a night, or during a single love fiesta . . . **Double header.**

Two coital bouts in one love session, have . . . **Double.**

Two females, a sexual orgy with . . . **Double event.**

Two males, sexual engagement of, with one female, as a team . . . **Double header.**

Two men, woman who engages in sexual practices with . . . BIVIRIST.

Two sexual bouts, complete the performance of, on a single erection, without entracte and without a withdrawal of the phallic line . . . **Double one's milt.**

Two sexual bouts, complete with orgasms, effected without an intermission and without withdrawal, on a single erection . . . **Double milt.**

Two women, male who engages in sexual play with . . . BIGYNIST.

Twot . . . Same as **Twat**, the lower toothless apparatus of the female.

TYLOS . . . A Greek synonym for the phallus, in allusion to a wooden nail used in shipbuilding.

U

Uglies . . . From the viewpoint of some females, the male genitalia.

Uglies . . . From the viewpoint of some male cognoscenti, the emaciated, pendulous, lumpy, flattened breasts of an older female who has borne children.

Uhlan . . . The phallus conceived as a spirited pudendal lover.

Unable to avail oneself of an attractive pudendal opportunity because just relieved by masturbation . . . **Caught with the spinnaker down.**

Unappropriated blessing . . . An unmarried female.

Unattractive girl or woman, usually the former . . . **Lemon.**

Uncle and niece relations, allegedly platonic . . . **Avuncular relations.**

Under age for the phallic thrust; said of a young female . . . **Few pence short of a shilling.**

Under sailing orders . . . Of the phallus, erected.

Undercover man . . . A male homosexual.

Underdevelopment of secondary sex characteristics in females . . . HYPOCOSMOSIS.

Underdevelopment of secondary sex characteristics . . . See also under *Secondary sex characteristics.*

Undergarments of the female, esp. those covering the desirables . . . **Angel's gear.**

UNDINISM . . . Sexual excitation aroused by the sight or thought of water. Ex *unda* (a water wave).

UNDINISM . . . Sexual excitation aroused by the thoughts of water nymphs. Ex *Undine* (a water nymph).

Undressed, completely, down to and including the pubic embellishments . . . **Down to buckle and bare thong.**

Unfaithful wife . . . **Wife out of Westminster.**

Unfaithfulness in marriage . . . APISTIA.

Unfaithfulness, spiritual or mental, to one's spouse; expressed by wishful or illusory engagements in amatory pleasures with another . . . PHRENAPISTIA.

UNGATION . . . The lubricating discharge of the female genitalia appearing during sexual excitation.

Unholy bedlock . . . 1. Bedlock without wedlock. 2. A common-law marriage.

Unmarried female . . . **Unappropriated blessing.**

Unmarried phallator . . . **Leg lifter.**

Unmonkeyable . . . Of a girl, not accessible to the phallus or to the lecherous fingers of possessor.

Unparliamentary . . . Erotic; lecherous; obscene.

Unparliamentary procedures . . . In lovemaking, the coarser procedures, at least from her point of view.

Unrelieved holocaust . . . A tenacious phallic erection which remains unappeased after an evening of provocative manueuvering, including several near hits.

Unvirgin a virgin . . . **Blaze the trail.**

Unwillingness of female to accept the male in coitus . . . ADECTIA.

Up . . . Of a male, upon the female, and phallating.

Up-and-down place . . . A house where a man may, for a consideration, exercise his up-and-down pudendal movement.

Up-and-downer . . . A male heaving his buttocks in pudendal concourse.

Up in Annie's room . . . Of a male, out with a girl.

Uphills . . . Of the posture in coitus, with her on top.

Upright man . . . A male who phallates standing, in a hurry.

Upsetting to the male, because erotically charming . . . BOULVERSANTE.

Urination, person who derives sexual pleasure from watching another in the act of . . . COPROSCOPIST; UROLAGNIAC.

Urination, sexual excitation aroused by the sight of another person in the act of . . . UROLAGNIA.

Urine, person deriving sexual pleasure from the odor of; esp. from urine voided by one of the opposite sex . . . RENIFLEUR.

Urine, sexual excitation aroused by the sight of . . . UROLAGNIA.

URNINDE . . . A female homosexual. Ex the German.

URNING . . . A male homosexual. Ex the German.

UROLAGNIA . . . Sexual excitation aroused by the sight of another in urination, or by the sight of urine. From *ouron* (urine) & *lagneia* (lust).

Usher of the hall . . . The clitoris as the vaginal usher.

Utopia of sexual pleasures . . . **Swiveland.**

UXORAVALENCE . . . Sexual impotence with one's own wife. Ex *uxor* (wife), *a* (not), & *valere* (to be able).

UXORAVALENT . . . Designating or pert. to a husband who is impotent with his own wife, but often potent with another woman; also, such male.

UXORIOSIS . . . Masochistic submissiveness to one's wife. From *uxor* (a wife).

UXORIOUS . . . Excessively fond of and slavishly submissive to one's wife.

UXORODESPOTISM . . . Excessive or morbid domineering by a wife.

UXOROSTHEN . . . A male potent sexually only with his wife. Ex *uxor* (wife) & *sthenos* (strong).

V

VAGINA . . . The female canal which receives the phallus in sexual intercourse.

Vagina as a cavity . . . **Hole.**

Vagina as a warm dress for the phallus . . . **Roast beef dress.**

Vagina as a warmer for the phallus . . . **Muff; Toaster.**

Vagina as an indispensable sewer . . . **Hole.**

Vagina as the best body cavity of the female . . . **Molly's hole.**

Vagina as the conventional route for the phallus, in sexual concourse . . . **Rural Route No. 1.**

Vagina as the female inlet for the male outlet . . . **Moey.**

Vagina as the home of the phallus . . . **Ken.**

Vagina as the receptacle of the genital end . . . **Tail box.**

Vagina as the way to pleasure . . . **Road.**

Vagina, by way of . . . PERCOLPAL.

Vagina; conceived as a fornicator's chamber . . . **Fornicator's hall.**

Vagina; conceived as a hot "bearing" around a shaft . . . **Hotbox.**

Vagina; conceived as a jelly jar from which the desirous male organon derives its gratification . . . **Jelly cruse.**

Vagina; conceived as a passage closed at the far end . . . **Blind alley.**

Vagina; conceived as a reception hall for the phallus . . . **Fumbler's hall.**

Vagina; conceived as an enclave between the urethra and rectum (Tigris and Euphrates) . . . **Mesopotamia.**

Vagina; conceived as the anterior receiving chamber . . . **Front parlor.**

Vagina; conceived as the "boot" in which the third lower extremity of one Matthew Buckinger went . . . **Buckinger's boot.**

Vagina; conceived as the fiddle for the male bow . . . **Fiddle.**

Vagina, construction of, where none exists . . . COLPOPOIESIS.

Vagina, dilatation of, as after childbirth, with a resulting loss of "bottle" . . . COLPECTASIA.

Vagina, dryness of interior of . . . COLPOXEROSIS.

Vagina, external opening of . . . INTROITUS VAGINAE; COLPYLE.

Vagina, Greek form for; in allusion to a cavity . . . **KYSTHOS.**

Vagina, Greek form for; in allusion to a hollow, as that between the female breasts . . . **KOLPOS.**

Vagina, Greek form for; in allusion to a sheath . . . **KOLEOS.**

Vagina, Greek form for; in allusion to its service as a covering for the phallus . . . **ELYTRON.**

Vagina, having a large, elephantine; as if she had two . . . **Double-cunted.**

Vagina; in allusion to the attrition upon the phallus . . . **Rasp.**

Vagina; in allusion to the touchhole of old-time cannons . . . **Sear.**

Vagina, laceration of, as by a dildo or a large membrum virile . . . COLPORRHEXIS.

Vagina, large, made capacious by childbirth, phallation, or masturbation . . . **Barge.**

Vagina, occlusion or blockage of . . . GYNATRESIA.

Vagina of a colored prostitute . . . **Black Maria.**

Vagina, operation for narrowing of . . . ELYTROSTENOPLASTY.

Vagina, pain in; as after coitus with a voluminous phallus . . . COLPALGIA; COLPODYNIA; VAGINODYNIA.

Vagina, plastic surgery on, as to improve the phallic embrace . . . COLPOPLASTY.

Vagina, regarded as an insatiable demander . . . **Bottomless pit.**

Vagina, roughness of lining or mucosa of . . . TRACHYCOLPIA.

Vagina, spastic contraction of, as in fear or aversion . . . COLPISMUS; COLPOSPASM; VAGINISMUS.

Vagina, spastic contraction of, due to aversion to the sexual act or to the male involved . . . MENTAL COLPISMUS; MENTAL VAGINISMUS; COITAL COLPOSPASM.

Vagina, virgin . . . PARTHENOCOLPOS.

Vagina, virgin, condition of having . . . PARTHENOCOLPIA.

Vaginal embrace pressure upon the incoming phallus . . . **Bottle.**

Vaginal embrace pressure upon the incoming phallus, gratifying . . . **High on the bottle.**

Vaginal embrace pressure upon the incoming phallus, inadequate . . . **Not much bottle.**

Vaginal entrance tight enough to break the male genital bat . . . **Crack-bat.**

Vaginal excitation by the male finger . . . **Finger dosing.**

Vaginal invasion by the male finger, for his pleasure . . . **A dose of finger.**

Vaginal privileges for the membrum virile erectum, given by her . . . **She-kindness.**

Vaginal secretion as lubricant for the phallus . . . **Fiddlestick rosin.**

VAGINISMUS . . . Same as COLPISMUS, a spastic closure of the vagina, due to various causes but often the result of a loathing by the woman of sexual intercourse, or of the phallator.

VAGINISMUS, MENTAL . . . Same as MENTAL COLPISMUS, a contraction of the vagina resulting from fear of or aversion to sexual intercourse, or aversion to a particular phallator.

VAGINORAPTUS . . . Sexual intercourse with one's wife against her will. Ex *vagina* & *rapere* (to seize).

VARIETISM . . . The craving for variety in sexual pleasures.

Variety in sexual pleasures, craving of . . . VARIETISM.

VASOSIPHLATE . . . To sterilize the male by ligation of the vasa deferentia. From *vas* (vessel) & *siphloo* (cripple).

VENEREAL . . . 1. Transmitted by sexual intercourse, as an infection. 2. Pert. to the organs of generation.

Venereal disease, abnormal fear of becoming infected with . . . VENEREOPHOBIA.

Venereal disease, esp. gonorrheal arthritis . . . **Bone ache.**

Venereal disease, in allusion to a district in London, England, once teeming with brothels . . . **Covent Garden ague.**

Venereal disease, in allusion to a theatrical district in London, England, where girls with loose pudendal strings, who would as lief lie down as sit down, were most likely to be seen and engaged, for the usual chores . . . **Drury Lane ague.**

Venereal disease, in allusion to its being not good . . . **Bad disease.**

Venereal disease, in allusion to its prevalence among harlots . . . **Harlotosis**

Venereal disease, in allusion to Mild Mercurial Ointment, one of the old remedies, known also as Blue Ointment . . . **Blueball.**

Venereal disease, in allusion to the ancient Italian goddess identified with the Greek Aphrodite . . . **Venus's curse.**

Venereal disease, in allusion to the Blue Boar Tavern, of 18th century London, England, located in a district where a man was as likely to pick up a case of V.D. as a mug of ale . . . **Blue boar; Blue boy; Blue board.**

Venereal disease, in allusion to the foam-born goddess of love . . . **Aphroditis.**

Venereal disease, in allusion to the ladies of the oldest profession who are often regarded as the only dispensers thereof . . . **Ladies' fever.**

Venereal disease, in allusion to the son of Venus . . . **Cupid's itch.**

Venereal disease, usually gonorrhea . . . **Burner.**

Venereal infection conceived as a taper passed from one bearer to another . . . **Torch of Venus.**

Venereal infection, have a . . . **Be in for the plate.**

Venereal infection, in allusion to the 16th century Bishop of Winchester who had jurisdiction over a large district studded with bagnios . . . **Winchester goose.**

Venereal infection . . . See also under *Venereal disease.*

Venereally infected, to be; in allusion to burning urination . . . **Piss fire.**

Venereologist . . . A medical practitioner specializing in the treatment of diseases transmitted by sexual intercourse.

Venereophobia . . . Abnormal fear of becoming infected with a venereal disease.

Venery . . . 1. Indulgence of one's sexual cravings. 2. Pudendal concourse. Ex *Venus,* the goddess of love.

Vernorexia . . . The increase in the romantosexual appetite in the spring; spring fever. Ex *ver* (spring) & *orexis* (appetite).

View of the land . . . The panorama of the female pudendum, stripped and spread for phallic reception.

Viewy . . . Tantalizingly visible; used esp., naturally, with reference to female embellishments.

Viracme . . . The sexual orgasm in the male. From *vir* (man) & *akme* (top).

Virgin along . . . Of a female with an unspavined pudendum, to hold on to the maidenhead, come hell or high water.

Virgin, blood escaping from, at her phallic initiation, or during the break-in post-nuptial period . . . **Christening wine.**

Virgin bottom . . . The pudendal slit of a girl who has not yet yielded to the phallic subversion.

Virgin bride, blood stains on bed sheet of, following phallic initiation . . . **Bed bugs.**

Virgin bride, wedding night of . . . **Christening night.**

Virgin, coital bleeding of a, or of a recent . . . **Christening nosebleed.**

Virgin, defloration of a . . . Parthenoclasis.

Virgin, deflower a; in allusion to the bat . . . **Bat-foul.**

Virgin, deflower a . . . See also under *Deflower.*

Virgin, draw blood from, in defloration . . . **Broach claret.**

Virgin, female . . . Parthena.

Virgin, female who is no longer a . . . Phallata.

Virgin, female who is no longer a; designating . . . Phallatic.

Virgin females, designating . . . Aphallatic.

Virgin girdle, unbind the . . . **Zonam solvere.**

Virgin hock . . . Phallically unsullied female pudendal flesh.

Virgin-hot . . . Of a female, experiencing the first sensations of erotic desire.

Virgin hymen . . . Parthymen.

Virgin hymen, condition of having a . . . Parthymenia.

Virgin jack . . . A bit of screw with a previously unscrewed mademoiselle.

Virgin, male . . . Parthenus.

Virgin, phallate a . . . **Play first fiddle.**

Virgin pullet . . . 1. A young female who has not borne. 2. A young female who is pudendally unfamiliar with the phallus.

Virgin, seducer of a . . . PARTHENOCLEPT; **Ken cracker; Blazer; Trail blazer.**

Virgin, status of a . . . PARTHENITY.

Virgin, take it from a . . . **Break the knee.**

Virgin unfamiliar with the phallus . . . **Virgin pullet.**

Virgin, unvirgin a . . . **Blaze the trail.**

Virgin-welded . . . Betrothed to a virgin female.

Virginal hemorrhage during first or early subsequent phallations . . . **Christening nosebleed.**

Virginal membrane which in the unphallated female partially or, sometimes, completely occludes the external opening of the vagina . . . HYMEN.

Virginity . . . APHALLATIA; PARTHENIA; PARTHENITY.

Virginity, deprive of; in allusion to breaking of an intact pie crust . . . **Crack a crust.**

Virginity, deprive of; in allusion to cracking a fragile object . . . **Crack a Jane; Crack a Judy.**

Virginity, loss of, in sexual intercourse . . . DEFLORATION.

Virginity, loss of, surgically . . . HYMENOCLASIS.

Virginity, mental depression resulting from squandering of one's . . . HYMENOPENTHY.

Virginity, science dealing with . . . PARTHENOLOGY.

Virgins, adoration of . . . PARTHENOPHILY.

Virgins, erotic interest in or veneration of . . . PARTHENOPHILIA.

VIRGOPHRENIA . . . The state of mind characteristic of spinsters. Ex *virgo* (spinster) & *phren* (mind).

VIRGYNATION . . . Sexual intercourse between husband and wife. Ex *vir* (man) & *gyne* (wife).

Virile fornicator . . . **Good fellow.**

VIRILIA . . . Male sex organs.

VIRILINGUS . . . The erotic licking of the male sex organs. Ex *virilia* (male sex organs) & *lingere* (lick).

VIRIMIMISM . . . Adoption of masculine manners by a woman. Ex *vir* (man) & *mimesis* (an imitating).

VIROCOSMIC . . . A secondary sex characteristic of a male, as the beard.

Visible, tantalizingly, as above-the-garter female thigh, etc. . . . **Viewy.**

Visit a whore, professionally, to her . . . **Go fishing.**

Vittles . . . The female breasts as victuals.

Volunteer . . . A girl who, as the saying goes, lies down when asked to sit down.

VOMER . . . A Latin figurative synonym for the penis, in allusion to a plow.

Vomitory . . . The space between the labia of the female pudendum.

VOYEUR . . . A person who derives sexual gratification from watching others in the nude or in the act of coitus. Ex the French "one who sees."

VOYEURISM . . . The derivation of sexual gratification by watching others in the nude or in the act of sexual intercourse; peeping.

Vrow-case . . . A house where female pudenda may be hired and consumed on the premises; a brothel.

VULVA . . . The sexual sanctum of the female situated, mostly, between the medial aspects of the thickest parts of the thighs and composed mainly of the rounded prominence covered, in the adult, by pubic hair, the larger lips, the smaller lips, the small erectile body homologous with the penis (the clitoris), and the entrance to the vagina.

Vulva, arse, and a pair of titties as the dowry of a fortuneless bride . . . **Tipperary fortune.**

Vulva as a bag of cute tricks . . . **Monkey.**

Vulva as a canning device for the phallus . . . **Can.**

Vulva as a catcher of the male burrowing organ . . . **Mole catcher; Mole trap.**

Vulva as a cooker of savory erotic dishes . . . **Kettle.**

Vulva as a delightful assuager of the phallus . . . **Jack's delight.**

Vulva as a dowry . . . **Rochester portion; Whitechapel portion.**

Vulva as a juicer . . . **Keester.**

Vulva as a milt extractor . . . **Milt market.**

Vulva as a naughty performer, from grandma's point of view . . . **The naughty.**

Vulva as a phallus warmer . . . **Muff; Toaster.**

Vulva as a place for attrition . . . **Rasp.**

Vulva as a pleasurable trinket . . . **Knick-knack.**

Vulva as a seminal robber . . . **Rob-the-ruffian.**

Vulva as a small thing . . . **Minge.**

Vulva as a tree of pleasure . . . **Plum tree.**

Vulva as an exotic pudendal desirable . . . **India.**

Vulva as an insatiable demander . . . **Hog-eye.**

Vulva as female's majesty . . . **Seat of majesty.**

Vulva as hole for male "key" . . . **Key-hole.**

Vulva as no small pudendal comfort . . . **Modicum.**

Vulva as real estate of female . . . **Premises.**

Vulva as recipient of male spew . . . **Spew alley.**

Vulva as the avenue to sensual pleasure . . . **Road.**

Vulva as the business end of the female torso . . . **Business.**

Vulva as the catcher of the male "mouse" . . . **Mouser.**

Vulva as the genital end of the female . . . **Tail.**

Vulva as the home of the phallus . . . **Ken.**

Vulva as the inexpendable part of the female . . . **The indispensable.**

Vulva as the interlabial slit . . . **Slot.**

Vulva as the receiver of the membrum virile . . . **Receiving set.**

Vulva as the road to male happiness . . . **Toby.**

Vulva as the toothless lower mouth . . . **Pan.**

Vulva as the trap for the male hole-crawler . . . **Mouse trap.**

Vulva, blood-stained, of a just phallically christened virgin (bride or no bride) . . . **Bloody Mary.**

Vulva; conceived as a circumhirsute center of amorous engagements . . . **Hairy ring.**

Vulva; conceived as a drain for the phallic lava . . . **Gutter.**

Vulva; conceived as a garden . . . **Hortus.**

Vulva; conceived as a girl's better end . . . **Sunny south.**

Vulva; conceived as a holy place or as a revelation . . . **Hairy oracle.**

Vulva; conceived as a male's rosarium . . . **Gentleman's pleasure garden.**

Vulva; conceived as a metr*opolis,* revealed by the female when she is in a certain de*cubit*us position . . . **Cubitopolis.**

Vulva; conceived as a milking apparatus for lecherous males (goats) . . . **Goat-milker.**

Vulva; conceived as a mouth . . . **Moey.**

Vulva; conceived as a presentation of goodies . . . **Basket.**

Vulva; conceived as a repository of pudendal food, for the male . . . **Green-grocery.**

Vulva; conceived as a sanctum of the female . . . **Holy ground.**

Vulva; conceived as a savory goody . . . **Bit of jam.**

Vulva; conceived as a sheath for the male's third lower extremity . . . **Boot.**

Vulva; conceived as a soft, moist, and furry animalcule . . . **Bun; Bunny.**

Vulva; conceived as a "sweet little animal" . . . **Beastie.**

Vulva; conceived as a warm, furry animal . . . **Puss; Pussy; Pussycat.**

Vulva; conceived as a work of art . . . **Masterpiece.**

Vulva; conceived as afflicted by erotic pruritus . . . **Itcher; Itching Jenny.**

Vulva; conceived as an arse shop . . . **Bum-shop.**

Vulva; conceived as an oat manger to assuage phallic hunger . . . **Oatbin.**

Vulva; conceived as bottled joy . . . **Jugful of joy.**

Vulva; conceived as capacious accommodator . . . **Omnibus.**

Vulva; conceived as fishing waters . . . **Fish pond.**

Vulva; conceived as junior sis . . . **Little sister.**

Vulva; conceived as locale of phallic festivities . . . **Joy spot.**

Vulva; conceived as receptacle of phallic ejaculation . . . **Bucket.**

Vulva; conceived as something to "eat," by a cunnilinguist . . . **Cunt-pie.**

Vulva; conceived as somewhat too well worn for phallic comfort . . . **Bag.**

Vulva; conceived as the arena for bull sessions . . . **Bull ring.**

Vulva; conceived as the bifurcation at the crotch . . . **Bit of fork.**

Vulva; conceived as the captor of the male pants fly . . . **Fly cage; Fly-catcher.**

Vulva; conceived as the female's choicest part . . . **The article.**

Vulva; conceived as the jewels of the female . . . **Jewelry.**

Vulva; conceived as the ornament at the root of the female leg . . . **Leg piece.**

Vulva; conceived as the proverbial can't-do-without-it abomination . . . **Hole.**

Vulva; conceived as the receiver of the male button . . . **Buttonhole.**

Vulva; conceived as the toothless biter of the phallus . . . **Twat; Twot.**

Vulva; conceived in the light of its central feature . . . **Crack.**

Vulva, condition of, in which the labia present a gaping slit . . . CUNNECTASIA.

Vulva, especially erotic about the; said of the male . . . NAOSIPHILOUS; CUNNIPHILOUS.

Vulva, esp. of a Negress . . . **Jemima.**

Vulva, esp. the interlabial slit, conceived as a pudendal tear, as it were . . . **Jag.**

Vulva, esp. the introitus . . . **Hell hole.**

Vulva, esp. the lip-lined, partly open female receptacle in the thighs-abducted position . . . **Christmas box.**

Vulva, esp. the mons veneris . . . **Mount Pleasant.**

Vulva, esp. the vagina, conceived as a passage closed at the far end . . . **Blind alley.**

Vulva, excessive talk about, or obscene language involving the . . . CUNNILALIA.

Vulva, folds of skin bordering the slit of the . . . LABIA MAJORA.

Vulva from viewpoint of a cunnilinguist, regarded as an eating place . . . **Dining room.**

Vulva, Greek form for; in allusion to something deserving of respect . . . AIDOION.

Vulva having its labia majora closely approximated . . . VULVA CONNIVENS; SYNLABIA.

Vulva having its labia majora gaping . . . VULVA HIANS; CHASMALABIA.

Vulva, in allusion to a hot bearing around a shaft . . . **Hotbox.**

Vulva, in allusion to a wedge . . . **Cunt.**

Vulva, in allusion to *cun*(e)*t,* spelled backward . . . **Tenuc.**

Vulva, in allusion to its water department . . . **Water mill.**

Vulva, in allusion to the interlabial hiatus . . . **Crack.**

Vulva, in allusion to the labia majora which resemble, in abduction, the collar of a horse . . . **Horse collar.**

Vulva, in allusion to the labia majora which resemble, in abduction, the shoe of a horse . . . **Horseshoe.**

Vulva, in allusion to the pigmentation of the parts . . . **Brown madam.**

Vulva, in allusion to the pubes . . . **Bushes.**

Vulva, in allusion to the pubic hair . . . **Parsley-bed.**

Vulva, in allusion to the reddish mucosa . . . **Rufus.**

Vulva, in allusion to the superimposed pubic brush . . . **Broom.**

Vulva inaccessible phallically, because chaste or prudish . . . **Fastidious cave.**

Vulva inaccessible phallically, because too young legally . . . **Jail bait; San Quentin pigeon; San Quentin quail.**

Vulva infected by *Neisseria gonorrhoeae* . . . **Tetbury portion.**

Vulva, interlabial slit of . . . ENTOMA.

Vulva, Latin form for; in allusion to something one keeps hidden or covered . . . **CUNNUS.**

Vulva, licking of . . . CUNNILINGUS; CUNNILINCTION; EDELINGUS; **Pearl diving; Biting the dog-end; Brushing with Miriam.**

Vulva, lubricating secretion of, during sexual excitation . . . UNGATION.

Vulva, lubricating secretion of, during sexual quiescence . . . HUMEX.

Vulva, male who licks the, for his pleasure . . . CUNNILINGUIST; EDELINGUIST; **Pearl diver; Cunt-sucker.**

Vulva of a colored prostitute, esp. the vagina . . . **Black Maria.**

Vulva of a fashionable whore . . . **Belgravia.**

Vulva of a female of substance . . . **Aristocratic vein.**

Vulva of a female who pretends to be, or is, chaste . . . **Righteous bush.**

Vulva of a learned female . . . **Ivy bush.**

Vulva of a luscious female . . . **Jammy bit of jam.**

Vulva of a mulattess . . . **Can of brown polish.**

Vulva of a Negress . . . **Black mouth.**

Vulva of a slattern whore . . . **Mespot.**

Vulva of a whore, regarded as being used in the "battle" for a living . . . **Battle bag.**

Vulva of an inaccessible teenager, because too young legally . . . **Teentalizer.**

Vulva of an under-age girl . . . **Holy ground.**

Vulva regarded as a night creature . . . **Fly-by-night.**

Vulva regarded as a slash in the female pudendum . . . **Gash.**

Vulva regarded as the abode of sinners . . . **Hell-box; Hell hole.**

Vulva regarded . . . See also under *Vulva conceived.*

Vulva, titillate the, with the male cream stick . . . **Tickle the toby.**

Vulva, touch the, for good luck, before embarking on an adventure . . . **Touch the bun for luck.**

Vulva, well-worked . . . **Turn-round pudding.**

Vulva with split labia, open to receive the phallus . . . **Split crow.**

Vulvae of colored females . . . **Black bagging.**

Vulvae, rubbing of, against each other; by tribades . . . **Pussy bumping.**

Vulvar secretion during sexual excitation . . . UNGATION.

Vulvar secretion during sexual quiescence . . . HUMEX.

Vulvar slit . . . ENTOMA.

Vulvar space bounded by the labia majora and vulvar floor . . . CHASMA.

Vulvette . . . The vulva of a young pretty girl, conceived as being petite, delightful, and savory.

Vulvocracy . . . A typical North American gynecocratic pattern of family life in which the female holds the reins by virtue of the man's subservience to and utter dependence on her vulvar favors.

VULVOLIMIA . . . An insatiable craving for the female pudendum, and for concourse with it.

W

Wag a mute tongue . . . To have an itch affecting an intimate part of the body while one is not alone, esp. an itch of the scrotum or the vulva.

Wait impatiently for a positive menstrual report from a phallated girl who might conceivably conceive . . . **Sweat for a sugar report from one's gadget.**

Walk in a restrained manner so as to conceal an embarrassing erection . . . **Walk with a limp.**

Walk the streets in search for patrons; said of a prostitute . . . **Go on the batter.**

Walk with a limp . . . To walk in a restrained manner, in an attempt to conceal an embarrassing erection, as at a party abounding in provocative quail.

Walk with an exaggerated movement of the buttocks; said of the female . . . **Walk with the hips.**

Walk with the hips . . . Of a female, to walk with an educated movement of the buttocks.

Waning of sexual desire in the male . . . OBSOLAGNIUM.

Waning of sexual power in the male . . . FLACCILATION.

Want sexual gratification . . . **Itch.**

Wappenschawing . . . An alluring display of titty cleavage, or other blandishments, in allusion to a mustering of armed might.

Warm the husband's supper . . . Of a woman sitting in front of a fireplace, to lift the skirt above the knees and warm the pudendum.

Warmup . . . The manual excitation of the phallus prior to normal sexual intercourse, by the bearer or the recipient, in order to aid the lethargic organ in coming forth with an ejaculation.

Warrenite . . . One of Mrs. Warren's girls, i.e., a female who lets her perineum make a living for her.

Warts . . . A pair of miserable female breasts, not bigger than respectable warts.

Wasted blessing . . . A chaste old maid.

Water mill . . . The genital suite of the female, in allusion to the enclosed water department.

Water nymphs, sexual excitation aroused by thoughts of . . . UNDINISM.

Water, sexual excitation aroused by the sight of . . . UNDINISM.

Way of life, a . . . Mrs. Warren's profession.

Wear a forker . . . Be a cuckold, i.e., to be the husband of an unfaithful wife.

Wedding night coitus, omission of, by a male who wants to spare his virgin bride the apparent ordeal . . . **Christian compliment.**

Wedding night of a virgin bride . . . **Christening night.**

Well fukked and far from home . . . Exhausted physically and/or mentally; bushed.

Well worked-over vulva . . . **Turnround pudding.**

Well-rigged frigate . . . A woman possessing unusually well-appointed physical attracitons, esp. fore and aft bulges.

Wet blanket . . . A female whose pudendal funnel is still wet with the dew of a previous sexual engagement.

Wet dream . . . ONEIROGMUS.

Whaler . . . A phallus of magnificent size, in allusion to the lady's remark, "It's a whale of a prick."

Whank off . . . Of a male troubled by a resistant phallic uprising, to bring it down with the palmar persuader.

What Harry gave Doll . . . A phallus erectus smack down the pudendum.

Whipped, erotic desire to be . . . MASTILAGNIA.

Whisker-splitter . . . A male who splits the pubic whiskers of the female, phallically, on the way to the interlabial hiatus.

White hot meat . . . Exposed good parts of a white girl.

White meat . . . The by far preferable tissues of a female. Also, such flesh specifically of a white girl.

Whitechapel portion . . . Same as **Rochester portion,** a dowry of cunt.

Whore as a capacious pudendal accommodator . . . **Omnibus.**

Whore, as a vulva personified . . . CUNNUS.

Whore, colored . . . **Black Maria.**

Whore, frequent an older . . . **Keep up an old queen.**

Whore; in allusion to her lower interlabial fissure . . . **Crack.**

Whore; in allusion to her "maggoty" pudendum . . . **Mawkes.**

Whore; in allusion to her professional dorsal posture . . . **Fiddleback.**

Whore; in allusion to her splitting the thighs . . . **Split-arse mechanic.**

Whore, of a, to marry . . . **Hammer the sword into a plowshare; Rehabilitate.**

Whore, of a, to remove pudendum from phallic traffic and dedicate to peaceful uses, in wedlock . . . **Convert.**

Whore, of a, to retire; by way of marriage or otherwise . . . **Hang up the fiddle.**

Whore of note, for her industry and/or coital dexterity . . . **Moll Peatley.**

Whore of proletarian vintage . . . **Bloss.**

Whore, youngish and not bad looking . . . **Q.T. cutie.**

Whorehouse . . . **Trugging-house.**

Whorehouse, as a moll dispenser . . . **Moll shop.**

Whorelet . . . 1. A cute harlot. 2. A young prostitute, in her lower teens.

Whoremaster general . . . **Brother of the gusset.**

Whoremonger, be a noted . . . **Play the giddy goat.**

Whoremonger conceived as hunter of pudenda . . . **Crack hunter.**

Whoremonger; in allusion to one who searches in shady walks (mall) . . . **Molrower; Mollrower.**

Whoremonger; in allusion to the female "rabbit" . . . **Cunny-hunter.**

Whores, male who hunts; for pudendal consumption . . . **Moll hunter.**

Whoring about, in allusion to the opening of the labial gates . . . **Split-arsing.**

Whoring, go out . . . **Go fishing.**

Whoring, practice the vocation of . . . **Let out one's parlor.**

Wide in the bows . . . Of a female, usually, more than average in width at the lower bulge; i.e., having a wide **hiposterior.**

Wife . . . A masturbator's right arm, if he is right-handed.

Wife . . . A child, usually a boy, whom a pederast phallates per rectum.

Wife, conceived as a good-to-have-around phallic comforter . . . **Conveniency.**

Wife; conceived as a licit phallic cover . . . **Lawful blanket; Lawful jam.**

Wife; conceived as an important or, at least, a necessary-evil adjunct to the life of the male, and also as an always-at-hand muff for the warming of the membrum virile . . . **Comfortable importance.**

Wife, excessively submissive to one's . . . UXORIOUS.

Wife, have a; for the sexual privilege . . . **Keep a cow.**

Wife in water colors . . . A mistress, in allusion to the impermanency of such colors.

Wife, masochistic submissiveness to one's . . . UXORIOSIS.

Wife, morbid domineering by a . . . UXORODESPOTISM.

Wife, morbid domineering of one's . . . MARITODESPOTISM.

Wife out of Westminster . . . A wife with a tenuous concept of faithfulness.

Wife, sexual impotence only with one's own . . . UXORAVALENCE.

Wife, sexual intercourse with one's own, against her will . . . SPHENOPHALLIA; VAGINORAPTUS.

Wife, sexual potency limited to one's own . . . UXOROVALENCE.

Wild oats . . . Amorous escapades to relieve the first twinges of seminal pressure, in the young.

Wild rogue . . . The man's phallic bayonet conceived as an untamed rascal.

Winchester goose . . . 1. A venereal infection. 2. A bubo of venereal origin. 3. A person afflicted with 1 and/or 2. An allusion to the 16th century Bishop of Winchester who had jurisdiction over a district rich in bordellos.

Winchester goose . . . A woman practicing the oldest profession.

Wine, sexual desire induced or enhanced by the drinking of . . . OENOLAGNIA.

Wish of good luck addressed to a man who is pudendum-bound, either at home or at some pudendal exchange, after a long period of deprivation, as after a voyage . . . **Have a good luck round!**

With both sheets fore . . . Masturbating with both hands, usually said of the male.

Withdraw forcibly from the coital act, after it has proceeded almost to the male's completion; said of the female . . . **Bluff the rat.**

Withdrawal of phallus before ejaculation, practice of . . . COITUS INCOMPLETUS; COITUS INTERRUPTUS; ONANISM.

Withdrawal of pudendal privileges, by a wife from her husband, as punishment or coercion . . . **Jamaica discipline.**

Withhold ejaculation to prolong phallation . . . **Keep it up.**

Withholding of ejaculation, coitus marked by . . . COITUS RESERVATUS.

Without a condom or a diaphragm, designating a bout of phallation . . . **A cappella.**

Without a condom, phallus plunging . . . **Skin diver.**

Woman as a female . . . **Skirt.**

Woman as a savory dish . . . **Pot.**

Woman as a warm and softly adipose pudendum . . . **Bit of mutton.**

Woman as bearer of the genital pore . . . **Hole.**

Woman, attractive; in allusion to gold nuggets . . . **Basket of oranges.**

Woman, big and masculine-looking . . . **Horse-godmother.**

Woman, desirous, in allusion to her figuratively hot pudendum . . . **Frigate on fire.**

Woman, fat, as a sexual target . . . **Bit of fat.**

Woman free with her pudendum, as gifts or sales . . . **Dant.**

Woman having large, bushel-size mammae . . . **Bushel bubby.**

Woman, inability of, to accept the male in coitus . . . ADECTIA.

Woman, marriage of, to more than one man at the same time; when not sanctioned by custom or law . . . POLYGAMY.

Woman, marriage of, to more than one man at the same time; when sanctioned by law . . . POLYANDRY.

Woman, masculine or man-like . . . GYNANDER.

Woman morally flexible . . . **Bitch.**

Woman no longer a virgin . . . PHALLATA.

Woman no longer a virgin, designating a . . . PHALLATIC.

Woman regarded as an appeaser of the male appetites . . . **Bit of goods.**

Woman, resembling a . . . GYNECOID.

Woman, the better tissues of a . . . **Bacon.**

Woman, unworthy, as phallus fodder . . . **Fagot.**

Woman well decorated bosom- and hip-wise . . . **Well-rigged frigate.**

Woman who dislikes men . . . MISANDRIST.

Woman who engages in sexual acts with two men at the same time, or with one in the presence of the other . . . BIVIRIST.

Woman who has borne several children . . . **Wrinkle-belly**; PARA.

Woman who has never had sexual intercourse . . . APHALLATA.

Woman who has never had sexual intercourse, designating a . . . APHALLATIC.

Woman who has sexual feelings of a man, state of . . . VIRAGINITY.

Woman who has strong sexual cravings and is obsessed by thoughts of the phallus erectus . . . MENTULOPHRENIAC.

Woman who is a man's wife in every way but is not married to him, legally . . . **Brevet-wife.**

Woman who is adept in sexual relations, although unmarried . . . **Graduate.**

Woman who masturbates a stallion . . . **Horse breaker.**

Woman who takes the penis into her mouth . . . FELLATRICE; **Sword swallower; Beef eater; Jaw artist; Mouther; Cocksucker.**

Woman whose vagina is still wet with seminal fluid of one phallator when she engages another male . . . **Buttered bun.**

Woman with a daring décolletage . . . **Bare brisket.**

Woman with a thoroughly phallated vagina . . . **Battered box.**

Woman with a wide hinterland . . . **Broad gauge.**

Woman with very large breasts . . . MACROMASTA; **Bushel bubby.**

Woman . . . See also under *Female, Girl,* etc.

Women as center of thoughts and interest, holding . . . GYNECENTRIC.

Women as female society . . . **Minge.**

Women as the female sex . . . **Gusset.**

Women, aversion for or fear of . . . GYNEPHOBIA.

Women, aversion for the company of . . . GYNERESPIA.

Women collectively . . . **Calico; The skirt**; DISTAFF.

Women, diseases of, branch of medicine dealing with . . . GYNECOLOGY; GYNIATRICS.

Women, hatred of; by a male . . . MISOGYNY.

Women, hunger for; as after a prolonged enforced deprivation . . . GYNELIMIA.

Women, lack of association and/or intercourse with, abnormal condition resulting from; as after prolonged enforced isolation . . . AMULIEROSIS.

Women, old, sexual lust for . . . ANILILAGNIA.

Women who bore children, bodily changes characteristic of; as discolored nipples . . . PAROSTIGMATA.

Women who may be talked into it, without too much breath . . . **Fadcattle.**

Women's clothing, practice of wearing, by a man . . . CROSS DRESSING; EONISM; TRANSVESTISM; TRANSVESTITISM.

Work the hairy oracle . . . To busy oneself with the phallus erectus in the female genital sheath.

Workable model . . . A dame who does what is expected of her, pudendally.

World of male homosexuals, real and imaginary . . . **Pansyland.**

Worship at the back altar . . . To obturate the rectum with the phallic plunger.

Wriggle . . . To phallate a female.

Wriggle navels . . . Fit the round peg in the round hole.

Wriggle off . . . To relieve seminal pressure by a manually induced spurt.

Wriggling pole . . . The male pole used in the act of wriggling a female pudendum. See **Wriggle.**

Wrinkle-belly . . . A woman who has borne several children, in allusion to the stretching of the abdomen during pregnancy and the subsequent wrinkling of the abdominal wall.

Wrong font . . . The anus as a substitute vagina.

X

Xassafrassed . . . Stung vaginally by the membrum virile; phallated.

Xeniaphilia . . . Female pudendal hospitality, without commercial overtones. Ex *xenia* (friendly relation) & *philein* (to love).

XENODYNAMIC . . . Sexually potent with an unfamiliar female, but impotent with one's own wife. Ex *xenos* (strange) & *dynamis* (power).

XENOLIMIA . . . The craving for unorthodox methods of sexual gratification, with a female. Ex *xenos* (strange) & *limos* (hunger).

XENOLYTRIA . . . Sexual infidelity on the part of a married man. Ex *xenos* (foreign) & *elytron* (vagina).

XENOMENIA . . . Menstruation from a part other than the uterus. Ex *xenos* (foreign) & *meniaia* (menses).

XENOPHALLIA . . . Sexual infidelity on the part of a married woman. Ex *xenos* (strange) & *phallos* (penis).

XERONISUS . . . An ineffectual effort at coitus in which orgasm is not attained. From *xeros* (dry) & *nisus* (effort).

XERONYMPHIA . . . Dryness of the vulvar interlabial parts, esp. of the labia minora.

Xerotripsis . . . A pudendal dry run, i.e., phallation terminated short of ejaculation. Ex *xeros* (dry) & *tripsis* (friction).

Xiphophagia . . . The act of dephlogisticating a tumefied male genital gladiolus by means of oral cuddling.

XIPHOS . . . The male genital perforator regarded as a sword.

Xiphosclerosis . . . A hardening of the membrum virile which responds admirably to vaginal massage.

X-legged . . . Of a female, pudendally unwilling; in allusion to crossed legs.

Y

Yack . . . The male instrument of phallation.

Yack-yack . . . To give the vagina the acquaintance of the phallus. Also, a course of sexual intercourse.

Yam . . . To phallate voraciously, as if there were no tomorrow.

Yankee heaven . . . Paris as a favorite girlie center, so regarded by American male tourists.

Yap . . . The upper, vocal mouth of the female, when assuming the role of the lower, silent mouth, as recipient of the phallus erectus.

Yap wagon . . . The pleasure wagon of the female, with the fringe on the top.

Yap wagon, hop the . . . Of the male, to mount the female pleasure wagon, with a hot rivet.

Yard . . . The able and willing male spar.

Yard . . . To do with the willing and able male spar what it's willin' to do.

Yard and a half . . . Sizewise, esp. lengthwise, a better than adequate phallus.

Yazz . . . To give the female pudendum what's coming to it.

Yehudi . . . The membrum virile of a Mosaic descendant.

Yelper . . . A female who, when spiked phallically, hollers erotically.

Yen for . . . Have that certain feeling for a female, fortified by erections.

Yen, have a . . . Of the male, suffer a phallic insubordination, expressed by an uprising.

Yen-on . . . A transitory sclerosis of the male stylus which is specifically responsive to the vaginal caress.

Yentz . . . To give a female vaginafuls of phallic reciprocations.

Yentzer . . . A male in the act of pudendal calisthenics.

Yeoman of the mouth . . . A person, usually a female, who gives oral sanctuary to erotically disturbed phalli.

Yes-woman . . . A female who, for love or money, buffers sex-hardened penes with warm vulvar receptions.

Yinker . . . A man with an effete genital poniard who engages a prostitute, nevertheless, to tinker with her genitalia, and to do with his hands what he cannot do with his zeek.

Yodel . . . To relieve the tense phallus by homing into the rectum.

Yogurt . . . The milk of phallic exuberance.

Yoni . . . In Sanskrit, the vulva.

Yoni . . . A figure of the female genitalia used as a symbol in the worship of Shakti.

York . . . To ogle voraciously an exposed or bold female part.

Yorkshire bite . . . In fellatio, a bite upon the oral visitor, not always resented.

Yorkshire compromise . . . An impotent male married to a frigid woman.

Yorkshire estate . . . A non-prostitutional pudendum muliebre to whose privileges a man has established dependable access.

Yorkshire hog . . . A steatopygous wench who takes the seminal hose per rectum.

Yorkshire muff . . . A toothless fellator or fellatrice.

Yorkshire pavilion . . . The muliebral *chef-d'oeuvre* conceived as a decorative shelter for the male pendant in its non-pendent posture.

You don't look at the mantelpiece when you are poking the fire . . . So what if her face is not pretty, so long as her pudendum is satisfyin'!

You have been doing naughty things . . . A quip addressed to a man and his spouse when the latter is visibly enceinte, in allusion, obviously, to the causative mattress jig.

You weren't born—you were pissed up against the wall and hatched in the sun . . . A plebeian imputation to one's antagonist of a fanciful non-uterine origin.

You wouldn't fuck it . . . You can bet your gonads that it's so.

Young blood . . . Young females regarded as targets for phallic maneuvers.

Young female pudendally accessible . . . **January chicken.**

Young female who has borne no children . . . **Virgin pullet.**

Young females or harlots, male attracted to . . . **Kid-stretcher.**

Young girl as a young gallinacean . . . **Pullet.**

Young girl, phallate a, esp. with a strapping organon . . . **To bull in a china shop.**

Young girls, male pudendally smitten by . . . **Pullet squeezer.**

Young girls, sexual craving for . . . Neanirosis.

Young girls, sexual desire for . . . Neanilagnia.

Young, incapable of bearing . . . Intictant.

Young prostitutes, in the teen-age class . . . **Kid-leather.**

Young strop . . . The phallus of a young man, esp. of a youth.

Young stuff . . . Young virgins with vulvi hardly pubescent.

Young thing . . . A girl of tender age, usually in the lower teen-age group, with better than average development, where it counts.

Yum-yum . . . The female pudendal confection, as seen through the aphakial genital periscope of the male.

Z

Zeal girl . . . A girl with a desirous, hence compliant, underbelly.

Zee titties . . . The areolated upper tenants of the female, as appellated by members of the 50 million who, certainly in such matters, can't be wrong.

Zeek . . . A still willing but hardly able male pudendal coupler.

Zipper-snapper . . . A thoroughly inflammatory female whose contour map is so diastrophic to the male genital bowsprit that she causes it to go rampant and, at least figuratively, snap the fly zip.

Zonam solvere . . . To unbind the virgin girdle, as of a bride at the time of her wedding.

Zonerotism . . . Erotic sensitivity peculiar to certain parts of the body. Ex *zone* (belt) & *eros* (sex love).

Zooerast . . . A male who has sexual intercourse with a female animal. From *zoon* (animal) & *erastes* (lover).

Zoofellatio . . . A form of fellatio in which the taker of the penis is an animal. From *zoon* (animal) & *fellare* (suck).

Zook . . . An old prostitute who is "sick and tired" of it all. i.e., has had it.

Zoolagnia . . . The desire to engage in sexual concourse with animals. Ex *zoon* (animal) & *lagneia* (lust).

Zoolinction . . . A sexual perversion in which the interlabial parts of a female are licked by an animal, usually somewhat trained for the act. Ex *zoon* (animal) & *lingere* (to lick).

Zoophallia . . . Sexual intercourse with a female animal.

Zoophallist . . . A male who has sexual intercourse with an animal. Ex *zoon* (animal) & *phallos* (penis).

Zoophilia . . . Love of animals associated with erotic pleasure. Ex *zoon* & *philein* (to love).

Zoophilism . . . Sexual love for animals.

Zoophilism, erotic . . . Sexual pleasure derived from the touching or fondling of animals, esp. animals of the opposite sex.

Zoophilist . . . A person whose love for animals is associated with an erotic element.

Zoophily . . . Same as Zoophilia, love of animals involving an erotic element.

Zoopsilagnia . . . The derivation of sexual pleasure from watching animals in copulation. Ex *zoon* (animal), *ops* (vision), & *lagneia* (lust).

Zoosadism . . . The condition in which sexual pleasure is derived from inflicting cruelty on animals.

Zygophilia . . . Erotic pleasure derived from the feeling of subjugation, esp. such feeling in a man dominated by a woman. Ex *zygon* (yoke) & *philein* (to love).

Zygophilist . . . A man who derives sexual pleasure from submitting to the domination by a woman.

APPENDIX

A

A mortarful of pestle . . . A vaginaful of membrum virile erectum.

Aberrationist . . . A person who indulges in unorthodox forms of sexual concourse or erotic play. Derived from *aberrare* (to go astray).

Ablutolagnia . . . The sexual desire aroused by taking baths, showers, or other ablutional procedures indulged in by addicts of ablutophilia. Derived from *ablutio* (washing) and *lagneia* (lust).

Ablutomania . . . A compulsive desire or mania to take baths, showers, etc. See discussion under *ablutophilia.* Derived from *ab* (off), *luere* (to wash), and *mainesthai* (to rage).

Ablutophilia . . . An excessive interest in taking baths, showers, or the other modes of washing oneself. There is usually a sexual background, the pactitioner deriving erotic pleasure from the act of self-exposure, from the act of rubbing or manipulating his body, or from the titillating effect of the water. The condition is more common in women. Some women are completely frigid before taking a bath but show marked eroticism after the bath. The term is derived from *ablutio* (washing) and *philein* (to like). A stronger form of the same condition is known as *ablutomania.*

Ablutophobia . . . A morbid fear of bathing or washing, usually based on a sense of guilt arising from the realization that one derives sexual pleasure from the act. Derived from *ablutio* and *phobos* (fear).

Ablutoskepsis . . . The desire or the practice of watching women in their bath. Men have gone to great lengths to make it possible for them to watch women bathing, as by boring holes in doors and walls, installing transparent mirrors, posing as female attendants, and burying themselves in sand at seashores reserved for women bathers. Ablutoskepsis is observed almost exclusively in men; the interest of women in male bathers is mild and seldom leads to desperate measures. The word is derived from *ablutio* (washing) and *skepsis* (viewing).

Abrophrenia . . . The ability to express thoughts and feelings pertaining to love and sex with grace and delicacy. The term is derived from *habros* (graceful) and *phren* (mind).

Abominable dream man . . . Incubus; an imaginary male who has sexual intercourse with women in their dreams. 2. The image of an attractive male, or of a favorite male, which a woman conjures while masturbating, to enhance the pleasure of the act.

Abominable pants worm . . . The urogenital tailpiece of the male, regarded as a toady "worming" its way into the sheath of the pudendum muliebre. It is often so regarded by newly pregnant women who were opposed to being enceinte.

Abraham's bosom . . . The female pudendal embellishments, regarded as a warm bosom for phallic cuddling.

Acclimation . . . The gradual diminution in sexual appetite in general or, especially, with regard to one's spouse, as a result of familiarity.

Acedolagnia . . . Complete indifference to sexual matters, without the slightest aversion or interest. This condition is common in women. Derived from *a* (negative), *kedos* (care), and *lagneia* (lust).

Ace of spades . . . The perineal genital mouth of the female, conceived as the figure of a spade, because of the adjacent hairy escutcheon having, in fact, a similar appearance.

Achlysio . . . The mild state of mental narcosis or drowsiness that follows a lengthy and satisfying sexual bout. Derived from *Achyls* (goddess of obscurity).

Acmasia . . . The highest point of sexual excitation and pleasure; in the male during the period of ejaculation. Derived from *akme* (the top).

Acokoinonia . . . Sexual congress which is not accompanied by or the result of sexual desire. The condition is common in women whose passive attitude in the act of intercourse does not make desire mandatory. Paradoxically, the condition is also observed in men, although rather rarely. The term is derived from *a* (without), *conatus* (desire or zeal), and *koinonia* (sexual intercourse).

Acomoclitic . . . Preferring a hairless vulva. While the average man has no definite liking or aversion for the pubic hair, there are some who have a phobia for it. The term is derived from *a* (without), *kome* (hair) and *clitic* (prone).

Acomovulvate . . . Having no hair in the pubic region; said of a woman. Derived from *a* (without), *kome* (hair), and *vulva* (the external genital complex of the female).

Aconorrhea . . . A discharge of seminal fluid not as a result of a conscious sexual climax or orgasm. The stimulus may be a mild erotic excitation, as the sight of a shapely leg or a low decolletage, and the subject is usually unaware of the discharge at the time of its occurrence. Derived from *a* (without), *conatus* (desire), and *rheo* (flow).

Acosmoclisis . . . A tendency toward disorderliness in matters pertaining to courtship, love play, coitus, etc. The term is derived from *a* (without), *kosmos* (order), and *clisis* (inclination or tendency).

Acousimia . . . Erotic hallucinations of hysterical girls during which the victims hear male voices summoning them to seduction. Derived from *akoustikos* (pert. to hearing) and *mimeisthai* (to imitate).

Acrasolagnia . . . Lack of self-control with regard to sexual behavior. Derived from *a* (without), *kratos* (power), and *lagneia* (lust).

Acritition . . . Sexual intercourse terminating without an orgasm, especially when due to partial impotence of the male. Derived from *a* (without), *krisis* (crisis), and *coition* (intercourse).

Acrocinesia . . . A condition in which the penis, though erected, possesses too much mobility which makes insertion into the vagina difficult. Derived from *akros* (extreme) and *kinesis* (motion).

Acrocoition . . . The habit of indulging in sexual intercourse with excessive frequency. Derived from *akros* (extreme) and *coition* (sexual intercourse).

Acrorthosis . . . The condition of having erections with abnormal frequency. Derived from *akros* (extreme) and *orthosis* (condition of being erect).

Actirasty . . . Pleasurable sexual lassitude aroused by exposure to sun, as at the seashore. Derived from *aktis* (ray) and *erastes* (lover).

Adelophilia . . . The state of giving the impression, by appearance and action, of not being interested in amorous or sexual matters, when the opposite is actually true. The term is applied primarily to women and is derived from *adelos* (not evident) and *philia* (a liking).

Adelphegamy . . . Marriage to a sister. This is akin to *casigamy*. except that it imputes the volitional part to the brother. It is derived from *adelphe* (sister) and *gamos* (marriage).

Adelphepothia . . . Sexual interest in a sister, regardless of age. The term is derived from *adelphe* (sister) and *pothos* (desire).

Adelphirexia . . . Sexual desire for one's nephew. The term is derived from *adelphideos* (nephew) and *orexis* (desire).

Adelphithymia . . . Sexual interest in one's niece. The term is derived from *adelphide* (niece) and *epithymia* (lust).

Adeption . . . The use of lubricating oils, jellies, etc. on the male organ during sexual intercourse, to facilitate entry or to avoid irritation. The word is derived from *adeps* (fat or grease).

Adventitious erogenesis . . . Sexual excitation, often accompanied by ejaculation, resulting from emotional phenomena which are not normally related to libido, as, for example, fear, anger. In addition, certain postures may often affect some persons, although they appear quite innocent to the average man or woman.

Aelurophobia . . . A strong aversion for or fear of cats. One form of this condition is attributable to a conscious or subconscious identification of the cat with a woman or, more specifically, with the vulva. The identification stems, undoubtedly, from the fact that the pet name for a cat happens to be an endearing name for a girl and in the indelicate patois of men also the appellation of a girl's vulva. The term is derived from *ailouros* (cat) and *phobia* (fear or aversion). The condition is observed in men who are victims of sexual frustration and in them the aversion is a form of rebellion. In women the condition arises from a sense of modesty.

Aftereffects . . . The gluteal sitting spherosites, usually of the female, in allusion to their rearguard position.

Agamobiosis . . . The status of life without marriage or without sexual experience. Derived from *a* (without), *gamos* (marriage), and *bios* (life).

Agamunia . . . 1. Sexual intercourse outside of wedlock. 2. A living together as man and wife without being married. Derived from *a* (without), *gamos* (marriage), and *eune* (bed).

Agapopingia . . . Pictorial art depicting the various phases of sexual love. The term is derived from *agapetikos* (in love) and *pingere* (to represent pictorially).

Agitocubia . . . A rapid succession of coital movement, leading to an early orgasm for the man. The condition is usually observed in nervous people or in sexually starved males, and is totally unsatisfactory to the female participant. The situation can be eliminated by discipline. Derived from *agitare* (to put in motion) and *cubare* (to lie).

Agnogenia . . . A period marked by an increase in sexual potency and craving of unknown etiology. The enhanced sexual capacity in this condition is not due to abstinence, exposure to temptation, etc. It has also no relation to physical well-being or other understandable stimuli. The term is derived from *agnos* (unknown) and *genesis* (origin).

Agnuopia . . . A peculiar lascivious stare characterized by submissiveness, observed in some women during pre-coital play or during the first stages of sexual intercourse. The term is derived from *agnus* (a lamb) and *ops* (eye).

Agomphathymia . . . Lack of sexual interest in a woman who has no teeth or who has dental caries. Derived from *a* (without), *gomphios* (tooth), and *epithymia* (sexual desire).

Agonorgasmos . . . Sexual orgasm attained only after a prolonged act of coitus and at the cost of great effort. Derived from *agon* (struggle) and *orgasmos* (orgasm).

Agonophilia . . . The preference of some men for an act of coitus which is delayed or made difficult by a pretended struggle of opposition on the part of the woman. Derived from *agon* (struggle) and *philia* (liking or preference).

Agraphobia . . . The fear of being "grabbed" or "pawed" by a lusty male. The fear is intuitive and not based on tangible evidence of an impending attack. The term is derived from *agra* (a catching of prey) and *phobos* (fear).

Agrexophilia . . . The condition of being more passionate when there are people in the proximity of the arena of sexual indulgence, as in an adjoining room. The phenomenon is a form of exhibitionism in which the participant fancies himself exposed in the act of coitus. The term is from *ad* (toward), *grex* (flock or crowd), and *philein* (to love).

Agrexophrenia . . . The condition of being unable to perform the sexual act because of the knowledge that someone is nearby, as in an adjoining room. The characteristic is a form of bashfulness or, at times, a manifestation of a sense of guilt. It is derived from *ad* (toward), *grex* (flock or crowd), and *phren* (mind or state of mind).

Agriophrenia... A state of almost uncontrollable sexual frenzy often observed in perverts and derelicts. The word is derived from *agrios* (wild) and *phrenia* (state of mind).

Agrypnolagnia . . . A state of sexual restlessness developing during a siege of sleeplessness. The term is derived from *agrypnos* (sleepless) and *lagneia* (lust).

Aidacratia . . . Sexual impotence in men which results from a sense of bashfulness. The term may also be applied to frigidity in women caused by bashfulness. The term is derived from *aidos* (bashfulness) and *akrateia* (impotence).

Aidocratia . . . The libidinous impulse aroused in a man by the bashfulness of a girl. Also, the additional sexual potency which the bashfulness of the female imparts to the man. Derived from *aidos* (bashfulness) and *kratos* (strength).

Aidomania . . . Abnormal sexual craving for the female pudendum. Derived from *aidoion* (female sex organs) and *mania* (frenzied desire).

Albalagnia . . . The sexual desire of a non-Caucasian male for a white woman. Derived from *alba* (white) and *lagneia* (lust).

Albedosynia . . . A sexual craving for girls with a tender white skin. The term is derived from *albedo* (whiteness) and *machlosyne* (lust).

Algogenesolagnia . . . Sexual excitation or pleasure resulting from the infliction of pain in another person. The term is derived from *algos* (pain), *genesis* (production), and *lagneia* (lust). Algogenesolagnia is the mechanism of sadistic pleasure.

Algolagnia . . . A sexual abnormality in which the infliction of pain or the suffering of pain affords sexual gratification or increases sexual excitement. The word is derived from *algos* (pain) and *lagneia* (lust).

Algophily . . . The condition of wanting to suffer pain because it affords sexual pleasure. Derived from *algos* (pain) and *philein* (to love).

Algoterpsia . . . A type of moral austerity which demands that every pleasure, especially sexual pleasure, be followed by physical punishment, as the infliction of pain. The term is derived from *algos* (pain) and *terpsis* (enjoyment).

Aliphineur . . . A man skillful in the application of ointments and inunctions on men or women for the purpose of inducing pleasant sexual excitation often accompanied by an orgasm. The term is derived from *aleiphein* (to anoint).

Aliphineuse . . . A woman skilled in the application of ointments and inunctions on men and, occasionally, women for the purpose of inducing pleasant sexual excitement often accompanied by an orgasm. The term is derived from *aleiphein* (to anoint).

Allantotribism . . . A form of masturbation practiced by women in which a sausage takes the place of the male organ. The term is derived from *allas* (sausage) and *tribein* (to rub).

Allassophily . . . The addiction to constant change in the procedures of sexual indulgence, as in finding new ways to stimulate the sexual appetite or to appease it. Derived from *allassein* (to alter or change) and *philein* (to love).

All-beef sausage . . . A male of small stature having a disproportionately large phallus.

Alleloknismus . . . A form of masturbation, often practiced by children, in which the participants tickle each other's sexual organs. The word is derived from *allelon* (of one another) and *knismos* (tickling).

Alloerasty . . . An unconventional method for initiating erotic thoughts in a man by exposing to him nudity which in itself has no attraction, such as that of a naked child, and serves only as a reminder. The method is often resorted to by wives who feel that a little indirect suggestion is all that is required. The term is derived from *allos* (other) and *erastes* (lover).

Allokinesis . . . The responsive sexual movements of a woman during intercourse. The word is derived from *allos* (other) and *kinein* (to move).

Allomulcia . . . The desire to caress or fondle a woman in the presence of another woman. The term is derived from *allos* (other) and *mulcere* (to fondle).

Allonemia . . . A mental maneuver in which one of the participants in a bout of sexual play or intercourse indulges in the illusion that the other member or participant is someone else, more desirable. The term is derived from *allos* (other) and *noema* (a thought).

Allopellia . . . The condition of having an orgasm from the stimulation obtained by watching others in the act of sexual intercourse. Derived from *allos* (other) and *pellere* (to eject).

Allotriorasty . . . The phenomenon of having a greater sexual interest in women of foreign nations or of other races as opposed to women of one's own race or country. The explanation lies in the conscious or subconscious reasoning that a woman of one's own nationality is in a sense "related" to one's tribe or family for whom the man has no sexual craving. The word is derived from *allotrios* (belonging to another) and *erastes* (lover).

Almanac . . . The female external genitalia, in allusion to their being replete, from the viewpoint of a desirous male, with interesting items.

Alphamegamia . . . A marriage between an older man and a young girl. Derived from *alpha* (first letter of Greek alphabet), *omega* (last letter of Greek alphabet), and *gamos* (marriage).

Altar . . . 1. The pudendum muliebre, as an object of phallic adoration. 2. The buttocks.

Altocalciphilia . . . The special interest in a girl wearing high heels. The term is derived from *altus* (high), *calcis* (heel), and *philein* (to love).

Alvojaction...A maneuver, often seen in burlesque shows, in which a female performer causes her abdomen to perform provocative gyrations. The word is derived from *alvus* (belly or abdomen) and *jacere* (to thrust or throw).

Alvolagnia . . . The centering of one's sexual interest on a woman's abdomen. The word is derived from *alvus* (abdomen) and *lagneia* (lust).

Amatory dextrality . . . The condition of being clever, subtle, and effective in expressing one's affection for a member of the opposite sex.

Amatory mancinism...Awkwardness in expressing one's affection for a member of the opposite sex. The term usually applies to a man.

Amatripsis . . . A form of masturbation in which the labia majora are brought together and rubbed against each other. The word is derived from *ama* (together) and *tripsis* (rubbing).

Ambibiosis...The living together of a homosexual person with a person of the opposite sex, as a homosexual man and a normal woman. Derived from *ambo* (both), *bios* (life), and *-osis* (a condition).

Ambibombe . . . A girl who has a prominent bosom as well as prominent buttocks; i.e., one who is rounded both in front and in the rear. The term is derived from *ambo* (both) and *bombe* (rounded or bulging). The word is also used as an adjective.

Ambivovalent . . . Having a sexual desire for, and capable of having intercourse with, a woman who is physically attractive but who shows and evokes a feeling of hostility. Ambivovalent men associate sexual desire and intercourse with the motive of conquest. The term is derived from *ambivo* (both for and against) and *valere* (to be strong).

Amblyrosis . . . The dulling of sexual appetite, as with the passage of time or because of excessive indulgence. The word is derived from *amblys* (dull) and *eros* (desire).

Ambosexual . . . Having reference to or affecting both male and female organisms or both men and women, as environment, feelings, behavior, etc. Also, pertaining to medicinal substances which stimulate activity common to both sexes. The word is derived from *ambo* (both) and *sexus* (sex).

Amendolette . . . A girl whose pleasant informality may deceive a man into believing that she is amenable to sexual exploitation. See discussion under *amendolia.* Derived from *amoenus* (pleasant, lovely) and *dolus* (deception).

Amendolia . . . A form of deceptive pleasantness in the behavior of a girl, which often leads a man to believe that she is amenable to sexual exploitation. The behavior may be calculated to deceive or it may be innocent. A girl or woman exhibiting amendolia is termed an *amendolette*. The term is derived from *amoenus* (pleasant) and *dolus* (deception).

Amenolagnia . . . A condition of mild sexual excitement which does not demand satisfaction and which is manifested by talkativeness, gaiety, and optimism. The term is derived from *amoenus* (pleasant) and *lagneia* (lust).

Amokoscisia . . . A sexual frenzy which expresses itself in the compulsion to slash women, as exemplified in the case of Jack the Ripper. The word is derived from *amuck* (in a state of frenzy) and *schizo* (slit).

Amomaxia . . . Love making or "necking" in a parked car, usually in the familiar setting of a lovers' lane. The term is derived from *amor* (love) and *amaxa* (a car).

Amplexia . . . A position assumed by the participants in sexual intercourse in which the woman, lying supine, embraces the loins of the man with her legs and thighs. The term is derived from *amplexus* (embrace).

Amychesis . . . A peculiar expression of sexual heat in which the woman, when excited sexually, resorts to scratching her male companion in the act. This is never a defense mechanism but an inexplicable release from the tension of the libido. The term is derived from *amyche* (scratch).

Angelina . . . The boy in the act of pederasty.

Ankle sprained, to have the . . . Of a female, to receive the membrum virile, esp. the first time.

Anophelophobia . . . A morbid fear of hurting the woman in sexual intercourse through the introduction of the erected male organ into her vagina. The term is derived from *anopheles* (hurtful) and *phobos* (fear). The condition is frequently the cause of sexual impotence, especially during the first months of married life.

Anophelorastia . . . A type of sexual craving which is motivated by a conscious or subconscious desire to ravage or defile. The term is derived from *anopheles* (hurtful) and *erastes* (lover).

Answer with rhythm . . . Of a female in act of coitus, to respond pudendally with a rhythmic movement.

Anthorexia . . . The creation of a romantic mood and the stimulation of erotic desires by flowers, especially in women. The term is derived from *anthos* (flower) and *orexis* (longing or desire).

Antidote . . . A physically unattractive girl, in allusion to her antaphrodisiac effect upon the male. Used since late 18th century.

Antipodes, the . . . The female pudendal bandbox, in allusion to its relative inaccessibility (as were once New Zealand and Australia) and its position on the opposite end of the trunk, with reference to the head. Known since mid-19th century.

Aperitor . . . A person who lays more stress on love play and less on the act of sexual intercourse. The term is derived from *aperire* (to open).

Aphrodette . . . A young and, usually, pretty girl who excites a man's passion in order to gain a mercenary advantage but does not yield to him. Also, an attractive girl who entices men into a brothel for the benefit of other less desirable girls. Derived from *Aphrodite* (goddess of love).

Aphrodisia . . . Strong sexual desire, especially when expressed with violence. Derived from *aphrodisiakos* (frenzied sexual pleasure).

Aphrodisiology . . . The study or science of sexual passion. Also, that branch of medical knowledge which deals with the methods used in enhancing or alleviating the normal and abnormal sex drive, the effects of sexual craving on the pattern of behavior, and the ways in which the erotic desires are satisfied. The term is derived from *Aphrodisios* (pert. to Aphrodite, the goddess of love) and *logos* (a discourse).

Aphrodism . . . The desire, on the part of a girl or woman, to excite a man's passion in order to torment him, but not to gain any advantage. Derived from *Aphrodite* (goddess of love) and *-ism* (conduct or policy).

Apoclisis . . . The doctrine which holds that true love for a person cannot coexist with sexual desire for the same person. Also, the belief that sexual desire and love are mutually exclusive emotions when directed toward one person. The term is derived from *apokleisis* (exclusion).

Apodeuse . . . A female performer whose specialty is a slow, provocative act of undressing, otherwise known as a striptease. Derived from *apodyo* (undress).

Apodyopsis . . . The habit of "undressing" women mentally, in trying to visualize their naked bodies. The word is derived from *apodyo* (undress) and *opsis* (vision). The term obviously applies to men.

Apostle's pinch . . . A pinch involving a delicate or indelicate part of the body of a female, usually a buttock or breast, or worse. Not noted before 1900.

Apple-dumpling shop . . . Well-formed female breasts, fancied as "something good to eat." Noted in mid-18th century.

Arbor vitae . . . The male begetting organ, visualized as the "tree of life." From late 18th century.

Arrhenocallia . . . Manly beauty or handsomeness. Derived from *arrhen* (male) and *kallos* (beauty).

Arrhenogynia . . . The condition of a female who has a masculine figure, face, or mien. Derived from *arrhen* (male) and *gyne* (woman).

Arrhenolagnia . . . In a woman, an excessive sexual desire for a man. Derived from *arrhen* (man) and *lagneia* (lust).

Arrhenothigmophilous . . . Desirous of seeing a man touching the sexual parts of a woman. Derived from *arrhen* (male), *thigma* (touch), and *philein* (to love).

Arrhenotropic . . . Pertaining to, or marked by, manly sex appeal. Derived from *arrhenotos* (manly) and *trope* (a turning).

Arrhenozygous . . . Seeking the company of males, often applied to homosexual men. Derived from *arrhen* (male) and *zygous* (paired).

Arse painter . . . One who licks the anus.

Article of virtue . . . A female whose pudendum has not yet been accosted by the organum virile durum. From mid-19th century.

Ass peddler . . . A female whose interlabial sanctum is available for phallic debasement, in return for a monetary consideration.

Artamesia . . . In a woman, the state of being left sexually unsatisfied or in "mid-air" as a result of a premature orgasm in the man. The term is derived from *artao* (to hang) and *mesos* (in the middle).

Asthenolagnia . . . Sexual desire aroused by weakness or humility. Applicable mostly to men. Derived from *asthenos* (lack of strength) and *lagneia* (lust).

Atelia . . . A state of mind or point of view with regard to sex pleasure in which the attainment of an orgasm is considered of secondary importance. It is the condition in which the "preliminaries" are considered the main issue. Derived from *a* (negative) and *telos* (end or aim).

Atelophallia . . . State of incomplete development of the male sexual organ, especially in size. Derived from *a* (without), *telos* (end), and *phallus* (penis).

Atelotremia . . . The condition of having an imperfectly developed vulva or female pudendum. Derived from *a* (without), *telos* (end), and *trema* (female pudendum).

Atelysis . . . Incomplete release from sexual tension, as the state following an unsatisfactory act of intercourse. The term is derived from *ateles* (incomplete) and *lysis* (solution).

Athenaeum, the . . . The penis. An "educated" slangonym known in the late 19th century. Recorded in 1903.

Aterpsia . . . The belief that sexual intercourse must be engaged in only for the sake of procreation and not for pleasure, and that any pleasure accompanying the act must be subdued as much as possible or atoned for. A person who believes in this doctrine is an *aterpsist*. The term is derived from *a* (without) and *terpsis* (enjoyment).

Aterpsist . . . A person who believes that sexual intercourse should be engaged in only for the purpose of procreation. See discussion under *aterpsia*. Derived from *a* (without), and *terpsis* (enjoyment).

Autoerotism . . . Sexual excitation or pleasure which comes from one's own person or action, rather than from another person or an outside source. Derived from *autos* (self) and *eros* (love).

B

Backgammon player . . . A sodomite; i.e., one who phallates per rectum.

Baculophallia . . . The condition of having a very rigid penis. Derived from *baculum* (a rod) and *phallus* (the male organ). The term is usually applied to an organ having a rather small diameter but remarkable rigidity.

Bagged, be . . . To be phallated with cyetic consequences, i.e., with a resulting pregnancy.

Bailiwick in the boat . . . The domain of the female in the region of the escutcheon, esp. the interlabial sanctum.

Balanism . . . The use of vaginal suppositories and pessaries. The use may be therapeutic, as in the treatment of vaginal ailments, or it may be for the purpose of sexual stimulation. Derived from *balanos* (an acorn).

Balanotage . . . A playful manipulation of the glans penis or head of the male organ. It is often part of the pre-coital love play. The word is derived from *balanos* (the head of the male organ) and *barboter* (to dabble or play).

Ball juice . . . Seminal fluid, esp. ejaculated.

Balls and bat . . . The penis and testicles. From 1900.

Baloney . . . The membrum virile, esp. one of impressive tonnage. Intro. in the 1920s.

Bananas . . . Enjoyment of the para-orthodox versions of sexual foreplay and play.

Bandicooting . . . Playing the vagino-phallic game; the act of so playing.

Barboteur . . . A man engaging in love play, especially in pre-coital love play. The term is derived from *barboter* (to dabble or play).

Barboteuse . . . A woman engaging in love play, especially in pre-coital love play. The term is derived from *barboter* (to dabble or play) and a feminine suffix.

Barefoot . . . Without a condom; (phallating) without a condom.

Barges . . . 1. The female breasts, when of Gargantuan proportions. 2. Queen-size falsies.

Barn-dance . . . A bout of pudendal concourse with a female whose introitus and vagina are prodigiously spacious.

Baroselgia . Sexual desire aroused in the woman by the weight or pressure of the male during love play or coitus. The term is derived from *baros* (weight) and *aselgeia* (sexual desire).

Barosmia . . . Erotic interest in strong-smelling flowers, perfumes, etc. Derived from *barycosmos* (strong-smelling).

Basculocolpia . . . A provocative swaying of the breasts, as observed in some loosely-garmented and fleshy females. Derived from *basculer* (swing or sway) and *kolpos* (breast).

Basculophilia . . . The desire to be dandled or rocked in order to obtain a pleasurable sexual excitation. It is observed more often in children and is said to be a yearning for the prenatal uterine swaying. Derived from *basculer* (to sway) and *philein* (to love).

Basette. . . A girl or young woman who kisses warmly, tenderly, and thrillingly. Derived from *basiare* (to kiss).

Basiter . . . A male kissing pervert, or a man who kisses women in unnatural ways in order to satisfy their sexual desires. Derived from *basiare* (to kiss).

Basitrix . . . A female kissing pervert, or a woman who kisses men in unnatural ways in order to cater to their sexual cravings. Derived from *basiare* (to kiss).

Basket-making . . . An act of concourse between two heterosexual pudenda.

Basket of goodies . . . Those of the perineal organa of a woman which have a natural provocative effect upon the male. 2. A brassiereful of titties.

Basorexia . . . A strong craving or hunger for kissing. The term is derived from *basium* (a kiss) and *orexis* (appetite).

Basorgasmus . . . Sexual orgasm attained by means of kissing. The term is derived from *basium* (a kiss) and *orgasmos* (sexual climax).

Basorthosis . . . An erection of the male sex organ caused by a kiss or kissing. The term is derived from *basium* (a kiss) and *orthosis* (condition of being straight).

Bat . . . The phallus, esp. erectus, regarded as a cudgel and the scourge of the pudendum muliebre. From mid-18th century.

Bathysect . . . A deep intermammary cleft. The term is derived from *bathys* (deep) and *secare* (to cut).

Be in a woman's beef . . . Of the male Homo sapiens, to have the instrumentum erectum in the vagina feminae, and to do what comes naturally.

Bean-tosser . . . The erectile urogenital pendant of the male, conceived as the "spiller of the beans," which are the spermatozoa.

Beard-splitter . . . The timid nether appendage of the male, fancied as the splitter of the female hairy escutcheon, in the course of its vulvar sortie.

Beast with two backs . . . A male and a female of Homo sapiens in the act of genital inosculation.

Beef . . . The pendent pendant of the male perineum, conceived, often by the female, as a hunk of "raw" or impudent meat.

Beigel . . . A pessary. An allusion to the doughnut-shaped roll of the same name. Also spelled *bagel* and *baigel.* From mid-1920's.

Belly-ruffian . . . The male genital club, regarded as a rowdy who "roughs up" the female objet d'art.

Belly-up . . . 1. Of the female, in position for genital concourse. 2. Desirous.

Bellyful of marrow-pudding . . . Vaginaful of petrified phallus; a vaginaful of phallic vomitus.

Bemascopia . . . The watching by men of a girl's calves, esp. during the process of climbing a stairway, getting on a bus, etc. The term is derived from *bema* (a step) and *skopein* (to observe or watch).

Berkeley . . . The female pudendum, from the viewpoint of a concupiscent male.

Best leg of three . . . The male interfemoral infidel, regarded, often by the recipient thereof, as the choicest of the three lower extremities.

Bidetonism . . . A form of masturbation practiced by women, now seldom encountered, in which the woman assumes a sitting position in a sitz bathtub provided with equipment for giving injections, and plays a stream of water upon her genitalia. The term is derived from *bidet* (a certain kind of sitz bathtub) and *onanism* (popularly masturbation, but actually *coitus interruptus*).

Biforatia . . . The condition of being equally interested in receiving the male organ in the vagina and in the rectum. The word is derived from *bi* (two) and *fora* (opening).

Bimodal coitus . . . A form of sexual intercourse in which the participants augment the copulation of the sexual organs by an auxiliary maneuver, as suckling of the breast.

Bird taker . . . A female who takes the membrum virile rectally or orally. Also a male who does same.

Bitch boy . . . The boy in the act of pederasty.

Bite . . . The female genital inosculating paraphernalia, esp. the labia, introitus, and the sheath, regarded as a mouth that "bites" the penetrating phallus.

Biuterine marriage . . . A pseudomarriage between two women for the purpose of practicing tribadism.

Blabber . . . A phallus that dies in flaccidity while in the act of diadochokinesia.

Black joke . . . The female genital slit or interlabial hiatus with its chevelure, the pubic escutcheon, especially of a Negress.

Block . . . To close the female adit with the male obturator; i.e., to phallate.

Boat . . . The vulva, conceived, on the basis of the labial folds and the inclosed recession, as a navicular structure.

Booby trap . . . The vulva, esp. the vulva hians. Also, the female breasts.

Botulinonia . . . A form of masturbation practiced by women in which a sausage, properly smoothed, lubricated, and usually heated, is introduced into the vagina in lieu of the male organ, and manipulated to imitate coital movement. The term is derived from *botulus* (sausage) and *koinonia* (sexual intercourse).

Bouginonia . . . A form of masturbation practiced by women in which various objects are introduced into the vagina to cause dilatation and sexual excitation. In some forms of this practice pain is a component part of the stimulation and thus objects having rough or angular surfaces are used. The term is derived from *bougie* (a device used to dilate an orifice) and *koinonia* (sexual intercourse).

Boyherder . . . An adult male who derives sexual gratification by introducing his phallus into the rectum of a child, esp. a boy.

Brachycolpia . . . The condition of having a short vagina or vaginal canal. Derived from *brachys* (short) and *kolpos* (vagina).

Brachycraspedonia . . The pleasurable excitation enjoyed by men when watching girls in miniskirts. Derived from *brachys* (short), *kraspedon* (hem or skirt), and *hedone* (pleasure).

Brachycubia . . . A short or fast bout of coitus, as performed by "minute men." Derived from *brachys* (short) and *cubare* (to lie down).

Brachyphallia . . . The condition of having a short penis. Derived from *brachys* (short) and *phallus* (penis).

Bradycubia . . . A form of coitus in which the male proceeds with slow, deliberate motions. This procedure is usually acceptable to the female participant, especially in the first part of the act. The term is derived from *bradys* (slow) and *cubare* (to lie down).

Bradyorthosis . . . The condition in which the penis is slow in acquiring complete erection. This defect is also observed in elderly men, in those who overindulge in coitus, and in men who are either ill or oppressed by fear, sense of guilt, etc. Some cases of bradyorthosis can be explained by the fact that the female partner in the act is not seductive. In such cases the situation can be remedied if the woman takes the trouble to learn the art of provocative exposure and erotic motion.

Bradyspermatism . . . A condition characterized by a slow ejaculation of the seminal fluid during orgasm. Derived from *brady* (slow) and *sperma* (semen or seminal fluid).

Brassiroregia . . . Man's lascivious interest in brassieres as expressed in mental preoccupation or in observing them in store windows, on clothesline, etc. The word is derived from *brassiere* and *oregomai* (to lust after).

Brassirothesauriast . . . A collector of brassieres. The term applies to a man who collects brassieres because of a libidinous interest as well as to one who collects them for scientific or historical study. Occasionally the term is used to describe a man who collects pictures of brassieres, cut from magazines, newspapers, catalogues, etc. The term is derived from *brassiere* and *thesauros* (a store or collection).

Break a leg . . . With reference to a sweet, young thing, to stuprate; to unvirginate.

Breech-loading . . . A phallic safari into the vaginal interior.

Bridle string . . . The fold of mucous membrane at the junction of the posterior ends of the labia majora.

Bristols...The lactopoietic glands of the human female, regarded not as such but as fascinating playthings for the lickerish hands of a satyric male.

Broken-kneed . . . 1. Of a female, probed by the abdominal pants worm. 2. Of an erstwhile virgin, a virgin no more.

Broken-legged . . . 1. Of a female, phallated and impregnated. 2. Of an ingenue, stung by the pudental serpent of the male.

Broom . . . The female sexual organa, esp. those of an older distaff, whose pubic mat is reminiscent of an inverted broom.

Broomstick . . . The virile stick, in allusion to the broom (*q.v.*), which it is meant to complement.

Brown eyes . . . The female nipples; also, the fleshy gibbosities supporting them.

Bucket broad . . . A prostitute who gives her pudendum an up-and-down movement in the course of coitus.

Bulldiking . . . Homosexual; said of a female.

Bunker . . . A man who introduces his phallus into the rectum of another, male or female.

Burn out . . . To suffer an embarrassing collapse of the inflated phallus in the course of phallation, before its vesuviation.

Bushel-cunted . . . Having a barn-like vaginal space, due to childbirth, harlotry, masturbation, etc. From early 19th century.

Butt . . . The rump; also, one or both of the rumpal mounds. Standard English from 15th century to 17th. Slang thereafter.

Butterflies, the . . . The labia minora, in allusion to the alar shape of the parts. From early 20th century.

Buttock jig . . . Sexual concourse, conceived as a springy dance of the hemispheres, in triple time. From 17th century.

Buttonhole . . . The vulva, conceived, on the basis of the approximated labia and the intermediate slit, as a typical recipient of a button. Used as early as first part of the 19th century. Recorded in 1879.

C

Caboose . . . The rump or its constituent domes.

Cacocallia . . . The condition of being ugly and yet sexually attractive. The term is derived from *kakos* (ugly) and *kalos* (beautiful).

Cacophallic . . . Having an inadequate phallus, as one lacking in size or in effective erection. Derived from *kakos* (vitiated or bad) and *phallus.* The state of having a cacophallic defect is called cacophallia.

Callibombe . . . The state of having attractive anatomical curves, as hips, buttocks, bosom, shoulders, etc. The word is derived from *calli* (beautiful) and *bombe* (rounded or bulging).

Callicacia . . . A state of mind brought about by love or passion in which even that which is bad or ugly in the sexual partner seems right and beautiful.

Callicolpia . . . The condition of having ravishingly beautiful breasts. The term applies especially to breasts which are both beautiful and larger than normal. The word is derived from *kalos* (beautiful) and *kolpos* (a bosom).

Callicunnate . . . Having a beautiful vulva or external genital organ. Derived from *calli* (beautiful and *cunnus* (the vulva).

Callipygette . . . A girl who has lovely buttocks. The term is derived from *kallos* (a beauty), *pyge* (buttock), and *ette* (suffix indicating a female subject). The adjective form is callipygian.

Can . . . 1. The sex organs of the female conceived as an area lacking in cleanliness, e.g., a slop can. 2. The rump, mostly of the female, or its two hemispheric butts.

Cannibal . . . 1. A male who indulges in cunnilingus. 2. A female who licks the male genitalia.

Cantharis . . . A kind of beetle, also known as Spanish fly or "blister bug," reputed to have stimulating properties when taken internally. It has been used as a sexual stimulant. The active principle of the beetle is called cantharidin.

Capnocratia . . . The sense of well-being and, especially, the fancied feeling of increased sexual potency that is often gained from smoking. The term is derived from *kapnizo* (to smoke) and *kratos* (strength).

Capnogeria . . . Sexual excitation or pleasure derived by some from the act of smoking. The term is derived from *kapnizo* (to smoke) and *egeiro* (to excite).

Capnolagnia . . . Erotic desires aroused in some men by watching a woman in the act of smoking. The term is derived from *kapnizo* (to smoke) and *lagneia* (lust).

Capnopnea . . . A mild and pleasant sexual excitation experienced by some men upon breathing the air of a room scented with the cigarette smoke of a beautiful woman. The term is derived from *kapnos* (smoke) and *pneo* (breathe).

Carvel's ring . . . The female sexual receptacle and the adjacent pudendal structures.

Casigamy . . . Marriage to a brother, as practiced among some primitive tribes. The word also applies to such marriage resulting from mistaken identity. The word is derived from *kasignetos* (brother) and *gamos* (marriage).

Casimeria . . . Sexual interest in a brother, regardless of age. Derived from *kasignetos* (brother) and *himeros* (desire).

Cat . . . The pudendum muliebre, conceived as a furry and pruriently purring animalcule. From 19th century.

Catatasis . . Among certain tribes, the practice of attaching a weight to the head of the male sex organ in order to increase its length by continuous stretching. Derived from *kata* (down) and *tasis* (stretching).

Cathouse bird . . . A female whose mercenary vulva is available for commercial engagements with desirous males.

Cavaulting . . . The normal act of sexual concourse between two heterosexuals.

Celerorgasmus . . . Same as *prochronorgasmus,* which see. Derived from *celer* (swift) and *orgasmus* (the sexual orgasm).

Cerassie . . . The female genital organs considered as a whole, especially the organs of a virgin. The term is derived from *cerasus* (a cherry) on the basis of a popular association. The word also indicates maidenhead, virginity, or the hymen.

Charmers . . . The female's pectoral excurvations, considered not as lactogenic organs but as fountains of sensuous felicity.

Charms . . . In the female, all the anatomical embellishments which have a stimulating effect on the male, esp. the breasts.

Cheaters . . . Padded brassiere worn to compensate for small breasts.

Cheilocunnidipity . . . A mental visualization of the mouth or lips of a woman as the counterpart of the vulva, a condition observed in men afflicted with satyriasis. Derived from *cheilos* (lip), *cunnus* (the vulva), and the suffix *dipity* (condition).

Cheilogusia . . . The tendency to enjoy things primarily through contact with the lips. A mild form of cheilogusia is demonstrated in the act of kissing. Derived from *cheilos* (lip) and *geusis* (taste).

Cheiloproclitic . . . Tending to lay the greatest amorous attention upon a girl's lips. Derived from *cheilos* (lip) and *proclitic* (inclined to).

Chelonia . . . A release mechanism of sexual excitement, usually observed in women, consisting of clawing and scratching. The term is derived from *chele* (claw).

Cherry . . . The virgin hymen. Based on its proneness to bleed when torn by phallus in coitus.

Cherry-crusher . . . 1. A newly-married man. 2. A male who deflowers a virgin.

Cherry juice . . . The cherry wine emanating from a deflowered virgin hymen during and after the phallic pogrom.

Cherry pie . . . A young, sexually desirable girl, esp. one not yet deflowered.

Cherry-ripe . . . A young girl old enough, legally and perhaps even morally, for the instrumentum virile erectum.

Chimaropia . . . The characteristic erotic stare of a man in passion, as during love play or the first movements of coitus. It embraces an element of frenzy. The term is derived from *chimaros* (he-goat) and *ops* (eye).

Chingus . . . The sex organon of the male, conceived as the master of the female pudendum, in allusion, by corruption, to Genghis Khan.

Chirapsis . . The practice of bringing about sexual orgasm in a man by friction of a woman's hand upon the phallus. Derived from *cheir* (hand) and *haphe* (a touching).

Chirapsolody . . . The practice of arousing sexual desire by hand friction. Derived from *cheir* (hand), *haphe* (a touching) and *lody*.

Chorophobia . . . The fear of or aversion for dancing, often based on one's unwillingness to become aroused. Derived from *choros* (dance) and *phobia* (fear or aversion).

Chorotripsis . . . The touching of or rubbing against one's partner while dancing and the resulting sexual excitation, sometimes followed by an orgasm. The term is derived from *choros* (dance) and *tripsis* (a rubbing).

Churner . . . The female receptacle for the membrum virile erectum, in allusion to its sometimes cooperative movement.

Chymocunnia . . . The condition of having a vulva which is generously moistened by lubricating discharges. The term is derived from *chymos* (juice) and *cunnus* (the vulva).

Cingulomania . . . A strong desire to embrace and hold in one's arms, especially the desire of a man to hold a girl in his arms. It is derived from *cingulum* (a girdle) and *mania*. When the urge is unusually strong, the word for it is hypercingulomania; *hyper* implying excess.

Claret-topped . . . Of the vulva, bloody or covered with a cruentous menstrual pad. Of the female, in the throes of Eve's curse, i.e., menstruating.

Cleopatralagnia . . . An interest in watching a woman in a reclining pose, in the manner of Cleopatra. Derived from *Cleopatra* and *lagneia* (lust).

Clitoridauxe . . . The enlargement

of the clitoris through hypertrophy. It may assume considerable size, occasionally matching the male organ. It may follow chronic masturbation.

Clitoris . . . In the female, a small organ homologous with the male penis and situated inside the anterior junction of the labia minora. It possesses erotic sensitivity, and, like the male organ, is capable of erection. In the young female, the clitoris is the only part of the body susceptible to excitation through manipulation, but later in life the vagina takes over or shares with the clitoris the role of erotic receptor.

Clitorism . . . A persistent state of erection of the clitoris, often accompanied by a strong sexual desire. Frequently observed in masturbators.

Clitoromania . . . Excessive, uncontrollable sexual desire in a woman.

Cnemopalmia . . . The choice by a man of a woman's legs as the most prized part of her body. The term is derived from *kneme* (leg) and *palma* (prize).

Cnemoscopy . . . The popular pastime of leg watching. Derived from *kneme* (leg) and *skopein* (to observe).

Cnemotaxis . . . The stimulating and orienting effect a girl's legs have upon a man. The term is derived from *kneme* (leg) and *taxis* (direction or influence).

Cnemotropism . . . The capacity of a girl's pretty legs to turn a man's head, literally and figuratively. Derived from *kneme* (leg) and *tropos* (a turning).

Cock, to . . . Of the male, to push the turgid bayonet into the female scabbard and proceed ad rem.

Cock alley . . . The female sex organs, esp. the vulvar slit, the introitus vaginae, and the sheath, in obvious allusion to the "garden lane" which the male pendeloque travels.

Cock buster . . . A male, sometimes also a female, who takes the male sex organon into the mouth, for titillation and sugescent alleviation.

Cock-chafer . . . The muliebral sex organa, esp. the vaginal corridor. 2. A female giving and taking all sexual coruscations but the ultima Thule. From 19th century.

Cock-hall . . . The distaff genital structures, esp. the reception chamber for the visiting phallus. From 18th century.

Cock Inn . . . The genital structures of a female concerned with phallation, esp. the vaginal hostel in which a visiting mogul exuberates. From 18th century.

Cock lane . . . The genital paraphernalia of the female of interest to the phallus and its bearer, but esp. the introitus and sheath. From 18th century.

Cock-pit . . . The female genital "trap," esp. the vaginal shaft, regarded as a concealed snare for the naif but desirous membrum virile. From 18th century.

Cock-sure . . . Confident, esp. with regard to sexual potency. Debut early 17th century.

Cock teaser . . . A girl who teases the tensor virile by liberal foreplay but refuses pudendal appeasement.

Cocked . . . No longer a virgin; phallated. 2. Erected, of the penis, sometimes of the nipples, clitoris, etc.

Cockshire . . . The female pudendalia, regarded as the county or shire of the male obturator. From 18th century.

Cockstipation . . . The condition marked by inability on the part of the male to arrive at a productive orgasm; delayed ejaculation.

Cockstupration . . . The interpolation of the "boneless stiff" in the female pudendal adit.

Coital accommodation . . The gradual adjustment to the act of intercourse with one's spouse, resulting from loss of anxiety, general relaxation, and the learning of sex technique. It usually leads to more enjoyable sexual sessions and more willingness to submit on the part of the woman.

Coital aditus . . . The collective name for the various love gestures and practices indulged in by man and woman before the act of sexual intercourse. Derived from *coitus* (sexual intercourse) and *aditus* (approach).

Coital adulteration . . . The practice of introducing into the vagina, for the purpose of sexual gratification, some object which resembles a male organ. It is a form of masturbation.

Coital ectrimma . . . A sore place either on the male organ or in the vagina caused by friction during the act of sexual intercourse. The term is derived from *ektrimma* (an ulcer caused by friction).

Coital effraction . . . Laceration of the vagina occurring during sexual intercourse because of the excessive size of the male organ.

Coital hypercinesis . . . Overactivity in the pursuit of the sexual act. The term is derived from *hyper* (excess) and *kinesis* (movement).

Coital magma . . . The fluid resulting from the mixture of the ejaculated semen and the vaginal secretions, as after coitus.

Coital malalignment . . . The condition at sexual intercourse in which the male organ and the vulva are not inclined in the same direction or at the same angle, making it difficult or impossible to perform the act satisfactorily. The condition may arise when one of the participants is excessively obese or when there are anatomical deformities.

Coital mancinism . . . Awkwardness in performing the sexual act. The term applies to a man.

Coitant . . . The male member of a pair engaged in sexual intercourse. The term is derived from *coitus* (sexual intercourse).

Coitante . . . The female member of a pair engaged in sexual intercourse.

Coitobalnism . . . The practice of having sexual intercourse in a filled bathtub. Derived from *coitus* (sexual intercourse) and *balneum* (bath).

Coitoperissia . . . Excessive indulgence in the act of sexual intercourse. Derived from *coitus* (sexual intercourse) and *perissos* (excessive).

Coitophthoria . . . The loss of interest in normal sexual procedures and the accompanying desire for coital perversions. Derived from *coitus* (sexual intercourse) and *phthora* (destruction).

Coitus acceptus . . . Sexual intercourse welcomed by the female participant.

Coitus adulterinus . . . 1. Out-of-wedlock sexual intercourse which begets a bastard. 2. An act of sexual intercourse involving adultery.

Coitus Bacchicus . . . Sexual intercourse which is part of an orgy; orgiastic coitus.

Coitus coactus . . . An act of sexual intercourse enforced by the male within wedlock.

Coitus delicatus . . . Any form of contraceptive sexual intercourse pursued exclusively for the pleasure it affords.

Coitus diurnus . . . A daytime performance of sexual intercourse. See *coitus nocturnus*.

Coitus fecundus . . . Sexual intercourse resulting in pregnancy. Derived from *coitus* (sexual intercourse) and *fecundus* (fruitful).

Coitus innuptus . . . Sexual intercourse involving an unmarried person, either the male or the female, or both.

Coitus legitimus . . . The act of sexual intercourse performed by a legally married man and wife. Derived from *coitus* (sexual intercourse) and *legitimus* (legal)

Coitus maritus . . . Sexual intercourse within matrimony, between man and wife.

Coitus miscegenatus . . . Sexual intercourse between members of different races.

Coitus nocturnus . . . Sexual intercourse taking place during the night, rather than daytime.

Coitus operosus . . . Sexual intercourse which is laborious or difficult, usually due to obesity in one or both partners. It may be hazardous medically, especially to the male.

Coitus pergratus . . . Sexual intercourse which is thoroughly gratifying to either or both participants, especially the male.

Coitus pluvius . . . Sexual intercourse which terminates in a seminal ejaculation.

Coitus primus . . . 1. The first experience of sexual intercourse. 2. The first engagement in sexual intercourse by a married couple.

Coitus profundus . . . Sexual intercourse in which the penis penetrates deeply into the vagina. It is more conducive to pregnancy.

Coitus siccus . . . Sexual intercourse which does not terminate in a seminal ejaculation.

Coitus sodomus . . . Sexual intercourse in which the penis is introduced into the rectum of the female, rather than the vagina.

Coitus sordidus . . . Sexual intercourse in which the female partakes for the sake of money.

Coitus usitatus . . . The conventional or normal form of sexual intercourse.

Coitus vadosus . . . Sexual intercourse in which the penis barely enters the vagina, or does not enter it at all; shallow coitus.

Coitus variatus . . . 1. A variant form of sexual intercourse. 2. The practice of engaging in sexual intercourse in a variety of ways.

Coitus venenatus . . . Sexual intercourse resulting in a venereal infection.

Coitus vetitus . . . Any illegal instance of sexual intercourse, as in adultery.

Coitus virgineus . . . Sexual intercourse involving a virgin maiden.

Cold meat . . . A flaccid, unwilling or unable, membrum virile.

Cold pig . . . A masculine pendant that cannot or will not stand up to the occasion.

Collement . . . The condition resulting when, due to vaginal spasm, the male organ cannot be withdrawn from the vagina after intercourse. The term is derived from *collement* (cohesion).

Colossus . . . The male sexual organon in its functional mood, conceived, by timorous females, as a frightening personification of manly youth, in allusion to the Colossus of Rhodes, the gigantic statue of Apollo, one of the seven wonders of the ancient world.

Colpachoresis . . . Gradual diminution in the capacity of the vagina resulting in a more satisfying act of coitus. Derived from *kolpos* (vagina) and *achorein* (to diminish room).

Colpachresis . . . A condition in which the woman is unable to utilize the vaginal stimuli of the coital movements to gain an orgasm. It is observed in women who have moral qualms about sexual intercourse or in others who suffer from an anesthetic state of the vagina. The term is derived from *kolpos* (vagina), *a* (negative), and *chresis* (use). Women having colpachresis depend on stimulation of the clitoris.

Colpalgia . . . Feeling of discomfort or pain in the vagina, from *kolpos* (a vagina) and *algos* (pain). Colpalgia may be caused by too frequent intercourse, by excessive stretching during intercourse due to a large penis, by manipulation, masturbation, etc.

Colpectasia . . . Dilation or distention of the vaginal canal, from *kolpos* and *ektasis* (distention). Excessive dilation may result from childbirth, frequent coitus, large male organ, and masturbation.

Colpette . . . A girl, usually a petite girl, whose bosom dwarfs all of her other physical attractions.

Colpile . . . Susceptible to sexual stimulation mainly or only through manipulation of the breasts.

Colpkinophilia . . . The preference, on the part of a man, for the small, not yet fully developed, breasts of a young girl, as those of a teenage girl.

Colpochoresis . . . The gradual enlargement of the vagina, resulting from continued intercourse. Derived from *kolpos* (vagina) and *chorein* (to make roomier). Marked colpochoresis may lead to unsatisfactory coitus and unduly delayed orgasm.

Colpocoquette . . . A girl or woman who is conscious of her beautiful breasts and uses them cunningly to get men's attention and admiration. The term is derived from *kolpos* (a bosom) and *coquette.*

Colpocunnocnemia . . . The triad which constitutes a girl's sexual armamentarium; i.e., the breasts, the vulva, and the legs. Derived from *kolpos* (breast). *cunnus* (vulva), and *knemis* (leg).

Colpofette . . . A girl or woman who displays her bosom to attract men's attention but who will not allow them to touch it. The term is derived from *kolpos* and *pheidolia* (parsimoniousness).

Colpoheterophrenia . . . In a woman, the condition of being susceptible to sexual excitation by the contemplation or manipulation of the breasts of another woman. The term is derived from *kolpos, heteros* (the other), and *phren* (the mind).

Colpohomophrenia . . . The condition of being susceptible to sexual excitation by the contemplation or manipulation of one's own breasts. The term applies to a woman. It is derived from *kolpos* (a bosom), *homos* (the same), and *phren* (the mind).

Colpopetia . . . The condition of being interested in the breasts only, to the exclusion of other parts of the body. The term applies to a man. It is derived from *kolpos* and *petere* (to seek or aim).

Colposinquanonia . . . The attitude or policy of a man who feels that no girl or woman is adequate unless she has beautiful breasts. Also, the policy of making beautiful breasts the essential condition or qualification in the selection of a wife. The term is derived from *kolpos* (a bosom) and *sine qua non* (an absolute prerequisite).

Colpotage . . . The act of sexual play involving the vagina, as by gentle rubbing of the vaginal opening. Derived from *kolpos* (vagina) and *barboter* (to dabble or play).

Colpotantia . . . The practice of making one's breasts prominent, either by low decolletage or by clinging garments, in order to entice male interest, but without any intention to submit to love play. The term is derived from *kolpos* and *Tantalus.*

Colpothymia . . . The belief on the part of a girl or woman that men are especially intrigued by her breasts. Also, an unfounded conviction on the part of a girl that every man who looks at her is obsessed by a desire to touch or pull her breasts. The term is derived from *kolpos* and *thymia* (condition of the mind).

Colpoxerosis . . . A condition marked by abnormal dryness of the vaginal wall and the vulva. The condition makes coitus rather difficult. Derived from *kolpos* (vagina) and *xeros* (dry).

Come . . . Of the male, to ejaculate; of the female, to experience the sexual orgasm. From mid-19th century.

Come through the front door . . . To phallate by the book, i.e., vaginally, as opposed to off-beat stupration.

Compass of the netherland . . The male pudendum in which the ithyphallos is conceived as the needle.

Contrectation . . . A general term applied to the act of fondling or "kneading" the anatomical parts of a female, as in a bout of petting. The term is also applied to the "warmup" activities preceding the sexual act. It is derived from the Latin *contrectatio* (to handle). The word for the act of fondling a woman's breasts is *mastocontrectation, masto* referring to the breast. Fondling or stroking a girl's legs is *tibiocontrectation, tibia* meaning a leg. The fear of a girl lest she be "pawed" is *contrectophobia,* while the love of it is *contrectophilia.*

Cooling pad . . . The female pudendalia regarded as a cooling assuager of the fervent phallus.

Coozie butcher . . . A female "candy-butcher" whose sweets are her pudendal benefactions.

Copper-stick . . . The penis, esp. when erected. 2. The phallating stick of an Ethiop.

Coprology . . . The study of or interest in obscenities as expressed in literature or art. The word is derived from *kopros* (dung) and *logy* (science).

Coprophilia . . . Love for the obscene, especially in art or literature. The word is derived from *kopros* and *philein* (to love).

Cornhole . . . To introduce the male organon into the rectum, in the practice of pederasty or sodomy.

Cow-cunt . . . A female whose vaginal embrace is unpleasantly relaxed as result of childbirth distention, thriving harlotry, or dildoism.

Coxinutant . . . Swaying the hips in walking. Derived from *coxa* (hip) and *nutant* (swaying).

Crack . . . 1. The interlabial slit of the female, as an adit to Eden. 2. The entire complex of female pudendalia.

Cracked mortar . . . 1. A female whose pudendal mortar is no longer unfamiliar with the male pestle. 2. A female mortar so familiarized.

Cranny . . 1. The female pudendal slit, introitus, and scabbard, conceived as an unworthy fissure which, nevertheless, is redolent of phallic hedonism. 2. The vagina or female sheath considered as an entity.

Cranny-hunter . . . The desirous colossus of the male pudendum, viewed as a chasseur in hot pursuit of the female pudendal crevasse.

Cratolagnia . . . Lust aroused in a woman by the manifestation of physical strength in a man. Derived from *kratos* (power) and *lagneia* (lust).

Cream-stick . . . The phallus, esp. erectus, viewed as the discharger of the male cream. Since 18th century.

Credo of a Jesuit . . . No phallation without insemination! A light-hearted allusion to the edict (now slated for revision) which prohibits the use of contraceptives by the members of a noted religious denomination.

Crib . . . To persuade a young one to give up her chastity, and to take same.

Criomedia . . . The condition of having a large, cruel, and relentlessly butting male organ, from the point of view of the woman. The term is derived from *krios* (a battering-ram) and *medos* (the male organ).

Crurormia . . . The teasing of the sexual desire by seeing or touching the legs. The term is derived from *crus* (leg) and *hormao* (to stir up).

Cryptoscopophilia . . . The curiosity of looking through the windows of homes that one passes by, as when walking or driving. The tendency is based on the desire to see people as they are and act when they consider themselves unobserved. Derived from *kryptos* (hidden). *skopein* (observe), and *philia* (desire for).

Cryptovestiphilia . . . The love for women's undergarments. More specifically, the term refers to the practice of collecting such articles as panties, brassieres, stockings, garters, etc. In a sense the term is related to thesauromania, but cryptovestiphilia refers specifically to undergarments. The term is derived from *kryptos* (hidden), *vestimenta* (garments), and *philia* (love).

Cuckold the parson . . . To join pudenda with the girl one expects to marry, before the issuance of the permit.

Cunniknismos . . . The practice of tickling the vulva (female slit), as with the fingers, tongue, etc. Derived from *cunnus* (vulva) and *knizo* (cause to itch).

Cunnilingus . . . The licking of the female genital organs. Derived from *cunnus* (vulva) and *linguere* (to lick).

Cunnitripsis . . . The rubbing of the female organs by a man. Derived from *cunnus* (the external female organ) and *tripsis* (a rubbing).

Cunnocnesis . . . An itching of the vulva or the external female sex organs in the absence of a demonstrable cause. This condition is often an expression of a neurosis and less frequently the result of sexual frustration. The term is derived from *cunnus* (the external female sex organs) and *knesis* (itching).

Cunnorasia . . . The habit of scratching or rubbing the vulva by manipulating the skirt or dress over the sex organs. Unlike medorasia, cunnorasia is usually a conscious attempt to alleviate itching. The term is derived from *cunnus* (the vulva) and *radere* (to scratch).

Cunnotage . . . A playful and leisurely rubbing of or playing with the external female sex organs or the vulva, especially precoital play. Derived from *cunnus* (a vulva) and *barboter* (to dabble or play).

Cunny . . . The coital palace of the female. Based on the Latin *cunnus,* the vulva. Current since about 1650.

Cunny-haunted . . . 1. Of the male, tormented by a compulsion to enter the coital gates of the female pudendum. 2. Of the female, desirous.

Cunt hooks . . . The fingers, esp. the lickerish fingers of a romantic male.

Cunt itch . . . 1. Sexual desire in women. 2. Sexual desire in men. Both from circa 1750.

Cunt party . . . A sexual concourse of two female homosexuals in which the juxtaposed pudenda are maneuvered as mortar and pestle.

Cunt-struck . . . Prurient; sexy; preoccupied with thoughts of women.

Cyeserasty . . . Increased desire for intimacy with a pregnant woman. Derived from *cyesis* (pregnancy) and *erastes* (a lover).

Cyesolagnia . . . The provocative effect which the sight of a pregnant woman has upon some men. Derived from *cyesis* (pregnancy) and *lagneia* (lust).

Cypridophobia . . . An excessive fear of acquiring a venereal disease. The term also means fear of sexual intercourse. It is derived from *Kypros* (Cyprus, the reputed birthplace of Aphrodite) and *phobos* (fear).

Cyprinolalia . . . Lewd or obscene language or jokes. Derived from *Kypros* and *lalia* (talking).

Cyprinomania . . . Strong urge to cohabit with lewd women.

Cyprinophilia . . . Love for lewdness or lewd women. Derived from *Kypros* (Cyprus, the supposed birthplace of Aphrodite, the goddess of love) and *philein* (to love).

Cyprinophobia . . . Excessive fear of lewd women, their manners, language, etc. Derived from *Kypros* and *phobia.*

Cytheromania . . . An abnormally urgent sexual desire in a woman. Derived from *Kythereia* (Venus) and *mania.*

D

Dacnolagnomania . . . A psychopathic urge to rape and kill women. The word is derived from *Dacus* (a warlike person), *lagneia* (lust), and *mania* (urge).

Dacrylagnia . . . The condition of being aroused sexually or susceptible to excitation by a woman's tears. The term is derived from *dakry* (tear) and *lagneia* (lust).

Dactylate . . . To introduce the finger into the vagina, especially for the purpose of masturbating. The term is derived from *daktylos* (finger).

Dairy arrangements . . . 1. The female breasts. 2. The size and form of the female breasts.

Dangler . . . A male who derives sexual pleasure by exposing his genital organs to members of the opposite sex, esp. in public. 2. A female in decolletage who finds frequent opportunities to lean forward.

Dasofallation . . . Sexual intercourse taking place in a forest or woods or in a sylvan setting. The term is derived from *dasos* (forest) and *phallation* (sexual intercourse).

Decoromedia . . . The sum total of what is considered correct sexual procedure for the male organ before and during intercourse. Less precisely, male sex etiquette. The term is derived from *decere* (be suitable or correct) and *medos* (the male organ).

Dendrophilia . . . Sexual interest in trees. The term is derived from *dendron* (tree) and *philein* (to love).

Deonteur . . . A man versed in the art of making love. One well versed in deontra.

Deonteuse . . . A woman skilled in the art of making love. One expert in deontra.

Deontra . . . All that one has to know and do to be a successful love partner. It includes the minutiae of pre-coital play and the masterful execution of the act. Derived from *deon* (that which is necessary).

Dermacentric . . . Especially interested in the physical appeal of the skin. Derived from *derma* (skin) and *kentron* (goad).

Dermagraphism . . . The penchant for leaving marks on the skin of a girl, as by pinching, biting, sucking, etc. The term is derived from *derma* (skin) and *graphein* (to write). It represents a form of possessiveness.

Dermaphilia . . . An erotic craving for a delicate female skin; the condition of being aroused by the delicate skin of a young girl. Derived from *derma* (skin) and *philein* (to love).

Derrick . . . The phallus conceived as an instrument of erection. From about 1840.

Derrieroscopia . . . Preoccupation with the rear view of girls, or with the view of their derriere.

Detumescence . . . The loss of erection of the male organ after the orgasm. The word is derived from *de* (down) and *tumere* (swell).

Deuterition . . . A second act of sexual intercourse, following the first within a short time. The word is derived from *deutero* (second) and *coition* (sexual intercourse).

Diaphanophilia . . . The desire to view nudity through the semi-transparency of sheer fabrics, as veils. Derived from *diaphainein* (to show through or be transparent) and *philein* (to love).

Diaphinia . . . A predilection for sheer, semi-transparent garments, as blouses, brassieres, panties, etc. The word applies to the woman who likes to wear such garments as well as to the man who prefers a woman to wear them. Derived from *diaphainein* (to show through or be transparent).

Diapiresalgia . . . Pain felt by the male in pushing a large penis through a small vaginal opening, as in a virgin. Derived from *dia* (through), *piresis* (a pushing) and *algia* (pain). The pain experienced by the female under these circumstances is gynepiresalgia, from *gyne* (woman), *piresis* (a pushing), and *algia*.

Diapnolagnia . . . A rather rare form of excitation wherein lust is aroused by blowing in one's ear. The term is derived from *diapnein* (to breathe through) and *lagneia* (lust).

Diasteunia . . . The practice of sleeping in separate beds, as applied to man and wife, in order to avoid sexual temptation. The term is derived from *diastatos* (separated) and *eune* (a bed).

Dick . . . The botuliform genital pendant of the male, conceived as the bullwhack of the female pudendum. Derived, apparently, from dick, a whip. Current since mid-19th century.

Dicked in the pudding . . . Of a female, transfixed by the sexual trocar of the male.

Diddly-pout . . . The perineal sexual implements of the female. From mid-19th century.

Diddly-pouter . . . A male who licks the primary sex characteristics of the female.

Dilberry bush . . . The pubic hair, more often of the female.

Dingbat . . . The male genital colossus, regarded as a missile whose target is, obviously, the female genital atrium. From about 1930.

Discinctophilia . . . The choice of the state of semi-nudity, rather than complete nudity, as the setting for sexual intercourse. The term is derived from *discingere* (to ungird).

Dishabilloerigesis . . . Sexual provocation by deliberate undressing. See discussion under *dishabillophobia.*

Dishabillopedia . . . 1. A passion for seeing nude children, or for undressing children. 2. A desire to undress before children. See discussion under *dishabillophobia.*

Dishabillophilia . . . See discussion under *dishabillophobia.*

Dishabillophobia . . . Fear or strong aversion for undressing in the presence of another. *Dishabillophilia* is the desire to undress in presence of another, especially before a member of the opposite sex. Dishabillophilia is a form of exhibitionism, often observed in perverts. The desire to undress before children is *dishabillopedia.* The terms are derived from *dishabiller* (to undress), *phobia* (fear), *philia* (fondness), and *pais* (child). The practice of exciting sexual desire in a man through deliberate undressing is *dishabilloerigesis.* The stimulating effect of the sight of a woman's shoulder strap, as under a thin blouse, is *loroerigesis,* from *lorum* (strap) and *erigesis* (excitation).

Diurnovalent . . . Potent sexually only or mainly during the day. This condition is practically unknown in normal men, but not uncommon in those who suffer from certain ailments having nocturnal exacerbations. It is also found in some neurotics whose anxieties assume alarming proportions during the night. The term is derived from *dies* (day) and *valeo* (be able).

Dive in the dark . . . 1. Sexual concourse. 2. To introduce the male sexual felon into the darkness of the female genital oubliette.

Divertissement . . . Sexual play or foreplay which is a departure from the orthodox. Based on *divertere* (to turn in different directions). Introduced in 1915.

Do a woman's job for her . . . Of a phallating male, to perform to the female's satisfaction. Current since mid-19th century.

Do an inside worry . . . Of the male, to introduce the allantoid process into the female genital pantry.

Don't feed the animals! . . . Don't sample the merchandise. A *verbum sapienti* of a maid to her beau, to keep his cunt hooks (*q.v.*) off her bubbies and, especially, out of the bailiwick of the little man in the boat, a territory roughly encompassed by the labia majora.

Dry-mortar work . . . Phallation without ejaculation.

Dulcicunnia . . . The condition of having a "sweet-smelling" vulva or vagina. The term is derived from *dulcis* (sweet) and *cunnus* (vulva).

Dulcistomia . . . The condition of having a mouth sweet enough to kiss. The term is derived from *dulcis* (sweet) and *stoma* (mouth).

Dyscalligynia . . . Antipathy for beautiful women. A condition based on frustration and emotional rebellion, and observed in men who for various reasons are rejected by attractive women. Derived from *dys-* (difficult), *kallos* (beauty), and *gyne* (woman).

E

Easy meat . . . A female whose resistance to pudendal invasion is notably labile.

Eat oneself sick . . . To make palpatory love to a female, short of coitus, until the phallic lava exudes.

Eat oneself stiff . . . To fool around a girl until the nether proboscis is perpendicular to the long axis of the body.

Ebrilagnia . . . Sexual craving aroused by drunkenness. Derived from *ebrietas* (drunkenness) and *lagneia* (lust).

Ecarteuse . . . A woman who helps her mate in sexual intercourse by pulling her labia apart, as by traction on the tissues of her thighs. Derived from *ecarter* (discard).

Ecdemolagnia . . . The tendency to be more lascivious when away from home, as when in another city or country. The term is derived from *ekdemos* (away from home) and *lagneia* (lust).

Ecdysiasm . . . An urge to take off one's clothes, especially when motivated by erotic tendencies. The term is derived from *ekdyein* (to take or put off).

Ecdysiast . . . A stripper.

Ecdysiophile . . . A man fond of strip teasers and strip joints. Derived from *ekdyein* (to shed) and *philein* (to love).

Echolagnia . . . The association of certain human or natural sounds with sexual ideas or motifs. The term also applies to the state of being aroused sexually by given sounds, as the playing of an instrument. The word is derived from *echos* (sound) and *lagneia* (lust).

Ecorcement . . . The act of removing one's clothes in order to awaken erotic desires in onlookers, as in a strip-tease show. The term is derived from *ecorcer* (to strip).

Ecorchement . . . A rare sexual perversion in which the perpetrator flays the female victim by whipping. The man who performs the act is an *ecorcheur*. A woman who flays a man is an *ecorcheuse*. The female victim of flaying is an *ecorchente*. A male victim is an *ecorchent*. Derived from *ecorchement* (a flaying).

Ecorchent . . . A man who is whipped by a woman. See discussion under *ecorchement*.

Ecorchente . . . A female who is whipped or flayed by a male.

See discussion under *ecorchement.*

Ecorcheur . . . A man who whips or flays a woman. See discussion under *ecorchement.*

Ecorcheuse . . . A woman who whips a man. See discussion under *ecorchement.*

Ectorexis . . . The inability to contain one's sexual cravings. The word is derived from *ektos* (outside) and *orexis* (desire).

Ectovalent . . . Able to perform the sexual act only outside one's own home or in a new environment. Derived from *ektos* (outside or without) and *valeo* (be able).

Edeocacosis . . . The belief by a woman that her genital organs are unattractive. The term is derived from *aidoia* (sex organs) and *kakos* (bad).

Edeapsis . . . Coitus or sexual intercourse. The term is derived from *aidoia* (sex organs) and *hapsis* (joining).

Edeormia . . . Stimulation of the sexual appetite by the sight or touch of the sex organs. The term is derived from *aidoia* (genitals) and *horme* (desire).

Edeotage . . . Love play involving the manipulation of the genital organs, male or female. Derived from *aidoia* (genital organs) and *barboter* (to dabble).

Ederacinism . . . The tearing out of one's sex organs. The practice may be the result of sexual frenzy or desire to punish oneself for having erotic cravings. The term is derived from *aidoia* (sexual organs) and *deracinate* (to pull out by the roots).

Egeiseur . . . A man skilled in the technique of arousing sexual desire in women, as by manipulating the nipples, clitoris, etc. The term is derived from *egeiro* (to arouse passion).

Egeiseuse . . . A woman skilled in the technique of arousing sexual desire in men, as by provocative exposure, erotic posturization, manipulation of the genitalia, etc. The word is derived from *egeiro.*

Electra complex . . . A tendency which arises early in childhood and causes the patient to become attached emotionally and sexually to her father. There is an accompanying hostility toward the mother. The name is derived from a character in Greek legend who brought about the death of her mother because of her love for her father. The Electra complex is the Oedipus complex in females. The word that sums up the concept of the Electra complex is *paternorexis,* derived from *pater* (father) and *orexis* (desire).

Eleutherophilist . . . A man or woman who believes in free love. The term is derived from *eleutheria* (freedom) and *philein* (to love).

Ellipseur . . . A man who omits every form of pre-phallation play and goes through the act itself with great haste. The term is derived from *elleipein* (to leave out or undone).

Ellipseuse . . . A woman who is not opposed to vagination but opposes pre-vagination play. Derived from *elleipein.*

Elytra . . . The vagina or canal which receives the male organ during copulation. It is derived from *elytron* (a sheath) and is based on the fancied assumption that the vagina forms a sheath around the penis during coitus.

Elytrocleisis . . . The closing of the vagina by operative procedure, as to preclude sexual intercourse. This practice is still common among some primitive nations. Derived from *elytron* (sheath) and *kleisis* (closure).

Elytrostenosis . . . Contraction or diminution in size of the vagina, from *elytron* (the vagina) and *stenosis* (a narrowing).

Elytrostomia . . . The popular but erroneous belief that the size of a girl's vagina can be estimated from the size of her mouth. Also, the supposed relation between the opening of the vagina and the size of the mouth. The term is derived from *elytra* (vagina) and *stoma* (mouth).

End-pleasure . . . That segment of the total pleasure derived from the sexual act which comes during the orgasm.

Enfant terrible . . . The suddenly petrified masculine pendant forming an irrepressible evagination in the owner's pantaloons, to the dismay of the victim and those about him.

Entorexia . . . The ability to repress one's sexual cravings. The word is derived from *entos* (within) and *orexis* (desire).

Epacmasia . . . The period of the sexual act characterized by a continued increase in tempo and lasting from the insertion of the penis into the vagina to the moment of ejaculation. Derived from *epakmazein* (to come to its high point).

Epentheuse . . . A woman who helps her mate in sexual intercourse by guiding his organ manually into the vagina. Derived from *epenthesis* (insertion).

Ephemerorthosis . . . An erection of the male organ which lasts but a short time. The condition is observed in elderly men, in those who indulge in frequent bouts of coitus, or in men who suffer from certain ailments. Ephemerorthosis is a frequent cause for the failure on the part of a man to satisfy the woman, or, often, even himself. Fear, anxiety, qualms of conscience, and a sense of guilt also account for many cases of ephemerorthosis. The term is derived from *ephemeron* (something lasting a short time) and *orthosis* (the condition of remaining erect or straight).

Erastophiliac . . . A person who harbors a strong desire to delve in and gossip about the sexual cravings of others. The term is derived from *erastes* (a lover) and *philiac* (one who is addicted to something).

Erection increment . . . The increase in size and rigidity of an already erected male organ occasionally observed when the erotic stimulus is unusually strong.

Eretithia . . . A feeding from the breast given to an adult male as a means of sexual pleasure. The term is derived from *eros* (love) and *tithenesis* (nursing).

Erotic achalasia . A form of tenseness or restlessness which results from conscious or subconscious sexual cravings or frustrations. The term achalasia is derived from *a* (negative) and *chalasis* (relaxation).

Erotic egregorsis . A kind of sleeplessness which results from sexual frustration. Derived from *egregorsis* (wakefulness).

Erotic foulage . . . A form of love play in which the sexually interesting parts of a woman's body are kneaded and squeezed.

Eunagoria . . . Sexual debauchery characterized by frequent visits to brothels, especially to different brothels, as when the subject travels from town to town in order to "sample" the various salons. The term is derived from *eune* (bed) and *agora* (an assembly).

Eunoterpsia . . . The belief that the only real pleasure in life is sexual indulgence and that one should spend as much time in such pleasures as possible. The term is derived from *eune* (a bed) and *terpsis* (enjoyment).

Euthistorgia . . . The doctrine which holds that love at first sight is not only possible but in fact represents the only true love, since it is devoid of any form of rationalization. The term is derived from *euthys* (instant) and *storge* (love).

Exhibitionism . . . A desire, based on sexual craving, to display or show parts of one's body usually clothed, especially as observed in men. Some exhibitionists make it a practice to expose their genitalia in public, especially in the presence of little girls.

Extravaginist . . . A male whose sexual desires are stimulated and satisfied by para-orthodox love-play and extravaginal phallic intrusions.

Eye openers . . . The labia minora, the "eye" here being the introitus, undoubtedly. From about 1890.

F

Faggoty . . . With regard to sex-pleasures, inclined to enjoy the unbeaten or unorthodox paths.

Fancy piece . . . A female merchant whose stock in trade is her own pudendal atrium, esp. one such who is rather cute.

Fanny . . . 1. The rump or the gluteal convexities thereof, esp. when attached to a female torso. 2. The pudendal panoply of the young female.

Fart-daniel . . .The female genital accouterments, esp. the receiving chamber for the phallus. Based on Daniel, a prophet, in allusion to the alleged fact that the vagina is the first "to feel a fart coming on."

Fart-smeller . . . A male sexual aberrationist, or one just famished, who derives pleasure from sniffing, when he has the opportunity, at feminine underthings worn about the loins, esp. those parts which in wear dandle the perineum.

Fart-sucker . . . An uxorious husband, esp. one who, allegedly, kisses the glutei of his pecking-hen wife, as an offering of homage or appeasement.

Fast-fuck . . . A hurried pudendal concourse, usually in a standing position, often in a hallway, and, obviously, with a harlot.

Faunadestia . . . An uneasiness felt by some people when animals are in sight, based on the fear that an embarrassing situation may arise if the animals scratch or lick their genital organs or engage in a bout of copulation. The term is derived from *fauna* (animal) and *modestia* (bashfulness).

Faunoiphilia . . . A strong interest in watching animals in the act of copulation, especially dogs. The term is derived from *fauna* (animal), *koinonia* (copulation), and *philia* (a liking).

Femormia . . . The awakening of sexual desire by seeing or touching the thigh of a girl. The term is derived from *femur* (thigh) and *horme* (desire).

Ficaro . . . A house of prostitution. A brothel, especially one catering to those who seek unusual ways to satisfy the sexual craving. Some *ficaroes* provide their clients with sexual complements, male or female, while others offer only the room and such equipment as the ficker may require, leaving the choice of complement to the client. The word is derived from *fica* and its allusion to sexual intercourse.

Fick . . . To do to a female what men who make babies do.

Ficken . . . To insert and withdraw, repeatedly, the turgid baby-maker into and from a woman's lower mouth, for the purpose of baby-making or just for the exercise.

Ficker . . . A man who *ficks*, especially one who would rather *fick* than eat.

Flabelleuse . . . A female dancer who augments the provocativeness of the act by affording the spectators brief glimpses of semi-nudity from behind deftly maneuvered fans. The term is derived from *flabellum* (a fan).

Flagellation . . . Sexual pleasure, often accompanied by an orgasm, derived from the act of whipping, usually a member of the opposite sex, or from being whipped. The term is derived from *flagellum* (a whip).

Flat floozie . . . A prostitute who is in business for herself, operating in her apartment or flat.

Flatus vaginalis . . . A noisy eructation of gas from the vagina, as when the male organ is inserted.

Fluter . . . One who phallates per rectum.

Fly the red flag . . . Of the menacmal female, to be indisposed because of the normal tetrahebdomadal sanguinary discharge, i.e., to be menstruating.

Fore-and-after . . . A woman who accepts the phallus both in the usual place and in the rectum.

Fore-pleasure . . . The pleasure of the sexual act which precedes the end-pleasure. Also, the pre-copulation shenanigans.

Free fishery . . . The copulating organs of the female, esp. those of a prostitute. From the 19th century.

Free with both ends of the busk . . Privileged enough, with a particular woman, to caress both the breasts and the vulva. Also, of a woman, taking the penis either in her mouth or vaginally.

French kiss . . . 1. A prolonged kiss applied with ardent pressure. 2. A kiss marked by a protrusion of the tongue into the mouth of the other. 3. A kiss of a male applied to the intralabial area of the pudendum muliebre.

Frenchified . . . Of a female, versed in ways and means of diversifying the standard procedures of the foreplay and play in sexual concourse.

Frigoamia . . . The condition of accepting a woman's frigidity without complaint. The term is derived from *frigor* (cold) and *amicabilis* (friendly).

Front door . . . The pudendum muliebre as the adit to carnal pleasure.

Frottage . . . This is a form of sex aberration in which sexual satisfaction or orgasm is obtained by a deliberate rubbing against the body of a person of the opposite sex. In a crowded place, as in a public conveyance, the perpetrator, usually a man, finds it not too difficult to rub against the buttocks of a woman and thus to attain an orgasm. The man who engages in the act is known as a *frotteur*.

G

Galateism . . . A tendency to fall in love with or to develop a sexual interest in figurines or statues of young women. The term is derived from *Galatea,* the legendary statue with which Pygmalion fell in love.

Gap-stopper . . . The male genital shaft conceived as a "stopper" for the female genital gap.

Gape over the garter . . . The female genital chink conceived as staring down upon the stocking garters.

Gaper . . . The female copulative organs, esp. the interlabial slit, conceived in its relaxed condition as an openmouthed cavern.

Gatty . . . A pet name for the vulva or female sex organs. It is based on the word *gat* which is derived from *gatos* (a cat), the animal proverbially associated with the vulva.

Geneclexis . . . The evaluation and selection of a wife on the basis of her sexual or physical appeal, as opposed to her intellectual qualities. The word is derived from *genos* (sex) and *eklexis* (selection).

Genital macies . . . The wasting or shriveling of the sex organs, as in old age. Derived from *macies* (leanness).

Genophobia . . . An aversion for anything that has to do with sex. The term is derived from *genos* (sex) and *phobos* (fear).

Gentleman of the back door . . . A "gentleman" who, in phallation, prefers the rectum, not the vagina.

Genuglyphics . . . The art and practice of decorating the female leg, esp. the knee, with pictorial embellishments to enhance its erotic impact. Derived from *genu* (knee) and *glyphein* (to carve).

Genuphile . . . 1. A male who is attracted by the female knee; a male who regards the knee as the cynosure of the female anatomical armamentarium. 2. A protagonist of the short skirt. Derived from *genu* (knee) and *philein* (to love).

Genuphilia . . . Fondness or adoration of the female knee; the fashion or style which emphasizes the sexual appeal of the female knee, especially as it appears under a short skirt. Derived from *genu* (knee) and *philein* (to love).

Gerafavic . . . Having a preference for older women, in matters of sexual affection. Derived from *geras* (old age) and *favere* (to favor).

Get Jack in the orchard . . . To place the membrum virile in the atrium of the pudendum muliebre.

Get shot in tail . . . 1. Of the woman, receive the phallus; be phallated. 2. To be inseminated in the old-fashioned way.

Girlometer . . . The male organon, conceived as a kind of yardstick for measuring the "business end" of a girl.

Give juice for jelly . . . Of the female, to give orgasmic vaginal "juice" in return for seminal fluid; i.e., to respond with the female sexual acme.

Glutobasiation . . . The practice of kissing a girl's buttocks as a manifestation of lust. The verb is *glutobasiate*. Derived from *gloutos* (buttock) and *basiare* (to kiss).

Glutoerigentic . . . Capable of being excited sexually through stimulation of the buttocks. *Glutoerigesis* is the act of stimulating through some form of manipulation of the buttocks. Derived from *gloutos* (buttock) and *erigo* (to raise).

Glutolatry . . . The state of being excessively interested in the female buttocks. An even stronger passion for the buttocks is called *glutomania*. *Glutophilia*, on the other hand, denotes a mild or normal interest in female buttocks. Derived from *gloutos* (buttock) and *latreia* (service).

Glutomania . . . See discussion under *glutolatry*. Derived from *gloutos* (buttock) and *mania* (a strong urge).

Glutophilia . . . A mild or normal interest in the buttocks of a female. Derived from *gloutos* (buttock) and *philein* (to love). See also under *glutolatry*.

Gomphipothic . . . Aroused sexually by the sight of beautiful teeth. The word is derived from *gomphios* (tooth) and *pothos* (desire).

Goose . . . 1. The unconditional and alacritous surrender of the female. From about 1870. 2. Deflower, ravish, possess, etc. 3. To sodomize. 4. To phallate between the thickest parts of the thighs. 5. To surprise by a sudden fingering of the female perineum, esp. from behind.

Grand walloper . . . The membrum virile erectum considered as the mastix of the pudendum muliebre.

Gravy . . . 1. Ejaculated seminal fluid. 2. The lubricating vulvar secretion in evidence during pudendal excitation.

Gravy-maker . . . The vulva conceived as the stimulator of the "gravy-giver," the phallus.

Grease the mortar . . . 1. To ejaculate into the vagina. 2. To inject lubricating or medicinal jelly into the vagina.

Gregomulcia . . . The desire of a woman to be fondled in the presence of other persons, especially men. The term is derived from *grex* (a herd or crowd) and *mulcere* (fondle).

Grinding tool . . . The phallus conceived as a triturating pestle.

Gut reamer . . . 1. A sodomite. 2. Phallus of a sodomite.

Gymnocryptosis . . . The tendency of some women to tell their friends about the intimate relations with their husbands.

Some women talk about the subject in order to impress their listeners with the attraction they exert upon their husbands; others do so in order to relive the pleasant experiences. Derived from *gymnos* (open; revealed) and *kryptos* (hidden).

Gymnographephilia . . . The yen for collecting and displaying pin-up pictures of scantily dressed girls. Derived from *gymnos* (nude), *graphe* (picture), and *philia* (a liking).

Gymnogynomania . . . An inordinate, often morbid, desire to look at naked women. This term is applicable to the psychopathic "peeping Tom" who will stop at nothing to get a glimpse of a naked girl. The person thus afflicted is a *gymnogynomaniac,* which is the noun form of the word. A mild desire to look at an undressed female is, of course, accepted as normal. The word describing this form is *gymnogynophilia.* The words are derived from the particles *gymnos* (naked), *gyne* (woman) and *mania* (strong urge) or *philia* (a strong but normal craving).

Gymnogynomaniac . . . A person afflicted with *gymnogynomania* (which see).

Gymnogynophilia . . . A mild or normal desire to see a female in the nude. Derived from *gymnos* (nude), *gyne* (woman), and *philein* (to like or love).

Gymnomania . . . An extremely strong desire or craving to see naked bodies, especially those of females. Derived from *gymnos* (naked) and *mania* (a strong urge).

Gymnophilia . . . A desire to see naked bodies, especially those of girls. When such a desire is extremely strong, the craving is *gymnomania.* Derived from *gymnos* (naked), *philia* (desire).

Gymnophobia . . . Fear or dislike of the naked body, especially as felt by a woman towards a naked man. Derived from *gymnos* (naked) and *phobos* (fear or aversion).

Gymnophoria . . . The sensation or illusion of being naked, though the facts are otherwise, as when a girl is ogled by a lecher. Derived from *gymnos* (naked) and *phoria* (a feeling).

Gymnoscelia . . . The fashion in women's clothes which exposes the entire leg and the knee, as it became popular in the 1960's. Derived from *gymnos* (naked) and *skelos* (leg).

Gymnoscopia . . . The viewing of a naked body, especially the pecular stare of a man looking at a naked woman. Derived from *gymnos* (naked) and *skopein* (to see or observe).

Gyneclast . . . A man who is very successful in having his way with women. A "lady killer." The term is derived from *gyne* (woman) and *klastes* (breaker or killer).

Gynecomimetic . . . Imitating women, in behavior, clothing, etc. Derived from *gyne* (woman) and *mimetes* (an imitator).

Gynecothalpos . . . The warmth of a woman's body. Derived from *gyneco-* (pertaining to a woman) and *thalpos* (warmth).

Gynecozygous . . . Seeking the company of females, as applied to homosexual women. Derived from *gyne* (woman) and *zygon* (a yoke).

Gynesteresis . . . A state of neurotic anxiety or restlessness observed in men who have been deprived of female companionship for long periods, as inmates of prisons. Derived from *gyne* (woman) and *steresis* (privation).

Gynonudomania . . . A strong compulsion to bare a woman's body, as by tearing off her clothes. Derived from *gyne* (woman), *nudus* (naked), and *mania* (a rage).

H

Halitalagnia . . . Loss of sexual desire and potency during love play or intercourse because of bad breath of the partner. The term is derived from *halitus* (exhalation), *a* (without) and *lagneia* (lust).

Hammock-happy . . . Of either the male or the female, "bed-happy," i.e., addicted to bed pleasures.

Hapalophallia . . . The condition of having a large, soft, non-erectible male organ. The term is derived from *hapalos* (soft) and *phallus* (the male sex organ).

Haphemania . . . 1. A keen desire to be touched or fondled, as felt by a woman. 2. A strong desire to touch, especially the female body, as felt by a man. Derived from *haphe* (touch) and *mania* (a rage).

Haphephilia . . . The desire to be touched, especially as felt by a woman. Derived from *haphe* (touch) and *philein* (to love).

Haphephobia . . . The fear of being touched, especially the fear of a woman at the thought of being touched by a repulsive male. Haphephobia is a strong aversion and may be considered pathologic. It is derived from *haphe* (touch) and *phobos* (morbid fear of). The opposite feeling, i.e. the desire to be touched by a member of the opposite sex is called *haphephilia.* When the desire to be touched is extremely strong and unmanageable, the word for it is *haphemania.* Haphemania is also applied to the compulsion itself or to the desire to touch things, especially the female form.

Haploist . . . A person, male or female, who believes that the sexual act should be as brief as possible and unaccompanied by expressions or avowals of love, love play, marital embraces, etc. The term is derived from *haploos* (simple or plain).

Happy juice . . . 1. The phallic climactic vesuviation. 2. The vulvar ungation in excitation.

Haptephilia . . . A strong desire to be touched, especially by a member of the opposite sex. The term is derived from *haptein* (to touch) and *philein* (to love).

Haptepronia . . . The condition of being disposed or inclined to accept amorous advances, especially from a stranger. The term is derived from *haptein* (to touch) and *pronus* (inclined).

Haptevoluptas . . . Somebody very

pleasant to touch, hold, or fondle. Derived from *haptesthai* (to touch) and *voluptas* (pleasure).

Haptic . . . Of a girl, sensitive and responsive to the touch of a man. The term is derived from *haptikos* (able to lay hold of).

Hard-head . . . 1. The phallus erectus. 2. A phallus that goes "diving" with the protection of a condom, in allusion to a diver wearing the conventional diving suit and helmet, known in the trade as a hard-head. 3. A condom-protected phallator.

Have one by the wool . . . Of a female, to dominate a male by virtue of his phallic infatuation with her pudendum.

Hawk one's brawn . . . Of the male, to submit to the homosexual cravings of another, for a remuneration; also, of a female, to prostitute.

Hawk one's meat . . . Of a female, to tantalize by exposing one's stimulating parts, as the breasts. Also, to sell sexual favors.

Heberogmus . . . Nocturnal emission (wet dream) occurring in boys or young men. Also the state of having such episodes in youth. Derived from *hebe* (puberty) and *oneirogmos* (a wet dream).

Hemeuner . . . A man who is potent only during the day or who prefers to have sexual intercourse during the day. The term is derived from *hemera* (day) and *eune* (bed).

Hemotigolagnia . . . Sexual curiosity or desire aroused by the sight of sanitary pads used by women during their menstrual periods, as in window displays, advertisements, drugstores, etc. The word is derived from *haima* (blood), *tigillum* (piece of wool), and *lagneia* (lust).

Heptic . . . Knowing one's way with girls; especially, knowing how to touch a girl without giving offense. The term is derived from *haptein* (to touch).

Hermaphrodism . . . The existence of both male and female sex organs in one person. In some animals the condition is very frequent, and in other animal forms it is normal. In man the condition is abnormal and not very frequent. In most cases one of the organs is not fully developed; in some cases both organs are only partly developed. The term is derived from *Hermaphroditos,* a character in Greek mythology and the son of Hermes and Aphrodite. While bathing, Hermaphroditos saw the beautiful nymph Salmacis and became united with her.

Hetaera . . . A concubine, mistress, or female paramour of ancient Greece. Some hetaerae were former slaves, but others were of noble birth.

Heterodromia . . . That type of body movement in a woman during sexual intercourse which is opposite to the man's movement and hence conducive to satisfactory results. It is that type of motion which thrusts the woman's genital organs upward when the man thrusts his organ downward. The term is derived from *heteros* (other) and *dromos* (running).

Heterovalent . . . Sexually potent or able to perform the act of coitus with another woman but not with one's own wife. Derived from *heteros* (other than usual) and *valeo* (to be strong or able).

Hijack . . . 1. To force a boy to submit to pederasty. 2. To persuade a young and naive one to partake in a vagino-phallic duet. 3. To remove a man forcibly from his quarry while he is in the act of coitus.

Hip-swishy . . . Walking with a diadochokinetic oscillation of the buttocks; characterized by the monronian movement.

Hirsutophilia . . . The condition of having a sexual interest in men who are especially hairy. Derived from *hirsutus* (hairy) and *philein* (to love).

Homoerotism . . . Erotic feeling directed toward a member of the same sex. In a typical case of homoerotism the erotic feeling remains passive and finds release or expression in acceptable behavior. The term is derived from *homos* (same) and *eros* (love).

Homunculate . . . To try ineffectually to perform the sexual act with a small organ. Also, to try hopelessly to insert a very small male organ into a vulva. The term is derived from *homunk* (a miniature male organ).

Homunk . . . A penis of rather miniature size. Derived from *homunculus* (the diminutive of *homo*, a man).

Hone . . . 1. The vagina, or the entire vulvar assembly, conceived as a whetstone upon which the phallic razor is honed. 2. To whet the phallus erectus in the female genesic oubliette.

Honest Mac . . . An unmarried man who insists on retaining a virgin phallus, in order to present it unfouled to the one-and-only, in marriage.

Honeydews . . . The female breasts of medium size, conceived as fruit having a "smooth rind and sweet flesh."

Hootenanny . . . The gluteal domes of a girl, conceived as poppling, exhilarating lollapaloozas.

Hot cockles . . . Genital organs in the mood, male or female.

Hot in the tail . . . Of either sex, but esp. of the female, desirous.

Hot meat . . . 1. The tantalizing instrumentalities of a desirable female. 2. The exposed parts of a female not normally uncovered.

Housewife . . . The female genitalia conceived as man's best friend, or his right arm.

Hunkies . . . The gluteal hemispheres of a girl, esp. of a young or small one.

Hygrophilematous . . . Pertaining to "wet" kisses; fond of long, "wet" kisses. Derived from *hygros* (wet) and *philema* (kiss).

Hymenomania . . . An inordinate desire to deflower a virgin. Derived from *hymen* (the virginal membrane) and *mania* (a raging desire).

Hymenorexis . . . The act of rupturing the hymen, the membrane which partially covers the entrance to the vagina. Derived from *hymen* (the virginal membrane) and *rhexis* (rupture).

Hypnolagnia . . . An erotic state induced by hypnotism. The term is derived from *hypnos* (sleep) and *lagneia* (lust).

Hypsilatry . . . The adoration of the line of cleavage of a woman's breasts, especially the upper portion as seen above a decolletage. Derived from the name of the letter "Y" (upsilon) whose form the upper portion of the line of cleavage often assumes, and *latry* (adoration).

I

Iatronudia . . . The desire on the part of a woman to expose herself to a physician under the pretext of being ill. Derived from *iatros* (physician) and *nudo* (to make naked or bare).

Iconolagny . . . Sexual excitement derived from the sight of certain pictures or statues. The term is derived from *eikon* (image) and *lagneia* (lust).

Ictor . . . A person but mildly interested in love play who lays the main stress on sexual intercourse. Derived from *ictus* (a blow or stress).

Idiogamist . . . A man who is sexually potent only with his wife or a few other selected women, but not with women in general. The term is derived from *idios* (one's own) and *gamos* (marriage).

Idrophrodisia . . . The excitation of the sexual urge by the odor of perspiration, especially from intimate parts of the body. Derived from *hidros* (perspiration) and *Aphrodite* (the goddess of love).

Imago . . . A childhood recollection or memory of some loved person which the adult retains in the subconscious. The memory is usually blended with phantasy.

Imatolibidin . . . A fancied preparation believed by some to be effective in arousing the passion of young women. It is assumed to be a liquid. The term is derived from *iama* (remedy) and *libido* (lust).

Imparcolpia . . . A condition of enforced virginity, as by virtue of religious vows, imprisonment, absence of men, etc. The term is derived from *impar* (without a fellow) and *kolpos* (vagina).

Imparkoinonia . . . An act of sexual intercourse in which one of the participants derives much more satisfaction than the other. It is derived from *impar* (unequal) and *koinonia* (sexual intercourse).

Imparlibidinous . . . Not matched favorably with regard to libido or sexual urge, as when either the husband or the wife is decidedly more ardent than the spouse. Derived from *impar* (unequal) and *libido.*

Imparphallia . . . A condition of enforced sexual abstinence, as by virtue of religious vows, imprisonment, absence of women, etc. The term is derived from *impar* (unpaired; without a fellow) and *phallus* (the male organ). The term applies to men.

Imparvalent . . . Not equally potent sexually at different times. The variation in potency may depend on one's state of mind, physical condition, exposure to temptation, etc. Derived from *impar* (unequal) and *valeo* (to be strong or able).

Impuberal virgin... A very young virgin whose vulva is not yet ringed by pubic hair. The expression is not, however, always used in the literal sense, often implying merely a young, delicate virgin.

Incest . . . Sexual relation between persons related closely enough to make marriage illegal.

Incoercible apathy . . . A form of sexual indifference in women which cannot be overcome by love play.

India . . . The female pudendum conceived as an exotic, slightly inaccessible area of the pre-jet age.

Indorser . . . 1. A male who, in phallation, shuns the vagina in favor of the rectum. 2. A sadist who pays for the privilege of tormenting a prostitute.

Inframamma . . . A female whose sexual attractions are below the waist or below the lower level of the breasts. It applies to a woman who is devoid of facial beauty or callicolpia but has interesting legs, hips, or buttocks. The term is derived from *infra* (below) and *mamma* (the breast).

Insertio . . . The first thrust of the male sex organ into the vagina at the beginning of sexual intercourse.

Inspectionism . . . An unusual interest in looking at genital organs, one's own or another's. Another term expressing the same idea is *scoptophilia.*

Invade . . . To perform an act of ingression into the lower interior of the female by the lower exterior of the male; to phallate. From 17th century.

Ipsithigmophilous . . . Enjoying the touch of one's own body; especially applied to women. The condition is extremely rare in men. The term also describes the desire of a man to watch a woman touch or handle her own sexual parts. It is derived from *ipse* (self), *thigma* (touch), and *philous* (fond of).

Ischiofrecosis . . . A sexual perversion consisting of rubbing one's hips against the hips of another, usually a woman. The practitioners of this perversion seek the company of crowds, as in a subway during the rush hour, where they may unobtrusively lean against the hips of a female. Derived from *ischion* (hip) and *freco* (to rub). While the habit is observed more often among men, the practice is not unknown in women.

Ischolagnism . . . See discussion under *ischolagny.*

Ischolagny . . . The avoidance of the company or even the sight of women, or anything reminiscent of women, in order to suppress one's lust for them. The practice is observed by men whose moral code dictates abstinence but whose sexual cravings are, nevertheless, easily aroused by contact with women. The term is derived from *ischein* (to check) and *lagnos* (lustful). During the Vietnam and Korean Wars and even during World War II there was a movement afoot to discourage female celebrities from visiting the armed forces, the argument being that such visits, while ostensibly intended to better the morale of the men, actually made the enforced abstinence more difficult to endure. The word for the movement is *ischolagnism.*

Isodromia . . . That type of up-and-down movement by a woman during sexual intercourse which is in the same direction as the man's thrusts and hence not conducive to good coital results. The term is derived from *isos* (equal or same) and *dromos* (running).

Isomulcia . . . The desire to caress or fondle a woman in the presence of a man. The term is derived from *isos* (alike) and *mulcere* (to fondle).

Itcher . . . The vulva, conceived as a part in need of "scratching" by the phallus.

J

Jack . . . 1. Indulgence of the sexual desire. 2. To subject the female to phallation. 3. The phallus, or the erection thereof.

Jactitation . . . The boasting of a man that he succeeded in having sexual intimacies or intercourse with a specific girl, whether he did or not. The term is derived from *jacto* (to boast).

Jacob's ladder . . . The female slit, regarded as an object to climb.

Jake-drinker . . . A fellator; a fellatrice. An allusion to *jake*, the seminal fluid.

Jam pot . . . The vulva, esp. its vaginal corridor, in allusion to its function as a "pot" for the ejaculated "jam."

Jam-session . . . The act of "canning" the phallic jam in the female Mason jar.

Jape . . . To have sexual intercourse, esp., of the male, to phallate.

Jay . . . One who indulges in sexual pleasures. 2. An inexperienced phallator.

Jazz-festival . . . A beating of the female drum with the phallic drumstick.

Jazzmania . . . 1. A maniacal desire to phallate or be phallated; an urge to anneal a hard poker by plunging it into the hairy underbrush of a supine female. 2. A prolonged bout of vulvophallic gymnastics.

Jazzmaniac . . . A male, or female, afflicted with *jazzmania,* which see.

Jazzmaniacal . . . Sexually frenzied; afflicted with *jazzmania,* which see.

Jazzmination . . . 1. Vaginal insemination with the original equipment. 2. The act of measuring the pudendal interior with the phallic yardstick.

Jerk off . . . To relieve one's sexual urge by masturbation. Of 18th century vintage.

Jewel box . . . The perineal sex equipment of the female.

Jiggle . . . To engage in sexual concourse. Of the male, to phallate.

Jink . . . To shake or thrust provocatively, as the bubbies, the arse, or the pubes.

Jink one's tin . . . To shake the bosom or posteriors.

Jink the jargon . . . Of female burlesque performers, to give the pudendal orchard a forward thrust.

Jobbing . . . The action involved in sexual concourse; a bout of such. From 17th century.

Jock . . . To spit a female with the male harpoon.

Jockstrop . . . 1. The female receptacle for the male intruder. 2. A female who alleviates males with a surplus inventory of seminal fluid.

Joey . . . A post-coital flaccid membrum virile, as conceived endearingly by the contented female.

Johnnie . . . The copulating device of the male. A term used, mostly, by non-misandristic females.

Join dissimilars . . . To bring together the membrum virile and the pudendum muliebre in a bout of sexual concourse.

Join giblets . . . To have sexual intercourse outside of wedlock. From late 18th century.

Join paunches . . . To juxtapose venters in coital embrace; to engage in phallation.

Joy stick . . . The erectile allantoid perineal process of the male, conceived as a joy-bringer to a willing pudendum muliebre. From late 19th century.

Jumbler . . . A participant in sexual concourse, either the male or the female.

Jump . . . To phallate; to engage in phallation. From 17th century.

K

Kick in the front door . . . Intromit the male eager beaver into Eve's hutch.

Kickback...The effluence of gratification from the vaginally mollified male ramrod. 2. The ejaculation.

Kiss-off . . . An orgasm induced by "kissing" the sex organs.

Knemeskepsis . . . The preoccupation of gazing at girls' legs or knees. *Mammaskepsis* is the ogling at a woman's breasts or their contour. Derived from *kneme* (leg), *mamma* (breast), and *skepsis* (a gazing).

Knemelatry . . . The adoration of the female knees, especially as they coruscate under a high hemline or a miniskirt. Derived from *kneme* (knee) and *latris* (a servant).

Knismolagnia . . . The practice of arousing sexual desire by applications which cause an itching or tickling about or in the genital area or other erotogenic places, such as the nipples, anus, etc. Derived from *knizo* (to make it itch) and *lagneia* (lust).

Knismophallia . . . The practice of tickling the phallus in order to obtain sexual gratification. *Cunniknismos* is the practice of tickling the female sexual organs, as by manipulation with the fingers. Derived from *knizo* (to cause an itching) and *phallus* (the penis).

Knock . . . 1. The male botuliform organ with which he "knocks" the female. From 18th century. 2. To do the man's part in sexual concourse. 3. A female as the object of phallation.

Knocked-up . . . Of the female, phallated and impregnated.

Knockup drops . . . The extruded lava of the orgasmic male organon.

Koinasthenia . . . A general loss of confidence and feeling of security, accompanied by restlessness and anxiety, resulting from self-blame for unsatisfactory sexual relations with one's spouse. The term is derived from *koinonia* (sexual intercourse) and *asthenia* (want of power or strength).

Koinocrasia . . . A bout of sexual intercourse which is composed of normal and abnormal acts. Derived from *koinonia* (sexual intercourse) and *krasis* (a mixture).

Kolpectasia . . . A stretching or

dilatation of the vagina, as in coitus. Derived from *kolpos* (vagina) and *ectasia* (a stretching).

Kolpeuryntalgia . . . The pain experienced by a woman from the stretching of the vagina by the phallus. It is akin to *megamedalgia,* but may be caused by a small vagina rather than a large phallus. It is derived from *kolpos* (the vagina), *eurynein* (to dilate), and *algos* (pain). The act of stretching the vagina is *kolpeurysis,* derived from *kolpos* and *eurysis.*

Kolpeuryntomania . . . A form of sexual perversion in which the man derives pleasure not so much from the physiologic thrill of coitus but from the sadistic desire to stretch or mutilate the female organs. The term is derived from *kolpos* (the vagina), *eurynein* (to dilate), and *mania* (craving for). Various devices have been contrived to assist the male in achieving his goal. They are usually condom-like sheaths provided with padding, ridges, or even rubber cleats. Such devices are known as *kolpeurynters,* from *kolpos* and *eurynein* (to dilate).

Kolpeurysesthesia . . . The sensation of having the vagina stretched by the introduction of the erected phallus. The term is especially applicable to the act of defloration or the initial act of coitus. A woman having a small vagina will, naturally, experience kolpeurysesthesia for a much longer period of her life than one with a large canal. Similarly, a woman who has had no children will continue to enjoy kolpeurysesthesia for a much longer time than one who has borne children. The phenomenon of kolpeurysesthesia also depends, quite understandably, on the size of the phallus. Men with large organs will produce the sensation much longer. A synonym for kolpeurysesthesia is *kolpeurysophoria.* The terms are derived from *kolpos* (vagina), *eurynein* (to dilate), *esthesia* (perception), and *phoria* (a feeling).

Kolpeurysis . . . The act of stretching or dilating the vagina, in women whose vaginas are abnormally small. Derived from *kolpos* (vagina) and *eurynein* (to dilate).

Kolpocingulaphoria . . . The sensation of having the penis tightly "embraced" by the vagina in the course of copulation, as when the act is with a virgin. The term is derived from *kolpos* (a vagina), *cingulum* (a girdle), and *phoria* (a feeling). Kolpocingulaphoria is absent in coitus with women who have had children, but it may be restored by plastic operations.

Kolpophobia . . . Fear of or aversion for sexual intercourse or the female sexual organs. Dеirved from *kolpos* (vagina) and *phobia* (fear or aversion).

Korophilia . . . The tendency to fall in love with a man younger than oneself. Also, of women, the condition of being sexually interested only in very young men or boys. The term is derived from *koros* (a youth) and *philein* (to love).

Krukolibidinous... Always watching the crotch, as of girl dancers, skaters, etc.

Kystapaza . . . A "snapping" vagina that "snatches up" the male organ. The term is derived from *kysthos* (vagina) and *harpazein* (to snap up).

L

Ladder . . . The vulva, in allusion to the male's "climbing" upon it, in coitus.

Lagnatrophy . . . Partial or complete disappearance of sexual craving, as in old age. Derived from *lagnos* (lustful) and *atrophy* (a withering).

Lagnechia . . . The condition of not being completely satisfied sexually after the orgasm. The failure of orgasm to give complete release from sexual tension. The term is derived from *lagneia* (lust) and *echo* (hold).

Lagnocopia . . . A sense of weariness resulting from sexual debauchery. The term is derived from *lagneia* (lust) and *kopos* (weariness).

Lagnodomnia . . . Sexual control on the part of a man as expressed in his ability to delay his orgasm in order to prolong the sexual act and thus afford the woman an opportunity to gain and enjoy her own orgasm. The term is derived from *lagneia* (lust) and *dominari* (to rule).

Lagnofugia . . . A conscious or subconscious avoidance of thoughts, activities, amusements, etc., which deal directly or indirectly with sex. The term is derived from *lagneia* (lust) and *fugere* (to flee).

Lagnolysis . . . Complete relief from sexual tension, as through a satisfying act of sexual intercourse. The term is derived from *lagneia* (lust) and *lysis* (solution).

Lagnonector . . . A man who kills girls or women in order to ravish the dead bodies. The term is derived from *lagneia* (lust) and *neco* (to kill).

Lagnopalindromia . . . A sudden return of both sexual desire and potency in elderly men. The term is derived from *lagneia* (lust), *palin* (again), and *dramein* (to run).

Lagnoperissia . . . The condition of having excessive sexual lust. Derived from *lagnos* (lustful) and *perissos* (extraordinary).

Lagnopetance . . . The orienting effect or influence which the sex urge has upon a person's activities, aims, moods, and behavior. Derived from *lagneia* (lust) and *petere* (move toward)).

Lagnoprivous . . . Lacking sexual interest, as a person, scene, story, etc. Derived from *lagneia* and *privare* (to deprive).

Lagnopyresia . . . A low grade fever which occasionally accompanies sexual excitation. The term is derived from *lagneia* (lust) and *pyretos* (fever).

Lagnoserotinous . . . Attaining full sexual capacity late in life, especially in men. Derived from *lagneia* (lust) and *serotinous* (ripe late in season or life).

Lapacratia . . . Sexual impotence in men, resulting from a peculiar aversion for the mucous secretion of the vagina and consequent unwillingness to insert the penis. The term is derived from *lape* (phlegm or mucus) and *akrateia* (impotence).

Lapactor . . . The male sex organ, especially in the erected form. The term is derived from *lapassein* (to discharge).

Lapper . . . A sodomite who phallates in accordance with his style, holding the recipient in his lap.

Lather . . . The disembogued lactescent syrup of the propitiated membrum virile.

Lavacultophilia . . . A penchant for watching girls in bathing suits. Derived from *lavatio* (bathing), *cultus* (suit), and *philein* (to love).

Leak . . . To have a slow effusion of seminal fluid before the orgasm, esp. during the foreplay.

Leather lane . . . The region of the female perineum dominated by the vulva.

Leather-stretcher . . . The male genital reamer viewed as a gentle dilator of the introitus vaginae and the vaginal corridor.

Lecheur . . . A man who indulges in licking the female sex organs. The term is derived from *lecher* (to lick).

Lecheuse . . . A woman who licks a man's sex organs.

Lechoitus . . . Sexual intercourse with a woman about to give birth. The term is derived from *lecho* (parturient woman) and *coitus* (sexual intercourse).

Lectamia . . . Love play performed in bed, not including sexual intercourse. The term is derived from *lectus* (a bed) and *amor* (love).

Lectamie . . . A bedmate or female participant in love bouts. The term is derived from *lectus* (a bed) and *amie* (a female friend).

Lectualia . . . Sexual orgies accompanied by drinking and acts of perversion. The term is derived from *lectus* (a bed), in allusion to arena of these events.

Lectulate . . . To wallow habitually in bed, especially in pursuit of sexual pleasures. The term is derived from *lectus* (a bed).

Legorastia . . . The condition of being aroused sexually by watching a girl's lips in the motions of speech. The term is derived from *lego* (to speak) and *erastes* (lover).

Lenirer . . . A person, usually a woman, who by mild, skillful manipulation of the erotic areas of the body of another person brings about sexual and general relaxation rather than excitation. The term is derived from *lenire* (to soothe).

Lesbian love . . . A term synonymous with sapphism and tribadism, referring to the mutual friction of the sex organs between two women. Many women who practice tribadism also enjoy and practice sexual intercourse with men, though the majority prefer bouts of Lesbian love with other females. Among the ancients, strangely enough, this practice was considered part of good behavior, and ladies of high repute spent much time in perfecting their style and skill in the practice of tribadism. Since the possession of a large clitoris was an advantage in this form of sex gratification, the participants spent both money and effort to enlarge the organ by every means available, including manual pulling. The term Lesbian love is derived from the name of the Greek island of Lesbos whose women were reputedly expert in the practice of tribadism.

Libermenseuse . . . A woman who gives herself to men without reward and without much persuasion. The term is derived from *liber* (free) and *mensa* (table or table board).

Libidacoria . . . A form of sexual craving which knows no satiety, no matter how frequently the victim indulges in sexual pleasures. It is found both in men and women, the latter being the more profoundly affected. Libidacoria may be considered a severe form of satyriasis or nymphomania but differs from both in the fact that the sufferer is never satisfied. The term is derived from *libido* (sexual desire), *a* (without), and *koros* (satiety).

Libidation . . . Love play or any form of sexual practice, whether conventional phallation or some extravaginal insertion.

Libido . . . Sexual craving or desire in its normal form. In certain uses it also refers to the motive force or energy as it stems from the sex instinct or the general urge to live.

Libidocenosis . . . The removal or release of pent-up sexual pressure by sexual indulgence or by abreaction. The term is derived from *libido* (lust) and *kenosis* (emptying).

Libidocoria . . . A form of sexual desire which is seldom satisfied without a sense of satiation and is often followed by a feeling of surfeit. It is more common in women. The term is derived from *libido* and *koros* (satiety).

Libidolambosis . . . The awakening of the libido by licking, as the vulva. Derived from *libido* and *lambo* (lick).

Libidolirium . . . A hysteria-like seizure observed in young women during which the subject becomes irrational and unresponsive and mutters fragmentary sentences having an erotic content. It occurs more frequently in the period preceding menstruation. The term is derived from *libido* (sexual desire) and *delirare* (to rave).

Libidopause . . . The period in the life of a man or woman when the sexual desires are on the decline. Derived from *libido* (sexual desire) and *pausis* (a stopping).

Libidophrenia . . . A state of mind characterized by sexual craving for which the person seeks no practical relief and from which he is relieved by discourse. The condition is more common in women. Derived from *libido* (sexual desire) and *phren* (mind).

Libidopiesis . . . The pressure of the sex urge, conscious and subconscious, as it affects one's aspirations, actions, motives, etc. Derived from *libido* (sexual craving) and *piesis* (pressure).

Libidoplasia . . . A gradual development of the sexual desire for each other in man and wife during the early years of marriage. Derived from *libido* (sexual desire) and *plasis* (formation). The term is also used to describe the increase of sexual interest on the part of a wife, for her husband.

Libidosyntonia . . . The condition of being sexually responsive to the demands of married life. The term is derived from *libido* (sexual desire) and *syntonia* (responsiveness).

Lie in state . . . To lie amorously between two females.

Lift the heels . . . Of a woman, to get into bed for coitus.

Light in the tail . . . 1. Of loose morals; wanton. 2. Receptive with regard to the membrum virile erectum.

Linguation . . . The practice of licking the anatomical parts of a man or a woman to obtain or impart sexual excitation. The word is derived from *lingua* (tongue).

Lip-service . . . The act of servicing the nether female labia and the inclosed donjon with the phallic moderator.

Lip-warmer . . . The membrum virile erectum, which, when properly introduced, forms, with the scrotum, an efficient labial calefacient.

Little man in the boat . . . The clitoris.

Long nose . . . A long nose pleases the lady because of the wishful relation between the nasal and phallic dimensions. From the 19th century.

Loosen the panties . . . Of the female, to indicate a disposition to unconditional surrender.

Lord of a pillicock-hill . . . A male who derives sexual pleasure or gratification from a lip-and-tongue safari into the wilds of the vulvar jungle.

Loroerigesis . . The sexually stimulating effect of the sight of a slip or brassiere shoulder strap, as under a thin blouse. Derived from *lorum* (a strap) and *erigere* (to erect).

Loroptosilagnia . . . Sexual desire aroused in a man by the sight of a slip or brassiere shoulder strap off the shoulder. Derived from *lorum* (strap), *ptosis* (a falling), and *lagneia* (lust).

Lose the last round . . . Of the male in copulation, to be overtaken by flaccidity before reaching the summit.

Love center . . . A "stock exchange" in which the stocks are female pudenda. 2. The female's interlabial niceties.

Lygerastia . . . The tendency to become romantic or erotic in a darkened or partly darkened room. Many persons are unable to acquire a romantic mood in daylight. The term is derived from *lyge* (twilight) and *erastes* (lover).

Lygerevirescence . . . A renewal of interest in lovemaking and sexual intercourse that comes late in life, especially in women. Derived from *lyge* (twilight) and *revirescence* (a renewal or a growing young again).

M

Machlobasia . . . Pleasurable sensation experienced by some women when walking. It is caused by the rubbing of the thighs and labia of the genital organs, and is found more often in obese women. The term is also applied occasionally to the lust aroused in men watching the walking gyrations of an attractive woman. The term is derived from *machlosyne* (lust) and *basis* (step).

Madefaction . . . The process or act of getting "wet" or having the genital organs oiled by natural secretions, as when a girl is aroused by love play. The term is derived from *madefacere* (to make wet). The word also applies to the "teasing" which causes the wetting.

Madidia . . . The discharge of a few drops of sexual fluid from a man's organ when in a state of keen excitement, as during love play, without the full course of an orgasm. The term is derived from *madidus* (dripping wet). The word is also applied to a somewhat similar phenomenon in a woman subjected to sexual heat. In the woman the secretions serve as a lubricant for the vaginal canal which facilitates the entry and movements of the penis. The phenomenon, as it occurs in women, is also known as *sexual lubrication* and *madefaction.*

Mageiria . . . A form of sublimation in which sexual cravings are expressed in preoccupations with cookery and dietetics. It is a mechanism by which sexual frustrations are satisfied. Derived from *mageirike* (cookery).

Mageria . . . A form of substitution in which a married woman, conscious of her inadequacy as a sex partner, attempts to make amends by skillful cooking. Derived from *mageirike* (cookery).

Maiden-wife widow . . . a widow who had never had sexual intercourse with her deceased husband.

Maid's ring . . . 1. The labia minora, conceived as a ring around Rosie. 2. The hymen.

Make free with both ends . . . To caress, esp. simultaneously, the mammae and the pudendum of a female. From 18th century.

Make free with the land . . . To do finger exercise with a girl's charm.

Make settlement in tail . . . 1. To have sexual intercourse. 2. Of a girl in debt, financially or similarly, to a male, to square things by a series of propitiatory pudendal offerings.

Make the chimney smoke . . . Make a woman experience the pudendal orgasm.

Malacus . . . A male sex organ which upon erection does not possess the necessary firmness to make it adequate for sexual intercourse. The term is derived from *malakos* (soft).

Malaxomania . . . A strong craving to "knead" the flesh of a woman, especially the breasts. Derived from *malaxatio* (a kneading). *Malaxophobia* is the fear of some women that they will be "kneaded" by their escorts, husbands, lovers, etc.

Malaxophilia . . . Of a male, to be fond of "kneading" a girl's tissues, especially the breasts. Derived from *malassein* (to soften by kneading) and *philein* (to love).

Malaxophobia . . . The fear of some women that their tissues, especially breasts, will be "kneaded" by their lovers, husbands, escorts, etc. Derived from *malassein* (to soften by kneading) and *phobos* (fear).

Malleation . . . A series of rapid, hammerlike thrusts made by the male sex organ in the act of coitus. It expresses an extreme state of eagerness, as after enforced abstinence. The term is derived from *malleare* (to hammer).

Mammagymnophilia . . . The desire of some women to wear a garment with a low neckline in order to show more of the line of cleavage. 2. A man's desire to see naked breasts. Derived from *mamma* (breast), *gymnos* (naked) and *philein* (to love).

Mammagymnophoria . . . A nervous preoccupation with the level of the neckline, based on the fear that it might slip down and show too much of the bosom. Observed in extremely modest women. Derived from *mamma*, *gymnos* (naked) and *phobos* (fear).

Mammaquatia . . . The bobbing or up-and-down oscillation of a woman's breasts, as when walking, dancing, exercising, etc. Derived from *mamma* and *quassare* (to shake). The term applies especially to the movement of the breasts when not supported or confined by a brassiere.

Mammaskepsis . . . The ogling of women's breasts, or, more often, merely their contour; the tendency to make the bosom the first region of observation, or the first part observed, in a woman. Derived from *mamma* (breast) and *skopein* (observe).

Mammathigmomania . . . A compulsion to touch the breasts of a woman. Derived from *mamma* (breast), *thigma* (touch), and *mania* (raging desire).

Mammilingus . . . The sucking or licking of the breast as a manifestation of lovemaking. Derived from *mamma* and *linguere* (to lick). The procedure was formerly considered by some as a form of perversion but it is now accepted as a normal expression of the libido, especially in the pre-coital love play.

Manevalent . . . Potent sexually only in the morning. This condition is frequent in older men whose full bladder, in the morning, initiates the erection reflex. After the bladder is emptied, the erection vanishes. The word is derived from *mane* (morning) and *valeo* (to be strong or able).

Manipulus . . . A handful of a girl's flesh or that which is seized by the hand of a man during love play. Derived from *manus* (hand) and *pleres* (full).

Manoplania . . . The tendency of a man's hands to "wander" or seek bodily contact with a girl's body. Derived from *manus* (hand) and *planasthai* (wander).

Manormia . . . Sexual excitation brought about by working upon some part with the hand. Derived from *manus* (hand) and *horme* (desire).

Manotripsis . . . The manipulation of the phallus by a woman until ejaculation is effected. Derived from *manus* (hand) and *tripsis* (a rubbing).

Marinatia . . . The state of mind of a woman who wishes her spouse to embody the spirit and character of both a husband and a son. The term is derived from *maritus* (husband) and *natus* (son).

Maritomania . . . A strong desire, bordering on the abnormal, to possess a husband. It is the frenzy that overtakes a young woman on the borderline of spinsterhood. The word is derived from *maritus* (a husband) and *mania* (raging desire).

Maritopatria . . . The state of mind of a woman who wishes her spouse to embody the spirit and character of both a husband and a father. The condition is observed in women who have an Electra complex. The term is derived from *maritus* (husband) and *pater* (father).

Marriage music . . . 1. The groans of the bedstead of a newly or recently married couple. 2. The audible manifestations of the foreplay and play (coitus) of a newly or recently married couple.

Marrow-pudding . . . The ejected sexual lava of the male. 2. The membrum virile conceived as the ejector of the genital lava.

Marrowbone-and-cleaver . . . The turgid male genital shaft, conceived as a marrow-filled cleaver of the female pudendal slit.

Martymachlia . . . A sexual perversion observed in men and women which demands the presence of several persons during the act of coitus or love play. It is a form of exhibitionism. The term is derived from *martys* (witness) and *machlosyne* (lust).

Maschalitosis . . . Malodorous underarm perspiration. It may act as an aphrodisiac. The term is derived from *maschale* (armpit) and *halitus* (emanation).

Maschalolagnia . . . Sexual desire aroused by viewing an exposed armpit of a girl. Derived from *maschale* (armpit) and *lagneia* (lust).

Masochism . . . The reverse of sadism or the derivation of sexual pleasure through the absorption of punishment. The name is derived from the poet Sacher-Masoch who submitted to cruel treatment in order to obtain sexual gratification. A certain amount of masochism may be regarded as normal in a woman, since her part in normal intercourse is subordination to the male.

Mason . . . A female homosexual who takes the part of the male in the act of tribadism.

Massolette . . . An instrument built on the order of an electric vibrator and having attachments for applying pleasurable stimulation to the pubic and inguinal region. Derived from *massein* (to knead).

Mastigothymia...An erotic pleasure derived from whipping, real or imaginary. The term also describes the erotic sensation aroused in the victim of a whipping bout. The word is derived from *mastizo* (to whip) and *epithymia* (lust).

Mastolator . . . A man who worships the female breasts. Derived from *mastos* (breast) and *latreia* (service).

Mastolatry . . . The adoration of a woman's breasts, as felt by a man. The various anatomical parts of a woman have special attraction for certain men, and those men who are especially enthralled by the breasts are *mastolators.* The word is derived from *mastos* (breast) and *latry* (worship).

Mastomyzosis . . . The suckling of a woman's breast by either a man or another woman for the purpose of gratifying the libido. Derived from *mastos* (breast) and *myzein* (suckle).

Mastopetal . . . Seeking the female breast. This term, like *vulvopetal* and *phallopetal,* refers to a subconscious interpretative craving expressed in creative work. It is derived from *mastos* (a breast) and *petere* (seek).

Mastormia . . . The awakening of the sexual appetite by the sight or manipulation of the breast. The term is derived from *mastos* (breast) and *horme* (to urge).

Matronolagnia . . . Sexual desire for older women. The term is derived from *matrona* (a married woman who is no longer young) and *lagneia* (lust).

Mazomyzia . . . A love play procedure in which a woman's breasts and nipples are stimulated with the tongue and lips. The term is derived from *mazos* (breast) and *myzein* (to suck).

Mazotropism . . . The influence or attraction which the female breasts exerts upon a man. The term is derived from *mazos* (breast) and *tropism* (influence).

Meat . . . Flesh as a source of sensual pleasure.

Meatosthesia . . . The phenomenon of having erotic sensitivity in the region of every body opening, as the mouth, anus, vagina, phallus, and nipples. The term is derived from *meatus* (opening) and *esthesia* (feeling or sensitivity).

Medanorthosis . . . The inability to produce an erected phallus. (The same as *anorthomedosis.*) The word is derived from *medos* (the male organ), *an* (inability), and *orthosis* (state of erection).

Medectasia . . . The bulging of an erected penis in the front of the trousers. Derived from *medos* (penis) and *ektasis* (a stretching out).

Medectophobia . . . Fear that the contour of the penis will be discernible, as because of tightness of pants, especially when brought to erection by the sight of a pretty girl. Derived from *medos* (penis), *ectasia* (a protruding), and *phobia*. Certain situations, as attending a party or a dance, are conducive to medectophobia. The bulging of an erected phallus through the front of one's trousers is *medectasia.*

Mederigentic . . . Stimulating the desire to have intercourse, as applied to men. Derived from *medos* (the male organ) and *erigentic* (exciting).

Medisect . . . The cleft between the two breasts of a woman. The term is derived from *medius* (middle) and *secare* (to cut).

Medlar . . . The female escutcheon with its subjacent labia, conceived, fancifully, as a small tree of the same name.

Medochnoia . . . From a woman's point of view, the condition of having a gentle, "thoughtful," or considerate male organ; i.e., one that does not inflict pain when entering the vagina. A male organ with a "light touch." The term is derived from *medos* (the male organ) and *chnoos* (the bloom of a peach).

Medocnesis . . . An itching of the sex organ in the absence of a demonstrable cause. It is often a manifestation of a neurosis or sexual frustration. The term is derived from *medos* (the male organ) and *knismos* (itching).

Medocure . . . The cosmetic care of the male sex organ and the genital area, as by clipping the hair, perfuming, etc. The term is derived from *medos* (the male organ) and *cura* (care). The term also applies to a male attendant who engages in the practice of medocuring.

Medocurix . . . A woman who engages in the cosmetic care of the male sex organ and genital area, as by clipping the hair, creaming the skin, massaging, etc. A number of medocurixes are also fellatrices, but the majority restrict their activities to the cosmetic care only. The practice of medocure is not a new occupation, as might be assumed, but dates back to ancient times, when slave girls and concubines applied fragrant inunctions to the genitalia of their masters. Certain articles used by the ancients in the practice of medocure, such as genital aprons, brushes, and oil dispensers, are on exhibition in the British Museum, although the nature of these articles was not understood till recently. A still larger collection of medocure adjuncts was discovered by the author in another European museum where they had been simply and erroneously labeled as "articles of the ancient bath." During a previous trip the author discovered another set of medocure equipment forming part of a large exhibit labeled "torture instruments used by the ancients." The label was not meant to be facetious; it was written in error, as far as the medocure articles are concerned.

Medomalacophobia . . . The fear, mostly as felt by the man, that the erected phallus will collapse during coitus. This fear is encountered with unusual and surprising frequency among men of all ages and the fear is often the cause of *medomalcosis,* the softening of the erected penis during coitus and before the orgasm. The term is derived from *medos* (the male organ), *malakos* (soft), and *phobia.*

Medomalacosis . . . The softening of the erected penis during sexual intercourse, before the orgasm. Derived from *medos* (penis) and *malakizo* (soften).

Medorthophobia . . . An aversion for or fear of the erected male organ. The term is derived from *medos* (the male organ), *orthosis* (state of erection), and *phobia* (aversion or fear). The condition is common in newly married women who have had no previous experience in coitus.

Medotage . . . Sex play involving the manipulation of the male sex organ. Derived from *medos* (the penis) and *barboter* (to dabble).

Medotractation . . . The handling or pulling of the phallus or male organ with the object of causing an erection or effecting an orgasm. Derived from *medos* (penis) and *trahere* (to draw).

Medotripsis . . . The practice of rubbing one's phallus against the buttock or buttocks of a woman, as in a crowd. Derived from *medos* (penis) and *tripsis* (rubbing).

Megamedalgia . . . The pain felt by the woman when an unusually large male organ is introduced into her vagina. The term is derived from *megas* (big), *medos* (the male organ), and *algos* (pain). For obvious reasons the virgin is more likely to be the victim of such pain. The pain felt by a virgin is called *vestimedalgia,* from *vestal* (pertaining to a virgin), *medos* (the male organ), and *algos* (pain).

Melcryptovestimentaphilia . . . A fondness for women's black undergarments. The term applies both to the woman who likes to wear such garments and to the man who likes to observe them. Derived from *melas* (black), *kryptos* (hidden), *vestimenta* (garments), *philia* (a liking).

Melolagnia . . . Sexual desire aroused by music. The term is derived from *melos* (song) and *lagneia* (lust).

Menodmia . . . The peculiar odor associated with a menstruating woman. Derived from *menses* (menstrual flow) and *odme* (odor).

Menolagnia . . . An increase in sexual desire during the menstrual period. Derived from *menses* (menstrual flow) and *lagneia* (lust).

Mentulagra . . . Frequent and sustained erections of the male organ not accompanied by sexual desire. Derived from *mentula* (penis), and *agra* (a seizure).

Mentulalgia . . . Pain in the male organ caused by excessive masturbation, frequent bouts of coitus, or sustained erections. It is derived from *mentula* (the male organ) and *algos* (pain).

Mentulate . . . Having an unusually large organ or penis. Derived from *mentula* (penis).

Mentulhedonia . . . A sense of pride or satisfaction in being a man or having a phallus. Derived from *mentula* (phallus) and *hedone* (pleasure). A synonym of mentulhedonia is *phallhedonia.*

Mentulomania . . . Masturbation or the constant preoccupation with one's penis, in thought or action. Derived from *mentula* (penis) and *mania* (urge).

Microedea . . . A peculiar delusion in which the subject believes that his sex organs are becoming smaller. The term is derived from *mikros* (small) and *aidoia* (the genital or sex organs).

Milk . . . 1. To knead or suckle amorously the breasts of a female. 2. To cause a phallic ejaculation by female manual stimulation.

Milk churners . . . The female breasts, esp. those that are confined but loosely in their undergarment hammock, with obvious results when the bearer is in motion.

Milk-jug . . . The pudendum muliebre, esp. the vaginal corridor, conceived as a container for the phallic ejaculant. From 18th century.

Milking pail . . . The vulva, esp. the receiving chamber thereof, conceived as a receptacle for the phallic milk. From 18th century.

Misandrist . . . A woman who dislikes men. The term is derived from *misein* (to hate) and *andros* (man).

Misogynist . . . A man who hates women. The term is derived from *misein* (to hate) and *gyne* (woman).

Misophileist . . . A person who dislikes kissing or being kissed. The term is derived from *misein* (to hate) and *phileo* (kiss).

Miss Horner . . . The female pudendal organa, in allusion to their "hornifying" effect upon the male pudendus.

Moll Peatley's jig . . . A lively bipudendal communion between man and maid, in allusion to one Moll Peatley, a 17th century hetaera.

Moneunia . . . The practice of having only one act of sexual intercourse during any reasonable period of time. The term is derived from *monos* (single) and *eune* (a bed). A person who believes in the practice of moneunia is a *moneunist.*

Moriaphilia . . . A fondness for telling or hearing "sexy" jokes or anecdotes. Derived from *moria* (folly) and *philia.*

Monkey bite . . . A passionate kiss terminating in a bite. Also, the mark left by such a bite.

Mortar and pestle . . . The pudendum muliebre and the membrum virile.

Mortar-grinding . . . The action of the male pestle in the female mortar.

Mortar-pounding . . . An act of trituration involving the phallic pestle and the vaginal mortar.

Mortar-work . . . Phallic trituration of the female pudendal channel.

Mortarful of pestle . . . 1. The female sheath brimful with phallus erectus. 2. A perfect vaginophallic occlusion. 3. To have a gratifying phallation; said of both coitant and coitante.

Mouth-pie . . . Vulvar substance as "pie" of the cunnilinguist.

Mouth that cannot bite . . . The mouth nefrens at the lower end of the female trunk. From 18th century.

Muff . . . The female pudendum, esp. the outer aspect thereof. From late 17th century.

Muff diving . . . An act of basiation or linguation of the pudendum muliebre.

Mulcage . . . The appeasement of the erected male organ by stroking it with the hand, especially by the hand of a girl. The term is derived from *mulcere* (to stroke).

Mulceur . . . A man who practices mulcage upon another man, whether to gratify his own lust or to gain some profit. Derived from *mulcere* (to stroke or soothe).

Mulceuse . . . A woman who practices mulcage, especially one who is expert at the art and who engages in the practice for profit. Derived from *mulcere* (to stroke or soothe).

Mulciber . . . A homely woman whose very sight cools a man's sexual desire and renders him at least temporarily impotent. The name is derived from the surname of Vulcan, the fire god, who was capable of softening hard iron.

Mulcierism . . . The practice of wearing a mulcierre or vulva-fondler. See discussion under *mulcierre.*

Mulcierre . . . An elongated pad of soft material, as gauze, secured against the vulva by straps or an appropriate belt, to provide pleasant friction when the subject walks or moves her thighs. The use of this device is called *mulcierism.* Mulcierism was once thought to be a practice of depraved women, but is now believed to be fairly common in better circles. Some girls use a sanitary pad as a mulcierre. The term is derived from *mulcere* (to rub, stroke, or fondle).

Muliebraphrenia . . . A condition characterized by a constant preoccupation with thoughts of the female organs. Derived from *muliebria* (female organs), and *phrenia* (state of mind).

Multicipara . . . A girl or woman who has participated in many acts of sexual intercourse. The term is derived from *multus* (many) and *recipere* (to receive).

Multimitia . . . The state of having had many experiences in sexual intercourse. The term applies to a man. It is derived from *multus* (many) and *emitto* (discharge).

Multimitus . . . A man who has participated in many acts of sexual intercourse. The term is derived from *multus* (many) and *emitto.*

Myzoerasty . . . 1. The act of suckling a woman's breasts by a man for the pleasure of the suckler. 2. The sexual pleasure derived by a man who suckles erotically a woman's breasts. Derived from *myzein* (to suckle) and *erastes* (lover).

Myzoerigentic . . . Aroused to sexual warmth through having one's nipple suckled. Derived from *myzein* (to suck) and *erigentic* (excitable).

Myzoeroticism . . . The state of being sexually aroused through having the breasts suckled. There are two forms of myzoeroticism. One refers to the practice of having the breasts suckled by a lover, as in the pre-coital stage. The other refers to the excitement incident to infant breast feeding. Many women first discover the erotic effect of suckling in the process of breast feeding. The word is derived from *myzein* (to suck) and *erotikos* (erotic). The sexual pleasure derived by the man when suckling a woman's breast is called *myzoerasty*. The same word also describes the act.

N

Nanophilia . . . The condition of having a strong urge to possess girls of small stature, as those under five feet in height. The term is derived from *nanos* (a dwarf) and *philein* (to love).

Natocallia . . . The condition in which the beauty of the hips or buttocks is the outstanding feature. The term is derived from *nates* (the buttocks) and *kallos* (beauty).

Necrophilism . . . A pathologic interest in dead bodies, especially when on a sexual basis. The term is derived from *nekros* (dead body) and *philein* (to love).

Necrosadism . . . A pathologic desire to mutilate dead bodies in order to excite or satisfy erotic feelings. The term is derived from *nekros* (dead body) and *sadism.*

Needle-book . . . The female pudendal "book" which, in sexual concourse, receives the male "needle."

Needle-case . . . The sexual sanctum muliebre, conceived as a sheath for the male "needle."

Negovalent . . . Potent sexually and able to perform the act of coitus only after a preliminary period of sincere or pretended refusal to submit on the part of the woman. The condition is observed most frequently in males having a mild masochistic inclination, the refusal or defiance then being accepted by the man as an act of exciting punishment. The term is derived from *negare* (to deny or to say "no") and *valere* (to be strong or able).

Neonatal charm . . . The special sexual attraction exerted by a woman who has just given birth to a child, as felt by some men.

Neophilism . . . A tendency to tire of old methods of sexual gratification and to seek new ones. The term is derived from *neos* (new) and *philein* (to love).

Nepiknisis . . . The practice of lulling an infant to sleep by gently stroking or tickling his or her genital organs. This device of putting an infant to sleep was once very common among child nurses and governesses. When such practices continue into childhood, they often lead to the habit of masturbation. The word is derived from *nepios* (an infant) and *knizo* (tickle).

Nepiomania . . . A strong desire to

bear a child, a condition occurring in childless married women and in spinsters. Derived from *nepios* (an infant) and *mania* (frenzied desire).

Nepirasty . . . Pleasure of a sexual nature derived from handling or fondling an infant, especially one of the opposite sex. The condition is much more common in women than in men and is especially common in spinsters. The word is derived from *nepios* (an infant) and *erastes* (a lover). *Nepiomania* is a strong desire to bear a child, a condition observed in childless married women and in spinsters.

Nictavalent . . . Potent sexually only at night, as opposed to the daylight hours. It is not uncommon to see men who are partly or completely impotent during the day but extremely virile at night. The term is derived from *nyx* (night) and *valere* (be able).

Ninnies-splitter . . . A male who prefers to phallate between the female breasts.

No money in the purse . . . Fresh out of seminal fluid, due to repeated ejaculations; said of a chain phallator. 2. Sexually impotent.

Nock . . . 1. The genital unmentionables of the female. From 16th Century. 2. Of the male, to do what comes naturally, with a young female, or even an older one.

Noeclexis . . . The evaluation and selection of a wife on the basis of her intellectual power, as opposed to her physical attraction. The term is derived from *noetikos* (intelligence) and *eklexis* (selection).

Nose, long . . . A long nose pleases the lady, because of the fanciful naso-phallic ratio, with regard to size. From 19th century.

Nosolagnia . . . The condition of being sexually interested in a sickly woman. The term is derived from *nosos* (illness) and *lagneia* (lust).

Notch . . . The perineal sexual sanctum of the female. From 18th century.

Notch girl . . . A girl, or a female not quite a girl, who is a financial dependent of her notch (q.v.), an appurtenance she lets, periodically, to pudendal jockeys.

Nototentia . . . The opinion held by many men that the back is the most beautiful part of a woman's body. The term is derived from *noton* (back) and *sententia* (opinion).

Nullcipara . . . A girl or woman who has never had sexual intercourse. The term is derived from *nullus* (none) and *recipio* (receive).

Nullciparity . . . The state of never having experienced sexual intercourse. The term applies to a woman. Derived from *nullus* (none) and *recipio* (receive).

Nullimitia . . . The state of never having experienced sexual intercourse. The term applies to a man. It is derived from *nullus* (none) and *emittere* (send out).

Nullimitus . . . A man who has never had sexual intercourse. The term is derived from *nullus* (none) and *emittere* (send out).

Nutarian . . . A woman or girl whose breasts bob up and down as she walks. The term is derived from *nutare* (to nod).

Nycteuner . . . A man who is potent only at night or who prefers to have sexual intercourse at night. The term is derived from *nyx* (night) and *eune* (bed).

Nyctotherus . . . A man who frequents night clubs and dance halls late at night in order to make the acquaintance of amorous females. Derived from *nyx* (night) and *ther* (beast).

Nyxia . . . The penetration of the hymen or virginal membrane by the male sex organ. The term is derived from *nyxis* (a pricking).

O

Obsidium . . . A bout of sexual debauchery. The term is derived from *obsidium* (a siege).

Ochlolagnia . . . Erotic sensation aroused by mingling with a crowd. The sensation is aroused by the mere presence of many persons or by the actual rubbing against the bodies of others. It is derived from *ochlos* (a crowd) and *lagneia* (lust).

Oculoplania . . . An ogling or wandering of the eyes in looking over a girl. Derived from *oculus* (eye) and *planos* (wandering).

Ocyjack . . . A man who, as some women describe it, "hops on and hops off," in the performance of the sexual act; or, in other words, a man who omits preliminary love play and performs the act itself with great haste, to the utter frustration of the female participant. The term is derived from *okys* (swift) and *jack* (a male).

Odaxelagnia . . . A condition in which sexual potency can be achieved only while biting the female participant. The act of biting may consist merely of holding a fold of skin between the teeth, without exerting too much pressure. While the term applies chiefly to men, some women fail to enjoy the act of coitus unless they are bitten by the male participant or, in some cases, bite him. The term is derived from *odaxesmos* (a biting) and *lagneia* (lust).

Odaxia . . . The biting of one's cheek or tongue during the height of sexual excitement. The term is derived from *odaxesmos* (a biting).

Oedipus complex . . . A tendency which arises early in childhood and causes the patient to become attached emotionally and sexually to the parent of the opposite sex and to be antagonistic to the parent of the same sex. Quite frequently the expression Oedipus complex refers to the appearance of the condition in males only. The terminology is based on an old Greek fable. Oedipus was the son of Laius and Jocasta, the king and queen of Thebes. Even before Oedipus was born, the father was told by an oracle that he would eventually be killed by his son. To avert this danger, Laius gave the infant Oedipus to a herdsman with instructions to abandon him to death. The herdsman did not expose the infant but gave him to a friend who let Oedipus be adopted by Polybus, king of Corinth. When Oedipus grew to manhood, he left his home and on a journey he met Laius, not knowing, however, that Laius was his father. Somehow a quarrel ensued, and Oedipus killed his father, thus fulfilling the prophecy. Later Oedipus became a hero and returned to Thebes where he married his mother. Some historians believe that Oedipus never knew Jocasta was his mother; nevertheless his name is linked to a complex which describes the craving of a boy for his mother or the attachment of a girl to her father. The word that sums up the concept of the Oedipus complex is *maternorexis*, derived from *mater* (mother) and *orexis* (desire).

Oikovalent . . . Potent sexually only in one's own home or in a familiar environment. Derived from *oikos* (a home) and *valere* (be able).

Old horny . . . The male mastix, in allusion to its "hornification" when emotional.

Old Peg . . . An older man who continues to have wet dreams. An allusion to the winged horse Pegasus whose stamp of the foot created the fabled fountain on Mount Helicon.

Old root . . . The male organon; either, endearingly, in its state of vigor, or, disparagingly, in its status effete.

Olesbos . . . A device fashioned to resemble the male sex organ and used by women in acts of masturbation. The term is derived from onanism or *Onan* (a Biblical character who practiced masturbation or, more correctly, coitus interruptus) and *Lesbos* (a country reputed for the sensuality of its inhabitants).

Olfactism . . . A peculiar condition in which sexual excitation causes the subject to "smell" odors which do not exist. It is observed in women. The term is derived from *olfacere* (to smell).

Olfactolagnia . . . The condition of having one's sexual desires aroused through odors or perfumes. It is derived from *olfacere* (to smell) and *lagneia* (lust). The aphrodisiac effect of perfumes is well known, but, paradoxically, some disagreeable odors have a similar direction, as, for example, body odor. Odor stimulation is quite understandably observed almost exclusively in men, and ancient courtesans were in the habit of beguiling their victims not only with delicate perfumes but also with the scent of armpit or breast perspiration dabbed cleverly on exquisite handkerchiefs.

Oligeunia . . . The practice of having sexual intercourse at long intervals or very infrequently, either for lack of desire or on moral grounds. The term is derived from *oligos* (little or scanty) and *pareunia* (sexual intercourse).

Omocoinia . . . The performance of the sexual act without the use of a condom or phallic sheath. Also, the ability to perform or enjoy the act of sexual intercourse only with a "naked" or uncovered organ. The term is derived from *omos* (raw) and *koinonia* (sexual intercourse).

Omognosis . . . To have carnal knowledge of a premenstrual girl, i.e., to have sexual intercourse with a girl not old enough to menstruate. Derived from *omos* (unripe) and *gnosis* (knowledge).

Omolagnia . Erotic desire aroused by nakedness, not necessarily the nakedness of one of the opposite sex. Derived from *omos* (raw, undressed) and *lagneia* (lust).

Omophallus . . . The penis uncovered by a sheath or condom; a "raw" phallus. Derived from *omos* (raw) and *phallus* (penis).

Omophilist . . . A man who is sexually interested in girls of a tender age, before they reach puberty. Derived from *omos* (undeveloped) and *philein* (to love).

On the grind . . . Of the male, superimposed on the female and grinding with the pestle in the female mortar.

On the shelf . . . Of the membrum virile, permanently desiccated seminally.

Oncophallia . . . A condition characterized by a permanent enlargement of the male sex organ, believed to be caused, in some cases, by frequent erections. Derived from *onkos* (bulk) and *phallus* (the male organ).

Oneirogmophilia . . . The desire to have wet dreams or nocturnal emissions for the pleasure they afford, observed in men who are deprived of the means of normal satisfaction. Derived from *onieros* (dream), *ogmos* (straight, erected), and *philein* (to love).

Oneirogmophobia . . . The fear of having a wet dream or an episode of oneirogmus. The fear arises from the fact that the telltale spot left on the linen by the discharged semen reveals the incident. Derived from *oneiros* (dream), *ogmos* (straight or erected), and *phobos* (fear).

Oneirogmus . . . An orgasm occurring in males during their sleep and usually accompanied by an erotic dream. Also known as a wet dream. Derived from *oneiros* (dream) and *ogmos* (straight or erected).

Oneiropornism . . . A dreaming, both literal and figurative, of harlots, sexual escapades, the pleasures of lovemaking and other matters pertaining to the libido. Derived from *oneiros* (dream) and *porne* (harlot).

Oneirotantia . . . The condition of having frequent dreams of an erotic nature, especially dreams of naked girls bidding the subject to follow them. The term is derived from *oneiros* (dream) and *Tantalus* (a mythological king who was tempted with food and drink which he could not reach).

Onion . . . A female breast, esp. in "peeled onions," the uncovered breasts of a professional uncoverer.

Oolala . . . Of a female, accessible for a pudendal symphony.

Open C . . . The entire pudendal complex known as the vulva, but especially the introitus and the scabbard (i.e., the entrance to the vagina and the vagina). From 19th century.

Open up . . . To spread the thighs apart, thus causing a dehiscense of the labia, in anticipation of the phallus. From mid-19th century.

Opsonousia . . . The belief that the face is the most important anatomical part of the woman; i.e., the belief that facial beauty is more important than beauty of the body. The term is derived from *ops* (a face) and *nous* (mind).

Orange . . . The organs of the female which partake in the act of sexual concourse, conceived as something palatable but not always easy to come by, in allusion to the fruit which was regarded as a luxury in many parts of the world until not long ago.

Orastorgia . . . The doctrine which holds that true and lasting love between man and woman can arise only when the subjects are mature. The term is derived from *oraios* (mature) and *storge* (love).

Orcheoknismos . . . The procedure of tickling the scrotum in order to produce an erection, to effect an orgasm, or, occasionally, to bring about relaxation. Derived from *orchea* (scrotum) and *knismos* (tickling).

Orcheotage...The gentle manipulation of the scrotum, usually by a woman, to arouse sexual appetite or, sometimes, to induce relaxation. Derived from *orchea* (scrotum) and *barboter* (dabble).

Orchiormia . . . The handling, rubbing, or gently squeezing of a man's testes, usually by a woman, to bring a pleasurable sexual excitation. The term is derived from *orchis* (testis) and *horme* (impulse).

Orchitripsis . . . The procedure of rubbing or massaging the testicles, to effect erection or orgasm. Derived from *orchis* (testicle) and *tripsis* (a rubbing).

Ormephthoria . . . The gradual deterioration of the normal sexual desire with the substitution of homosexual tendencies. Derived from *horme* (desire) and *phthora* (corruption).

Orthocoitus . . . Sexual intercourse performed in the normal, accepted manner with regard to anatomical juncture, position, timing, etc. Derived from *orthos* (right or correct) and *coitus* (sexual intercourse).

Orthocubia . . . Orthodox or accepted methods of love play and sexual intercourse. The term is derived from *orthos* (right or correct) and *cubare* (to lie down).

Orthogen . . . Any stimulus, as a thought, action, vision, agent, etc., which causes the erection of a man's sex organ. The term is derived from *orthos* (straight) and *gignesthai* (to be produced).

Orthokoinonia . . . The sexual act performed in the conventional, unembellished form, especially coitus without preliminary love play. Derived from *orthos* (correct) and *koinonia* (sexual intercourse).

Ortholagnia . . . Lust aroused by the sight of an erected penis. Derived from *orthos* (straight, i.e., erected) and *lagneia* (lust).

Orthophallia . . . The state of having an erected penis, as during coitus. It is derived from *orthos* (straight) and *phallus* (the male organ). A man whose organ is erected is an *orthophallos*. A scene, an act, or a thought that causes the male organ to become erected is *phallorthific* (making erect). Pre-coital love making is *phallorthific.* So is a strip tease act or, in some cases, a low decolletage.

Orthophallic . . . Pertaining to, or having, an erected penis. See under *orthophallia.*

Orthophallogenic . . . Causing, or capable of causing, an erection of the penis, as *orthophallogenic* pictures, thought, etc. Derived from *orthos* (straight, i.e., erected), *phallus* (penis), and *gignesthai* (become).

Orthophallos . . . A male having an erected penis; a male sustaining an erection. Derived from *orthos* (straight, hence erected) and *phallos* (penis).

Orthostatic coitus . . . Sexual intercourse performed in the standing position. Derived from *orthos* (straight), *stare* (stand), and *coitus* (sexual intercourse).

Osculocentric . . . A person whose erotic cravings are expressed in the desire to kiss. The term is derived from *osculum* (a kiss) and *kentron* (a goad).

Osculoduce . . . Of two persons in the act of kissing, the one who is the aggressor, or the one who does the kissing as opposed to being kissed. The term is derived from *osculari* (to kiss) and *ducere* (to lead).

Osculoscopophilia . . . A strong desire to watch lovers in the act of kissing. The term is derived from *osculari* (to kiss) *skopein* (to view), and *philein* (to love).

Oxyrosis...The sharpening of the sexual appetite, as because of improved coital technique, loss of anxiety, improved health, etc. The term is derived from *oxys* (keen or sharp) and *eros* (desire).

Ozoamblyrosis . . . Loss of sexual desire and potency during love play or intercourse because of bad body odor. The word is derived from *ozein* (to smell), *amblys* (dull), and *eros* (desire).

P

Pageism . . . A sexual fancy in which a man imagines himself to be a page or menial to a beautiful woman. It is a form of masochism. 2. The tendency of some men to seek employment, especially menial work, with attractive female employers, for the sexual pleasure it affords them.

Pan . . . The female copulating organs, esp. as conceived in the haze of unfamiliarity by a lay man.

Paneunia . . . The condition of having a "girl in every port" or of being sexually promiscuous. The term is derived from *pan* (all) and *eune* (bed).

Panmixia . . . Promiscuous sexual activity. The term is derived from *pan* (all) and *mixis* (a mixing).

Panselgia . . . The condition of being interested in every phase of sexuality or in all women. The term is derived from *pan* (all) and *aselgeia* (licentiousness).

Pants worm . . . The mebrum virile, conceived, in good-natured contempt, as a "worm" bent on inching its way into the female pudendal gimcrack.

Pappostorgia . . . The doctrine which holds that true and lasting love between male and female can arise only when the subjects are very young. The term is derived from *pappos* (the first growth of a beard) and *storge* (love).

Paracmasia . . . That part of the sexual act characterized by anti-climax and the cooling of passion. It begins with the finale of the orgasm and lasts until the penis is flaccid. Derived from *para* (past) and *akme* (top).

Parapareunia . . . Sexual intercourse with one who is not the usual or legal coital partner. The term is derived from *para* (beside) and *pareunia* (sexual intercourse).

Parhedonia . . . A sexual behavior abnormality characterized by a strong urge to touch, observe, or exhibit one's own sexual organs or those of another person. The term is derived from *para* (beyond normalcy) and *hedone* (pleasure).

Parthenomazia . . . The condition of having a breast characteristic of a maiden or a woman who has not borne children; i.e., a breast marked by firmness, delicacy of texture, lack of pendulousness, and adorned by a small, pink nipple. The term is derived from *parthenos* (a maiden) and *mazos* (a breast).

Pasononia . . . The condition of being interested in all forms of sexual pleasure and in all modes of sexual intercourse. The term is derived from *pas* (all) and *eune* (bed).

Paternorexis . . . The sexual love of a daughter for her father. Derived from *pater* (father) and *orexis* (appetite). See also *Electra complex*.

Pecker . . . The male genital beak, conceived, not groundlessly, as a pointed object used in pecking the female pudendum. From early 19th century.

Pectobombe . . . A girl having an attractively bulging bosom. Derived from *pectus* (breast) and *bombe* (bulged).

Pectotage . . . The lascivious manipulation of the female breasts, especially as part of precoital love play. Derived from *pectus* (breast) and *barboter* (dabble).

Pederastor . . . The man who performs the act of pederasty (which see).

Pederasty . . . An abnormal act of sexual gratification in which the penis is inserted into the rectum of a child, usually a boy. Derived from *pais* (child) and *erastes* (lover). The man performing the act is a *pederastor*.

Pederosis . . . Sexual gratification obtained through any act with immature girls. Sexual affection for young children, male or female, is *pederotosis*.

Pederotosis . . . Sexual affection for young children, male or female. It is usually controlled and does not express itself in molestation. Derived from *pais* (child) and *eros* (love).

Pedomentia . . . The popular but groundless belief that the size of a man's sexual organ can be estimated from the size of his feet. Also, the purported relation between the size of the organ and the size of the feet. The word is derived from *pes* (foot) and *mentula* (the male organ).

Pencil . . . The male genital jotter, in allusion, apparently, to the seminal "lead." From late 19th century.

Penultima . . . A woman who indulges freely in sex play but stops short of the last act. Derived from *paene* (almost) and *ultima* (last).

Perdurorthosis . . . An erection of the male organ which lasts a considerable time. Sustained erection is of great importance to the female partner in coitus because she is slower than the male in arriving at the orgasm. The term is derived from *perdurable* (extremely durable) and *orthos* (straight, i.e., erected).

Pestle . . . To triturate erotically in the female mortar with the male pestle. 2. The penis.

Pestle spasm . . . A persistent erection of the penis; priapism.

Peter . . . The male erectile fillet, conceived as man's auxiliary, probably in allusion to Pete, a succedaneous circus clown. From mid-19th century.

Phagacia . . . The condition of having one's sexual desires stimulated by watching the motions of a girl's lips, as in eating. The term is derived from *phagein* (to eat) and *ciere* (to excite).

Phallaneuria . . . The absence of a strong erectile tone in the male organ. Derived from *phallus* (penis), *a* (without), and *neuron* (nerve).

Phallate . To insert the male sexual organ into the vagina of a woman and proceed with the act of intercourse. This is the word which describes the activity of the male in the process of sexual intercourse and it may be used both as a transitive verb and as an intransitive verb. In the sense of a transitive verb it implies the transference of the action to the female partner, as in the sentence: "The husband fallated his wife without preliminary love play." In the intransitive sense the verb can be used without an object, as in, "The husband had no desire to fallate with a penis that had so recently been circumcized."The word phallate is new, and now for the first time the English language has the means to designate without circumlocution this vital, timeless activity. The reader will note that until now one could only speak of a man having intercourse or cohabiting, or perhaps engaging in coitus; but there was no lexicographically legitimate equivalent for the consummately expressive but embarrassingly vulgar term "screw" or "fuck." The philologic injustice has now been corrected. Derived from *phallus* (the penis).

Phallation . The act of phallating a woman. It is similar in meaning to coitus or sexual intercourse but is more specific because it designates the action the male participant performs in the sexual act. See under *phallate.*

Phallauxesis . . . An increase in the size of the male sexual organ in its soft, un-erected state, as from the administration of hormones. Derived from *phallus* (penis) and *auxein* (increase).

Phallesthesia . . . The feeling or illusion that one has a phallus, as experienced by some hysterical women. Derived from *phallus* (penis) and *aisthesis* (feeling). Occasionally a woman has the impression that the phallus which she supposedly possessed was taken from her. The word for this is *phalloperdasia* from *phallus* and *perdo* (lose).

Phalleuse . . . A woman expert in teasing the male organ. The term is derived from *phallus* (the male organ).

Phallic anabasis . The process of becoming erect, as applied to the male organ. It is the sum of the changes which bring it from a state of flaccidity to full erection. Derived from *anabasis* (ascent).

Phallic catabasis . . . The process of becoming flaccid, as applied to an erected male organ. Derived from *katabasis* (a going down).

Phallic dedolation . . . The bruising of the male organ in the process of sexual intercourse, due to prolongation of the act, sensitivity of the organ, dryness of the vagina, etc.

Phallic impaction . . . A condition in which the erected male organ becomes tightly wedged in the vagina so that movement or withdrawal is difficult or impossible. It may result from a marked disparity in the size of the male organ and the vagina or from a spasm of the vagina.

Phallic incompetence . . . The condition resulting when the male sex organ cannot remain in a state of erection long enough to consummate the act of coitus.

Phallic insufficiency . . . The condition resulting when there is a striking disparity between the size of the male organ and that of the vagina.

Phallocacosis . . . The belief by a man that his sexual organs are repulsive to a woman. The belief often leads to sexual impotence. The term is derived from *phallus* and *kakos* (bad).

Phallodipsia. . . A state of excessive preoccupation with thoughts of the male sex organs, as by a woman afflicted with nymphomania. Derived from *phallus* (the male organ) and *dipsia* (thirst).

Phallomalacia . . . A softening of the erected male organ, as after the orgasm. Derived from *phallus* (the male organ) and *malacia* (a softening).

Phallomeiosis . . . The state of mind of a man who considers his penis too small for effectual intercourse, although the fact may be otherwise. The term is derived from *phallus* and *meion* (less).

Phallomecism . . . The condition of having an unusually long male sex organ. The term is derived from *phallus* (the male organ) and *mecism* (abnormal lengthening).

Phalloneuria . . . The condition of having a strong erectile tone in the male organ. Derived from *phallus* (penis) and *neuron* (nerve).

Phalloperissia . . . Excessive preoccupation with the male sexual organ. Derived from *phallus* (penis) and *perissos* (extraordinary).

Phallopetal . . . Seeking the male creative organ. Derived from *phallus* and *petere* (to seek).

Phallophobia . . . Fear of or aversion for the male sexual organ, as felt by some women. Derived from *phallus* (the male organ) and *phobia*. The condition is occasionally observed in women who enjoy coitus. *Kolpophobia,* on the other hand, is very seldom found in men who enjoy intercourse. (*Kolpophobia* is the fear of or aversion for the female sex organs.)

Phallopleiosis . . . The state of mind of a man who considers his penis too large and who abstains from sexual intercourse for fear of causing injury to his spouse. The term is derived from *phallus* and *pleion* (more).

Phallormia . . . The practice of manipulating a man's sex organ, usually by a woman, in order to afford sexual excitation and pleasure. The term is derived from *phallus* (the male organ) and *horme* (urge).

Phallorthific . . . Causing, or capable of causing, an erection of the penis; orthophallogenic. Derived from *phallus* (penis), *orthos* (straight, hence erected), and *facere* (to make).

Phallorthosis . . . A state of persistent erection of the penis or of frequent erections. This word does not imply the presence of pain. Derived from *phallus* (penis) and *orthos* (straight, hence erected).

Phallospasm . . . A condition in which the male sexual organ remains erected after an orgasm and in the absence of sexual desire. Derived from *phallus* and *spasmos* (a spasm).

Phallostosis . . . A condition of extreme rigidity of the male sex organ. The term is derived from *phallus* (the male organ) and *osteon* (a bone).

Phanerolagniast . . . A psychiatrist or a psychologist who investigates and demonstrates the lust patterns of men and women. The term is derived from *phaneros* (manifest), *lagneia* (lust), and *iast* (one who).

Phanormia . . . The stimulation of the sexual appetite by a demonstration of nudity. The term is derived from *phaneres* (visible) and *horme* (urge).

Pherbasia . . . A kiss which is endured without manifest opposition but which elicits no response. The term is derived from *phero* (to bear or endure) and *basium* (a kiss).

Philadelphia lawyers . . . The sexciting legs of a girl which, in a court of law, argue more eloquently than a baker's dozen of expert attorneys, as far as male jurors are, allegedly, concerned.

Philemalagnia . . . The condition in which sexual desire is aroused by kissing, either in the kissing male or in the female being kissed. Derived from *philema* (kiss) and *lagneia* (lust).

Philemalgia . . . The condition of being unresponsive or "cold" to kissing. Derived from *philema* (kiss) and *algidus* (cold).

Philemamania . . . A strong urge to kiss; an uncontrollable yearning to be kissed. Derived from *philema* (kiss) and *mania* (frenzied urge).

Philemaphobia . . . An aversion for kissing or for being kissed. Derived from *philema* (kiss) and *phobos* (fear or aversion).

Philematology . . . The art or skill of kissing. It is derived from *philema* (a kiss). A strong urge to kiss is *philemamania.* An aversion to kissing is *philemaphobia.* Sexual desire aroused by the act of kissing is *philemalagnia, lagneia* meaning lust. The state of being unresponsive to kissing is *philemalgia,* literally "cold to kissing." A person who enjoys short, dry kisses is *xerophilematous,* and one preferring long, "wet" kisses is *hygrophilematous.* Derived from *xeros* (dry) and *hygros* (wet).

Philemaxenosis . . . The practice of unorthodox kissing, especially with regard to the anatomical part that is kissed, as the nipple, foot, etc. Derived from *philema* (kiss) and *xenos* (strange, exotic).

Philemette . . . A girl who allows herself to be kissed even by a casual acquaintaince, as on a first date. Derived from *philema* (kiss).

Philemorthotic . . . Preferring or tending to kiss in the usual, accepted manner, i.e., on the lips or face. Derived from *philema* (kiss) and *orthos* (straight, conventional). The majority of American men may be thus described. On the other hand, some men, proverbially the French, like to indulge in kissing various parts of the female anatomy other than the face or lips. The general term for unorthodox kissing is *philemaxenosis*. Philemaxenosis is derived from *philema* and *xenos* (strange, foreign, or exotic). There are many words to describe the various eccentricities of kissing, as *pygophilema* (a kiss on the buttocks), *mammillaphilema* (a kiss on the nipples), etc.

Philemyosis . . . Kissing while the eyes are kept closed. The term is derived from *philema* (a kiss and *myo* (to keep one's eyes shut). Another word having the same meaning is *typhlobasia,* derived from *typhlos* (blind) and *basium* (a kiss).

Philomolysmist . . . One who loves obscenity in any form. Derived from *philein* (to love), *molysma* (filth), and *ist* (one who).

Philophileist . . . A person who likes to kiss and to be kissed. The term is derived from *philein* (to love) and *phileo* (to kiss).

Philopornist . . . One who loves loose women or prostitutes. It is derived from *porne* (a harlot) and *philein* (to love).

Pigeon hole . . . The vagina. The vulva in entirety, conceived as the housing of the sheath.

Pillicock-hill . . . The vulva. Shakespeare: "Pillicock sat on pillicock-hill."

Pillows . . . Large female breasts, conceived as too much of a good thing.

Piss-proud . . . Erected because of the fullness of the urinary bladder; said of the male genital organon. 2. Of an older, generally impotent, male, enjoying the luxury of an erection, in the morning, not because of rejuvenation, but because of an assist from a full bladder.

Pisser . . . 1. The phallus as a urinary petcock. 2. The vulva as a urinary outlet.

Piston . . . The male genital shaft, conceived as an oscillating piston in the "cylinder" of the pudendum muliebre.

Pizzle chewer . . . A female who relieves a male of his phallic tension by fondling the instrument in her mouth.

Plain-clothes man . . . A male who phallates without a condom.

Play at hot cockles . . . Stimulate a female sexually by titillating her labia or clitoris.

Play at itch-buttocks . . . To have sexual concourse. Introduced in 16th century.

Play at up-tails all . . . Of an amorous man and his maid, to do what newlyweds do.

Play pickle-me-tickle-me . . . To be in sexual intercourse. From 17th century.

Play solitaire . . . To relieve oneself of sexual tension by manual, or similar unilateral, means.

Play top-sawyer . . . Of the male, to be mounted on the female, and to proceed in the manner of a male, so situated.

Pleasure boat . . . The external and internal parts of the female pudendum with which the male is concerned in the act of sexual concourse.

Plug for posterity . . . Of the male, with reference to a subjacent female, to do a man's job for her.

Poitrinographia . . . A form of doodling in which the figures have the shape of a woman's breasts. Also, an unusual interest in writing about breasts. Derived from *poitrine* (breast) and *graphein* (to write).

Poitrinolalia . . . An abnormal desire to talk or tell jokes about a woman's breasts. Derived from *poitrine* (breast) and *lalia* (talkativeness).

Poke-hole . . . The pudendum muliebre, esp. its sheath for the membrum virile cupidum, i.e., the vagina.

Pole-work . . . The physical integration of the membrum virile and the pudendum muliebre, esp. the phallating action of the former.

Polyvaleur . . . A man who can perform the act of sexual intercourse an indefinite number of times during one night. The term is derived from *polys* (many) and *valere* (to be strong or able).

Pornoepy . . . Discourse pertaining to obscene subjects. Derived from *porne* (harlot) and *epos* (word). The term applies to what is commonly known as "dirty talk." *Pornerastic* means obscene or licentious and describes such talk as *pornoepy.*

Pornocracy . . . Government by prostitutes or licentious women. The suffix *-cracy* refers to a form of government and *porne* is a harlot. There is a historical justification for the existence of this term, for in the 10th century a woman named Theodora rose to great power in Rome. Theodora was a demimonde.

Pornological . . . Showing an interest or preoccupation with the obscene side of sex. Derived from *porne* (harlot) and *logos* (description).

Poscovalent . . . Potent sexually and able to perform the act of coitus only when forced, sincerely or in the spirit of play, to beg for the woman's co-operation. This condition is similar to *negovalency* and is found in men of a mildly masochistic personality. Derived from *poscere* (to beg or ask for urgently) and *valere* (to be able).

Poseuse . . . A married woman who mimes a professional strip teaser or burlesque entertainer by assuming various seductive poses often seen on the stage, or by stripping her clothes in imitation of a strip act. A more conservative poseuse may merely imitate a provocative style of walking, or she may offer her husband such blandishments as an excessively low decolletage, short-skirt, sheer negligee, and other forms of seminudity. The term refers especially to women who behave in this manner at the request of the husband.

Post-coital malaise . . . A sense of discomfort or indisposition that occasionally follows an act of sexual intercourse.

Potato finger . . . 1. The membrum virile. 2. A dildo or artificial penis used by female masturbators. 3. A long and thick finger introduced into the rectum of an anal erotic. 4. A finger stuffed in the vagina as a phallic substitute. 5. A finger used in "goosing" a female.

Prat . . . From the point of view of a desirous male, the more practical end of the female trunk, esp. the labia and the enclosed scabbard. From 19th century.

Precoital acedia . . . A complete disinterest in love play prior to sexual intercourse. This condition is observed in both men and women and in both the frigid and the ardent. Derived from *a* (without) and *kedos* (care).

Premastorgia . . . The enjoyment of seeing, or merely contemplating, women engaged in certain activities which cause intimate parts of the body to be subjected to pressure or friction, as riding a bicycle, on horseback, etc. The term is derived from *premo* (to press) and *storge* (love).

Prenuptiophrenia . . . The excitement, generally the sexual excitement, preceding marriage. It refers specifically to the psychogenic awakening of the libido, usually in the husband, at the contemplation of the pleasures of intercourse following the marriage ceremony. It is this resurgence of lust that often accounts for premarital pregnancies in couples who have been discreet during many months of courtship. It is derived from *pre* (before), *nuptiae* (marirage), and *phrenia* (a specified state of mind). In spite of the exciting effect of premarital reveries, the actual ceremony often leaves a husband completely impotent on the first night of married life. Various theories have been offered to explain this phenomenon, and the most likely explanation is the anxiety caused by the "challenge" of married life. Now that restraint is removed, and with it the lure of the "forbidden fruit," the husband shrinks at the thought of having to prove himself a "man." Whatever the explanation, the word that describes the condition is *postnuptasthenia,* from *post* (after) *nuptiae* (marriage), *a* (without), and *sthenia* (strength).

Pre-phallation . . . Before sexual intercourse.

Pre-phallation play . . . Amorous play, in bed, before the act of sexual intercourse.

Pre-vagination play . . . Same as *pre-phallation play,* above.

Priapism . . . A state of persistent erection of the penis, often accompanied by pain and seldom accompanied by sexual desire.

Prick . . . The membrum virile. Standard English from 15th century to end of 16th. Slang thereafter. A functional term based on the allusion to the "piercing" habit of the organon.

Pride of the morning . . . A morning erection due to fullness of the bladder. From 19th century. Based on the conventional meaning of the phrase, which refers to an early morning shower. See also under *piss-proud.*

Primaphallation . . . The first act of sexual intercourse partaken by a man. Derived from *primus* (first) and *phallation* (which see).

Primavagination . . . The first act of sexual intercourse partaken by a woman. Derived from *prima* (first) and *vagination* (which see).

Primicipara . . . A girl who is having or who has had her first experience in sexual intercourse. Also, a woman who has been vaginated but a few times. The term is derived from *prima* (first) and *recipio* (to receive).

Primiciparous . . . Engaging in sexual intercourse for the first time. The term applies to a woman. It is derived from *prima* (first) and *recipio* (to receive).

Primitia . . . The state of partaking in the act of sexual intercourse for the first time. The term applies to a man. It is derived from *primus* (first) and *emitto* (to emit; hence ejaculate).

Primitous . . . Engaging in sexual intercourse for the first time. The term applies to a man. It is derived from *primus* (first) and *emitto* (to emit, hence ejaculate).

Princock . . . The totality of the female pudendum concerned with sexual concourse. From 16th century.

Private property . . . 1. The membrum virile. 2. The pudendum muliebre. Current since 19th century.

Prochronorgasmus . . . The premature arrival at the orgasm in the act of coitus, either by the male or the female, with regard to the coital partner. It is derived from *pro* (before), *chronos* (time), and *orgasmus* (orgasm or the last thrill of coitus). The word is also used to describe a speedy or premature ejaculation, without regard to the orgasm of the female. The term is not applied to the naturally quicker orgasm of the male, but to an abnormal discrepancy between the orgasm of the male and that of the female, when the former is premature. *Prochronorgasmus* is usually an affliction of youth. It is common in males who have long been deprived of sexual gratification and whose reflex pathways of genital reactions are tense. Pre-coital play also hastens the arrival of the orgasm. So does a good figure, a virginal vagina, and an exciting reaction from the female. *Prochronorgasmus* is frustrating to the female who is thus deprived of the fruition of her aroused passion. It may lead to a neurosis if the condition persists. *Prochronorgasmus* is practically never observed in females, although as time slows the male reaction and speeds the female reaction, a point may be reached when the orgasm of the woman precedes that of the male. *Celerorgasmus* is a synonym of *prochronorgasmus*.

Proctoerigentic . . . Easily aroused to sexual excitement by stimulation of the anus, manually, with the penis, etc. The term applies to both male and female. Derived from *proktos* (anus) and *erigere* (to erect). The man who performs the act with a woman is a *proctorator* while the woman is a *proctorix*.

Proctophilia . . . The condition of having one's interest centered around the rectum or anus. *Proctophobia* is the fear of anything dealing with the rectum. This term also applies to the state of anxiety observed in some people with rectal ailments.

Proctophobia . . . Fear of, or aversion for, any sexual involvement of the anus or rectum, as in precoital play. Derived from *prok-*

tos (anus) and *phobos* (fear).

Proctorator . . . A male who excites a female sexually by stimulating her anus, either manually (as by gentle massage) or by playing the penis against her anus. Derived from *proktos* (anus) and *patrare* (to effect).

Proctorix . . . A female whose sexual appetite is aroused by having her anus gently stimulated, either manually (as by a man's hand) or by the penis of a coital partner. Derived from *proktos* (anus) and *patrare* (to effect).

Proctotitillia . . . The gentle tickling of the anus, especially in a female, to arouse the sexual appetite. The tickling or stimulation may be accomplished by hand, by means of the penis, or by the use of medicinal substances which are mild irritants. Derived from *proktos* (anus) and *titillare* (tickle).

Prolegomenophrodesia . . . The act of preparing a woman for sexual intercourse by discourse, usually professions of love. The word also describes the state of needing such preparation. The condition must be differentiated from the usual pre-coital love play, such as manipulation of the sexual organs, kissing, etc. The term is derived from *pro* (before), *legein* (to speak), and *Aphrodite* (the goddess of love).

Pseudomacrophallia . . . The condition of having a male organ which appears large in the flaccid state but does not increase much in size when erected. The term is derived from *pseudo* (false), *makros* (big), and *phallus* (the male organ).

Pseudomicrophallia . . . The condition of having a male organ which seems unusually small when flaccid but which becomes remarkably large when erected. Derived from *pseudo, mikros* (small), and *phallus.*

Psilerastomaniac . . . A person who is obsessed with a maniacal craving to expose and publicize widely men's and women's erotic aspirations and practices. The term is derived from *psilos* (stripped bare or naked), *eramai* (to love or long after) and *maniac* (one driven by a compulsion).

Psychrotentiginous . . . Aroused sexually by cold (as cold weather). Derived from *psychros* (cold) and *tentigo* (lewdness).

Psychrotentiginy . . . The condition of being aroused sexually by cold, as cold weather.

Pubephilia . . . An abnormal interest in pubic hair, especially the practice of collecting pubic hair of women as a focus of erotic interest. The term is derived from *pubes* (genital hair) and *philein* (to love).

Pucker-water . . . An astringent solution, usually of alum, used by seasoned prostitutes to "pucker" or narrow the relaxed vaginal canal. Recorded in 1785.

Pudendacure . . . The toilette or cosmetic care of the female sex organs. It consists of grooming the pubic hair, washing and perfuming the vulva, syringing the vagina, etc. The application of soothing creams and odoriferous ointments to the genital area is often part of the procedure. In most instances the woman performs her own pudendacure, but in some cases a professional attendant is called in. Pudendacure may remain an asexual procedure; i.e., one in which erotic feelings play no part. On the other hand, many pudendacures have an erotic basis or component; some are undertaken for the sole purpose of providing sexual pleasure. The term is derived from *pudendum* (female genitalia) and *cura* (care).

Pudendal jockey . . . A male who is a devoted phallator, esp. one who "plays" the rentable female grooves.

Pudendojacosis . . . A maneuver, often seen in burlesque houses, whereby a girl performer "throws" the genital area forward. It constitutes one of the many erotic gestures of a "girlie" show. Derived from *pudendum* (the external genital organs of a woman) and *jacere* (to throw).

Puellaphilist . . . One who loves girls. The term is derived from *puella* (girl) and *philein* (to love).

Pump . . . To do the male's part in the act of sexual concourse. From 19th century.

Punch . . . To phallate, esp. to deflower a young one.

Punchable . . . Of the female, phallatable; i.e., ripe or ready for the male punch.

Purser's grind . . . Coitus which brings the female no reward except the satisfaction of a massive phallus. From mid-19th century.

Puss . . . The perineal complex of the female which is functional in the act of sexual concourse, esp. the labia, the intervening slit, and the decorative pubic hairpiece. Originally spelled *pusse.* From mid-17th century.

Pussy bumping . . . Tribadism; i.e., the rubbing of the genitalia between female homosexuals.

Pussy-cat . . . The perineal apparatus of the female concerned with sexual concourse, esp, the labia, the interlabial slit, and the crowning escutcheon.

Pussyologist . . . 1. A man who "chases after" girls, esp. after harlots. 2. An alleged connoisseur of girlie flesh; a "student" of the pussy.

Puttilagnia . . . Erotic feeling aroused by the sight of naked children as represented in sculpture or painting. The term is derived from *putti* (figures of naked children in art) and *lagneia* (lust).

Pygies...The buttocks, esp. those of the female, conceived as sexual spherosities. From about 1940.

Pygobombe . . . A girl having a well-rounded derriere or bulging buttocks, especially one whose buttocks oscillate as she walks. The word is derived from *pyge* (buttock) and *bombe* (rounded or bulging).

Pygophallia . . . The practice of rubbing the penis against the buttocks of a female, or of inserting it in the cleft between the domes. Derived from *pyge* (buttock) and *phallus* (penis).

Pygophilema . . . A kiss on a buttock. The practice of kissing the buttocks is *pygophilemia.* Derived from *pyge* (buttock) and *philema* (a kiss).

Pygormia . . . The excitation of lust by means of the buttocks.

Derived from *pyge* (buttock) and *horme* (passion).

Pygosemantics . . . The international language of hip swaying or buttock oscillation. The term is derived from *pyge* (buttock) and *semantics* (the science of meanings).

Q

Quarry . . . The pudendum muliebre conceived as the target desideratum of the prurient organum virile.

Quatiosis . . . The procedure of arousing a man's sexual appetite by shaking the various anatomical parts of a woman, as in burlesque houses. Derived from *quatio* (to shake).

Quatopygia . . . The shaking of the buttocks in walking; applied especially to the erotic walk of a woman. Derived from *quatio* and *pyge* (buttock).

Queenies . . . A term of respectful endearment for the prize faggots which fill the concavities of a brassiere.

Quim-stake . . . The organum virile conceived as the mandrel of the female cannula.

Quim-sticking . . . The introduction of the male fifth column into the "soft underbelly" of the female.

Quim-wedging . . . The act of occluding the female sheath with the phallus tumefactus.

Quoniam . . . The pudendum muliebre conceived as the first and the last of carnal pleasures, in allusion to "quoniam" as the first word of the closing part of the hymn Gloria in Excelsis.

R

Raked fore and aft . . . Bored by the phallus both in the vagina and the rectum, intermittently. Said of a female who submits to sodomy, in addition to the usual.

Ram . . . To give hard for soft, i.e., to phallate.

Ramrod...The male genital shaft, conceived as a device for ramming down the charge of seminal fluid in the muzzle of the female pudendum. From early 19th century.

Rathole . . . The introitus and sheath of the female pudendum.

Reamer . . . A man's begetter conceived as a vaginal dilator.

Rear altar . . . The gluteal spheroids of a female, conceived as a secondary altar of sexual worship. From about 1910.

Rear guards . . . The cheeks of the thickest parts of the thighs.

Recumbofavia . . . The preference for the reclining position as the posture in coitus. Derived from *recumbere* (to lie or recline) and *favere* (to favor).

Red flag . . . The menstrual pad conceived as a red signal of inaccessibility of the pudendum muliebre to the membrum virile erectum.

Rhabdolagnia . . . Sexual desire aroused by the beating with a cane. The term applies to both the one who administers the beating and the person who is beaten, but it is used more frequently in the former sense. Derived from *rhabdos* (rod) and *lagneia* (lust). The condition is a form of sadism when the lust is aroused in the one who punishes, and a form of masochism when the sexual desire is aroused in the victim of the beating.

Rheononia . . . A form of masturbation practiced by women in which a stream of water, as from a faucet or rubber hose, is directed against the exposed genitalia. Derived from *rheos* (stream) and *koinonia* (sexual intercourse).

Roppus . . . An esoteric or pet name for a large male organ. The term is derived from *rhopalon* (a cudgel).

Rumbusticate . . . To phallate; to have sexual intercourse.

Rump . . . To phallate a woman from behind.

S

Sacofricosis . . . A form of sexual perversion, indulged in by men, in which the practitioner handles his genitalia while walking along the street, riding a public conveyance, or mingling in a crowd, through an opening cut in his pants pocket. The practice is common among habitual drunkards, drug addicts, and derelicts deprived of normal cohabitation. The term is derived from *sacculus* (pocket) and *fricare* (to rub).

Schizerastia . . . The excitation of the sexual appetite by gazing at the so-called "line of cleavage" of a girl's bosom, as above a low neckline. The act of looking eagerly at the area above a decolletage is *schizoscopia;* and the person so preoccupied is a *schizoscopist.* The words come from *schizein* (to split), *erastes* (lover), and *skopein* (to view).

Schizoscopia . . . The act of ogling the "line of cleavage" of a girl's bosom, as above a decolletage. Derived from *schizein* (to split) and *skopein* (to observe).

Schizoscopist . . . A man fond of looking at the "line of cleavage" of a girl's bosom, or at the slightest hint of cleavage, as above a low neckline. Derived from *schizein* (to split or separate) and *skopein* (to inspect visually).

Screw . . . To give the female pudendum its due reward, with phallic obturation, followed by vesuviation.

Second line of defense . . . The labia minora, the first line of defense being the labia majora. From about 1930.

Selgolalia . . . The telling of stories having a sexual motif. The term is derived from *aselgeia* (licentiousness) and *lalein* (to talk or babble).

Semen-banking . . . The pump-priming which usually leads to a seminal deposit in the vaginal bank.

Semenagogue . . . Something that hastens the arrival of the orgasm in sexual intercourse, as pre-coital play, coital accompaniments, visual stimulation, etc. The term is derived from *semen* (the ejaculated seminal fluid) and *agogos* (leading).

Sempereria . . . The quality of retaining everlasting influence on man's lust, as some famous beauties of the screen and stage. The term is derived from *semper* (always) and *eros* (desire).

Sergeism . . . The infliction of pain

upon oneself, as by self-mutilation, in order to subdue sexual craving. The term is derived from Sergius, the character in a story by Tolstoy, who severed his finger with an axe when his monkish chasity was being threatened by a conniving temptress.

Sexacmenia . . . The period in a person's life characterized by the acme of sexual development, capacity, or desire. The word is derived from *sexus* (sex) and *akmenos* (full grown).

Sexamnesia . . . A form of forgetfulness in which sexual experiences cannot be recalled. It is a defense mechanism against painful memories. The term is derived from *sexus* (sex), *a* (not), and *mnasthai* (to remember).

Sexanhedonia . . . The loss of one's ability to enjoy sexual acts which formerly gave pleasure. The word is derived from *sexus*, *a* (without), and *hedone* (pleasure).

Sexautism . . . The condition characterized by daydreaming about matters relating to sex. Constant preoccupation with thoughts about sexual gratification. The term is derived from *sexus* and *autism* (the condition of being preoccupied with daydreaming).

Sexechia . . . The capacity to retain sexual power late in life or the state of being sexually potent late in life. The word is derived from *sexus* and *echein* (to hold or retain).

Sexedonia . . . The doctrine that complete happiness is not possible without complete satisfaction of the sex urge. The term also means happiness derived from sexual pleasure. The term is derived from *sexus* and *hedone* (pleasure).

Sexegeric . . . Stimulating the differentiation of the secondary sex characteristics in both men and women, as certain hormones. The word is derived from *sexus* and *egeiro* (arouse).

Sexoclitic . . . Tending to show more sympathy for a member of the opposite sex; usually said of men. The word is derived from *sexus* and *klinein* (to lean).

Sexodrome . . . Any outward manifestation of the inner sex urge, as blushing, trembling, stammering, etc. The word is derived from *sexus* (sex) and *dromos* (a running).

Sexogamy . . . A marriage based on sexual attraction only. Derived from *sexus* and *gamos* (marriage).

Sexograde . . . Getting along, or forging one's way, on the basis of one's sexual appeal. The term is derived from *sexus* and *gradi* (to walk).

Sexolepsy . . . A strong sexual craving, usually of unknown etiology, coming on suddenly and characterized by restlessness, change in personality, loss of insight, and a tendency for sexual violence. One occasionally reads about a well-behaved man suddenly turned sex maniac with resulting rape and murder. Sexolepsy describes the mental condition which is the background of such attacks. The word is derived from *sexus* and *lepsis* (a seizure).

Sexolimia . . . The condition of being chronically hungry for sexual gratification, as observed in prison inmates and others deprived of the opportunity for satisfying the libido. Derived from *sexus* (sex) and *limos* (hunger). A chronic sex hunger is occasionally discovered in men who do have sexual contact but who crave for sexual experience with other, to them unavailable, women.

Sexomentia . . . A form of mental derangement caused by sexual frustrations. Derived from *sexus* and *mens* (mind).

Sexophilia . . . A more than average interest in matters dealing with sex; a preoccupation with objects depicting, or otherwise related to, sex, as books, paintings, statues, etc.; a liberal or permissive attitude toward sex. Derived from *sexus* (sex) and *philein* (to love).

Sexophobia . . . Fear of or aversion for matters dealing with sex. Derived from *sexus* (sex) and *phobos* (fear). The interest in matters pertaining to sex is *sexophilia,* from *sexus* and *philein* (to love).

Sexophrenia . . . The state of mind of one whose thoughts are colored or motivated by a conscious or subconscious sex urge. The term is derived from *sexus* and *phren* (mind).

Sexorman . . . A general name applied to anything exerting a stimulating effect upon the libido, as a woman's leg, shoulder, breast, etc., or a picture, statue, or other form of art. The term is derived from *sexus* (sex) and *horme* (passion).

Sexoschizia . . . 1. The condition of being both heterosexual and homosexual, i.e., of having heterosexual and homosexual cravings. 2. The condition of being both sadistic and masochistic; the condition of deriving sexual pleasure from sadistic acts as well as from masochistic practices. Derived from *sexus* (sex) and *schizein* (to split).

Sextonia . . . 1. The state of erection of sexually erectile structures, as the penis, clitoris, nipples, etc. 2. The state of tension resulting from sexual excitement, whether appeased or not. 3. The stimulus provided by the libido to a person's activities, expressions, ambitions, etc. Derived from *sexus* (sex) and *tonos* (tension).

Sexotrophic . . . 1. Stimulating or enhancing the sexual appetite; increasing sexual potency. 2. Catering to sexual desires; serving the sexual impulse. Derived from *sexus* (sex) and *trephein* (to nourish).

Sexotropic . . . Having a tendency to center one's thoughts on matters pertaining to sex. Derived from *sexus* (sex) and *tropos* (a turning).

Sextelia . . . The belief that the entire pattern of human behavior can be explained on the basis of the sex urge. The term is derived from *sexus* and *telos* (end or aim).

Sexual abreaction . . . The process of relieving suppressed sexual cravings by talking about them, especially to a physician.

Sexual adiaphoria . . . The condition characterized by a lack of pleasurable response to the various stimuli accompanying love play and coitus. It is the result of a nervous surfeit which comes, usually, from overindulgence.

Sexual adjuvants . . . The collective name for the various auxiliaries that add to sexual excitation and enjoyment, such as perfumes, music, lights, fancy undergarments, love play, etc.

Sexual adynamia . . . The inability to perform the act of coitus because of general weakness, as the inability to sustain one's self upon the woman. It does not refer to impotence or the absence of a satisfactory erection. The term is derived from *a* (without) and *dynamis* (might). While the phrase applies primarily to males, it may also describe a similar condition in females, who, although passive in the act of coitus, find themselves incapable of supporting the man during coitus or unable to be the host to sexual passion.

Sexual aequum . . . That amount of sexual preoccupation or participation which is judged sufficient for one's emotional and physical well-being. It represents a dose of sexual enjoyment which is neither too little nor too much.

Sexual agonist . . . The chief element in love play or the part which gives the most effective stimulus.

Sexual amusia . . . A lack of sexual harmony in the approach to coitus or in its performance. This may assert itself in a discordance with regard to the time when each of the participants is in the mood for coitus. If the time of sexual propensity is no issue, there may be a lack of concinnity regarding precoital play, position, the choice of sexual adjuvants, etc. Sexual amusia is a frequent cause of marital discord which often leads to divorce. It is derived from *amusia* (lack of harmony).

Sexual anempeiria . . . The loss of sex technique or finesse which was acquired from experience. Derived from *an* (without) and *empeirein* (to be experienced).

Sexual aphthongia . . . Loss of the power of speech during sexual excitement, due to spasm of speech muscles. The term is derived from *a* (negative) and *phthongos* (sound).

Sexual apnea . . . A transient cessation of breathing due to sexual excitation and the resulting failure of the respiratory muscles. Derived from *a* (without) and *pnoia* (breath).

Sexual audility . . . The tendency to be impressed most easily about matters pertaining to sex by that which one can hear, as by erotic narratives, jokes, etc.

Sexual balbuties . . . A stammering or stuttering which results from sexual heat, as during love play.

Sexual bruxism . . . A grinding of the teeth during the height of sexual excitement. It is observed more often in men.

Sexual camnosis . . . Extreme fatigue following sexual intercourse. The condition is observed more frequently in women of slender build or habitus. Derived from *kamno* (to be exhausted).

Sexual cheromania . . . A form of abnormal exaltation and cheerfulness occasionally observed in sexually excited women. Derived from *chairein* (to rejoice).

Sexual decubation . . . The period after sexual intercourse when the participants recover from the fury of the orgasm. Derived from *de* (down) and *cubare* (recline).

Sexual deflagration . . . A sudden and usually transitory burst of sexual desire and power. The term is derived from *deflagrare* (to burn up).

Sexual defluvium . . . A sudden and usually transitory loss of sexual desire. The term is derived from *defluere* (to flow down).

Sexual depravation . . . A gradual deterioration of the sex habits of a person. A change from orthodox sexual procedures to a practice of perversions.

Sexual dereism...An escape from reality and available sexual pleasures and a resort to phantasy. Derived from *de* (away) and *res* (thing).

Sexual detrition . . . The gradual loss of sexual desire and capacity that comes with time. Derived from *deterere* (to wear away).

Sexual dyspnea . . . A transitory shortness of breath resulting from sexual excitement, sexual intercourse, or a libidinous desire. It is usually due to a spasm of some of the muscles concerned with the mechanism of breathing. Derived from *dys-* (difficult) and *pnoia* (breath). Sexual dyspnea occurring during intercourse may be the result of both the physical exertion incident to coitus and the spasm caused by excitement.

Sexual eburnation . . . An erection of the penis or the clitoris. Derived from *eburnus* (of ivory), an allusion to the hardness of ivory.

Sexual eclecticism . . . A form of sexual perfectionism in which no one woman seems to possess all the required physical charms, so that the ideal woman is a mental combination of the outstanding attractions of many beautiful women. The term is derived from *ek* (out) and *legein* (select).

Sexual erethisia . . . The condition of being sexually excitable and active. Derived from *erethismos* (irritation).

Sexual fetish . . . A part of a woman's body or, sometimes, an object used or worn by a woman which represents, to a given man, the sum of all the sexual attraction of the woman.

Sexual haptics . . . The science of touch as it relates to sex and the pleasure derived from touching a member of the opposite sex. Derived from *haptikos* (able to lay a hold of).

Sexual hegemon . . . In the sexual relation between man and woman, the person who shows leadership, as in the matter of frequency, manner of coitus, duration, etc. The term is derived from *hegemon* (leader).

Sexual inanition . . . A form of nervous exhaustion, marked by fatigability, restlessness, partial loss of memory, etc., resulting from complete lack of sexual contact. Derived from *inanis* (empty).

Sexual inappetence . . . Lack of sexual desire, especially when following a period of increased sexual craving.

Sexual incubation . . . The period before sexual intercourse when the passions of the participants grow ripe for the act.